FOR REFERENCE

NOT TO BE TAKEN FROM THE ROOM

Native Americans and Political Participation

Political Participation in America
Raymond A. Smith, Series Editor

African Americans and Political Participation,
Minion K. C. Morrison, Editor

Gay and Lesbian Americans and Political Participation,
Raymond A. Smith and Donald P. Haider-Markel

Jewish Americans and Political Participation,
Jerry D. Stubben and Gary A. Sokolow

Latino Americans and Political Participation,
Sharon A. Navarro and Armando X. Mejia, Editors

Women and Political Participation,
Barbara Burrell

Native Americans and Political Participation

A Reference Handbook

Jerry D. Stubben

A B C 🌊 C L I O

Santa Barbara, California • Denver, Colorado • Oxford, England

Cataloging-in-Publication data is available from the Library of
Congress

09   08   07   06   10   9   8   7   6   5   4   3   2   1

This book is also available on the World Wide Web as an e-
book.
Visit abc-clio.com for details.

ABC-CLIO, Inc.
130 Cremona Drive, P.O. Box 1911
Santa Barbara, California 93116-1911

This book is printed on acid-free paper.
Manufactured in the United States of America

I have heard all through my life that "one does not exist without one's people." This book would never have come to be if it were not for the assistance, advice, faith, humor, prodding, ridicule, teasing, trust, understanding, and willingness to share of a great number of American Indian people. I owe a special debt of gratitude to the over 400 tribal leaders who have patiently participated in three political opinion and participation surveys over the past ten years. Without their words and insight, this book would be another empty academic report of what has already been written, rather than an example of what should be written.

I owe a special debt of gratitude to Dr. David Wilkins, Dr. Diane Duffy, Terry Crossbear, Saunie and Mona Wilson, Lance Foster, Dr. Kaye Tatro, Reuben Snake, and Dr. Pei-te Lien for placing their knowledge and research in specific sections of this book. And to the countless individual American Indians and others who offered their stories, experience, and resources that otherwise would have never been identified. Finally, I offer this book to my children and grandchildren, who will continue to participate in tribal, local, state, and national politics long after I have joined my ancestors. For it is through their generations that the political influence of American Indians will continue on to future generations, influencing America and the world forever.

Aho Dr. Jerry Stubben, Ahgaha Ska

Contents

American Indian History Timetable   319

Series Foreword

Native Americans, American Indians, and *indigenous Americans* are terms invented by those who attempt to conquer and control rather than live with the world that those who read this book presently inhabit. Peoples who fit these terms come from over a thousand different tribes and tens of thousands of different bands and clans and hundreds of thousands of different families. Many now share the blood of many tribes, groups, and peoples. But we the first peoples to inhabit what is now called "America" share one common experience: the constant fight for the continuation of our cultures, beliefs, and ways of life so that they may be passed on to the next generation and beyond.

Why do I focus on this point in a book on political participation? Native people participate in both internal (tribal) and external politics in order to protect their very existence as human beings. My own life has been a struggle against external political forces that threaten my existence as an Oglala-Lakota and Northern Cheyenne. This way of life is based on political rights passed on to me, my children, and grandchildren by ancestors who fought to maintain the sovereign status of our tribes and peoples. We are not a racial or ethnic group; we are a political entity based on our sovereign status as a people and the rights that come with that status. We fight daily with local, state, federal, and even international governments in order to protect and enhance this status. Hopefully, the reader will come to understand, respect, and honor it by supporting our struggle to maintain our rights as a people as we pass that right on to future generations.

This book, as I would like to see it, is of a scholarly character. It utilizes scientific data and academic publications as well as the historical writings of Indians and non-Indians. This is the mind of the book.

The book also offers personal experiences of Indian people, often appealing to the reader to understand the impact of political policies and actions from an individual rather than group perspective. This is the soul of the book.

The book appeals to a wide readership. Its audience includes people who take pains in thinking about such themes as the history and present state of human societies, their possible evolutions and destiny, and their order and governance. It also considers freedoms and their inevitable limitations, the rarity of fairness, the strengths and shortcomings of American democracy, and the possibility of spiritual guidance and intervention as American government and society move into another generation.

To write in full the political history of any one tribe would fill a volume by itself. Thus, to attempt to offer insight into the political participation of American Indians, even in modern times, is a vast undertaking. My brother offers the reader a map—one based both on oral and written facts—that will guide the reader to other sources of knowledge. Yet much of the knowledge of our ancestors lies in stories that will never be written down. It will be up to our children and grandchildren to learn this knowledge and pass it on to all.

Lastly, the reason why this book exists lies in the words of our Omaha grandmother, Elizabeth Springer. She often asked those of us who had obtained degrees from the white man's universities, "What do they know?" Our common response was, "Nothing." She would laugh and say, "Told you. Now go teach them."

In a Good Way,

Richard (Rick) B. Williams
Executive Director
American Indian College Fund

Preface

A recent review of the predominant writings used in political science classes at most American universities and colleges revealed that none mentioned Native American political participation. Those that did normally spent two to four pages on negative issues such as high alcoholism rates, poverty, inadequate housing, discrimination, and high mortality rates.

Some textbooks (Lowi and Ginsberg 1992, 68; Bardes et al. 1993, 51; Burns et al. 1993, 225) do briefly mention (less than one page each) the influence of the Iroquois Confederacy on the founding of the Articles of Confederation and the U.S. Constitution. Unfortunately, none of the major texts on American government describe the cultural resiliency, economic gains, or spiritual enlightenment of American Indian society. The lack of such information fosters "a distorted viewpoint of American Indians and their governmental systems, both past and present" (Stensgar 1989).

As we enter the twenty-first century, not one article about Native Americans has been published in the most prestigious journals of political science, such as the *American Journal of Political Science, American Political Science,* or *Journal of Politics.* This apparent lack of interest is especially distressing since during the 1990s the number of articles on African Americans, Asian Americans, Hispanics, and women in these and other major political science journals has increased dramatically.

The *Canadian Journal of Political Science* did publish several articles on tribal-national intergovernmental relations, environmental issues on tribal lands, and tribal governmental policy issues. And the *Policy Studies Journal* and *Policy Studies Review* have devoted a symposium to and published articles on American Indian issues. Major journals in other disciplines such as anthropology (*Human Organizations, Journal of Anthropological Research*), ethnic studies (*Ethnic Racial Studies*), history (*American Historian, Ethnohistory*), and sociology (*American Sociological Review, Rural Sociology, Social Science Journal,* and *Social Science Quarterly*) do contain articles on Native American political and social issues. There are also specialty journals that focus on American Indians such as *American Indian Quarterly, American Indian Culture and Research Journal, American Indian Law Review, Northeast Indian Quarterly,* and the *Journal of the National Center of American Indian and Alaska Native Mental Health Research.*

In political science, however, there remains a great deal of ignorance of Native American political participation, institutions, issues, governmental relations, and values. Yet Native American politics and political participation must be understood in their rightful context in order for such ignorance to end and a true understanding of the relationship between Native American nations and democracy can begin (Yerington Paiute Tribe 1985; Lyons et al. 1992). It is my belief that students and scholars of the twenty-first century are willing to make the effort to bridge the knowledge gap that presently exists regarding Native Americans and political science.

This book offers some insight into the political participation of Native American Indians in their own tribal politics and in American politics. The first chapter offers a theoretical analysis of ancestral Native American political participation, institutions, structures, and values. It also offers a historical analysis of the tribal-federal relations that have laid the foundation of present relationships between individual sovereign tribes and state and federal governments. Chapter two offers empirical analysis of participation in electoral politics at the federal and tribal levels and data accumulated from tribal elected officials' surveys regarding their opinions on several political, cultural, and societal issues. Chapter three offers insight into Native American political officeholders at various levels of government, from tribal to national. Chapter four looks at Native American social and political movements and the organizations that have come forth to champion the issues they raised. Chapter five analyzes the political issues, both internal and external, that have dominated Native American protest responses and movements.

The findings and research data reported in this book are derived from the literature of both Native American and non-Indian academics; the writings and oral stories of past and present American Indian leaders; government and tribal documents and surveys of tribal leaders, American Indian families, and individuals; and personal conversations with countless Native American relatives and friends. Yet, even with all of these resources, this book represents only a small fragment of the vast amount of American Indian political knowledge—knowledge that begs for further research by political scientists willing to devote the time and patience necessary to understand the immense diversity of American Indian culture and society. Their efforts will greatly add to the knowledge base of the discipline of political science. They will also strengthen the bridge between the worldviews of indigenous tribal people and Western culture so that both can exist in harmony and help to preserve each other (Cajete 1994; Duran and Duran 1995).

The terms *American Indian, Native American,* and *Indian* are used throughout the book to refer to the indigenous populations of what presently is called North and South America. *Native Alaskan* or *Alaska Native* and *Native Hawaiian* are utilized when these groups are specifically mentioned.

References

Bardes, Barbara A., Mack C. Shelley II, and Steffen Schmidt. 1993. *American Government and Politics Today: The Essentials.* St. Paul, Minn.: West.

Cajete, Gregory. 1994. *Look to the Mountain: An Ecology of Indigenous Education.* Durango, Colo.: Kivaki Press.

Duran, Eduardo, and Bonnie Duran. 1995. *Native American Postcolonial Psychology.* Albany: State University of New York Press.

Lowi, Theodore J., and Benjamin Ginsberg. 1992. *American Government— Freedom and Power.* New York: W. W. Norton.

Lyons, Oren, John Mohawk, Vine Deloria, Jr., Laurence Hauptman, Howard Berman, Donald Grinde, Jr., Curtis Berkey, and Robert Venables. 1992. *Exiled in the Land of the Free.* Santa Fe, N.Mex.: Clear Light.

Stensgar, Ernest L. 1989. (Chairman, Coeur d'Alene Tribal Council, Plummer, Idaho.) Letter to author. December 14.

Yerington Paiute Tribe. 1985. *Introduction to Tribal Government.* Yerington, Nev.

1

Introduction to Native Americans

*N*ative American, American Indian, Native American Indian, and Indian all refer to the indigenous populations of North and South America. There is an academic norm that is evolving to use the term indigenous or indigenous American.

There are nearly 2.5 million Native Americans in the United States, and 4.12 million Americans claim Native American blood and that of another race (U.S. Census Bureau 2001). This means that 1 to 2 percent of those eligible to participate in American politics consider themselves Native Americans. Table 1.1 offers a further breakdown of the Native American and Alaska Native population based on the 2000 U.S. Census.

Even though Native Americans make up a small percentage of the eligible U.S. voting population, their political participation affects all levels of American government (tribal, federal, state, and local). Unlike other racial or ethnic groups in America, Native American tribes are political entities as presently defined by federal law. When members of other racial or ethnic entities in the United States deal with the federal government, they are seen as individual citizens dealing with a political entity. When a tribe and its citizens have dealings with the United States, two political entities stand face-to-face and come to terms. Individual Indians are treated that way because "they are members of a political entity, the tribe" (Bureau of Indian Affairs 1984).

TABLE 1.1
General Demographic Characteristics of Native Americans

	Native American	Native American/Another Race
Total	2,465,956	4,119,301
Male	1,223,982	2,033,242
Female	1,241,974	2,086,059
Over 18	1,635,644	2,735,799

Source: U.S.Census Bureau, 2001.

A political entity is a group of people living within a certain territory under a government that has some sovereignty. In international law, sovereignty is the state of supreme and independent rule. Native American governments possessed totally independent rule until the European invasion and conquest. Today Native American tribal governments maintain their sovereign (independent) status through recognition by the U.S. government based on constitutional and treaty law. Native American tribes are part of the constitutional structure of the U.S. government. Article VI of the Constitution states that "all Treaties made . . . shall be the Supreme Law of the Land," and Article I states that Indians are "not taxed." The Constitution recognizes tribal sovereignty in terms of the reaffirmation of previously negotiated treaties, and relations between Indian tribes and the U.S. government were similar to those between other sovereign nations, cemented through treaties and treaty substitutes (Wilkinson 1987, 103). Thus federally recognized Indian tribes fall within the definition of independent rule. Federal recognition acknowledges that a tribe has a government-to-government relationship with the United States. Some tribes possess state recognition but not federal, and yet others exist as cultural entities without federal recognition.

Federal recognition allows tribes to receive services from the Bureau of Indian Affairs and other federal agencies. While that may seem to be an advantage, it has been seen by some as a disadvantage to federally recognized sovereignty; government programs generate rules, requirements, and sanctions that have been used against Native American people, culture, and society. My aunt told me that federal programs (such as termination, welfare, and even rural electrification) "have killed more Indians than Custer." Her view was that such programs promote dependency on the federal government that denies the people their natural right to self-governance and independence.

Federal recognition also means that certain lands and natural resources of tribes fall under the jurisdiction of the tribe and the trust Bureau of Indian Affairs 1984). Thus, a Native American who is enrolled in a tribe may participate in his or her tribal politics and also in the political institutions that all other Americans have the opportunity to participate in. In order to understand Native American political participation today, one must first understand the long history of Native American tribal sovereignty and its relationship with the U.S. government.

Indigenous American Ancestral Political Participation

Recent archeological discoveries in Central America identify a democratic political structure existed among the Copa'n Maya around A.D. 650–750. Nine men known as *hol-pop* ("he at the head of the mat") are represented on the facade of this building; there were nine such representatives who met with the kings to make decisions and deliberate about social problems (Fash and Fash 1990).

These representatives were identified not by their personal names but by the name of the geographic area that they represented. This institutionalized set of jurisdictions and representatives implied that late classic Maya political organizations were beginning to move beyond the confines of kinship ties to more institutionalized forms of democratic government that cut across traditional family lines and interests. Such a decentralized—almost "derulerized"—approach to government was particularly significant from a social evolutionary perspective, for it points to the concurrent weakening of the personal authority of the king and the emergence of direct political participation (Fash and Fash 1990).

The ancestral Ponca government is an example of the democratic structures that flourished for thousands of years across North America.

Ponca Ancestral Political and Economic Traditions

Archaeological findings place the Ponca in the area that is now southern Ohio from 10,000 B.C. until their move westward to the plains of present-day Nebraska around A.D. 600 with other kinship tribes. They are of the Degiha division of the Siouan language family, which also includes the Omaha, Osage, Kansa, and Quapaw and is further related to the Chiwere division, which includes the Iowa, Oto, and Missouri tribes (Howard 1965). The Ponca and Omaha were one tribe until their separation sometime between 1390 and 1700 (Dorsey 1884 and 1886; Connelley 1918, 449). After separating from the Omaha, the Ponca traveled as far west as the Black Hills of South Dakota before establishing a village near the mouth of the Niobrara River in northeast Nebraska in the early to mid-1700s (Howard 1965, 24; Wishart 1994, 6).

Economic trade was common among indigenous Americans, offering peaceful interchanges between tribes and stability to the government. The strategic location of the Ponca fostered trade with the Arikara, Omaha, Pawnee, upriver Dakota, Lakota-speaking Sioux, and other tribes in the region. Archaeological findings at the Ponca Fort site, located west of the Niobrara River's entry into the Missouri River, reveal that Ponca trade with other tribes was both extensive and lucrative. Pottery, stone mauls, mealing slabs and mullers, bone knives, hoes, tubes, shaft wrenches and picks, catlinite pipes and disks, twined mats, and strip bark in rolls have been found at the Ponca fort site from tribes as far away as the southeastern United States (Wood 1959; Howard 1965, 11–12; LeRoy 1990). Corn was a basic article of trade, and although the Ponca raised corn, they often preferred to trade robes and meat to the Omahas for corn (Jablow 1974, 40).

The Ponca lived by a strict set of moral and social rules (Province 1955), as described by the late Ponca leader Peter Le Claire (1947), which were passed on to him by previous Ponca leaders:

1. Have one god.
2. Do not kill one another.
3. Do not steal from one another.
4. Be kind to one another.
5. Do not talk about each other.
6. Do not be stingy.
7. Have respect for the Sacred Pipe.

Individual violations of specific tribal laws of the Ponca were often enforced by the victims or their relatives, as was common among Plains tribes. The punishment of an adulterer, for example, was left to the injured husband, who might kill, scalp, or cut off the hair of a man whom he caught with his wife. A wife could kill another woman with whom her husband eloped (Skinner 1915, 800–801).

Ponca women participated in Ponca government, including going to war and becoming braves, whereas Omaha women did not (Skinner 1915, 794; Jablow 1974, 60). Killing as a form of capital punishment or in warfare was not considered murder. When murder was committed, retaliation was left to the relatives of the murdered individual and was often swift, due to the belief that "the spirit of a murdered person will haunt the people, and when the tribe is on the hunt, will cause the wind to blow in such a direction as to betray the hunters" (Fletcher and La Flesche 1911, 216). Religious sanctions acted as a powerful deterrent to illegal acts. The murderer "can never satisfy his hunger, though he eat much food" (Dorsey 1894, 420).

Tribal laws required that property belong to families, individuals, or the tribe as a whole. Community buildings and land belonged to the tribe. Individual "property" might be a man's gun and clothes. People had to ask to use another's individual property, and stealing was not tolerated. Families owned the tent or house. If a family member left, he lost his rights to the house. If a man left his wife, she kept the tipi (Le Claire 1965, 96). Divorce was simple in Ponca society. "If a man and wife didn't get along, or weren't satisfied, they just split up" (Le Claire 1965, 148). The children could go with their mother, her mother, or their father's mother, unless the father would not allow it. In that case, the wife could take the children with her. Each could remarry (Dorsey 1884, 262).

The political structure of the Ponca clans was hereditary and patrilineal. An individual's position in Ponca society depended upon his or her position in their family, their family's position in the clan, and the clan's position in the tribe. Certain clans outranked certain others socially and had special rights and prerogatives that others did not (Howard 1965, 81). The terms *clan, band,* and *gente* are used synonymously throughout past literature. The Ponca, like the Omaha, were divided into two moieties or half-tribes, the earth and sky (Fletcher and La Flesche 1911, 140). The Ponca had seven clans until the mid-1800s, when the *Wa-ge-ziga* or "White Men's Sons" clan became the eighth clan (Ponca Census 1860, 1). The eight clans of the Ponca and their duties are as follows.

The Ponca camp, called *Hu-thu-gah,* is round with the entrance in the east. Each of the bands has duties in the camp (Ponca Census 1860; Skinner 1915; Le Claire 1947). From the entrance left to right are the *Wazaze* (Skinner 1915, 799) or *Wah-ja-ta* (Le Claire 1947) ("snake" or "osage") who guard the entrance and are expert trackers. Touching snakes is taboo to members of this clan. The *Nikapasna* ("skull" or "bald head") know all about the human head and how it should be dressed. The *Dixida* (Skinner 1915, 799) ("blood") or *Te-xa-da* (Le Claire 1947) performed magic and, when the camp was getting short of meats, would get their bows and arrows out and make believe they were shooting animals, saying "I'll shoot this fat one."

The band in the center of the circle is the *Wasabe, Washabe,* or *Wahshaba.* The principal chief of the tribe was always selected from this clan, and members were forbidden from touching the head of an animal because they were of the head clan. The *Maka* or *Miki* ("medicine") knew all about medicines and contained the best herbalists in the tribe. The *Nuxe* or *Nuxa* ("ice") knew everything about water and ice. The *Hisada* or *He-sah-da* ("stretching of a bird's leg when running") were the tribal rainmakers. The *Wageziga* (White Men's Sons), which originated in the 1850s, was founded to accommodate the sons of white traders who took Ponca wives. This clan had a similar taboo to that of the *Dixida,* in that they could not touch mice (Skinner 1915, 799). Ponca subagency records identify that members of *Wageziga* often were interpreters between the Ponca and the whites. Some clans had one or two subclans or subgentes who also had specific clan duties and rules.

Although the principal chief of the Ponca came from the *Wasabe,* there were seven chiefs of the first order, one from each of the other seven clans, which were older chiefs, and from five to twelve second-order chiefs per clan. Both first- and second-order chiefs could inherit their position, chosen by their bravery or trustworthiness, or they could buy their positions with acts of bravery in war, usually the number of times they counted coup in battle. Seven first-order chiefs, which included the principal chief, met in council to decide most matters. A third class of chiefs has been mentioned in past literature but were most likely younger warriors who had demonstrated that they were "not just interested in themselves, but in the tribe as a whole" (Howard 1965, 92). Each clan also had a hereditary clan head or chief and a group of subchiefs, who were appointed by the clan head. A chief of the first, second, and third order might also be a clan head (Howard 1965, 92). In contrast with the Omaha, who chose their subchiefs through heredity, a clan head among the Ponca could choose his successor or subchiefs based on trustworthiness or bravery in battle (Skinner 1915, 795). Thus Ponca chieftainships, unlike those of the Omaha, were both autocratic and democratic in nature (Jablow 1974, 55–58).

The clan heads and their subchiefs enforced the laws of the clan and settled conflicts within the clan. Conflicts between members of different clans were often settled by the council of seven, which was made up of the first-order chiefs and the principal chief (Howard 1965, 92–93). Intragroup loyalty and cooperation required that even the clan heads must follow tribal rules. Tribal clan heads and sub-chiefs were required to be good to the old, good to orphans, and good to the needy. Any violation could mean removal as clan head and shame to the clan (Le Claire 1965, 98). Tribal legend also indicates that women were not barred from becoming chiefs. Often women who became chiefs were those with great supernatural power—medicine women (Le Claire 1965, 93).

The summer buffalo hunt was one instance where tribal law predominated since all the clans were together for an extended period of time, and a successful hunt was essential to tribal survival. The *Washabe* and the *Maka* clans "were given charge of the tribal buffalo hunt—the direction of the journey, the making of the camp, and preservation of order" (Fletcher and La Flesche 1911, 48). The leaders were in complete charge of the hunt and maintained discipline through the hunt police or Buffalo police. Those selected to be buffalo police were the bravest warriors of some clan but not the whole tribe—the bravest of some other clan served at another time. The hunt police "were chosen from those who had the right to wear the 'Crow,' a decoration possessed by those men who more than once had achieved war honors of the first three grades" (Fletcher and La Flesche 1911, 441; Skinner 1915, 794–795).

When the Ponca were not on the tribal hunt, tribal responsibility and rules continued to be enforced by one or two buffalo police appointed by the head of each clan. These buffalo police did not have to achieve the war honors necessary to wear the Crow, but personal leadership and character were important factors in becoming buffalo police. The buffalo police could be very severe in their punishment, even to the point of killing the offender. Ponca justice was directed more at preserving order than at social revenge. Conformity rather than revenge was sought, and immediately after a promise to conform was secured from the perpetrator, steps were taken to reincorporate him or her into the society once more (Province 1937, 350). For example, after the buffalo police had whipped a man for violating the rule against individual hunting during the tribal bison hunt, they would give him gifts so that "his heart would not be bad" (Howard 1965, 96).

The main functions of the buffalo police were to regulate the communal hunt; to regulate ceremonies; to settle disputes, punish offenders, and preserve order in the camp; and to regulate war parties and restrain such at inopportune times (Province 1937, 351; Howard 1965, 95). Being a clan head, subchief or buffalo police in a small, highly interrelated tribe such as the Ponca was not easy. Right or wrong, the actions of these political and legal leaders were liable to earn the ill will of not only the persons directly involved, but the clansmen of all those persons as well. In conclusion, the well being of the tribe was always a major influence on the implementation of the political and legal traditions of the Ponca. As a Ponca elder (Elder Story 1979) stated over twenty years ago, "Not like the white people who put their laws in large, heavy books and forget them. We Ponca carry our laws in our hearts, where we never live a day without them."

The Iroquois Confederacy

Nearly two thousand miles to the northeast of the Ponca homelands, democratic principles were practiced within the Iroquois Confederacy and other confederacies in the northeastern parts of what is now the United States and Canada for centuries before Europeans arrived. Iroquois oral history places the origin of the Great Law of Peace and the Iroquois League derived from the Great Law at somewhere between A.D. 1000 and 1100. The Great Law provided for the hereditary position of sachem (representative) to the Grand Council and declared that they "shall be mentors of the people for all time. Their hearts shall be full of peace and good will and their minds filled with a yearning for the *welfare of the people* of the League" (Johansen 1982).

Most accounts of the ideological origins of democracy give nearly full credit to European precedents, such as the Greeks, the Roman republic, the Magna Carta, and Swiss and Dutch experiments. These were very important, but we also owe an intellectual debt to American antecedents (Johansen 1988, Grinde and Johansen 1991 and 1996). Some historians have expressed very strong sentiments about the American Indian role in the development of democratic theory:

> Long before the Magna Carta, the document that American anglophiles occasionally point to as the start of civil liberties and democracy in the English-speaking world, Native American peoples were utilizing representative democracy. Egalitarian democracy and

liberty as we know them today owe little to Europe. They are not Greco-Roman derivatives somehow revived by the French in the eighteenth century. They entered modern western thought as American Indian notions translated into European language and culture. (Weatherford 1988)

Many Americans would find such statements hard to believe. This is understandable, for even the colonial settlers of America, who relied upon American Indian agriculture, housing, medicine, and even cooking techniques to survive in the unfamiliar American environment, did not give much credit to Native Americans for their governmental or political knowledge. As a result, pre-European American Indian political institutions and participation are widely misunderstood, both within academia and within American society (Carter 1980, Grinde and Johansen 1991). Vine Deloria Jr. (1990) points out a major reason for these misunderstandings:

The knowledge and technology of tribal peoples, primitive peoples and the ancient ones does not really appear in the modern scientific scheme unless it is to be found with the minor articulations of the concept of cultural evolution hidden in the backwaters of anthropology, sociology, and history.

This knowledge which served our ancestors so well emerges from time to time when modern scientists advocate a novel interpretation of data and, in order to claim some historical roots for their ideas, since new ideas are forbidden in academia, ancient or tribal peoples are cited as societies which once used certain practices or held certain beliefs. But the presentation of the ideas is usually accompanied by the patronizing view that although tribals and primitives did originate the idea or the practice, they could not have possibly understood its significance.

Native American Political Thought versus European Conquest

The vast majority of seventeenth- and eighteenth-century European philosophers and settlers considered the native peoples of America to be uncivilized "heathens." This thought was further complicated by the state of the world at the time in which anything "heathen" must be Christianized or be wiped from the face of the earth. Political philosophers such as Rousseau, Locke, and even

Roger Williams felt that it was right because these were heathens; it was right because these were savages; it was right because the Word of God must be penetrated into the interior; it was right because they were the conquerors; it was right because they had the might (Mohawk 1987).

In the process of conquest it was necessary to convince the monarchical governments of the time that there were no intellectuals or philosophers among these "barbarians." The Spanish burned the manuscripts of the great libraries of the Aztec and Maya, burning and maybe forever destroying the scholarship of these great people and then called them "barbarians and savages." The destruction of such American Indian masterpieces may be one reason why American Indian history has remained mostly an oral history (Mohawk 1987).

In modern times, the American and European colleges and universities continue to celebrate the great philosophers of the West, as they should. The dilemma lies in the fact that the academic world has so entrenched itself in Western thought that the validity of any other philosopher or culture is difficult, if even possible, to be considered. Few academics or students possess knowledge of the political theories or institutions of cultures other than those of Western society. It is almost as though there were no great thinkers except the thinkers of the West (Mohawk 1987; Deloria 1990).

> This denial of thinking among peoples other than European peoples was so great (among the Europeans, especially European scholars) that when these two worlds came together, the people who wrote the history wrote the Indian thinking right out of the history because by the theories of the conquistador, the Indian could not think, a burro cannot think.
>
> So the very idea that Indians could have helped thinking among Europeans has been negated by the very people who gained the most from contact with American Indians, the Europeans. (Mohawk 1987)

To understand American Indian political participation, one must understand the cultural, social, and tribal norms prior to European contact and after European contact, including federal Indian policy. Participation in tribal societies was governed by rules of conduct, status, and norms that still exist in many modern American Indian tribes. The following sections of this chapter offer insight into the historical dynamics that continue to influence modern American Indian societies and participation.

Native American Nations called "Tribes" by the Europeans

For thousands of years, each Native American nation has considered itself a separate nation and, indeed, a separate race. They did not consider themselves generically or genetically identical. The term *Indian* was coined by Christopher Columbus in 1492 when he mistakenly thought he had reached India. Other terms were given to groups of Indians. The Europeans applied the word *tribe* to Native American nations in order to avoid giving Native American peoples legal or ethical status as nations. By using the word *tribe,* with its connotation of primitiveness, Europeans could rationalize behavior that was not in accord with international law governing relations between equal nations (Yerington Paiute Tribe 1985).

With the arrival of the Europeans, tribal societies began to be viewed as a homogeneous race. Later, Europeans gave Indian groups names that were often unflattering. For example, Navajo means "stealer of crops," Apache means "enemy," and Mohawk means "man-eater." The Delaware were named after a European who never set foot in America (Yerington Paiute Tribe 1985).

Each tribal group already had its own name in the native language before the Europeans arrived. Usually the tribal name translated as "the People," "the Human Beings," or something similar. The Navajo refer to themselves as *Dineh* ("the People"), the Chippewa as *Anishinawbe* ("the Original People"), the Northern Paiute as *Numu* (Human Beings), the Ponca as *Punka* ("Head People"), and the Delaware as *Lenni Lenape* ("True Men") (Yerington Paiute Tribe 1985; Ponca Oral History).

Among the North American Indians, the word *tribe* originally meant a body of persons bound together by blood ties who were socially, politically, and religiously organized and who lived together, occupying a definite territory and speaking a common language or dialect (Bureau of Indian Affairs 1987). However, the term *tribe* has achieved some validity as the equivalent of *nation* through repeated use in legal documents (Yerington Paiute Tribe 1985). Throughout this book, tribe and nation will have the same meaning.

Precontact Participation in Government and Leadership

Some tribes had to move to keep up with the herds of animals they depended on for food, so they tended to be smaller. Since these tribes were very small, they could utilize *direct democracy,* a political system in which each member of the group helps decide each problem or policy (Yerington Paiute Tribe 1985), oftentimes through a unanimous decision. (New England town hall meetings are an example of direct democracy in the European tradition.)

These smaller, nomadic tribes also developed a political system that allowed for shifting leadership, depending on the particular problem the tribe faced. Different kinds of problems would call forth different people to lead (Yerington Paiute Tribe 1985).

Larger and less mobile tribes had more representative, or *republican,* forms of government. Some tribes, as they grew larger and had more and more contact with one another, developed intertribal government systems that were much like confederal governments. Each of several tribes or villages would retain basic internal control, but the groups worked as a single unit in external matters (Yerington Paiute Tribe 1985).

The Iroquois Confederacy, which stretched from present-day north-central Pennsylvania through New York, presently includes the Mohawk, Oneida, Onondaga, Cayuga, and Seneca nations. The neighboring Wabanaki Confederacy, which embraced all the speakers of Eastern and Western Abenaki dialects, in the early 1600s held the territory in the present states of Maine, New Hampshire, and northeastern Massachusetts (Penobscot Indian Nation 1989).

Tribes often split into subtribes or new tribes if they felt they had become too large. The ancient Anasazi, who pioneered urban development in their multifamily units that housed as many as five thousand people at a time, broke up into the several Pueblo tribes that exist today (Pueblos 1989). However, these break ups of a tribe were not always caused by population increases but also by climate changes, changing hunting patterns, intertribal conflict, or conflict with another tribe.

Although tribal size influenced participation, subdivisions in the tribe influenced participation as well. In many tribes, the bands and clans often acted like "mini" tribes, with band or clan members living and traveling together. The band chief, clan matron or patron, and elders would act as the local government within the band or clan area, settling disputes within the band or clan and setting in place the rules that governed band or clan behavior. Participation in certain religious ceremonies were band or clan specific, that is, only band or clan members could participate in them. The particular practices performed in such ceremonies were known only by specific band or clan members and were carried down from generation to generation within the band or clan (Standing Bear 1933).

Values played a role in shaping different tribal governments. Some tribes emphasized physical strength and military success, and the traditional tribal leaders were often war heroes (Yerington Paiute Tribe 1985). Prior to the coming of the Europeans, individual acts of bravery were viewed as a sign of potential leadership ability. Skin paintings describing raids by other tribes upon the Lakota and Dakota (Sioux) from 1778 to 1784 focus on acts of bravery by particular Lakota. During the winter of 1779–1780, an Oglala warrior named Long Pine fought many Crow raiders but was killed by an enemy, as evidenced by the absence of his scalp. In 1783 the Mandans and Rees made a charge on a Dakota village. The Dakota drove them back, killed twenty-five of them, and captured a boy. An eagle's tail, which is worn on the head, stands for the Mandan and Ree (Powell 1886). Acts of bravery during such raids did not always include killing one's adversary. Oftentimes it meant taking horses or women and children or counting coup. Counting coup meant coming as close to an enemy as physically possible and touching or hitting them with a lance or club without causing serious injury or death. The purpose of counting coup was to show one's bravery and to shame the one that is counted coup upon, although one also extracts some of the power of the one who is counted coup upon. In the heat of battle warriors often would count coup upon a dead or wounded enemy, and it was regarded as an act equal in bravery to killing an enemy (Powell 1886).

Besides being brave, ancestral leaders tended to be nonauthoritarian. No matter how great the number of coups a warrior may count or their degree of bravery, their leadership was greatly limited by tribal law and customs. Leaders could not make many decisions unless they had been discussed and agreed to by the people. Leaders who stepped beyond the authority they had been given were either ignored or replaced (Yerinton Paiute Tribe 1985), thus increasing and diversifying participation in all stages of tribal decision making.

After the coming of the Europeans, warriors such as Massasoit (called King Philip by the English) of the Wampanoags (Grinde and Johansen 1991), Bashabes of the Penobscot (Penobscot Indian Nation 1989), Little Wolf and Dull Knife of the Cheyenne (Northern Cheyenne Tribe and Reservation 1988), Red Cloud, Sitting Bull, and Crazy Horse of the Lakota in their great victory over Custer (Ellis 1972; Freel 1990), Geronimo of the Chiricahuas Apache (Ogle 1972), and countless others were thrust into leadership roles in order to protect their peoples from utter annihilation.

The institution of leadership among Native Americans underwent considerable change as a result of white contact. Individuals rose to leadership positions that did not exist previously; traditional leaders were replaced by new leaders who possessed qualities demanded by intercourse with whites; and where there had been several leaders or representatives on more or less the same level, there was now a transmutation to choosing the one of greatest importance. These individual leaders, identified by the whites as "chiefs," were the principal, responsible leaders from the intergovernmental viewpoint, mainly concerning treaty making and warfare. But the chief who appeared most important to the whites may not have been, from the traditional point of view (Jablow 1974).

Pueblo governments were called theocracies. A theocracy is a government ruled by leaders who claim to rule with divine authority. (The kings and queens of Europe fall into this category.) In the case of the Pueblo, the religious leaders appointed the governing leaders of the tribe (Yerington Paiute Tribe 1985, 20). This governmental process continues today at the Pueblo De Acoma, where tribal council members are appointed by the traditional religious leaders. The theocracy of the Acoma Pueblo is unique in comparison to many other Native American tribal governments, but because of historical contact, it is similar to the systems of other Pueblos in the southwestern United States (Pueblo De Acoma 1989, Acoma Government).

Ancestral American Indian societies did not separate religion from government. They made little distinction between the political and religious worlds. Political wisdom was synonymous with spiritual power. All political actions were undertaken "with spiritual guidance and oriented toward spiritual as well as political fulfillment" (O'Brien 1989, 14). Tribal leaders sought spiritual advice in nearly every decision they made. Since Native Americans place spirituality as the paramount aspect of their daily living, American Indian spirituality impacted all aspects of American Indian society, including political participation.

Europeans commonly imagine that American Indian tribes interacted minimally, if at all, with other tribes before the arrival of the Europeans. However, Native American tribes maintained continual interaction with one another since the beginning of time. Ponca legends speak of ancestral meetings with the Aztec as well as the Iroquois, Ojibwa, and Lakota. Ancestral stories of Ponca travels stretch from the land of the Iroquois and Huron to the lands of the Seminole and Creek and into the sacred Paha Sapa (Black Hills) of the Lakota.

Tribal interaction led to verbal and recorded agreements between tribes in such matters as territorial boundaries, seasonal ceremonial gatherings among tribes, and protective alliances. The Ponca and Pawnee, for example, maintained a territorial boundary at the Elkhorn River in Nebraska that was utilized to prevent overhunting by either tribe in the other tribe's essential hunting areas. Both tribes respected the other's right to an adequate food supply through maintenance of this boundary. Clan and/or band heads of each tribe often met and exchanged the staffs of their respective clans or bands so that tribal members could cross this boundary and travel in the other tribe's territory for social, trade, or political visits and hunt in the other tribe's area if game was sparse in their own lands. If either crossed the Elkhorn River boundary without the clan or band staffs, it meant war. To Pawnee and Ponca warriors, crossing the Elkhorn into the other tribe's territory and counting coup brought great honor and power (Ponca Oral History).

Interaction with other tribes led to changes in tribal governments as tribes learned from one another. Tribes continually adopted ideas that had been developed by other groups. Of course, when one tribe was conquered or absorbed by another, changes in government were very swift (Yerington Paiute Tribe 1985). Many of the aforementioned confederacies were made up of tribes that came together to instill peace among themselves and to unite to protect all within the confederacy. Governing systems changed as tribes learned from one another, conquered one another, and sought peace through unity (Grinde and Johansen 1991).

Family Representation and Participation: Bands and Clans

Almost all pre-European tribal governments were based on family relations, or kinship. Usually leadership was inherited in two ways—the son took his father's place as leader or the new leader was chosen by the leaders of family groups (Yerington Paiute Tribe 1985). Family identity specified and required participation in family, clan/band, and tribal government and society. The following example from the Creek Nation of Oklahoma offers insight into kinship nature of Native American tribal governments.

Family ties are strong among the Indian people of the Creek Nation. There are a number of small Indian communities scattered throughout rural areas of the Creek Nation. In these communities, sons and daughters have built their homes simply because they want to be near their (elders and ancestors). The young people of the Creek Nation have great respect for their elders; these young people are taught during childhood to respect their elders and gain their heritage and cultural values from their elders. These people have a strong belief that this (living with or near their elders) is where they belong and the possibility of their wanting to leave is remote. (Muscogee Creek Nation 1990)

The Native American idea of kinship is much broader than that of the Europeans. Europeans view their family as their mother and father, grandparents, aunts and uncles, children, and cousins. Normally they do not see themselves related to anyone beyond their second or third cousin. In most cases the Native American family includes all the relatives included in the European family structure plus all members of their clan, adopted members from their tribe and other tribes, and even non-Indians. According to Lakota Luther Standing Bear (1933), "outside of family membership every person was an aunt, uncle, cousin, or "brother's keeper" to someone else. Relationships that white people would never recognize, because of their distance, were recognized by the Lakota."

Also included in the concept of family may be those from other tribes, bands, or clans who honor you by calling you "grandson" or "granddaughter," "niece" or "nephew," "brother" or "sister," and "son" or "daughter," even though they are not biologically related to you. This process of adoption is an honor-based tradition among many tribes. A person gains recognition from an elder as that elder's "granddaughter" or "nephew," etc., due to spiritual practices, family friendship, cultural preservation, and even to bring peace among warring tribes. It would be very difficult to fight one's grandmother's band or clan, whether she is your biological grandmother or not (Ponca Oral History, Standing Bear 1933; Black Elk and Lyon 1990). Kinship through adoption, whether "legal" or traditional, continues among modern-day tribes. Adoption ceremonies are sacred, special events, especially for the one who is to be accepted into the family, band, or clan of another.

Family ties were extremely influential within ancestral tribal government participation and structure. It is quite possible that the reason the facade of the building at Copa'n did not contain the names of the Mayan representatives but rather the names of the people they represent is that the people were more than just their "wards"; they were their family band or clan. And it is likely that the individual representatives shared the same name as the family band or clan that they represented, so the representative's name and that of those being represented were the same because they were both from the same family structure, the band or clan.

Bands

The term *tribe* often labeled something that did not exist. Not all members of a tribe lived together in permanent villages. A tribe was often comprised several bands that resided within a certain territory yet rarely came together as an entity. Quite naturally, they never saw themselves as one tribe. For example, the Northern Paiute are actually composed of a number of bands, including the *Tobusi Ticutta, Agai Ticutta, Cuyui Ticutta,* and *Pugwi Ticutta* (Yerington Paiute Tribe 1985).

Lakota elder and band chief Luther Standing Bear (1933) offered an insight into the civil arrangements of the Lakota (Sioux) and its bands:

> The *Lakota Oyate,* or Lakota Nation, was made up of *Tiyospaye,* or bands. These two words, *Oyate* and *Tiyospaye,* were the only two terms in the Lakota language that pertained to the civil or governmental structure of Lakota society, there being but two bodies or departments making up the organization.
>
> In size, bands might be small, medium or large, say from thirty or forty families to one hundred or more families. They erected their villages close together for social activities, which also added protection and strength to the bands. Each band was a social unit under a separate chieftainship, yet each band was an integral part of the nation. Bands were usually called by the name of some leading chief, such as Little Wound's Band or Red Leaf's Band. After the [U.S. government's Indian] agency was established, many different bands came together to be all known as *Oglalas.* (Standing Bear 1933)

Among the Lakota (Sioux) children were members of both the father's and the mother's band. Luther Standing Bear (1933) wrote: "My father was a member of the One Horse band and my mother was a member of the Swift Bear band, while I was claimed by both bands. I could not, therefore, have married within either one of these bands."

Each band of the Lakota (Sioux) had one, perhaps two, and sometimes a number of chiefs, depending somewhat, of course, on the size of the band; the greater the number of chiefs in a band, the greater its worth and importance, for only the finest of men became chiefs. So the fame of a band rested upon the number of tipis, horses, or other goods it might possess (Standing Bear 1933).

A major difference between a band and a clan appears to be geographic in nature. Bands were often geographically separated from one another, which is one reason the Europeans often mistook them for tribes. Clans, on the other hand, often lived within the same geographic area or village with one another, though even clans sometimes split off into separate geographic locations away from the main tribal body (Jablow 1974).

Clans

Clans, as opposed to bands, appear to have been responsible for a certain duty within the overall tribe, which specified clan participation in governmental matters. One clan might take care of military matters, another perform the religious duties, and a third might be in charge of hunting or the harvest. Sometimes one clan might provide the tribal leaders. These governing duties were passed down from father to son, or mother to daughter, with each clan training its young to administer the clan's tribal duties (Yerington Paiute Tribe 1985).

The number of clans within a tribe varied by the population of the tribe and also among tribes. Among the Ponca were seven clans for around twelve hundred persons prior to 1860. Each clan was fairly equal in both size and the number of families within it, thus preventing conflict based on size. Another clan was added in the latter part of the 1860s for half-breeds. Although this half-breed clan was slightly smaller than the other clans, its importance in tribal affairs was not diminished by size, for the leaders of this clan were very useful in negotiating with non-Indians and the U.S. government. Members of this clan spoke both English and Ponca and acted as interpreters for the other clan leaders (Howard 1965).

The maintenance of clan size was important. If a clan became too small, it might be absorbed by another clan; if it became too large, it might separate and develop its own tribal government. (Some feel that is what happened when the Omaha and Ponca split up.) This is one reason why adoption of persons from outside the biological origins of the clan was important, for the size of the clan often was correlated with the power and duties of the clan. The splitting off of clans also occurred when a conflict arose between clans that could not be simply resolved. The minority clan in the tribe would agree to move to a different area and live as a separate government (Yerington Paiute Tribe 1985).

Clan membership was hereditary, either through the maternal or paternal side of one's family. In most tribes, heredity was maternal—that is, the clan one belonged to was determined through heredity on the mother's side. In a maternal clan there would be a clan matron who would make many of the decisions of the clan. For example, the clan matron heads of the Iroquois chose the male representative from the clan to the Grand Council (Grinde 1977).

In the early history of the Creek Nation, the entire population of the Creek Nation was divided into clans. The children born of a married couple would belong to the same clan as the mother. According to this tradition, the women controlled ownership of belongings and property. In some instances, the Creek people have changed tradition to accommodate the changing times: if a Creek man marries a non-Indian woman or a woman from another tribe, the children born to this couple would belong to the same clan as their father (Muscogee Creek Nation 1990).

Tribes such as the Ponca (Nebraska and Oklahoma) and Quapaw (Missouri and Oklahoma) determined clan membership through heredity on the father's or paternal side (Jablow 1974; Quapaw Tribe of Oklahoma 1989). Clan membership could also come through adoption, either within the tribe or from another tribe or even racial group. Often adoption of a member of another tribe captured in a raid was done in order to substitute that person for a deceased relative. If a member of one clan died, members of another clan were responsible for his or her burial ceremonies.

Quapaw society was based on large family units. Each family unit was subdivided into many clans and subclans, which took their names from the animal kingdom (Deer, Elk, Black Bear, Grizzly Bear, Beaver, Buffalo, Dog, Panther, Fish, Turtle, Eagle, Crane, etc.) or some cosmic phenomenon (Star, Thunder, Sun, etc.). The clan or subclan to which a Quapaw belonged was determined through heredity on the father's side. The Downstream People, as the Quapaws called themselves, grouped the clans in two major divisions or moieties: one associated with the land, the other with the sky. The clan system gave individual Quapaws a spiritual identity and morally obligated each to help shield the other in times of crisis. Fellow clan members were related by blood or were considered relatives, so they could not marry each other (making the tribe exogamous). Occasionally a husband would take a second wife, but polygamy was not common among the Quapaws. Divorce was common and easy to accomplish. There was no ritual or process to go through; couples simply separated. Despite easy divorces, children were cherished and adoption was common among Quapaw clans (Quapaw Tribe of Oklahoma 1989).

Moiety

Another kind of division, a twofold division or moiety, also occurred within the tribe. Every individual definitely knew to which one of the two divisions he or she belonged. Certain names and functions were associated with the moieties, and today the moieties connote different ideas in different tribes (Yerington Paiute Tribe 1985).

Among the Omaha in the late nineteenth century, the moieties were known as *Ictacunda* and *Hanga,* probably connoting Sky People and Leaders; among the Ponca as *Wajaje* and *Tciju,* Earth and Thunder; among the Kansa as *Yata* and *Ictunga,* Right Side and Left Side; among the Osage as *Tciju* and *Hanga,* Peace and War (Bureau of American Ethnology 1919). The Quapaw, too, grouped their clans into two major moieties: one associated with the land, the other with the sky (Quapaw Tribe of Oklahoma 1989).

The moieties existed and continue to exist for specific purposes and occasions: when the tribe was on the tribal hunt, in which the clans that belonged to one moiety would hunt together or clans would share their kill with other clans in that moiety; and during ceremonial gatherings that could be attended by clans from their particular moiety only (Bureau of American Ethnology 1919).

Moiety-type subtribal groups leagued together for mutual protection, since the clan or moiety might be too small a group to adequately defend itself from attack. The Maskoke (Creek) tribes were leagued together for mutual protection, for example, the Kasihta and the Coweta who became the nucleus of the Lower Creek (or Lower Towns) and the Abihka and the Coosa who thus formed the beginning of the Upper Creek (or Upper Towns). This trend in uniting for a common purpose resulted in the great Creek Confederacy, in which the Maskoke-speaking peoples were dominant. The Maskoke proper comprised approximately twelve separate tribal groups, including the *Kashita, Coweta, Coosa, Abihke, Wakokai, Eufaula, Hilabia, Atasi, Kolomi, Tukabahchee, Pakana,* and *Okchai.* In the Lower Creek division, the *Kashita* were the White or Peace group, and the *Coweta,* the Red or War group (Muscogee Creek Nation 1990).

Kinship Influences on the Individual

The clan system gave (and still gives) individual Native Americans a spiritual identity and morally obligated each to help and shield the other in times of crisis. Clans still influence position and participation in modern Native American tribal governments, as evidenced by the following statements:

> Tribal council members are selected on the basis of clan.
>   (Pueblo De Acoma 1989, Acoma Government)

> Traditional clan influence is still evident in council meetings. Meetings open in traditional prayer with maternal clans creating a network of close relations (a first cousin is referred to by the word that also means sister/brother, etc.), and these close blood-ties create a tight bond in the structure. Tradition allows for anyone wishing to speak being given that opportunity. (Forest County Potawatomi Community 1990)

> The Tribal Clans have great influence in the tribal government. Two (clan) people are allowed to sit in on a council meeting. (Santa Clara Pueblo 1990)

In some modern tribes that elect their tribal council members by district, the district may have evolved from band or clan settlement areas and may be named after the particular band or clan that settled the area. Several members of a particular band or clan may continue to live in a particular district. The district may also have the same name as the band or clan that initially inhabited the area, for example, Red Shirt or Bear districts.

Factions within modern-day tribal governments are often based along family-clan lines. Some tribal leaders see these factions as destructive to the tribal government by protecting the policies favorable to that family-clan at the expense of other families or clans. Others see these family-clan-based factions as keeping an eye on those in power so that they do not use their powers at the expense of the people. One thing is certain: family-clan relationships have always played a key role in tribal government and politics, and their demise will not occur in the near future. Among Native Americans, one can truly say that family comes first in all relations, including participation in tribal politics ("Tribal Officials' Political Survey" 1998).

The Collective Attitude: Tribal Consciousness

Although respect for individual autonomy and freedom was important in tribal culture, the individual's inclusion within the wholeness of his or her tribe was (and still is) critical to his or her existence. Ancestral American Indian societies, as a rule, were egalitarian, without the kinds of centralized authority and social hierarchy typical of Western societies. Leadership was generally based on "personal qualities and not on any formal or permanent status" (Waldman and Braun 1985).

Ancestral American Indian hierarchical leadership, unlike the rigid style of the Europeans, was very fluid. Leaders led when called upon to lead and left leadership when they were no longer needed or when they were told to do so by their governing bodies, elders, or family heads. Section 14 of the *Gayanashagowa* (Iroquois constitution) allows for the speaker of the Grand Council of the Iroquois Confederacy to be appointed daily, so a person may serve as a speaker for years or one day (Grinde 1977).

Within the ancestral Native American family, each member had a place or position, often given at birth or a young age, based on family or clan recognition. Later in life members might gain another position or additional status based on particular events (bravery in battle), spiritual intervention (a dream, vision, or spiritual event), particular behavior (special or contrary living), or an age-related event (becoming a grandparent). Children were taught from birth to respect the status of each member of their family and clan and their place in the family or clan. Children knew which members of their clan or family to address, and when and how to do so. A son-in-law in some Plains tribes could never look his mother-in-law directly in the eyes. Young women in some tribes would not look young men straight in the eyes. Elders were not to be interrupted when speaking (this would be a difficult concept for European parliamentary procedure to deal with) (Duran and Duran 1995).

Tribal government decision making was often by consensus through unanimous decisions. Some present-day Indian leaders feel that a return to unanimous rule is needed—a departure from the European-style majority rule that the federal government imposed upon tribal governments and that still survives in the vast majority of tribes ("Tribal Political Officials' Survey" 1998). Majority rule, they maintain, only serves to perpetuate factionalism and minority agitation within modern tribal governments (Little Bear et al. 1984).

The collective attitude that dominated nearly all ancestral tribal governments meant that each tribal member considered himself or herself in terms of the group. The idea of people doing things or owning things individually did not make sense, because each individual was only a part of the whole. Because of this collective attitude, most tribal decision-making procedures were highly democratic. Due to their size, the smaller tribes were probably direct democracies. Each decision was discussed by all the members, and each member's voice counted. No decision was made until every person agreed to it (Yerington Paiute Tribe 1985).

One must realize that even though each individual's opinion was valued, if a unanimous consensus could not be reached, those in the minority who remained opposed to the beliefs of the majority often agreed to move to a different area and live as a separate government (Yerington Paiute Tribe 1985). Maintenance of the collective tribe was of the greatest importance. To ancestral American Indian societies, the words "we the people" were not just written into a constitution; they were a way of life that influenced each and every day of their lives.

Some argue that the collective aspect of Native American life is greatly diminished among modern-day tribal governments, replaced by individualistic rule tied to individual economic gain, imposed from outside. Yet one does not need to look far to find the collective attitude among today's Native Americans; one need only attend a *give away*. At a give away, which normally takes place after a death, adoption, naming ceremony, marriage, powwow, or other family- or clan-oriented ceremony, the host gives away personal belongings or gifts to all that attend. A guest may not refuse a gift, even though he or she may know that giving the gift is a financial burden on the family or clan. A give away is a very respected event for the family and/or clan doing so. It is an honor to receive a gift, and it is an honor to give away. Poverty does not alter the honor and joy of gift giving (Springer 1981 and 1991; Wilson 1991; Pearson 1992; Carufel 1994).

Involvement with one's tribe was and continues to be integral to the very existence of each tribal member. Ostracism or banishment was considered to be a living death (Little Bear et al. 1984). To place one's individual wants and needs above that of the tribe was inconceivable. To steal from or bring shame to one's tribe was unthinkable. To violate a custom of one's tribe was to violate one's own family.

The lack of lawlessness among Native Americans amazed the Europeans, as noted by Christopher Columbus on October 16, 1492:

> Although earlier Indians had seemed without law . . . in Hispaniola "there is government"; "there is a judge or lord whom all obey." And the lords are "men of few words, and excellent memories" who maintains "a very marvelous state, of a style so orderly that it is a pleasure to see it." They have, in brief, "very good customs" (Cohen 1969).

> I have not been able to find out if they have private property. As far as I could see, whatever a man had was shared among all the rest. (Morison 1955)

Amerigo Vespucci noted a similar finding:

> They live amongst themselves without (punishment by) king or rulers . . . yet we never saw disputing among them.
> They are so liberal in giving that it is the exception when they deny you anything. (Eden 1553)

Later European political philosophers were likewise impressed by the lack of state-sponsored coercion in most American Indian societies. Karl Marx and Frederich Engels (1968) offered an intricate account of the Iroquoian polity that directly examined the league's ability to maintain social cohesion without an elaborate state apparatus.

Lakota elder Luther Standing Bear explained this concept of "self-government" that has so intrigued non–Native Americans for centuries:

> The Lakotas were self-governors, and the rules and regulations that governed the conduct of people and established their duties as individuals, families, and bands came from a great tribal consciousness. Deep within the people, mingling with their emotions, was an inherent sense of solidarity—a tie between one and all others that the nation

might be expressed. Though each person became individualized—could be as truthful, as honest, as generous, as industrious, or as brave as he or she wished—could even go to battle upon his initiative, he could not consider himself separate from the band or nation.

Tribal consciousness was the sole guide and dictator, there being no human agency to compel the individual to accept guidance or obey dictates, yet for one to cut himself off from the whole meant to lose identity or to die. (Standing Bear 1933)

Written laws were not a part of tribal consciousness.

Such laws are written to be, in time, rewritten or unwritten, and that means to be kept and broken.

It is a mistake, therefore, to believe that a people without written laws are a lawless people. The Lakotas were, in fact, bound by the only codes that endure—those written into the essence of living. (Standing Bear 1933)

The Bureau of Ethnology of the Smithsonian found that "the Indians have a system of tribal laws which are notably fair, comprehensive, and efficient. In the absence of writing there are no statutes, yet through the intricate system of prescriptorial association the laws are perpetuated almost as completely as, and inculcated much more generally than, the statutes of civilized people; in nearly all tribes the code was crystallized in the tribal organization" (Bureau of American Ethnology 1881).

Tribal Code of Ethics

As we have seen, proper behavior has always been emphasized among Native American people and their tribal governments. Proper behavior was and continues to be impressed upon Native American children by their elders. In fact, "old people were revered for their knowledge and were never considered worthless members to be got rid of" (Standing Bear 1933). Tribal codes of behavior were passed down verbally from generation to generation and among ancestral tribal governments and in written form among many modern tribal governments.

Winnebago elder Reuben Snake (1989) of Nebraska offered the following "American Indian Governmental Code of Ethics" to modern-day tribal governments:

1. Treat all the people equally in assignment of responsibilities and distribution of tribal resources.
2. Immediately step forward when a threat confronts your people from any quarter.
3. Be the last in line to accept any largesse coming to the people.
4. Always seek the creator's blessings on your endeavors and the counsel of your elders in your efforts to lead your people.
5. Always exhibit the utmost compassion, respect, and honor toward your fellow man and woman.
6. Always maintain your personal dignity in any and every situation.
7. Always put the welfare of the people first.

Federal Indian Policy: Native Americans in Transition

White people have always tried to make us [Indians] like them. And we have always fought to remain Indian. I think we have won this war for we still practice the ways of our ancestors and the white people don't. They now come to us to learn our ways. (Black Elk 1991)

Thousands, perhaps even millions, of cultural conflicts have arisen between Euro-Americans and Native Americans in terms of their life philosophies, beliefs, and practices. Many of these conflicts, especially in terms of land ownership, ended in bloodshed and death. The majority of these conflicts were caused by U.S. government policies concerning Native Americans that were designed to assimilate Native Americans into "civilized" Euro-American society. This section discusses some of the assimilationist government policies and their impact on American Indian governments and political participation.

Federal Indian policy is a plan or course of action designed to influence and define decisions affecting Native American tribes and Alaska Natives. It is a guiding principle, determining the direction the U.S. government takes in its relations with tribal governments and in the general conduct of Indian affairs.

In the more than two centuries since the United States came into being, federal Indian policy has fluctuated greatly. Its intentions have been captured in self-explanatory names describing periods of history, such as "forced removal," "assimilation," "termination," and "self-determination." Each reflects an attitude of the federal government toward Native Americans (Bureau of Indian Affairs 1984, 1), and each has directly affected the ability and desire of Native Americans to participate in all levels of politics.

Native American land and resources have been entrusted to the U.S. government for over two hundred years. A trust relationship stipulates that the property of one party (Native Americans) is under the charge of a trustee (the United States) or trustees. But the trust relationship between the United States and Indian tribes and Alaska Natives is complex and cannot be so precisely defined. For this reason, misunderstandings sometimes arise and parties often disagree on the extent of the trust. The trust agreement is not spelled out in any single document. Rather, the trust is an evolving doctrine that has been expanded over the years to meet changing situations and changing times (Bureau of Indian Affairs 1984).

It is wrong to conclude, however, that because the trust relationship is not specifically defined, it is lacking in importance or significance. The trust agreements that presently exist between the United States and over three hundred Native American nations are derived from historically established legal and moral obligation that require the United States to protect and enhance the property and resources of Indian tribes.

The Shift from Independent to Dependent Nations

The implementation of federal trust responsibility began in the 1830s under President Andrew Jackson, who had been raised among tribes in Tennessee and, during the War of 1812, sought the assistance of tribal allies, who fought side by side with him. In the 1820s, the Cherokee, Choctaw, Creek, and other "civilized" tribes were very prosperous across the present states of Georgia and the Carolinas. The Cherokee had their own newspapers, schools, tribal capital, and government and held millions of acres of land in tribal and individual ownership. They also owed thousands of slaves. Non-Indian settlers coming to the area were jealous of the Cherokee's wealth and land and sought assistance from the state of Georgia and the federal government in moving the Cherokee westward so that their lands would be open to settlement. Jackson obliged by spearheading the passage of the Indian Removal Act of 1830, and the tribes saw their old ally become their new enemy.

THE INDIAN REMOVAL ACT OF 1830

CHAP. CXLVIII.—An Act to provide for an exchange of lands with the Indians residing in any of the states or territories, and for their removal west of the river Mississippi.

Be it enacted by the Senate and House of Representatives of the United States of America, in Congress assembled, That it shall and may be lawful for the President of the United States to cause so much of any territory belonging to the United States, west of the river Mississippi, not included in any state or organized territory, and to which the Indian title has been extinguished, as he may judge necessary, to be divided into a suitable number of districts, for the reception of such tribes or nations of Indians as may choose to exchange the lands where they now reside, and remove there; and to cause each of said districts to be so described by natural or artificial marks, as to be easily distinguished from every other.

SEC. 2. And be it further enacted, That it shall and may be lawful for the President to exchange any or all of such districts, so to be laid off and described, with any tribe or nation within the limits of any of the states or territories, and with which the United States have existing treaties, for the whole or any part or portion of the territory claimed and occupied by such tribe or nation, within the bounds of any one or more of the states or territories, where the land claimed and occupied by the Indians, is owned by the United States, or the United States are bound to the state within which it lies to extinguish the Indian claim thereto.

SEC. 3. And be it further enacted, That in the making of any such exchange or exchanges, it shall and may be lawful for the President solemnly to assure the tribe or nation with which the exchange is made, that the United States will forever secure and guaranty to them, and their heirs or successors, the country so exchanged with them; and if they prefer it, that the United States will cause a patent or grant to be made and executed to them for the same: Provided always, That such lands shall revert to the United States, if the Indians become extinct, or abandon the same.

SEC. 4. And be it further enacted, That if, upon any of the lands now occupied by the Indians, and to be exchanged for, there should be such improvements as add value to the land claimed by any individual or individuals of such tribes or nations, it shall and may be lawful for the President to cause such value to be ascertained by appraisement or otherwise, and to cause such ascertained value to be paid to the person or persons rightfully claiming such improvements. And upon the payment of such valuation, the improvements so valued and paid for, shall pass to the United States, and possession shall not afterwards be permitted to any of the same tribe.

SEC. 5. And be it further enacted, That upon the making of any such exchange as is contemplated by this act, it shall and may be lawful for the President to cause such aid and assistance to be furnished to the emigrants as may be necessary and proper to enable them to remove to, and settle in, the country for which they may have exchanged; and also, to give them such aid and assistance as may be necessary for their support and subsistence for the first year after their removal.

SEC. 6. And be it further enacted, That it shall and may be lawful for the President to cause such tribe or nation to be protected, at their new residence, against all interruption or disturbance from any other tribe or nation of Indians, or from any other person or persons whatever.

SEC. 7. And be it further enacted, That it shall and may be lawful for the President to have the same superintendence and care over any tribe or nation in the country to which they may remove, as contemplated by this act, that he is now authorized to have over them at their present places of residence.

(Bureau of Indian Affairs 2002)

The U.S. Supreme Court became involved in the dispute between the Cherokee and Jackson in the case of *Cherokee Nation v. Georgia,* which was decided in 1831. The significance of the high court opinion in this case, written by Chief Justice John Marshall, is found in a discussion of the legal status of Indian tribes and their relationship with the federal government. Marshall characterized this relationship as "perhaps unlike that of any other two people in existence" and said it was "marked by peculiar and cardinal distinctions that exist nowhere else." He then invoked the trust relationship between the United States and Indian tribes by saying it "resembles that of a ward to his guardian" (*Cherokee Nation v. Georgia* 1831). The use of such words as *guardian* and *ward* may have seemed appropriate in the 1800s, but today the relationship is properly described as involving a "trustee" and "beneficiary."

In common law, a guardian is under the supervision of a court and is not required to consult with the ward in carrying out his duties. A trust relationship, on the other hand, is more like a partnership agreement. For example, the consent of Native American tribes is required in order to dispose of property. Also, broader accountability is required of the trustee to the beneficiary than would be found in a guardianship (Yerington Paiute Tribe 1985).

This obligation has often been referred to as "fiduciary," meaning founded on trust or confidence. Through the years, courts have agreed with Marshall that our law has no direct parallel to this trust relationship, which has been described as "unique," "solemn," "special," or "moral." The trust responsibility of the United States with regard to the land and other natural resources of Indian tribes and Alaska Natives is a direct outgrowth of English law and practice. It held that title to newly discovered lands belonged to the Crown, or government, but was nevertheless subject to a compensable right of occupancy by the aboriginal people. Title to land is held in trust for tribes by the United States. In certain instances, land is held in trust by the United States for individual Indians. Some tribal funds also are held in trust, and, in some cases, funds are held in trust for individual Indians (Yerington Paiute Tribe 1985).

Regarding land, the trust responsibility is extensive, encompassing not only the land itself but anything to do with the land. Thus, the minerals under it, the water flowing over it, and the grass that grows upon it all are elements of the trust estate. As the operating arm of the secretary of the Interior, the Bureau of Indian Affairs has a responsibility to carry out the management and protection of these resources, which includes taking whatever steps are necessary to prevent waste.

Although *Cherokee Nation v. Georgia* involved a treaty, court decisions have held the trust relationship may be created by other means, such as statutes, agreements, and executive orders. The overall trust relationship between Indian nations and the U.S. government and its subpolitical entities, the states, consists of a series of laws passed by Congress, regulations promulgated pursuant to these laws, and federal administrative practice. A separate body of Indian trust law has been developed by the federal courts based on federal court decisions that include Alaska Natives and Native Hawaiians.

While the secretary of the Interior is responsible for carrying out the trust responsibility, the ultimate trustee in Indian affairs is the Congress, and therein lies a unique aspect of the federal-tribal relationship. Congress has plenary, or absolute, power in its dealings with Indian tribes. And, unlike other trust relationships, it can unilaterally dissolve the trust agreement with tribal groups. The Congress does not need to consult with, or seek approval from, the tribes to terminate this relationship.

On the other hand, tribes do have recourse in courts if the trust responsibility is breached. Though tribes cannot bring suit against Congress, officials who administer the trust are directly accountable through court actions. Accordingly, Native American tribes and individuals have recourse against the Department of the Interior or any other agency of government that violates the trust agreement.

The executive branch of the federal government—which includes the Department of the Interior and the Bureau of Indian Affairs (BIA)—is the agent responsible for carrying out the trust. As an agent, it cannot terminate the trust or change the manner in which it is carried out. Only Congress can do this.

Likewise, financial trust services also are maintained by the BIA to enhance the trust estate. In FY 1983, $1.7 billion in trust fund revenues were invested with per annum earnings of $171 million. Some 262 tribes received financial services, and individual Indian money accounts were maintained for 250 tribes (Bureau of Indian Affairs 1984). Yet mismanagement, fraud, and the loss of Indian trust funds by the BIA have led to calls by tribal officials for the elimination of the trust relationship between the Bureau of Indian Affairs and tribal governments (Tribal Officials' Political Survey 1998). Recent tribal self-governance legislation is a move in that direction.

Looking closer at the history of federal Indian policy, we can identify two areas in which Congress frequently refused to deal with the complexities of this government-to-government relationship. The two areas are "the use and ownership of property and the efforts to establish a modicum of self-government" (Deloria 1990, 27).

Federal Indian policy during the nineteenth century was inextricably tied with federal land policy. Although Native American nations were viewed by the courts as dependent nations, the U.S. government negotiated treaties with Indian tribes as it did with independent foreign powers until 1871. Many of the treaties extinguished Native Americans' title to land. Other agreements related to the pursuit and maintenance of peace further defined the status of tribes as dependent nations and regulated trade. Many of the treaties are still significant in the defense of Indian land claims, hunting and fishing rights, and tribal autonomy. (All treaties between the United States and Indian nations are held by the National Archives in Washington, D.C.)

It seemed that the national government was eternally involved in negotiating land surrender treaties with the Native American tribes to make room for settlers. At first these cession treaties provided for diminution of tribal domain; later, as the frontier settlements intruded to the very edge of the diminished tribal ranges, the policy of relocation developed (Gibson 1966). Throughout the early and mid-1800s many Indian tribes were forcibly removed from their ancestral lands. Many tribes were removed by the federal military, often with the assistance of state militia and the land-grabbing citizenry of the area. From the Cherokee to the Ponca to the Lakota, such "trails of tears" are common in tribal history.

Normally, tribes that were removed through peaceful or forced removal were promised better lands, military protection from the tribes and others that they were forced to move among, annuity payments, food, clothing, shelter, and even self-rule over the new lands that they were to occupy. Few of these promises were ever kept. Even after the treaty making and removal had ended, Indians continued to lose land, due mostly to differences in values regarding land ownership between Indians and non-Indians. In the nineteenth century (and still today) the U.S. government and the vast majority of its non-Indian citizens viewed individual ownership of land as man's God-given right. The entrepreneurial philosophies of the time, dominated by the capitalistic goals of the new nation, had no use for any other type of land ownership, especially tribal ownership, which nearly all Indian tribes clung to with a vengeance.

In the 1880s the eastern religious and social groups that promoted Indian rights, such as the Indian Rights Association, the Women's National Indian Association, and the Lake Mohonk Conference of the Friends of the Indian, had gained enough political clout in Congress to seek out what they considered to be more humane policies toward American Indians (Hauptman 1992). The reformers sought assimilation of the Indian into "mainstream" culture. Without such an assimilation policy many reformers felt that Indian people would be killed off by the turn of the century. In fact, Congress began appropriating funds to the Smithsonian in order to gather as much information on as many tribes as possible before they all disappeared (Bureau of American Ethnology).

Eighteenth- and nineteenth-century scientific philosophy and research attempted to define the different racial groups by many factors, including mental and even spiritual ability. In the case of Native Americans, the size of their skulls was found to contain brains adequate enough to think nearly as well as a white man, whereas blacks were found to have inferior-sized skulls that held inadequate brains. Religious philosophies defined Native Americans as savages in the eighteenth century, requiring either their conversion to Christianity or their extermination. By the nineteenth century, Christian leaders (perhaps influenced by the new Mormon religion) began to view American Indians as the lost tribes of Jesus.

Based on these racist factors, a new "enlightened" policy of making Indians like the white man was implemented. In terms of federal land policy, most of the available land in America had been settled by 1880, and new land was needed. Federal Indian policy changed from treaties and removal, which were both very expensive in terms of manpower and money, to "freeing the Indian from the chains of tribalism and bestowing upon him the freedom of Individual land ownership" (Meriam et al. 1928; Hauptman 1992). After 1880 and for the next fifty years, federal Indian policy nearly eliminated participation by Indians in their own tribal government and all other political activity.

Allotment

Few of the U.S. government's attempts to create a workable Indian policy offer a more vivid record of failure than the Dawes Allotment Act of 1887. The Dawes Act sought to resolve the Indian "problem" by persuading, or forcing if necessary, Indians to abandon their traditional tribal-communal way of life for the life of independent, individualistic yeomen farmers. To pave the way for the elimination of the tribes as distinct, social, political, and legal entities, the Dawes Act provided for the division of community-held reservation lands into individual 160-acre holdings ("Prairie Potawatomie" 1976). The act specifically stated that

> Tribal relations must be broken up; that the practice of massing large numbers of Indians on reservations must be stopped; that lands must be alloted in severalty; where there is more land in any reservation than the Indians on that reservation can profitably use, such surplus lands must be so disposed of that the whiteman may get possession of

them and come in contact with the Indian. ("Proceedings and Debates" 1887, 190)

The Bureau of Indian Affairs and its Indian agents implemented this new federal policy in a variety of manners, mostly to the benefit of the government and often themselves, rather than to the benefit of the Native American people. The Dawes Act utilized two strategies to dissolve participation in traditional tribal government and the control over lands within reservation boundaries. First, it took away the lands that the tribal government had previously held control over through communal ownership and redistributed them to individual Indian ownership, which was much more difficult for tribal governments to control. Second, it distributed (stole) "surplus" lands to the thousands of white settlers (many new immigrants) who demanded land, totally removing these lands from tribal government control ("Proceedings and Debates" 1887; "Prairie Potawatomie" 1976). Traditional tribal members saw their governmental powers dissolve away with their lands:

One of the principal advances made in the (Santee) tribe during the year was the abandonment of the hereditary chieftainships. This was accompanied by regular ballot, and new men elected in the same manner to serve as councilors for the term of two years. The chiefs and headmen were generally old men; the councilors are young men who are taking the lead in work, & c. (civilization). ("Santee Agency Report" 1878, 595)

The Dawes Act wreaked havoc without accomplishing any of its major goals except that of making Indian lands accessible to white settlement. Between 1887 and 1934, when allotment was ended by the Indian Reorganization Act, the landholdings of American Indians diminished from 130 million acres to 50 million acres, and much of the remaining acreage was too poor for white settlement.

Even after the loss of most of their land, most tribes clung to their traditional tribal patterns of life ("Prairie Potawatomie" 1976) and traditional tribal government (Springer 1993). Some traditional tribal leaders, such as Wah Quoh Bosh Kuk of the Prairie Band Potawatomie, led their people in the fight against allotment. "When the allotment commissioners arrived at the Prairie Band Reservation," *Indian Historian* reported (1976) they found not a single member of the tribe willing to discuss allotment. Tribes mainly resisted allotment by petitioning the president, filing lawsuits, hiring lobbyists, and appealing to Indian reform groups. Direct contact with members of Congress, however, was relatively rare, perhaps because tribal leaders wanted to speak directly with the president, or perhaps because of Congress's long history of passing laws that sought to exterminate Native Americans. In the end, the struggle of Native American leaders to stop the policy of allotment proved futile, and nearly every tribe had their reservation lands allotted. The allotment issue did bring many tribes together for the first time, even those who had once been bitter enemies, and a sense of nationalism arose among the tribes. They began to realize that in standing alone, none would survive, and that uniting with other tribes against government policies that were detrimental to all might be their only salvation against the continuous encroachment of Western civilization upon their tribal governments and societies.

Reorganization

The following section is coauthored with Terry Crossbear, Potawatomi/ Standing Rock Sioux.

> First (Indian) Nation to adopt IRA of 1934
> (Rosebud Sioux Tribe, Tribal Letter writen July 2, 1990)

> Big Pine is a Non-IRA tribe. We have our own Tribal Constitution and Bylaws the Government of our tribe operates by (Big Pine Band of Paiute-Shoshone Indians, Tribal Letter written July 2, 1990)

Within a period of twenty years (1934–1953), two significant pieces of legislation, directly opposite in purpose, were enacted by the Congress and imposed upon the Native American people. The first, in 1934, was the Indian Reorganization Act (Wheeler-Howard Act), which not only prohibited the further allotment of tribal land to individual Indians as prescribed by the Dawes Act but also authorized the secretary of the Interior to add lands to existing reservations and to create new reservations for landless tribes. Under this new policy, Native American landholdings did increase by over 2 million acres from 1935 to 1953. Unfortunately, the U.S. government's commitment to increase tribal land dwindled at the onset of World War II. However, it is safe to assume that despite the good intentions sought by the IRA, a consistent, 100 percent commitment by the federal government to keep replenishing Indian lands and building Indian reservation economies would have been met by fierce opposition sooner or later from a variety of sources—from non-Indian groups seeking enactment of anti-Indian legislation (which is taking place as I write) to state governments demanding the power to tax these lands through P. L. 280 policy.

A number of factors brought about the Indian Reorganization Act, ranging from the onset of the Depression to mounting public criticism of the handling of Indian affairs by the federal government. The most recognized factor for precipitating this abrupt policy change was the Meriam Report of 1928. It documented "the failure of the allotment period and gave an in-depth analysis on the poor state of health and living conditions faced by the Indian population throughout the United States" (Meriam 1928; Taylor 1980, 13–14). Although the publication of the Meriam Report in 1928 slowed allotment parceling significantly, the overall damage "had already been done" (Getches, Rosenfelt, and Wilkinson 1982, 79).

In 1926, Mr. Lewis Meriam and nine selected "specialists," while on the staff of the Institute for Government Research, began a survey of the economic and social condition of the American Indians. Their findings would later be compiled into a report to the secretary of the Interior, Hubert Work. Because of the diversity and complexity of Indian affairs, the report was detailed and divided into the following eight sections: (1) A General Policy for Indian Affairs, (2) Health, (3) Education, (4) General Economic Conditions, (5) Family and Community Life and the Activities of Women, (6) The Migrated Indian, (7) The Legal Aspects of the Indian Problem, and (8) The Missionary Activities among the Indians (Meriam 1928).

Overall these eight sections found that Indian people were in a state of severe poverty with no desire to adjust to the economic and social system of the dominant white civilization. When an Indian family obtained a small amount of wealth, they quickly distributed it among their friends and family and remained at the same socioeconomic level as everyone else, a common practice among Indian people even today. (Much of the Meriam Report of 1928 fits the socioeconomic circumstances found among many reservation and urban American Indian families in 1994.) Upon publication, the Meriam Report brought into sharp focus the problems of governmental administration of Indian affairs, thereby initiating a movement toward change and the Indian Reorganization Act (Meriam 1928, 3–51).

During the early 1930s the BIA held a number of meetings on Native American reservations across the nation to discuss the findings of the Meriam Report and to promote the concepts of the IRA. These discussions were successful in making people aware that not only would the Indian tribes be in existence indefinitely, but above all, they should participate in their own governmental decision making.

Yet, as noted earlier, the crucial provision of the IRA was the end to the practice of allotment, the culprit that caused Indian-held lands to drop from 138 million acres in 1887 to 48 million in 1934. Another important objective of the law was the elimination of the "absolutist" executive discretion previously exercised by the Interior Department and the Office of Indian Affairs. During congressional hearings on the IRA, Commissioner of Indian Affairs John Collier revealed that not only had administrative power grown beyond control, but its exercise depended on the attitude or whim of any given commissioner. This practice, also exercised by the local agency superintendents, led Senater Wheeler to refer to the local agent as a "czar." The IRA sought "to get away from the bureaucratic control of the Indian Department and give the Indian people control over their own affairs" (Canby 1981, 23–25).

Tribal self-government was the heart of the operative provisions defined by the IRA:

> Section 1 of the IRA ended the policy of allotment: "No land of any Indian Reservation . . . shall be allotted in severalty to any Indian." This provision alone assured the Act's historical significance.
>
> Section 2 "extended and continued" the existing periods of trust placed upon Indian lands.
>
> Section 3 "authorized the Secretary of Interior to restore to tribal ownership the remaining surplus lands of any Indian reservation. . . ."
>
> ("Proceedings and Debates" 1934, 11724)

Section 4 related to alienation. This provision prohibited the transfer of Indian land or shared assets of tribal corporations to no one other than the tribe. This section further strengthened the tribal land base and tribal control over it.

Section 5 authorized the secretary of the Interior to obtain additional lands "for the purpose of providing land for Indians." Section 7 authorized the secretary of the Interior "to add lands acquired pursuant to any authority conferred by this act to existing reservations ("Proceedings and Debates" 1934, 11724).

Sections 9 and 10 authorized and funded "Indian chartered corporations to promote their individual and collective economic welfare and the economic welfare of the tribe" ("Proceedings and Debates" 1934, 11725).

Section 19 provided that the act "would not apply to any reservation wherein a majority of the adult Indians voted against its application at a special election to be held within one year after the Act's approval" ("Proceedings and Debates" 1934, 11725). Section 19, by allowing the Indian people themselves to determine whether to implement an "IRA government" or not, was another significant change in the application of Indian legislation. In the past, there had been two types of legislation. One, being special, applied its terms to only one tribe or group of tribes. Two, the general, applied to all Indians without consideration of tribal differences. Through this section the IRA became somewhat of an enabling act, giving each tribe a voice and opportunity to decide for themselves whether or not they wanted to come under the act. The major flaw in this approach was that the tribe could hold an election only once. "There was no option for reconsideration" (Pevar 1983, 5–6).

Sections 16 and 17 "encouraged tribes to adopt their own constitutions, to become federally chartered corporations and to manage their own government and business affairs" (Pevar 1983, 6). And Indian preference in hiring at the Bureau of Indian Affairs to bring forth Indian involvement in government programs for Indians was ordered under section 13 as follows:

The Secretary of the Interior is directed to establish standards of health, age, character, experience, knowledge, and service laws, to various positions maintained, now or hereafter, by the Indian Office, in the administration of functions or services affecting any Indian tribe.

Such qualified Indians shall hereafter have the preference to appointment to vacancies in any such positions. ("Proceedings and Debates"1934, 11725)

During the two-year period in which tribes could reject or accept the IRA, 258 elections were held. One hundred and eighty-one tribes (129,750 individuals) voted to accept the IRA, while seventy-seven tribes (86,365 individuals, including 45,000 Navajos) rejected it. Sponsors and supporters of the IRA felt that a major change in Indian governance had been born. However, a recent survey of Indian legal experiences since the passage of the act suggests that the IRA was just an overhaul of past forms and concepts of federal Indian policy designed to make tribal governments more alike rather than giving tribes a stronger voice in their own policy-making process (Getches, Rosenfelt, and Wilkinson 1982).

Several tribes opposed the IRA, and many, through lobbying and legislative support, received exemptions from several sections of the act. Section 14 exempted tribes in Alaska from sections 1–8 and 15–21. Section 14 states that "Sections 2, 4, 7, 9, 17, 18, and 19 of this Act" shall not apply to the "following tribes in Oklahoma: Cheyenne, Arapaho, Apache, Comanche, Kiowa, Caddo, Delaware, Wichita, Osage, Kaw, Otoe, Tonkawa, Pawnee, Ponca, Shawnee, Ottawa, Quapaw, Seneca, Wyandotte, Iowa, Sac and Fox, Kickapoo, Pottawatomi, Cherokee, Chickasaw, Choctaw, Creek, and Seminole" ("Proceedings and Debates" 1934, 11725).

Some of the fears of tribal leaders opposed to the IRA were outlined by Representative Alfred Florian Beiter (D-NY), who wanted to have New York Indian tribes exempted from the act for the following reasons:

First. Passage of this bill would absolutely revoke the rights of free citizens granted to the Indians by act of Congress on June 2 1924 [Indian Citizenship Act].

Second. Passage of this bill would destroy all existing treaty rights of the various tribes and leave the new chartered communities with no protection.

Third. This bill will not do what it is supposed to do, provide for the freedom of self-government by the Indians, because all power and authority is left in the hands of the Secretary of Interior and the Commissioner of Indian Affairs, where it has been for 100 years past.

Fourth. This bill seeks to set the Indians apart as a separate race, means only continued segregation and would foster race prejudice.

Fifth. Passage of this bill would force the Indians backward into the status which existed 100 years ago.

Sixth. It does not give Indians any voice in the control and management of their own affairs, the selection of employees or reservations, the spending of tribal funds, nor the right to employ legal counsel. All such statements contained in the bill are carefully followed by words to this effect: "as the Secretary of the Interior shall see fit, shall consider competent, in his discretion, or according to such rules and regulations as shall be prescribed by the Secretary of the Interior."

Seventh. It provides only for a bigger and better Bureau and increased and more detrimental power for the Indian Bureau than has ever before been passed. ("Proceedings and Debates" 1934, 11736)

Several tribes agreed with Representative Beiter that the IRA concentrated power over the tribes in the hands of the secretary of the Interior and the Bureau of Indian Affairs, where it had always been. As for increased control over their own affairs, Indian tribal governments were no better off than before. One example of the power of the secretary of the Interior over implementation of the provisions of the IRA came in congressional testimony in 1975 on noncompliance to section 13 (Indian Preference) by Representative Don Young (R-AK):

> Mr. Speaker, the 1934 Wheeler-Howard Act, which completely reformed the administration of Indian Affairs, provided for preferential hiring of Indian people in the Bureau of Indian Affairs. For reasons not entirely clear, the Interior Department did not enforce the provisions dealing with Indian preference in promotions and these important Indian rights remained on the books virtually unnoticed. ("Proceedings and Debates" 1975)

Although the IRA did stop the erosion of tribal land bases and reorganized several tribal governments to their present-day structure, it did not eliminate the control of the secretary of the Interior and the Bureau of Indian Affairs over Indian people, which eliminated their ability to control or even participate in their own economic, political, or social success. This problem confronts American Indian governments today, even though several modern tribes are attempting to take over several programs and duties that were previously in the hands of the Bureau of Indian Affairs.

The 1950s: Termination and State Encroachment

> Termination hurt the people, economically, culturally, and psychologically. One day we were Indians and the next we were not. Many were lost and restoration of the tribe is the only way for our people to be found. (Northern Ponca Elder 1990)

> We are a P. L. 280 tribe. We have a contract with the county sheriff and he has Indian deputies on the reservation. This arrangement has worked out fairly well, but we have had some trouble with the state over tribal hunting licenses, so we may have to retrocede someday, if we have too much trouble with the state. (Daniel Denny, Santee-Sioux Tribal Chairman 1991)

> We used to have Indian police, then in the 50s, I think it was when we
> went under P. L. 280 and that was the end of them (Indian Police).
> There is no law enforcement on the reservation as we are under P. L.
> 280 and the young people are trying to do as they please. (Los Coyotes
> Band of Mission Indians 1989)

The 1950s proved to be a time of hardship for American Indian
governments, since two pieces of legislation sought to end tribal
sovereignty and the federal trusteeship that protected sovereign status. The first blow to tribal sovereignty came when the goals of the
IRA were abandoned and replaced with a disastrous new policy
called "termination." In 1953, Congress adopted House Concurrent
Resolution No. 108, declaring that various Indian tribes would no
longer be entitled to federal benefits and services and should be cut
off at the earliest possible time.

Termination meant eliminating tribal enrollment rolls, selling off
tribal assets, and distributing the funds raised from such sales to individual tribal members (fewer BIA expenses) and taxing of allotted
lands by local and state governments. Over a hundred tribes were
terminated in the following decade. Thousands of Native Americans
lost their lands, and many were forced by economic factors to move
away from their ancestral lands, often to cities.

In his presidential address of July 1970, Richard Nixon argued "that
the termination of the federal trust relationship and the privatization
of tribal resources among those terminated tribes failed to achieve the
goal of economic advancement, jeopardized or destroyed tribal
sovereignty and implicitly weakened cultural self-determination"
(McGuire 1990, 207). The removal of federal trusteeship responsibility
has produced considerable disorientation among the affected Indians
and has left them unable to relate to a myriad of federal, state, and local assistance efforts. Their (tribes) "economic and social condition
has often been worse after termination than it was before" (Price
1973, 599).

Reinstatement of federal trusteeship to the terminated tribes became the norm during the Nixon and future administrations. In
November 1990, the Northern Ponca Tribe of Nebraska (Ponca Nation of Nebraska) became the 108th tribe to have their federal recognition restored. Officials of the BIA informed the Northern Ponca
Restoration Committee that only one or two terminated tribes remained to be restored as of the spring of 1991 (LeRoy 1990).

As if termination wasn't enough, in 1953 the federal government
sought to reduce its own responsibility to tribal governments even

further by passing Public Law 83-280. This statute, normally called Public Law 280, gave "powers and responsibilities to the states which displaced past federal law and responsibilities and left the tribes with an almost invisible role and irrelevant status" (O'Brien 1989). This law conferred "upon certain designated states full criminal and some civil jurisdiction over Indian reservations and consented to the assumption of such jurisdiction by any additional state which chose to accept it" (Canby 1981).

Specifically, P. L. 280 allowed states to assume all civil and criminal jurisdiction on reservations in five specified states: California, Nebraska, Minnesota (except Red Lake Reservation), Oregon (except Warm Springs Reservation), and Wisconsin (except the Red Lake Chippewa and the Menominee) (O'Brien 1989, 276–277). Alaska was added to this list in 1958. Whereas the Indian Reorganization Act attempted to rebuild tribal lands and governments, Public Law 280 attempted to impose the will of yet another Great White Father, the one in the state capitol. Without the consent of the concerned tribes, P. L. 280 provided "that any other state could assume jurisdiction by statute or state constitutional amendment" (O'Brien 1989).

Public Law 280 represented a compromise between termination and continuation of the relative immunity of the tribes from state jurisdiction. Both the tribes and the states have been left dissatisfied ever since. The tribes do not want state jurisdiction forced upon them. The states do not want the financial responsibility of their newly acquired jurisdiction powers.

The practical application of P. L. 280 has become very confusing, since it did not allow states to take total control of Indian affairs. The federal government retained the power to manage Indian trust lands. And no state was allowed to make laws changing Indian hunting and fishing rights that were protected by treaties. P. L. 280 did not technically extinguish tribal powers but allowed the state to exercise jurisdiction. In practical terms, however, state jurisdiction, when exercised, tended to supplant tribal power. From the tribes' point of view, P. L. 280 was one of the most destructive bills to tribal sovereignty ever passed by Congress (Bennett et al. 1986; O'Brien 1989).

The scope of jurisdiction offered by P. L. 280 has been an ongoing conflict between states and tribes. The state of Minnesota, for example, withheld social service funding until some control of tribal social services could be placed under state jurisdiction. In Idaho no criminal laws are enforced on reservations, but state laws dealing with school attendance, family relations, mental illness, traffic, welfare, and juvenile delinquency are enforced (O'Brien 1989).

In 1968, a shift in federal Indian policy from the pro-assimilation stand of the 1950s to a greater emphasis on increasing tribal economic development and strengthening tribal governments was evidenced by the passage of the Indian Civil Rights Act. Congress provided in the Indian Civil Rights of 1968 (ICRA) that no state could acquire P. L. 280 jurisdiction over the objections of the affected tribe(s). States that had already assumed jurisdiction were allowed, with the secretary of the Interior's permission, to return it to the tribes. As of the late 1980s, the states of Nebraska, Washington, Minnesota, Nevada, and Wisconsin had returned all or part of their jurisdiction to the tribes within their borders (O'Brien 1989). Returning jurisdiction to the tribe is called "retrocession."

Once tribal consent became a prerequisite to state jurisdiction, and jurisdiction could be acquired in one area at a time, the negotiating table was opened to the tribes and states to negotiate state jurisdiction in cases where it would be beneficial to both parties. More recently, states and tribes have begun to realize that negotiations and mutual cooperation are less costly than court suits, and some have worked together to solve mutual problems (Officer 1984; O'Brien 1989). Many tribes have cross-deputized law enforcement and mutual aid agreements with state and local government entities in such areas as fire protection, ambulance service, etc. (Bay Mills Indian Community 1990; Chitimacha Tribe 1990; Grand Traverse Band 1990; Sault Ste. Marie Tribe 1990). Also some tribes have agreements that exempt tribal members from state income, sales, gasoline, cigarette, and automobile taxes and have replaced these state taxes with tribal taxes (Chitimacha Tribe 1990; Eastern Band of Cherokee 1990). Over 75 percent of present-day tribal governments have intergovernmental agreements with other state, local, or tribal governments ("Tribal Government Survey" 1990).

Presently, the jurisdictional stakes are much larger in scope than they were when P. L. 280 was first enacted, especially with the rise in tribal gaming ventures. Social, economic, and political developments existing today have made the tribes and the states more assertive in making their individual interpretation of the statute prevalent to their own favor. States' interests often lie in regulating and exploiting development of trust lands, especially on reservations with substantial energy resources (Yerington Paiute Tribe 1985).

On the other hand, tribal governments must keep a close eye on actions to promote state interests in order to preserve their special status as sovereign entities, which offers tribes an advantage over other "localized" governments in such areas as law enforcement, courts, taxation, gambling, and free trade zones. Recent comments from tribal council members reveal that state/tribal relations continue to be very strained at this point in time:

> "They [states] are in the process of finalizing termination of Indigenous people in Alaska."
>
> "State government is all over the reservation in social services, education requirements, police force certification to our gaming compact."
>
> "They want to control Indians, like they do their own people. The states want to tax us and put us under their laws. South Dakota has the most prejudice state government in the union. They [state officials] are working hard against Indians." ("Tribal Government Survey" 1990)

Even with such divisive feelings between tribal and state officials, tribal governments have been required to increase their participation at the state level in order to both maintain their freedom from state power (Sault Ste. Marie Tribe 1990) and to influence state policies toward tribes (Giago 1999).

Self-Determination: Externally Imposed? Or the Rebirth of Sovereignty?

Progress has been made for Indian people in health and education, but alcoholism and unemployment continue to plague the reservations as well as Indian-populated urban areas. Although tribes have cast state governments in a villainous shadow, many urban Indians are almost totally reliant on state social service programs because of their distance from their reservations. Urban Indians are also victims of a dual system of social service delivery: although they have no access to the federal Indian programs on the reservations, urban Indians are ineligible for state services because they are entitled to assistance from federal Indian programs.

Many persons from states with large Indian populations incorrectly believe that the "federal government is responsible for the education of Indian children" (Rosenfelt 1978). American Indians have been turned away from public and private hospitals due to the fact that they "should" be served at an Indian Health Service (IHS) facility (Crossbear 1994).

Another thorn in the side of those who develop and implement federal Indian policy is the continued practice of handpicking and shuffling around the top administrators in the Bureau of Indian Affairs and the Indian Health Service. This is a burning issue among tribal governments. Several tribal officials have argued that such officials should be democratically elected by the Indian people themselves and not chosen by a non-Indian administration, namely the president and the executive bureaucracy. Most other federal agencies are dominated by the interest groups that are impacted by these agencies, so it would seem appropriate that administrators of the BIA, the IHS, and other federal agencies that deal with Indians be chosen by Indians, since Indians are the major interest group that these federal agencies impact (Yerington Paiute Tribe 1985, 89–92).

The extent of tribal sovereignty seems to be defined by nontribal governmental entities, such as the Bureau of Indian Affairs, Indian Health Service, the U.S. Supreme Court, Congress, the states, the president, and even Peabody Coal. These political and bureaucratic entities continue to compound the frustrations and sense of futility felt by Native American people both on and off the reservations.

The Native American people have never met Indian policies enacted by Congress and administered by the executive branch of the federal government with whole-hearted trust and faith, because of the countless promises broken since Western civilization first stepped upon this continent. The federal and state governments seem to want to forget as quickly as possible the atrocities that were committed against the Indian people in the hope of somehow "fitting" the Native American into the Western world. Native American values have been under attack for nearly five hundred years by Western civilization. But Native American values are based upon an age-old history, and such traditional beliefs will never die (French 1987).

A major problem arises when Native Americans do not participate in determining what they require from the federal and state governments to make their communities, on or off the reservation, better places for their children to grow up in. There is some question as to whether or not adopting Western values has made Indian communities better places to live. Many elders say that such non-Indian values have made Native American communities worse off. Federal and state Indian policies "must take in to account American Indian values and beliefs or else such policies will fail" (Yerington Paiute Tribe 1985, 36–37).

The federal government since the mid-1970s has promoted the idea of self-determination for Indian tribes and their people (Yerington Paiute Tribe 1985, 41). How self-determination is defined by the tribal, federal, and state governments will determine how successful Indian communities will be in the twenty-first century. If self-determination entitles the federal and state governments to abstain from their financial responsibilities to the Native American people to develop better communities, then it is another anti-Indian policy, much like termination, which leaves the Native American people to sink or swim on their own without any acknowledgment of past or present promises. If self-determination means allowing Native American people the policy control necessary to determine what is best for their communities, and the financial, technical, and managerial resources necessary to implement such policies, then it will be a turning point in the history of Indian policy making in which Indian people will finally obtain their rightful place as directors rather than followers of such policy.

But if self-determination means the continued external domination of Indian policies, it will not work. The key to true self-determination lies in the fact that after nearly five hundred years of such domination, those of the dominant society must admit that Indian policies must come from the Indian people themselves. As Terry Crossbear's grandfather once said, "The next time the great white father passes out a new Indian policy, I hope he provides tall boots to go along with it." Perhaps the federal and state governments will finally allow full participation by the Native American people in the development and implementation of all policies directed at them, so that the Native American people will not need those tall boots.

Will there ever be true tribal sovereignty independent of non-Indian entities? Perhaps the increase in economic resources among gaming tribes will lead to further discussion and implementation of such a policy. Presently, this question remains unanswered.

Conclusion

To some this first chapter may seem long on historical and cultural concepts, but one must first understand how Native Americans participated in their tribal societies before attempting to understand their political participation today. Native American tribal culture still affects how individual tribal members view the world around them and how they individually and collectively participate in all aspects of that world, including both tribal and nontribal politics. Assimilation has changed many Native Americans, but it has not eliminated their tribal roots or the tribal entities that they pay allegiance to.

Some tribes share international enrollment, whereby tribal members are U.S. citizens and Canadian citizens. They have a choice in which society they participate in, a choice that is not available to other Americans, a choice that arises directly from their ancestral ties. These ties existed long before 1492 and were altered but not eliminated after 1492.

References

Bay Mills Indian Community. 1990. *Tribal Government Survey.* Brimley, Mich., March.

Bennett, Robert L., Robert Burnette, Alexander (Sandy) Mac Nabb, and Helen M. Schierbeck. 1986. "Federal Indian Policy, 1960–1976." In *Indian Self-Rule,* edited by Kenneth R. Philp. Salt Lake City, Utah: Howe Brothers.

Big Pine Band of Paiute-Shoshone Indians. 1990. Tribal Government Survey. Big Pine, Calif. February.

Black Elk, Frank. 1991. Phone interview. Denver, Colo.

Black Elk, Wallace H., and William S. Lyon. 1990. *Black Elk: The Sacred Ways of the Lakota.* San Francisco: Harper & Row.

Bureau of American Ethnology. 1879–1964. *Annual Report of the Bureau of American Ethnology.* Vols. 1–81.Washington D.C.: Government Printing Office.

———. 1881. *Annual Report of the Bureau of American Ethnology.* First Annual Report. Vol. 1: *Wyandot Government.* Washington, D.C.

Bureau of Indian Affairs. 2002. "U.S. Government Statutes." Washington, D.C.

Bureau of Indian Affairs, Department of the Interior. 1984. *American Indians, U.S. Indian Policy, Tribes and Reservations, BIA: Past and Present Economic Development.* Washington, D.C.: Government Printing Office.

———. 1987. "Answers to Your Questions." In *American Indians Today.* Washington, D.C.: Government Printing Office, 0-179-782.

Canby, William C., Jr. 1981. *American Indian Law.* St. Paul, Minn: West.

Carter, George F. 1980. *Earlier Than You Think.* College Station, Tex.: Texas A&M University Press.

Chitimacha Tribe of Louisiana. 1990. Tribal Government Survey. Cherenton, La., May.

Cohen, J. M. 1969. *Four Voyages of Christopher Columbus.* New York: Penquin Classics.

Connelley, William E. 1915–1918. "Notes on the Early Indian Occupancy of the Great Plains." *Collections.* Vol. 14. Topeka: Kansas State Historical Society.

Deloria, Vine, Jr. 1990a. "Property and Self-Government and Educational Initiatives," *Winds of Change,* Autumn.

———. 1990b. "Traditional Technology," *Winds of Change—A Magazine of American Indians,* Spring.

Denny, Daniel. 1991. Conversation with Denny, the Santee Sioux Tribal Chairman, during Northern Ponca of Nebraska Tribal Restoration Committee meeting, Lincoln Indian Center, Lincoln, Nebr., November.

Dorsey, J. O. 1884. "Omaha Sociology." In *Third Annual Report of the Bureau of American Ethnology.* Washington, D.C.: Smithsonian Institute Bureau of Ethnology.

———. 1886. "Migrations of the Siouan Tribes," *American Naturalist* 20 (3).

———. 1894. "A Study of Siouan Cults." In *Eleventh Annual Report of the Bureau of American Ethnology.* Washington, D.C.: Smithsonian Institution.

———. 1897. "Siouan Sociology." *Fifteenth Annual Report of the Bureau of American Ethnology.* Washington, D.C.: Smithsonian Institution.

Duran, Eduardo, and Bernita Duran. 1995. *Native American Postcolonial Psychology.* Albany: State University of New York Press.

Eastern Band of Cherokee Indians. 1990. Tribal Government Survey. Cherokee, N.C., March.

Eden, Richard, trans. 1895 [1511, 1553]. "A Treatyse of the Newe India." In *The First Three English Books on America,* edited by Edward Arber. Birmingham: Westminster, A. Constable, p. 55.

Elder Story. 1979. *Stubben's Discount Store.* Niobrara, Nebr., July.

Ellis, Richard N. 1972. "Plains Warfare." In *The Western American Indian.* Lincoln: University of Nebraska Press.

Engels, Frederick. 1968. "The Origin of the Family, Private Property and the State." In Karl Marx and Friedrich Engels, *Selected Works.* New York: International.

Fash, William L., Jr., and Barbara W. Fash. 1990. "Scribes, Warriors and Kings: The Lives of the Copa'n Maya," *Archaeology,* May/June.

Fletcher, Alice C. 1909. "Tribal Structure: A Study of the Omaha and Cognate Tribes." In *Anthropological Essays.* New York: Putnam.

Fletcher, A. C., and F. La Flesche. 1911. "The Omaha Tribe." In *Twenty-Seventh Annual Report of the Bureau of Ethnology.* Washington, D.C.: Smithsonian Institution.

Forest County Potawatomi Community. 1990. Tribal Government Survey and information packet, Kansas, Spring.

Freel, Danny. 1990. "Digging for Answers" *Dodge Adventurer,* Spring.

French, Laurence. 1987. *Psychocultural Change and the American Indian: An Ethnohistorical Analysis.* New York: Garland.

Getches, D., D. Rosenfelt, and C. Wilkinson. 1982. *Federal Indian Law.* St. Paul, Minn: West.

Giago, Tim. 1999. "Before Casino Santee Out of Sight," *Omaha World Herald,* November 12.

Gibson, A. M. 1966. "The Chickasaws," *Sooner Magazine,* January. Included in information packet from the Chickasaw Nation, Ada, Okla., December 12, 1989.

Grand Traverse Band of Ottawa and Chippewa Indians. 1990. Tribal Government Survey. Peshawbestown, Mich., January.

Grinde, Donald A., Jr., and Bruce E. Johansen. 1991. *Exemplar of Liberty: Native America and the Evolution of Democracy.* Los Angeles: American Indian Studies, UCLA Press.

_____. 1996. "Sauce for the Goose: Demand and Definitions for 'Proof' Regarding the Iroquois and Democracy." *William and Mary Quarterly* 53 (3), July.

Hauptman, Lawrence M. 1992. "Congress, Plenary Power, and the American Indian." In *Exiled in the Land of the Free*. Sante Fe, N.Mex.: Clear Light Books.

Howard, James H. 1965. *The Ponca Tribe*. Bureau of New American Ethnology Bulletin 195. Washington, D.C.: Smithsonian Institution.

Jablow, Joseph. 1974. *Ponca Indians*. "Ethnohistory of the Ponca with Reference to their Claim of Certain Lands." A Report for the Department of Justice, Lands Division, Indian Claims Section. New York: Garland, pp. 40–68.

Johansen, Bruce. 1982. *Forgotten Founders*. Ipswich, Mass.: Gambit.

———. 1988. "Vox Americana," *Northeast Indian Quarterly* 5.

Le Claire, Peter. 1947. "Letter Written on Tribal History by Ponca Indian." In *Ponca History*. Niobrara, Nebr., August 26.

———. 1965. Interview with tribal elder. In *The Ponca Tribe,* by J. H. Howard. Bureau of New American Ethnology Bulletin 195. Washington, D.C.: Smithsonian Institution.

LeRoy, Fred. 1990. Phone interview with Fred LeRoy, executive director, Northern Ponca Restoration Committee, Tribal Enrollment, December.

Little Bear, Leroy, Menno Boldt, and J. Anthony Long. 1984. *Pathways to Self-Determination: Canadian Indians and the Canadian State*. Toronto: University of Toronto Press.

Los Coyotes Band of Mission Indians. 1989. Tribal Government Survey. Warner Springs, Calif., December.

McGuire, Thomas R. 1990. "Federal Indian Policy: A Framework for Evaluation," *Human Organizations* 49 (9): 206–216.

Meriam, Lewis, et al. 1928. *The Problem of Indian Administration*. Baltimore, Md.: Johns Hopkins University Press.

Mohawk, John. 1987. "The Indian Way Is a Thinking Tradition," *Northeast Indian Quarterly* 4 (4), Winter, and 5 (1), Spring.

Morison, Samuel E. 1955. *Christopher Columbus: Mariner*. Boston: Little, Brown.

Muscogee Creek Nation. 1990. "Cultural Characteristics." Tribal information packet, received January 24.

Northern Cheyenne Tribe and Reservation. 1988. "The Morning Star People." Information packet. Lame Deer, Mont.

Northern Ponca Elder. 1990. Northern Ponca Restoration Committee meeting. Omaha, Nebr., April.

O'Brien, Sharon. 1989. *American Indian Tribal Governments*. Norman: University of Oklahoma Press.

Officer, James E. 1984. "The Indian Service and Its Evolution." In *The Aggressions of Civilization,* edited by Sandra L. Cadwalader and Vine Deloria, Jr. Philadelphia: Temple University Press.

Ogle, Ralph H. 1972. "The End of Apache Resistance." In *The Western American Indian,* edited by Richard N. Ellis. Lincoln: University of Nebraska Press.

Parker, Arthur, C. 1977. "The Constitution of the Five Nations." (1916). In *The Iroquois and the Founding of the American Nation,* edited by Donald A. Grinde, Jr. Washington, D.C.: Indian Historian Press.

Pearson Family Giveaway for John Pearson. 1992. Ames, Iowa, March.

Penobscot Indian Nation. 1989. *Bur-Nur-Wurb-Skek.* Department of Tribal Resources, November.

Pevar, Stephen L. 1983. *The Rights of Indians and Tribes.* New York: Bantam Books.

Ponca Census. 1860. Census Roll of the Poncas Tribe Taken at the Poncas Camp, by I. Shaw Gregory, U.S. Special Agent. Niobrara, Nebr., July 6.

Ponca Tribe of Nebraska. 1988. "The Ponca Restoration Act—History of the Ponca Tribe of Nebraska." Information packet. Omaha, Nebr.

Powell, J. W. 1886. *Annual Report of the Bureau of America Ethnology to the Secretary of the Smithsonian Institution.* Vol. 4, 1882–1883.

"The Prairie Potawatomie: Resistance to Allotment." 1976. *Indian Historian,* Fall.

Price, Monroe E. 1973. *Law and the American Indian: Readings, Notes and Cases.* Indianapolis, Ind.: Bobbs-Merrill.

"Proceedings and Debates of the Forty-Ninth Congress, Second Session." 1887. In *Congressional Record.* Vol. 18. Washington D.C.: Government Printing Office.

"Proceedings and Debates of the Second Session of the Seventy-Third Congress of the United States of America." 1934. Vol. 78, part 11. Washington. D.C.: Government Printing Office.

"Proceedings and Debates of the 94th Congress, First Session." 1975. Vol. 121, part 6. Washington, D.C.: Government Printing Office.

Province, J. H. 1955. "The Underlying Sanctions of Plains Indian Culture." In *Social Anthropology of North American Tribes,* edited by Fred Eggan. Chicago: University of Chicago Press, pp. 341–374.

Pueblo De Acoma. 1989. *The Pueblos: History.* Tribal Government Survey and information packet. Received December 18.

Pueblos. 1989. Information packet from the Eight Northern Indian Pueblos Council.

Quapaw Tribe of Oklahoma. 1989. "Indians of Arkansas." Information packet, received December 16.

"Report of Santee Agency, Nebraska. Isaiah Lightner. United States Indian Agent. Eighth Month, 20, 1878." 1878. In *Report of the Secretary of Interior.* Vol. 1. Washington, D.C.: Government Printing Office.

Rosebud Sioux Tribe. 1990. Tribal Government Survey. Rosebud, S. Dak., July 2.

Rosenfelt, Daniel M. 1978. "Toward a More Coherent Policy for Funding Indian Education." In *American Indians and the Law,* edited by Lawrence Rosen. New Brunswick, N.J.: Transaction Books, p. 79.

Santa Clara Pueblo. 1990. Tribal Government Survey, Spring.

Sault Ste. Marie Tribe. 1990. Tribal Government Survey, January.

Skinner, Alanson B. 1915. "Ponca Societies and Dances," *Anthropological Papers of the American Museum of Natural History.* Vol. 11. Washington, D.C.: American Museum of Natural History.

Snake, Reuben A., Jr. 1989. "Tribal Code of Ethics," *Winnebago Indian News,* June 6.

Springer, Elizabeth. 1981 and 1991. Omaha grandmother. Give Aways for Grandson Kenneth Wayne Springer. Macy, Nebr., September 1981 and August 1991.

———. Personal interview, eldest living female of the Omaha Tribe. 1993. Carl Curtiss Clinic and Nursing Home. Macy, Nebr., November.

Standing Bear, Luther. 1933. *The Land of the Spotted Eagle.* Cambridge, Mass.: Riverside Press.

Taylor, Graham D. 1980. "The Administration of the Indian Reorganization Act, 1934–45." In *The New Deal and American Indian Tribalism.* Lincoln: University of Nebraska Press, pp. 13–15.

"Tribal Government Survey." 1990. Tabulation of data obtained from nearly 200 tribes and other federal, state, and local governments, September to November. Unpublished.

"Tribal Officials' Political Opinion and Participation Survey." 1996–1998. Mail survey to 480 elected tribal council members by Dr. Jerry Stubben. Ames, Iowa, December 1996 to January 1998.

U.S. Census Bureau. 2001. General Demographic Characteristics by Race for the United States: 2000. Table 5: General Demographic Characteristics for American Indians and Alaska Native Populations. Special Tabulation. Internet Release, October 1.

Waldman, Carl. 1985. *Atlas of the North American Indian.* New York: Facts on File.

Weatherford, Jack. 1988. *Indian Givers.* New York: Crown.

Wilkinson, Charles F. 1987. *American Indians, Time, and the Law.* New Haven: Yale University Press.

Wilson Family Giveaway. 1991. Pine Ridge, S. Dak., August.

Wishart, David J. 1994. *An Unspeakable Sadness—The Dispossession of the Nebraska Indians.* Lincoln: University of Nebraska Press.

Yerington Paiute Tribe. 1985. *Introduction to Tribal Government.* Yerington, Nev.: Yerington Paiute Tribe.

2

Native American Political Activism

Native American political activism, dissent, and protest are thousands of years old and were fully developed by the time the first European arrived in America. Native American traditional society and governments had processes that fostered open debate and activism. Consensus was the rule, and as long as even one dissenter remained, the tribe believed they had not reached consensus. Thus conflicting views, dissent, and even protest have always been an important component of Native American society and government (Yerington Paiute Tribe 1985; Grinde and Johansen 1991).

The first European settlers in America were amazed to find a tradition of political activism and protest on a level that they had never witnessed in Europe. They were astonished to find that Native American nations were not ruled by one king and that the people were free to disagree with their leaders, often forcing those leaders to abdicate their position of power. The discovery of this sort of freedom had major implications on sixteenth- and seventeenth-century political scholars, and these influences are gradually being understood today as the roots of modern American democracy, political activism, protest, and even women's suffrage and the civil rights movement (Grinde and Johansen 1991; Stubben 2001).

According to De Tocqueville (1969, 29), "The Europeans made but little impression when they landed on the shore of North America;

they were neither feared nor envied," and yet "the Indian was a very real influence upon the mind and morals as well as upon the institutions of frontier New England" (Hutchinson 1764, 129). Frederick Turner (1920, 44–45) observed that "the half-breed children of captive Puritan mothers . . . are clear evidences of the transforming influence of the Indian upon the Puritan type of English colonist." In terms of political activism, historian Turner (1920, 30) speculated that "the most important effect of the Indian frontier has been in the promotion of democracy here (America) and in Europe." Grinde and Johansen (1991) postulated the "influence theory," which states that "16th through 18th century European and American democratic activism and institutions (such as the United States Government) were influenced by Native Americans, as much as they were influenced by European political theorists, such as John Locke." Stubben (2001) found that sixteenth-century Native American political activist thought offered the intellectual grounding for the writings of many early European scholars and promoters of democracy.

Roger Williams:
The First Euro-American Political Activist

Roger Williams, who came to America in 1631 "longing after the natives' soules" (Chupack 1969, 63), "was their [Indians] first missionary from among the English" Straus (1970 [1894], xlii). Williams met Massasoit, the Narragansett sachem, and in Williams's words, they became "great friends" (Brockunier 1940, 47). After only a few months in the New World, Williams had learned the Algonquian language and would soon master the dialects of other tribes in the region (Ernst 1932; Grinde and Johansen 1991). Williams's friendship with the Indians was leading to major controversies with the Puritan leadership and the king of England (Avery 1905).

Williams's activism on behalf of native peoples came in 1632, when he wrote a pamphlet "giving his arguments and proofs against their (the Puritans) right to Indian lands." He accused King James of having told "a solumn public lie, because in his patent he blessed God that he was the first Christian prince that had discovered land" and went on to warn the settlers that "they could have no title . . . except they compounded with the natives" (Winthrop 1853). Williams's writings openly condemned the king's patent to the Pilgrims and questioned the right of Plymouth to the Indian lands unless by direct purchase from the Indians in a voluntary sale (Ernst 1932, 80; Winthrop and

Weld 1644). Based upon what he considered the Puritans' illegitimate land title, Williams declared the Mayflower Compact, one of the most often cited examples of early European-based democracy in America, invalid (Ernst 1932, 79).

Williams understood that his denouncement of the king's rights and the Mayflower Compact subjected him to the charge of disloyalty and even treason (Straus 1970 [1894], 36) and the consequences of such a charge (Gaustad 1991). After initially calling him to task for disloyalty by a summons to appear before the next court and be censured, the magistrates were willing to accept an apology from Williams, "as they seemed to have found the matters not so evil as had first appeared" (Straus 1970 [1894], 36–37).

Williams's conflict with church leaders over Indian-related issues continued, especially with John Cotton, and finally, on October 9, 1635, he was sentenced by the court "to depart out of our jurisdiction (Massachusetts Bay) within six weeks" (Winthrop 1853, 171). Later Williams wrote of his banishment, "When I was unkindly and unchristianly, as I believe, driven from my house, and land and wife and children, in midst of a New England winter . . . that ever honored Governor Winthrop privately wrote to me to steer my course to the Narragansett Bay and Indians" (Mason 1670, 32; Winthrop 1853, vol. 1, 172; Winthrop Papers 1929–1947, vol. 3, 502–503).

In January 1636, the General Court in Boston, after trying "discussion, reprimands, warnings and even banishment . . . decided to ship Williams back to England" (Avery 1905, vol. 2, 272; Dunn 1962, 17). They summoned him to Boston, and "a few days later [when] Captain John Underhill was sent by the general court to Salem to arrest Roger Williams, the nest was empty." It seems that Roger Williams had taken Governor Winthrop's advice and "had flown into the night and the wilderness and the winter's snow" (Avery 1905, vol. 2, 272; Winthrop and Weld 1644, 26; Winthrop 1853; Gaustad 1991; Grinde and Johansen 1991). Williams traveled for "four days in knee deep snow to the home of Massasoit" and "was sorely tossed from place to place for fourteen weeks" among the tribal communities in the Narranganset Bay region, northwest of Massachusetts before "purchasing" land from Canonicus, the statesman sachem of the Narragansetts, and with no other patent, he began to build and plant (Avery 1905, vol. 2, 273; Brockunier 1940, 90; Giddings 1957).

In his old age Williams recalled that when the hearts of his countrymen had failed him, God had "stirred up the barbarous heart of Canonicus to love me as his son to his last gasp" (Narragansett Club Publications, Letters 6, 407; Brockunier 1940, 96). A couple months later, Williams and his growing party of dissident Puritans moved further toward the northwest arm of the Narrangansett Bay, after being informed by Governor Winslow that they had settled on lands still within the boundaries of the Plymouth grant. In April 1636, Williams founded Providence, Rhode Island, "a shelter for persons distressed for conscience" (Avery 1905, vol. 2, 273–274). Brockunier (1940), and Covey (1966) acknowledge that the banishment among the Indians had a major impact on Williams's views of Puritan religion and English society.

Williams and the Influence of Native American Society on European Political Thought

William's first major work, *A Key into the Languages of America,* was compiled on the voyage from America and appeared in Gregory Dexter's bookshop in London in September 1643. There were "216 duodeimo pages full of valuable and curious information about the language, manners, and customs, government and religion, trading and economy of the Indians" (Ernst 1932, 227; Brockunier 1940, 140). The *Key* changed the English view of Indian society in that "it was the English, both in the New World and the Old, who most needed the Key, for without it, they tended to think only in terms of the Indians' barbarity and their own superiority" (Gaustad 1991, 29). What the *Key* offered political theorists of the time was a much-needed counterpoint to the existing English power structure, namely the monarchy and its God-given right to rule. The most cited examples from the *Key* and personal correspondence of Williams's use of Native American examples as counterpoints to English society follow:

> Boast not proud English, of thy birth and blood.
> Thy Brother Indian is by birth as Good.
> Of one blood God made Him, and Thee, & All.
> As wise, as fair, as strong, as personall. (Williams 1973, 61; Brockunier 1940, 141; Gaustad 1991, 29)

> For the temper of the braine in quick apprehensions and accurate judgements . . . the most high and sovereign God and Creator hath not made them inferior to Europeans . . . Nature knows no difference between Europeans and Americans in blood, birth, bodies . . . God having of one blood made all mankind. . . . (Rider 1904, 22)

I've known them to leave their house and mat
  To lodge a friend or stranger
  When Jews and Christians oft have sent
  Jesus Christ to the Manger. (Williams 1973, 17)

They were hospitable to everybody,
  Whomsoever cometh in when they are eating, they offer them to
eat of what they have, though but little enough prepared for themselves. . . .
  It is a strange truth that a man can generally find more free entertainment and refreshment amongst these Barbarians than amongst the
thousands that call themselves Christians. . . .
  There are no beggars amongst them, nor fatherless children unpro-
vided for. (Williams 1973, 129; Grinde and Johansen 1991, 83)

In Summer-time I have knowne them lye abroad often themselves, to
make roome for strangers, English, or others. (Williams 1973, 46)

The sachims . . . will not conclude of ought that concerns all, either
Lawes, or Subsidies, or warres, unto which people are averse, or by gentle perswasion cannot be brought. (Williams 1973, 123)

Native American Influences on Early Political Philosophers

Williams's political ideals and knowledge of American Indian societies
arrived in Europe at a pivotal point, as much of modern political
thought began to emerge. But even prior to Williams, Michel de Montaigne (1533–1592) had introduced the image of native America and
the Noble Savage to the European world in his work *Essais* (Essays)
(1575). Montaigne did not view European society as superior to Native
American society, and he was the first to defend Native American society against the cultural biases that existed at the time. "I find that
there is nothing barbarous and savage in this nation, by anything that
I can gather," he wrote, "excepting, that every one gives the title of
barbarism to everything that is not in use in his own country." He felt
that the problem of understanding Native Americans lay with Europeans, who had great difficulty understanding other cultures due to
their limited points of cultural comparison. "Seeing so clearing into
their [Indians'] faults, we should be so blind to our own." Montaigne
hoped to enlighten Europeans by describing many aspects of Native
American society, such as family interaction, religion, government,
marriage, and even food. He attempted to tie Native American society

to earlier Greek philosophers by identifying Native American society as one where "the laws of nature govern them still."

Montaigne did not visit or live in America, as Williams had. He did meet with three American natives in the court of King Charles IX, but he was hindered by an inept interpreter. Instead, his sources for *Essais* were other Europeans who had been to America. "I long had a man in my house that lived ten or twelve years in the New World . . . a plain ignorant fellow, and therefore the more likely to tell the truth . . . and besides, he has at divers times brought to me several seamen and merchants who at the same time went the same voyage." Williams may have read or attended lectures on *Essays,* prior to coming to America, although it was not translated into English until 1686.

Locke (1632–1704), Montesquieu (1689–1755), Voltaire (1694–1778), Hume (1711–1776), Rousseau (1712–1778), Kant (1724–1804), and others had access to the writings of Montaigne and Williams. Grinde and Johansen (1991) theorize that since Locke never visited America, his research on American Indians had to have come from secondary sources, some of which were Williams'. Locke's writings express many of the ideas found previously in Williams's writings, such as inalienable rights, state of nature, and religious freedom. His theories on "natural peoples living in a state of liberty" appear similar to Williams's writings on American Indians in the *Key* and also to Montaigne's *Essays.* However, the idea of natural rights originated long before Montaigne, Williams, and Locke. Plato, Aquinas, and other philosophers turned "to the idea of natural law to delineate the contours of political society" (Sommerville 1986, 105), but Locke, to a much lesser degree than Williams, added an American Indian comparison to his work, as evidenced by the following passages:

> Thus, we see that the kings of the Indians, in America, which is still a pattern of the first ages in Asia and Europe, whilst the inhabitants were too few for the country, and want of people and money gave men no temptations to enlarge their possessions of land or contest for wider extent of ground, are little more than generals of their armies; and though they command absolutely in war, yet at home, and in time of peace, they exercise very little dominion, and have but a very moderate sovereignty, the resolutions of peace and war being ordinarily either in the people or in a council, though the war itself, which admits not of pluralities of governors, naturally evolves the command into the king's sole authority. (Locke 1690)

> In the beginning all the world was America. (Locke 1690)

The study of American Indian society was not a primary interest for Locke, as it was to Williams, but it can be surmised that the writings of Williams, including those on Native Americans, did influence Locke (Stubben 2001). Gaustad (1991, 197) states that although Locke does not cite Williams as a source for his own writings in quarrels on religious freedoms, Locke came off "sounding like Roger Williams" and that both "argued that all civil power originates with the people" (83). Although there are no direct references to Williams in Locke's writings, or evidence of them ever meeting or corresponding, they both knew John Owens, the dean of Oxford University. Owens was "a member of Cromwell's Independent sect and a colleague of Roger Williams" and as a teacher was a "major influence on the evolution of Locke's political philosophies" (Granston 1957, 30, 41; Orme 1826). Roger Williams visited Owens on his return trip to England with the *Key* (Granston 1957), and his "elaborate theory of natural law had been dissolved into a denial of the competence of any man to determine indifferency for any other" (Abrams 1967, 46), a theory shared by Owens (Abrams 1967, 33). Henry Stubbe, a colleague of Locke, reported that all the scholars from Oxford, including Locke, were entirely Dr. Owen's creatures" (Abrams 1967, 32). Through Owens and Oxford, Locke would have read the works of Williams and heard lectures in regard to both his theories and life in America.

Grinde and Johansen (1991) offer the writings of Rousseau, *The Noble Savage* and *The Social Contract* (1950), Voltaire, "The Huron, or Pupil of Nature" (1940), and Montesquieu (1777) as other examples of the use of American Indian societies as counterpoints to European government and their influence on the political ideals that flowed through seventeenth- and eighteenth-century Europe. Axtell (1981) concludes that American Indian governments and societies did play a key role in the philosophical debates and protests (including the Boston Tea Party) of seventeenth- and eighteenth-century Europe. European political philosophers of the time utilized Native American society as an example and counterpoint in defining the emerging democratic dogma (Grinde and Johansen 1991; Stubben 2001).

Native American Protests against European and American Rule

During the time that many European scholars were using the Native Americans as a source and reference for their democratic ideals,

Native Americans themselves found warfare with the British, French, and, later, Americans as their major form of protest. More peaceful Native American protest did arise with religious revitalization movements such as the Delaware Prophet (1760–1763), inspired by a Delaware Indian seer known as "The Enlightened," and the Ghost Dances of 1879 and 1890, which were inspired by Paiute visionary Wovoka and ended in bloodshed (Nabokov 1991). Wovoka (whose American name was Jack Wilson) described his vision, which foretold of the return of the old ways:

> I, Jack Wilson, love you all, and my heart is full of gladness for the gifts you have brought me. When you get home I shall give you a good cloud which will make you feel good. I give you a good spirit and give you all good paint. I want you to come again in three months, some from each tribe there.
>
> There will be a good deal of snow this year and some rain. In the fall there will be such a rain as I have never given you before.
>
> Grandfather says, when your friends die you must not cry. You must not hurt anybody or do harm to anyone. You must not fight. Do right always. It will give you satisfaction in life. This young man has a good father and mother.
>
> Do not tell the white people about this. Jesus is now upon the earth. He appears like a cloud. The dead are still alive again. I do not know when they will be here, maybe this fall or in the spring. When the time comes there will be no more sickness and everyone will be young again.
>
> Do not refuse to work for the whites and do not make any trouble with them until you leave them. When the earth shakes do not be afraid. It will not hurt you.
>
> I want you to dance every six weeks. Make a feast at the dance and have food that everybody may eat. Then bathe in the water. That is all. You will receive good words again from me some time. Do not tell lies. (quoted in Nabokov 1991)

Such movements sought a cataclysmic event that would restore the Native American nations to pre-European times (Johnson, Nagel, and Champagne 1997). Such eighteenth- and nineteenth-century Native American protest movements were repressed by the U.S. government, mostly through military means. Sometimes the followers lost faith as the white men remained and their influence over Native Americans grew stronger. On Christmas Eve of 1890, more than two hundred Sioux men, women, and children were massacred by the

Seventh Cavalry at Wounded Knee for practicing the Ghost Dance (Nabokov 1991).

Other Native American leaders found that they could take their protests against white encroachment to another battle ground, the federal courts. Ponca clan head, Standing Bear, was one of these leaders who took the old Indian fighter, General Crook, to federal court in 1879 in order to prove that he, Standing Bear, was a human being and thus entitled to the same protection of the U.S. Constitution as those of General Crook's race.

Standing Bear of the Osni Ponca: "Our Blood Is Red"

In the winter of 1876 the eight Ponca clan heads were approached by their agent, who offered to take them from their ancestral home in northeast Nebraska, near the Niobrara River, to Oklahoma to look over several alternative reservation sites (Ponca Agency 1876–1877, C186). The agent promised the clan heads that if they didn't like the land they saw, they could return to their Nebraska homeland. The Ponca clan heads made the journey to Indian Territory, visiting many different land reserves, which were equally barren and unsuitable for agriculture. The clan heads agreed that they did not want to exchange their land but wanted instead to return home. When they informed the agent of their decision, he threatened to withdraw all money and support for their return journey, including the interpreter. Nevertheless, the clan heads stubbornly refused to relinquish their Nebraska homeland, so the agent departed without the Ponca clan heads (Ponca Agency 1876–1877, C771).

Clan heads White Eagle and Standing Buffalo then telegraphed the secretary of the Interior, requesting "assistance to return to their reservation" (Ponca Agency 1876–1877, 100). Government officials did not respond, and the clan heads, some of whom were advanced in years and ill, were forced to make the journey in the middle of winter on foot without money, food, or an interpreter. Fifty days later, near starvation, the Ponca clan heads reached the Otoe Reservation along the Kansas-Nebraska border. The Otoe provided them with enough food and ponies to make their way back to Niobrara (Ponca Agency 1876–1877, C1089; Howard 1965, 33). When the clan heads returned home, they found their people already preparing for the move. Appeals were made by Rev. J. O. Dorsey and other white friends of the Ponca to leave the Ponca in Nebraska (Ponca Agency 1876–1877, C1212; Howard 1965, 33). In spite of all their appeals, U.S. Indian Inspector E. C. Kemble ordered the Ponca removal. On April 12, 1877, the removal of the Ponca to their new home in Oklahoma began, although the exact location was not yet known (Howard 1965, 33).

E. A. Howard was appointed agent for the removal, and federal troops were called in to enforce the removal orders. About 170 Ponca members had begun the long trek in late April 1877. Clan head Standing Bear and his brother, Big Snake, were briefly imprisoned when they urged that the remainder of the Poncas resist the removal. By May, the remaining six hundred or so Poncas—including Standing Bear and his brother—were forced to join in the march, leaving behind their homes, farms, and many of their possessions. Nine persons died in the course of the journey, including a daughter of Standing Bear.

The nine deaths turned out to be a grim prelude to much further hardship and death for the Poncas in their new locale. They suffered from diseases, such as malaria, which afflicted a large number of Indians transported from northern climates to the humid Indian Territory. Estimates of the number of deaths vary greatly, from nine to three hundred, but even Indian Bureau reports indicate that a sizable portion of the tribe perished in the course of the first year. Standing Bear and several other leaders went to Washington, D.C., in the autumn of 1877, seeking President Rutherford B. Hayes's approval of their request to return to Nebraska. Hayes reportedly vetoed the request but allowed the Ponca leaders to select a more desirable location for their reservation within the Indian Territory. Although the Poncas eventually settled on a more favorable site 150 miles away, the ravages of disease and poverty continued. Standing Bear's last living son was among those who had died by 1878.

The death of Chief (clan head) Standing Bear's eldest son set in motion events that were to bring a measure of justice and worldwide fame to the chief and his tribe. Despair over the situation of the Poncas in Indian Territory, together with the desire to bury his son in the tribe's Nebraska homeland, led Standing Bear to make the move that made him famous, though it cost him the leadership of his tribe. In early January 1879, he led a small band of thirty Poncas on a return march to Nebraska, determined to resettle on the old land or die in the attempt. Another group of nearly 150 Ponca left shortly after Standing Bear but were arrested by the U.S. Army and taken to Fort Smith, Arkansas (Ponca Agency 1878–1879). There they were released on the condition that they return to their lands in Oklahoma, so most of the roughly six hundred members of the tribe were forced or chose to remain in the Indian Territory. But Standing Bear and several dozen followers arrived at the Omaha Indian agency at Decatur, Nebraska, on March 4, 1879. Even though the Omaha welcomed their kinsmen and invited them to settle there, because Indians were not allowed to leave their reservation without permission, Standing Bear and his followers were labeled as a renegade band (Howard 1965; Tibbles 1972).

The Indian Bureau had been informed of Standing Bear's flight from the Indian Territory soon after his departure. Secretary of the Interior Carl Schurz ordered General George Crook, commander of the U.S. Army Department of the Platte, at Omaha, to arrest the chief and his followers and return them to the territory in Oklahoma. Schurz and his advisers feared that if Standing Bear and his band were allowed to remain in Nebraska, it would set a precedent for all Native Americans in the Indian Territory to demand a return to their respective homelands. Although General Crook obeyed the order and arrested Standing Bear and his followers, he is said to have personally sympathized with the Poncas and believed that they had been repeatedly wronged by the government. Crook convinced Thomas Henry Tibbles, an Omaha newspaperman, to undertake a publicity campaign and institute a case in the federal district court to have Standing Bear and his group released (Wishart 1994).

With the help of Thomas Tibbles and two lawyers, John L. Webster and A. J. Poppleton, and probably General Crook, Standing Bear petitioned the court by a writ of habeas corpus (King 1969). He appeared before Judge Elmer Dundy (Wishart 1994). The trial of *Standing Bear v. Crook* was held from April 30 to May 2, 1879. Tibbles saw to it that the plight of Standing Bear and his followers was well publicized not only in his own Omaha newspaper but in papers nationwide. The case was of great significance, not only as a means of righting the wrongs inflicted on the Ponca tribe but also because it raised the larger question of Native American citizenship and the rights of Indians to appear in and to sue in the courts of the nation (Tibbles 1972).

The federal district attorney, G. M. Lambertson, argued that Standing Bear was not entitled to the protection of a writ of habeas corpus because he was not a citizen or even a "person" under American law. Standing Bear spoke briefly but eloquently on his own behalf. He stated that "my hand is not the same color as yours, but, if you pierce it, I will feel the same pain. The blood will be the same color. We are men. God made us . . . All I ask is what is mine—my land, my freedom, my dignity as a man" (Mardock 1979). Judge

Elmer S. Dundy, in the decision he handed down several weeks later, held that an Indian was, indeed, a person within the meaning of the laws of the United States, although he avoided the larger question of what rights of citizenship an Indian might have. He also ruled that the federal government had no rightful authority to remove the Poncas to the Indian Territory by force; Native Americans, he stated, possessed an inherent right of expatriation—that is, a right to move from one area to another as they wished. Dundy therefore ordered the release of Standing Bear and his followers from custody (Tibbles 1972).

Thomas Tibbles and other leaders of the movement for Indian rights hoped to carry the case of Standing Bear to the U.S. Supreme Court in order to secure a more definitive statement on Indian citizenship and rights. Tibbles himself made a tour to Chicago, New York, and Boston in the summer of 1879 to publicize the case and to raise money for the Supreme Court appeal. By October of that year, he had arranged for Standing Bear to lecture in key cities in the eastern United States. As interpreters for the chief, who spoke no English, Tibbles included in the party two Omaha Indians: Susette La Flesche (better known by her Indian name, Bright Eyes) and her brother, Francis La Flesche, both of whom had been educated in English-speaking schools. The tour generated great enthusiasm in urban social and literary circles, especially in Boston. Standing Bear, an impressive figure in his full Indian regalia, including feather headdress, related his story and that of his people in simple but emotional terms, while Bright Eyes, also in Indian dress, translated it into poignant English. A good deal of money was raised for the court appeal and for relief of the Ponca, and reform leaders were moved to become active in the cause of Indian rights. Standing Bear and Bright Eyes also testified before committees of Congress in Washington. The tour finally ended in April 1880 (Green 1969; Mardock 1971; Tibbles 1972).

Secretary of the Interior Schurz was able to quash the proposed appeal of the Ponca case to the Supreme Court. However, the agitation over the affair did lead to both congressional and presidential investigations. On February 1, 1881, President Hayes recommended to Congress that the Poncas be allowed to live where they chose and that they be compensated for lands relinquished and losses sustained during the forced removal to the Indian Territory in Oklahoma. Congress voted the necessary legislation and funds on March 3, 1881 (Howard 1965; Wishart 1994). Although the majority of the Ponca tribe remained in the Indian Territory, Standing Bear and his group lived quietly on the old Nebraska reservation near the mouth of the Niobrara River, and the Northern (Osni) Ponca Tribe was born. Standing Bear died in September 1908.

Native American Influence on Women's Suffrage

It is important for the scholar or student of Native American political participation to understand that women's suffrage was never an issue in pre-1492 America. Women have always played a major role in most American Indian governments and continue to do so today, as nearly 38 percent of modern-day tribal councils are composed of women ("Tribal Government Survey" 1990). Few American Indian tribal governments today restrict women from holding tribal office, and those that do, such as the Pueblos, have traditional avenues through which women can express their viewpoints on governmental and other issues (Pueblo De Acoma 1989, Acoma Government).

The founding mothers of feminism were familiar with and utilized works of early American anthropologists to show the importance and equality of women in Native American societies. Elizabeth Cady Stanton and Susan B. Anthony pointed to the influence of Iroquois women on their government institutions and to the fact that many Native American societies descended through the female line (Grinde and Johansen 1991). Stanton (1891) noted that "our barbarian ancestors seem to have had a higher degree of justice to women than American men in the 19th century, professing to believe, as they do, in our republican principles of government."

Oral history reports that an Iroquois sachem asked a group of newly arriving Dutch traders in 1510, who came to negotiate a trade agreement with the Iroquois Confederacy, "Why are your women not here?" In the Iroquois Confederacy, even though the Grand Council was all male, the lords were chosen by women and could be removed by women. This reflected the fact that, in Iroquois and many other American Indian societies, the head of the family was a woman. Each family consisted of the woman, her children, plus all of her blood relatives and their descendants through the female line. One or more of these maternal families comprised a clan. Three or more clans made up a tribe or nation. Each clan was headed by a matron, usually the oldest or most respected female member of the clan. The wishes of the clan matron were seldom disputed. If there was dissension among the lords of the Grand Council when one of the lords wanted to go to war, the lords who did not want to go to war would approach the clan matrons, who would, in turn, approach the dissenting lord's mother. She could forbid him to go to war, and he would not disobey her. If the women of the tribe refused to place the warrior's weapons outside their homes in preparation for battle, the warriors could not go to battle. The Council of Women could also exert its power in overturning decisions of the Grand Council (Brownell 1865; Parker 1916; Grinde and Johansen 1991).

The use of Indian women to provide an exemplar of feminist liberty continued into the nineteenth century. On May 16, 1914, only six years before the first national election in which women had the vote, the periodical *Puck* printed a line drawing of a group of Indian women observing Susan B. Anthony, Anne Howard Shaw, and Elizabeth Cady Stanton leading a parade of women. A verse under the print read:

SAVAGERY TO CIVILIZATION

We, the women of the Iroquois
Own the Land, the Lodge, the Children
Ours is the right to adoption, life or death;
Ours is the right to raise up and depose chiefs;
Ours is the right to representation in all councils;
Ours is the right to make and abrogate treaties;
Ours is the supervision over domestic and foreign policies;
Ours is the trusteeship of tribal property;
Our lives are valued again as high as man's.
(Grinde and Johansen 1991)

Native American Activism in the Twentieth Century

The twentieth century saw far less religious activism and far more secular Indian movements than earlier centuries. This was probably due to the influences of boarding school education and assimilation policies that produced educated Native Americans who worked toward economic and social empowerment. A new Indian elite emerged in the first decade of the twentieth century to advocate on behalf of Indians as a whole. The institutional expression of what scholars would label as modern "Pan-Indianism" began on October 12, 1911. On that occasion about fifty Indians convened for three days in a stately hotel in Columbus, Ohio, to launch the Society of American Indians (SAI) (Nabokov 1991).

Some of the leaders of the Society of American Indians were Dr. Charles A. Eastman, Santee-Sioux, who graduated from Dartmouth and authored the best sellers *Indian Boyhood* (1902) and *The Soul of the Indian* (1911). Another leader, Charles E. Dagenett, Peoria from Oklahoma, rose through the ranks of the Bureau of Indian Affairs (BIA) to become its highest-placed Indian. Also included in the list was Henry Roe Cloud, Winnebago, who chaired the meeting at Columbus. He had grown up in a wigwam on the banks of the Missouri River in Nebraska and later graduated from Yale University. Roe Cloud was instrumental in the development of Indian policy through the 1920s and 1930s, the Indian Reorganization Act, and the New Indian Policy. Angel Decora, a young Winnebago woman and artist, became a successful designer and influenced the direction of new Indian art (Nabokov 1991).

The SAI worked to remove Native Americans from the poverty and even starvation of the reservation through education and political action that fostered policies of assimilation. SAI's lobbying and political activities were a model for later organizations such as the National Congress of American Indians (NCAI) described in chapter 3 (Johnson, Nagel, and Champagne 1997).

Native American activism in the 1960s and 1970s was mainly a response to government policies and actions, which were seen as a direct assault on tribal sovereignty and the people themselves. First, the Indian Reorganization Act (IRA), which was viewed as a radical shift toward Indian self-government by liberals, was seen by many tribal people as another attempt to deprive them of their sovereign rights and assimilate them into white society. Some Indians labeled several tribal business committees created under the IRA as tools of the federal government and the IRA itself as "a blueprint for elected 'Tyranny'" (Burnette and Koster 1974). The response to these "externally imposed" governments was direct. In 1946, 30 percent of the Oglala Sioux Tribe boycotted tribal elections, and many of these "IRA Councils" became the focus of "Red Power" militancy that sought to restore traditional governments to the reservations (Hauptman 1992).

Second, the policy of tribal termination of the 1950s, although reversed in the 1970s with the reinstatement of federal recognition of the Menominee Tribe, had diminished tribal resources and made survival of IRA tribes difficult if not impossible. The Pick-Sloan project in Nebraska and South and North Dakota flooded over a million acres of tribal land. In passing the Public Works Appropriations Act of 1958, Congress overruled previous treaties, devastated the Seneca people, and allowed the U.S. Army Corps of Engineers to take tribal lands without adequate compensation or legal protection. Later the federal courts ruled in favor of the army, expanding plenary power to a level previously unimaginable in U.S. constitutional history (Hauptman 1992). Native Americans, once again, saw that the U.S. government was not living up to its trust responsibility guaranteed by U.S. law as well as treaty law. Many felt it was time to take a more militant stand.

By the 1960s, Kennedy's New Frontier policies and Johnson's War on Poverty, along with federal civil rights laws and actions, fueled increased protest and militant actions, mainly by African Americans. Native Americans became more militant in the late 1960s, when the best-known Native American activist group was born, the American Indian Movement (AIM).

The American Indian Movement

The American Indian Movement was first organized by Clyde Bellecourt, Chippewa, on July 28, 1968, to help Indians in Minneapolis–St. Paul, Minnesota, with what they felt were deplorable living conditions and unbearable racism (Banks 1994; O'Brien 1989). "It wasn't that we didn't know there was racism in the cities," Dennis Banks, one of the AIM leaders, would later recall. "It was how racism forced us into squalid slum tenement buildings, closed doors to job opportunities, and fostered racist laws, jails, courts, and prisons. Beginning with our foundation meeting, we immediately set out to bring about change in those institutions of public concern: housing, education, employment, welfare, and the courts" (1994).

Ironically, during the time that Banks and his parents' generations were experiencing extreme racism in the Twin Cities, Hubert Humphrey was mayor of Minneapolis. Humphrey was a champion of civil rights, social justice, and economic opportunity across the nation but could not provide these things to the Native American citizens in Minneapolis.

During the twentieth century Native American culture had been weakened in most Indian communities due to U.S. policy, the boarding schools, and other efforts to extinguish Indian secular and spiritual life. AIM was founded to turn the attention of Indian people toward a renewal of spirituality, which would impart the strength of resolve needed to reverse the ruinous policies of the United States, Canada, and other colonialist governments of Central and South America (Means 1995). In the more than thirty years of its history, AIM sponsored a revival of culture by helping to restore spiritual leaders and elders to their former positions of esteem for the wisdom and the history they hold. It also supported the refusal by Indian people and nations to relinquish their sovereign right to exist as free and uncolonized people (Dewing 1985; Means 1995). AIM transformed policy making into programs and organizations that have served Indian people in many reservation and urban communities, and these policies have consistently been made in consultation with spiritual leaders and elders.

The founding of AIM in 1968 saw a new period of American Indian militancy across the United States (O'Brien 1989). But unlike the American civil rights movement with which it has been compared, desegregation was not a goal of AIM, and individual rights were not placed ahead of tribal sovereignty and culture.

In 1969, a group of Indians called the United Indians of All Tribes, which included AIM members, occupied Alcatraz Island in San Francisco Bay. Alcatraz, a maximum-security federal prison portrayed in movies and books, was abandoned in 1963. The activists claimed the island as Native American property under the Fort Laramie Treaty of 1868, which permitted any male Indian over the age of eighteen whose tribe was a party to the treaty to file a homestead on abandoned federal lands (O'Brien 1989; Johnson, Nagel, and Champagne 1997). The group occupied Alcatraz Island for nineteen months.

In November 1972, AIM led a protest march to Washington, D.C., named the Trail of Broken Treaties and made up of representatives of native nations. The group occupied the BIA headquarters for six days and presented a twenty-point solution paper to President Nixon:

1. Restoration of treaty making (ended by Congress in 1871).
2. Establishment of a treaty commission to make new treaties (with sovereign native nations).
3. Indian leaders to address Congress.
4. Review of treaty commitments and violations.
5. Unratified treaties to go before the Senate.
6. All Indians to be governed by treaty relations.

7. Relief for native nations for treaty rights violations.
8. Recognition of the right of Indians to interpret treaties.
9. Joint Congressional Committee to be formed for reconstruction of Indian relations.
10. Restoration of 110 million acres of land taken away from native nations by the United States.
11. Restoration of terminated rights.
12. Repeal of state jurisdiction on native nations.
13. Federal protection for offenses against Indians.
14. Abolishment of the Bureau of Indian Affairs.
15. Creation of a new office of Federal Indian Relations.
16. New office to remedy breakdown in the constitutionally prescribed relationships between the United States and native nations.
17. Native nations to be immune to commerce regulation, taxes, trade restrictions of states.
18. Indian religious freedom and cultural integrity protected.
19. Establishment of national Indian voting with local options; free national Indian organizations from governmental controls.
20. Reclaim and affirm health, housing, employment, economic development, and education for all Indian people.

(Means 1995; aimovement.org, 2001)

Even though the occupation of the BIA headquarters brought attention to AIM and Native American activism, it was AIM's occupation of the tiny hamlet of Wounded Knee, South Dakota, in 1975 that gained worldwide attention.

Wounded Knee

Wounded Knee, on the present-day Pine Ridge Reservation in South Dakota, is the site of the massacre of nearly four hundred Minneconjou women, men, and children on December 29, 1890, by the U.S. Army under the direction of Colonel James Forsyth and the infamous Seventh Cavalry. Many historians consider this to be the last major battle between the Sioux and the U.S. government (Dewing 1985; O'Brien 1989).

In 1972, AIM was contacted by Lakota elders for assistance in dealing with the corruption within the Bureau of Indian Affairs and

Oglala Sioux Tribal Council on the Pine Ridge Reservation (Matthisessen 1991; aimovement.org 2001). Violent confrontations between the traditional people and the GOONS (Guardians of Our Oglala Nation) became an everyday occurrence (Matthisessen 1991). Between February 27 and May 8, 1973, roughly two hundred Indians under AIM leadership occupied Wounded Knee in a military standoff between forces of the U.S. government, the Oglala Sioux Nation tribal government, and the American Indian Movement (O'Brien 1989; Dewing 1985). The occupiers commandeered the trading post at Wounded Knee, seized eleven hostages, traded gunfire with federal officers, and fired on automobiles and low-flying planes that dared come within rifle or shotgun range.

Heavily armed and helmeted federal marshals established a cordon around Wounded Knee, and federal forces brought armored personnel carriers into the Pine Ridge Reservation. Federal mediators maneuvered to obtain release of the hostages. U.S. Senator James Abourezk (D-SD) announced from Washington that he had talked by telephone with AIM leader Russell Means at Wounded Knee and told him he was ready to negotiate with the militants if they released the hostages (Means 1995; Dewing 1985). Means demanded that the Senate Foreign Relations Committee hold hearings on Indian treaties, that the Senate make a full-scale investigation of government treatment of Indians, and that Abourezk launch an inquiry into all Sioux reservations in South Dakota. They vowed to stay at Wounded Knee until they got answers from Washington and that no harm "by Indians" would come to the hostages (Dewing 1985).

When AIM took control of Wounded Knee, over seventy-five different Indian nations were represented, with more supporters arriving daily from all over the country. After three weeks of the occupation, with little movement on either side, federal authorities began to tighten the noose around Wounded Knee. The press and many outside supporters were denied access; outside supplies, including food, were cut off; and nighttime disturbances such as flares, bright lights, and loud noises were focused on the occupiers. The government action to cut off Wounded Knee led to more activity to drum up support for the besieged occupants among left-leaning antiwar and civil rights organizations (Dewing 1985).

The FBI identified twenty-one different groups sponsoring and participating in demonstrations across the United States for AIM. These included Students for a Democratic Society, Socialist Workers Party, Workers World Party, Youth against War and Facism, Young Socialist Alliance, Vietnam Veterans against the War, Black Panther

Party, Venceremos Organization, Progressive Labor Party, Republic of New Africa, National Committee for Defense of Political Prisoners, United States Committee to Aid the National Liberation Front, Medical Aid for Indochina, Red Collective, Black Workers Medical Committee for Human Rights, Pittsburgh Peace and Freedom Center, and Committee for Asian American Action (Dewing 1985).

Many church-related organizations also tried to intervene and/or supported AIM. These included the United Council of Churches, United Methodist Board of Christian Concern, United Methodist Church Midwest Dioceses, Church of God, National Council of Churches, and other individual churches. The Episcopal and Catholic dioceses owned churches at Wounded Knee that were occupied (Dewing 1985).

For the rest of that winter, the men and women inside Wounded Knee lived on minimal resources while they fought the armed aggression of federal forces. Daily, heavy gunfire was issued back and forth between the two sides, but true to their word, the occupiers refused to give up. They attempted to live in their traditional manner, celebrating a birth, a marriage, and mourning the death of two of their fellow warriors inside Wounded Knee. AIM member Buddy Lamont was hit by M16 fire and bled to death inside Wounded Knee. AIM member Frank Clearwater was also killed by heavy machine-gun fire inside Wounded Knee (Dewing 1985; Means 1995).

After seventy-one days, the siege at Wounded Knee had come to an end with the government making nearly twelve hundred arrests. But this would only mark the beginning of what was known as the "Reign of Terror" instigated by the FBI and the BIA. During the three years following Wounded Knee, sixty-four tribe members were murdered, and their murders remained unsolved; three hundred were harassed and beaten.

Over five hundred American Indians were arrested, and trials were held in Cedar Rapids, Iowa; Lincoln, Nebraska; and St. Paul, Minnesota, in an attempt to convict the organizers and occupants of Wounded Knee. However, fewer than a dozen people were ever convicted of any crimes.

Tensions between the U.S. government and AIM continued on the Pine Ridge Reservation after Wounded Knee. On June 26, 1975, two FBI agents and one young Lakota man were killed in a shootout on the Pine Ridge Reservation. Leonard Peltier still sits in Ft. Leavenworth Federal Prison in Kansas, convicted of murdering the two FBI agents (Dewing 1985; Matthisessen 1991; Means 1995).

AIM Legacy

Thirty years later, AIM continues, mainly through local chapters, and many of AIM's early leaders continue to be politically active, but nearly all have gone on to other interests. Russell Means was arrested in 1999 for protesting alcohol sales in White Clay, Nebraska, a town a few miles south of the Pine Ridge Reservation. Several deaths have been attributed to the use of alcohol purchased in White Clay, including unsolved murders. Means's life has turned to acting, starring in both movies and TV series. John Trudell also has expanded his acting and musical careers. Dennis Banks also has gained notoriety as an actor and remains involved in AIM and Native American activism. The Bellecourt brothers have been involved in tribal politics on their own White Earth Reservation and in urban Indian issues. Vernon Bellecourt is the president of the National Coalition on Racism in sports and the media. AIM protests still arise but now usually in a more localized manner, because more tribes are involved in their own activism. For example, even though AIM members were involved, Wisconsin and Minnesota tribes fought against anti-Indian sentiment, both in the courts and on their lakeshores, when they won back their legal right to spear fish. Tribal members and non-Indian sportsmen clashed at many lakes throughout the region, and local and state law enforcement found themselves enforcing treaty rights.

John Trudell has said that "AIM died years ago. It's just that some people don't know it yet" (Johnson, Nagel, and Champagne 1997). But Russell Means and others view AIM as continuing through the rebirth of tribal spirituality, tribal activism, and sovereign strength. Indigenous rights and third world power are now a norm on the international political scene (Means 1995; Johnson, Nagel, and Champagne 1997). But the question remains: "If AIM had not come along, would tribes be able to enforce sovereign rights, such as spear fishing, gaming, religious freedom and self-governance . . . and would urban Indians had any political power at all?" This author feels that AIM did more to educate Native Americans to their tribal responsibility than to force non-Indians to take notice, and as a result, Native Americans will continue to be politically active in protecting their right to exist as First Americans.

A chronological listings of major AIM activities since its birth in 1968 is available at AIMGGC@worldnet.att.net and at www.aimmovement.org.

Internal Tribal Activism

As we have seen, the Native American tradition of activism and protest began as internal tribal politics. The traditional rules under which internal tribal conflicts were settled did not include external intervention, for one must settle one's own disputes before attempting to intervene in another's. Internal tribal politics plays a significant role in today's tribal governments and can be divisive, personal, and even violent. Winning or losing a tribal election can mean the difference between continued employment and loss of jobs for relatives and supporters; it is also a factor in clan and family feuds and tribal division in public, personal, and professional arenas. Some feel the internal tribal political conflict has been caused by the lack of traditional values and norms that maintained consensus rather than division. In some instances, internal tribal conflict spills out onto the national and international scene, as evidenced by the conflict between the American Indian Movement and Ogalala Sioux Tribal President Richard Wilson in the 1970s.

Richard "Dick" Wilson:
Tribal Leader and AIM Antagonist

Native American tribal leaders have experienced both the positive and negative sides of activism, and several have found themselves in the national political spotlight due to such activism, in both positive and negative manners. Richard (Dick) Wilson, tribal chair of the Oglala Sioux Nation, was thrown into the national spotlight when the community of Wounded Knee, on the Pine Ridge Reservation in South Dakota, was taken over by members of the American Indian Movement in 1973. Wounded Knee brought more attention to the plight of the Native American people than any previous event. Wilson was portrayed, by the American Indian Movement and many non-Indian authors, as crooked and a leader of a half-breed goon squad (Matthisessen 1991).

Having worked with the American Indian Movement during the Wounded Knee trials and then later becoming personally related to the Wilson family, the author has grown to know that Dick Wilson was respected by many of the Oglala people, who saw him as striving to better their condition. At Wilson's memorial give away, I witnessed the beauty of Oglala strength, as the Wilson family and friends and some AIM members came together to honor him. At a give away, one gives away personal belongings, gifts, and other items, normally after a death, adoption, naming ceremony, marriage, pow wow or other family- or clan-oriented ceremony, to all that attend. At Richard Wilson's memorial and give away, family members, Oglala tribal members, and other indigenous peoples, including members of the Means family, offered words of love, respect, and forgiveness to honor Dick Wilson and his family.

One highly overlooked fact in the AIM-Wilson conflict is that both AIM and Wilson had common enemies, the U.S. government and the state of South Dakota. Wilson and AIM were used by both in an attempt to bring negative public attention to Native American issues during a time of high civil rights activity in our nation. As one Oglala friend said, "What the U.S. government and the state of South Dakota do not realize is that no outsider can divide a family, and the Oglala are a family, forever" (Wilson 1991).

The following comes directly from the writings submitted by the Wilson family who have requested that it be included in this chapter, as written by them. In traditional Ponca ways, such a request is an honor and must be honored.

On his deathbed Richard Wilson left his family a message to share with the Oglala people:

> The Oglala Sioux Tribal Constitution has everything you need to operate as a sovereign nation. We have a beautiful reservation. Help clean it up. I went to Kyle the other day and saw trash all along the way. Get something started to clean it up and show the beauty of our reservation. . . . Remember to always help people. Feed them if you can, give what you can. It is very rewarding. And most of all, get involved with the Tribe. Get involved with your districts, communities, and schools. . . . Make a difference.

Even on his deathbed, Dick Wilson was concerned about the Oglala people, the reservation, and the future of the Oglala Sioux Tribe. The message printed on the obituary card at his funeral read:

> Because we are Indian people with strong connection to the next world, the manner in which we die and the type of funeral is a reflection of the respect people have for the individual. Father Bill Pauly had just come to the Pine Ridge Indian Reservation in January 1990. Father Bill came into the room to meet my father and said, "I just wanted to meet you Dick, I have heard so much about you." They talked at length about some of Dick Wilson's accomplishments and about life

and death. Father Pauly asked if he could say a prayer with my father or if that would offend him as Father Pauly was Catholic and Dick Wilson was not. My father said "It is all the same thing and I am sure we all pray to one God, so I have no problem with you being Catholic." There were so many calls that the hospital switchboard asked to have a family member stay by a waiting room phone to take the calls. The people that came to the hospital to say good-bye to him were stopped at the entrance and asked to wait until a family member could come from the waiting room and inform them of his condition. The local radio station ran hourly reports on his condition and a basketball game was stopped at Pine Ridge School for a moment of prayer for him.

People and institutions cause and perpetuate division, and a true leader must transcend that division in the best interest of the people. Richard "Dick" Wilson was such a leader. In a speech that was delivered and aired on NBC in 1973, Mr. Wilson told the world that the urban militants who took over the BIA headquarters in Washington, D.C. and trashed the building and then declared that they were willing to die were "suddenly ready to live again when the BIA offered them $63,000 to leave town." Dick Wilson also told the world and residents of the Pine Ridge reservation that there was no doubt that the $63,000 that was given to AIM members in D.C. would come out of the annual BIA allocation for the Pine Ridge reservation. It was the Pine Ridge residents that would not have the roads repaired, or public safety protection, or education payments to the schools because the $63,000 would be taken from those projects. He was concerned that the kids would be going to school in July instead of having a summer break because the roads across the reservation had been sealed off to all traffic because to the take over. These were not the children of Dick Wilson, but children of the Oglala tribal members that he was concerned about.

Dick Wilson was accused or murder, he was accused of being a dictator, and he was accused of being a thief. Very recently (2000), American Indian Movement leaders that accused Dick Wilson of murder were themselves named as suspects in the murder of Anna Mae Auquash and others. These so-called leaders never did bring anything back to this reservation, nor have they made any contribution to the reservation. They have only capitalized on the plight of the very poor Oglala people in their movies, records, and other public engagements. For all of the accusations they made, Dick Wilson was never charged with murder. Anything and everything he done, was done for the Oglala people.

With all of the recent disappointment with tribal leaders, there is hardly a day that goes by that somebody doesn't stop by my office and tell me how they think Dick Wilson would have handled the situation.

Many people that live on the reservation remember that people had jobs and homes during the 4 years that Dick Wilson was tribal chairman. A dictator doesn't get this kind of respect 11 years after his death. It is leadership, concern and provision for the people, that make people remember what a leader is about.

Dick Wilson was extremely proud of the year-end audit at the end of his first term. The auditor told him the only disallowed cost for the entire tribe was the tribal member use of station wagons for a death in the family. Families were permitted to borrow the tribal vehicle and move their loved one's bodies to the wake and funeral because the reservation did not have a funeral home at that time. Each family was given $50 from the tribal general fund to help with the funeral and to honor the tribal member's life. The auditor told Dick Wilson that he would never cite the tribe for that disallowed cost due to the culture of the Oglala. (Wilson and Wilson 2001)

The accompanying letter was sent to the *Lakota Times,* a widely read and respected newspaper among Native Americans, and published in 1998. This is the original letter sent to the author by the Wilson family from Mona Wilson. It illustrates an important aspect of Native American politics and political participation that one must never overlook: everything is personal. An action, a vote, a column in the local newspaper by a person or group is not seen as a political or professional action but as a personal action. And the response to a political action is often personal and direct, as witnessed in the following letter. When a person makes a political promise, it is often seen as a personal promise. If it is not kept, even because of a difficult political problem such as lack of supporting votes, it is still taken as breaking a personal promise.

January 27, 1998
Indian Country Today
Editor in Charge
Rapid City, SD 57701

Dear Editor,

On Sunday the Denver Broncos won a memorable Super Bowl title. For a week prior I had mixed emotions, 8 years ago was the last time the broncos went for the title, 8 years ago my brother Billy D. Wilson was calling home from Texas betting various family members the Broncos would win. A few days before that gem he died on Texas Interstate and the broncos lost that weekend. A lot of memories flooded my heart this past week.

My father died at my brothers' funeral, my sister revived him and we lost him the next day for the last time. Shortly after, his only living Uncle "John Lee" was found in his living room chair. Family believed it was after he received the news of his nephew's death.

My father was Richard "Dick" Wilson, the ONLY Oglala Lakota Tribal Chairman to serve two consecutive terms in our Tribal history to date. He was also Tribal Chairman during what is known as Wounded Knee II.

Last week our tribal council passed a resolution proclaiming a holiday at the end of February officially to celebrate Wounded Knee II. There was one vote to table this resolution and take it back to the people and their districts by Mr. Ton Conroy. This failed, as he could not get a second. Then council turned around and changed it into an ordinance. I am shocked and disgusted to think I voted for some of these people! You were voted in office to represent the Lakota people as a whole not just a handful. It should have been the right of the people to have that say not just your personal opinion. Now you changed this resolution to an ordinance! You are sworn in office to protect our people and the constitution of Oglala Sioux Tribe and to give careful and dedicated thought to the laws you are making in the name of the Oglalas.

In passing this ordinance you are honoring people who tried to overthrow the Oglala Sioux Tribes a group of terrorists who burned alive a tribal councilman. A group who can murder and yet twenty-five years later be honored for it. Is this no different than the United States Government when they gave out medals of honor to the soldiers who murdered our defenseless people at Wounded Knee I?

You are arbitrarily throwing out ordinances making them the law of the land without rightful consultation from our people. This is wrong. I say arbitrarily because you did not give the people proper notice to comment prior to having this resolution brought to council floor. You did not take this to your respectful district. I live in Pine ridge and I know for a fact this was never brought to the people of Pine Ridge Village. It has been so long since this village has had a meeting of the people I can't even recall when it happened last? A new village council was elected and to date they were never soared. I ask the voting people of the Lakota Nation to check yourself if this issue came to your district floor for discussion and approval prior to your representative voting.

The people of the Pine ridge reservation need to know what our council is doing and have a rightful voice in these decisions. Once an ordinance is passed; it is the law of the land, people please pay attention to what is happening. The very same council that took an oath of office to uphold our constitution and voted on this action have two councilman that have disgraced our people with being our leaders our role models and have been convicted of federal charges, yet you do not have the courage to due your job and remove them. They should have not been able to have a vote in this and done the honorable thing by stepping down from office. This alone should void any action they have voted on since their conviction.

I realize for having spoken out the political backlash I will receive. I realize I may even lose my job. That next week I will probably join the rank of the unemployed. So be it. I watched my father, who was then 35 years old take a stand. I watched those that stood by him fighting not only aim but also the FBI the BIA the United States Marshals and other branches of the Federal Government because of the actions of aim. I have spoken to people who were of this era but I have decided not to mention their names but let them tell it in their own words because the feelings are so deep for each and every one of us and our families. I thank those people that have called me or returned my calls as well as calls to my family. I thank you for your words, your shred anger over this issue because you have endured what we know the people actually went through during that time.

Talk about dictatorship. Most of you that had an opportunity to vote in the secretarial vote did not even realize you were voting this administration in for another year. This very council put themselves in for three years instead of two years. A few years back when the council pay was on the agenda that council that would replace them in some instances. The present Tribal council had a secretarial vote that should have included all enrolled members of the Oglala Sioux Tribe wherever their address should be. This did not happen.

It was sudden and only a few thousand ballots were sent out. I am an enrolled member of this tribe. I reside here and I have voted in several elections and I had to go to the BIA office and ask for a ballot because I did not receive one. The majority of our people living here did

not get a ballot. Law provides that the Secretary of Interior must vali-
date a secretarial vote. The people were never informed to date of this
validation, was it ever? Otherwise, this would make it illegal that our
elections have not yet taken place. I tell you what, I for one am ready
to change my vote and I encourage others to give serious thought to
this also.

Why on earth would you want to celebrate something that tore our
people apart! It took twenty years for the people, for families to start
talking again. Our people seem to be our own worst enemies. After all
this time, we are finally looking in the same direction, working together. Coming together for the health and welfare of our people.
Now a handful of people want to pour salt in old wounds. Why? Why
do you want to divide us once again? Why do you only care about
putting yourself into the headlines and maybe get a vote and get a
vote there and not about the effect this has all of us that lived here during that era and live here now. Why are you trying to re-create "AIM"
days and hard feelings when you should be trying to create jobs! How
high is our unemployment Council? What are you doing today for
those suffering the results of welfare reform other than talking about it?
Where are the jobs? You should show us rather than talk about it. How
many jobs has this council created in the two years you have been in
office to this date, today. January 27, 1998? Do not include political
appointees please.

No administration has been able to match the industry and employment during my fathers' administration. Research your data. We had a
moccasin factory, plastics factory, and electronics and pottery factory.
We had the Indian Action Team. People had jobs, people had money.
All this disappeared AFTER my Fathers' administration. When he was
only a councilman for Pine Ridge Village in the early sixties, his dream
was to bring education to the people. Research your data. He accomplished this it was coming, Piya Wiconi main office was scheduled to be
placed near where the new Pine ridge Hospital is now located. But
change of administration put it elsewhere.

I commend Mr. Thomas Shortbull, President of Oglala Lakota College to have the courage a few years ago over KILI radio to mention
the support he received from Dick Wilson when the college was devastated by fire. He said dad helped obtain modular units that are still being used today. More recently at the dedication of the Lloyd Eagle Bull,
Jr. College Center, Mr. Shortbull once again gave credit to my father,

Dick Wilson, for taking immediate action on the issue of OLC needing a building. Mr. Shortbull said he stopped other Executive Board members right on the Tribal Building steps and made them take a voting action right then and there! That is the man Dick Wilson was.

Crazy Horse School doesn't even have a picture of the man who helped bring their school to this reservation. It was Dick Wilson with the support of the National Congress of American Indians, which was held in Sarasota Florida that year.

I also with to commend Elaine Quiver, Director of the Foster Grandparent Program for remembering my father this past summer for starting their program during his administration and giving a jacket in his honor.

I am so tired of the false stories of who my father was and of those of you that make him out to be a hateful man. This is so untrue and I will fight for the truth to be out so his grandchildren do not have to read bias one-sided stories.

There are people that grew up with my dad, who went to school with him, who knew that he was a good person and cared about his people. He grew up hard just like everyone else and he would take the shirt off of his back if he could to help. He didn't marry a white woman and come back proclaiming to be the ultimate "Mr. Indian" like many of you or getting rich like Russell Means starring in movies or making records. This goes on while the people here still have hard times and living poor. If Russell Means was so traditional, where was he when his grandmother Myrtle Means died? I was at her wake and funeral because she was a long time friend of Grandmother Emma Whalen.

Ask the real Lakota people, the grassroots people who really knew him. Ask an elder. Ask Ida Bullman, Potato Creek, what kind of man Dick Wilson was.

Ask one of the men who in their early twenties at the time, stood by his side ready to lay their life on the line for what he and they believed in. they were not goons as your dictionary describes, but rather deputized tribal policeman by the Tribal Council. Ask someone who knew him all his life. Ask Vincent Brewer, Sr. A few days after my father passed away, I seen Vincent then Judge Brewer in our tribal court house, he told ma a story about the Oglala community Boarding School. Of how there was this little boy standing there crying his eyes out, big tear rolling down his cheeks, he pitied him so he took him under his wing. It was my father being left at the school even before he was first grade as most of our people were as his parents went back to Red Shirt Table. With this story I knew Vincent knew him all of his life and I know Mr. Brewer to be an honest man. Not just a bunch of you who proclaim to have known him but yet never seen nor spoke to him in your life. You, that know nothing of my fathers life. I ask the people; the Oglalas that knew my dad from childhood to his death to please call me at (605)867-1229. It is time the family and friends of Dick Wilson spoke out. Please help me prove who my dad really was.

Why didn't you people have the courage to speak up when my father was alive? I know this, my father always thought 25 years ahead of his time. He was concerned what would be here; he was concerned if we would have a reservation. You people only care about today and yourselves and THAT frightens me! Why aren't you people being the leaders we elected and do something about the Senator from Montana who is threatening our serenity and Indian Lands?

Well, part of him is still alive through his children and I am one of them and proud. President John Steele, your father was killed by AIM, yet you bring this resolution to the council floor. I know the political repercussions but, I know who I am and Proud. Bogi Carlow, you should be ashamed of yourself being a "yes" man. Mr. Tapio, out of respect for your wife, Shirley Shangreau Tapio, whom my grandma Julie considered a daughter until her death, I just want to ask you where is your loyalty to my grandparents who treated you like son in their home, to my father who grew with you like a brother, and to all of us that are not aim but were at your sons' bedside during his last hours and at his funeral? It was not my father who forgot a lifetime. This is what aim accomplished, this is what aim historically done to our people and succeeded—they destroyed friends, families and almost our people. Now they are trying to do it again. Manuel, you say your brother-in-law was killed by aim and then turn around and vote for this. Where are your family values and loyalty and you say you are a leader. Where was your backbone on Council day?

You may rationalize, but I know this, I owe this letter and my sincere love to my fathers' memory and what he believed in. I owe this letter to my father who on his deathbed asked for prayers for his people first, then his family and lastly himself. I owe this letter to my mother. Yvonne "Sister" Wilson, who stood by his side for 24 years, 7 children many elections from school boards to council representative to Tribal Chairman twice and through Wounded Knee II. I owe this letter to those who stood beside him and would have put your lives down as you fought beside him because you knew he believed in and fought for the Tribal Constitution and Treaty Laws. I owe this letter to those whose family members died during this time and the pain and anguish this resolution/ordinance has brought you once again. I owe this letter to Tribal Councilman, Mr. Leo Wilcox, whose murder was never solved. I owe this letter to the real residents and members of the Oglala Nation. I owe this letter and commend Mr. Tom Conroy for having the courage, to be the only one to speak up, go against the majority with no support and ask to take this issue back to the people.

Sincerely, Mona R. Wilson on behalf of and with consent of my mother, sisters, Saunie, Holly and Connie and brother Richard Wilson Jr.

Spiritual Activism

American Indian Religious Freedom Act

Spirituality is the main factor in every aspect of American Indian tribal life, including political participation and government. The strongest driving force among American Indians is their traditional spiritual beliefs and practices. In fact, after nearly fifty years of living among many different American Indian tribal people, the author has never met an American Indian atheist. Native American activism, in terms of preserving spiritual rights, sites, and freedom, has been a major conflict between native peoples and the U.S. government. From the massacres of the Ghost Dancers (Lesser 1933), through the forced Christianization by church-controlled boarding schools, to modern-day legal battles, Native American spiritual activists have prevailed. Although all Americans are guaranteed the right to religious freedom under the First Amendment to the U.S. Constitution, Native Americans have had to rely on federal law and court interpretations of their religious freedoms.

The American Indian Religious Freedom Act (AIRFA) of 1978 specifically reaffirms the First Amendment rights of American Indian people to have access "to lands and natural resources essential in the conduct of their traditional religion, even though the lands and natural resources are located beyond the boundaries of a tribal reservation" (Stoffle et al. 1990, 4). The AIRFA acknowledged that the First

Amendment had not adequately protected Indians' rights to practice their religions without interference. Indeed, federal officials had often worked actively both to support and destroy Indian religions (O'Brien 1989, 90). Members of Congress admitted that "America does not need to violate the religions of her Native peoples. There is room for great value in cultural and religious diversity. We would be poorer if . . . American Indian religion disappeared" (United States Commission on Civil Rights 1980, 1).

In Section 2 of AIRFA the Congress asked the president to direct various federal departments and agencies to consult with native traditional religious leaders to determine appropriate changes in policies and procedures necessary to protect and preserve American Indian religious practices. If such consultation indicates that a proposed federal agency action may infringe on the free exercise of religion, then the federal agency will engage in additional consultation with the American Indian traditional religious leaders (Stoffle et al. 1990, 4).

A federal agency task force, chaired by C. D. Andrus, secretary of the Interior, issued the first set of department and agency responses to AIRFA in 1979. The Federal Agencies Task Force resolved that "Henceforth it shall be the policy of the United States to protect and preserve for American Indians their inherent right of freedom to believe, express, and exercise [their] traditional religions . . . including, but not limited to, access to sites, use and possession of sacred objects, and freedom to worship through ceremonials and traditional rites" (Andrus 1979, 8–12).

Federal authorities made it clear that they considered AIRFA a statement of ideals, not a binding law, and the judiciary has continued to rule against Indian rights. In *Lyng v. Northwest Indian Cemetary Protections Association* (1988), the Supreme Court held that the Forest Service could build a road through a mountain area sacred to three Indian tribes. The Court declared that the government could act if its purpose was secular and didn't specifically aim to harm a religion. In dissent, Justice William Brennan called this a "cruelly surreal result," in which "governmental action that virtually destroys a religion is nevertheless deemed not to 'burden' that religion" (Schmidt 1994).

The Supreme Court further diminished the intent of AIRFA in *Employment Division of Oregon v. Smith* (1990). Although the U.S. Constitution does prohibit federal and state governments from sanctioning a particular religion over another religion, Christianity has always been and remains the predominant religion in the United States. Until recently, most Christian-oriented religious practices that may violate a particular state law were protected by the Constitution. However, this practice may be changing with the Supreme Court's recent decision in *Oregon v. Smith,* which allowed for state sanctions in regard to the religious practices of the Native American Church. This church is an Indian approach to Jesus that blends Christian and Indian beliefs; peyote, a hallucinogenic cactus bud, is used sacramentally to attain visions (Burnette and Koster 1974, 37). However, the controversy over the use of peyote in the services of the church continues to this day. Many of the Christian missionaries who practiced among American Indians opposed the use of peyote, even though the Native American Church blends American Indian religious values with Christian beliefs. Congress and the courts have tried to ban the use of peyote, but each has found the same result, that "the Native American Church's use of peyote is a religious institution (far older than the U.S. government) and comes within the Constitution of the United States" (*Lake Mohonk Proceedings* 1914, 76).

In *Oregon v. Smith* the Supreme Court in April 1990 ruled that "states can forbid religious use of drugs in religious practices" (*Chicago Tribune* 1990, 1). In *Oregon v. Smith,* the Oregon Department of Human Resources fired two American Indian counselors because of their use of peyote in Native American Church services and their refusal to quit attending such services. The two workers, Smith and Black, filed an employment appeal on the basis that their religious freedoms were being violated by the action of the state of Oregon.

The majority opinion written by Justice Antonia Scalia concluded that the First Amendment guarantee of free exercise of religion did not require states to carve out religious exemptions from criminal and other laws applicable to all citizens. If a religious practice violates a state law that is not specifically directed at religious beliefs, the state can restrict it. Since peyote is an illegal drug in Oregon, it cannot be used for religious purposes unless the state exempts the use of peyote in religious practice from its general statutes. The federal government and twenty-three states (excluding Oregon) permit the religious use of peyote in ceremonies of the Native American Church (*Chicago Tribune* April 18, 1990, 1; *Des Moines Register* April 18, 1990, 14A).

Imagine the uproar if the Supreme Court denied the use of wine in Catholic communion. (In fact, during Prohibition the Catholic Church used "illegal" wine during communion and continues to serve it to minors today [Pearson 1992].) American Indian political values would view any denial of the use of peyote in Native American Church services in much the same way—as unconstitutional according to both the U.S. Constitution and the traditional laws of all tribes.

American Indians have fought for religious freedom for centuries and will continue to maintain their strong religious beliefs, no matter what action a foreign invader, such as the Europeans, may take. In discussions with members of the Native American Church about the possible denial of their religious practices in several states due to *Oregon v. Smith,* I have encountered the following belief: If American Indians are denied the use of peyote in our religious practices by the national or state government, we will still use peyote. No Supreme Court or governmental body can take away a religious right that has been given to us by the creator when time began.

It was the hope of many Indian people interviewed for this book that the AIRFA would protect their religious sites, objects, ceremonies, and rituals. But most were skeptical and felt that Secretary Andrus's words were just another false promise by the U.S. government. Many tribes are still locked in legal and even militant battles to protect their present religious sites and to be able to use the ones that have been stolen from them. Floyd Hand, Oglala Sioux, sums up these concerns over the implementation of the AIRFA:

> We as Indian people have the right to go to our sacred places to practice our sacred ceremonies. That is what the U.S. government says. But you must remember we live in a land where most of the people practice Christianity. Christianity teaches that no other religion can exist. So, Christian people don't favor us practicing our religion and since Christians control the United States government they are not willing to give back our religious sites their government stole from the Indian people. Even if they have a law that says we have the right to use these sacred sites. (Hand 1992)

Spiritual Activism and New Age Spirituality

The U.S. and state governments are not the only ones who infringe upon the spiritual ceremonies, sites, and practices of American Indians. Many non-Indians have come to tribal peoples to gain knowledge, utilize, and even practice the ceremonies, some with good intentions and others who seek to profit from such knowledge. The New Age movement, which fosters such action, is of concern to many Indian holy persons, tribal officials, and people. They hope that one who truly respects the spiritual ceremonies, sites, and practices of Indian people will also realize that the traditional and religious ways of American Indian tribes are not always open to non-Indians or even to nonmembers of the tribe. People who are not tribe members may attend some cultural activities of the Northern Cheyenne Tribe of Montana, for example, with some restrictions; other activities may be attended by invitation only; still other sacred ceremonies may not be attended by nonmembers. The public may attend Sundances, but only American Indian males may participate. No cameras or tape recorders are allowed. Activities that may be attended by invitation only include Native American Church services, Bear Butte religious ceremonies, and Indian weddings. Sweat tipis and Sacred Hat tipis are not open to the public (Northern Cheyenne Tribe 1988).

Derogatory Racism

Recently, Native American activists have taken on the derogatory use of tribal names and other words that are offensive to Native American people. The University of North Dakota has been caught in this turmoil over the use of the term "Fighting Sioux" by their athletic teams. Tribe members feel that such terms demean the Sioux people and stand as a barrier to the progress of Native Americans in general. Similarly offensive to Native Americans are Florida State's Seminoles and their Osceola mascot and the University of Illinois's Chief Illiniwek. Professional sports teams such as the Washington Redskins, the Cleveland Indians and their Chief Wahoo mascot, the Atlanta Braves and their tomahawk chop, and the Kansas City Chiefs and their Sacred Ground end zone continue to demean Native Americans (Harjo 1999).

After thirty years of complaints and protests from Native Americans, the woo-woo-woo of war chants and Indian dances on ball fields is beginning to fade. The Miami Tribe requested discontinuation of the University of Miami of Ohio's sports teams' name, the Redskins, in 1996, stating that "society changes, and what was intended to be a tribute, is no longer perceived as positive." University of Miami trustees immediately voted the name out, "as a sign of respect and to preserve Miami's long-standing relationship with the tribe." Its team is now the Red Hawks (Harjo 1999).

In 1996, the state legislatures of Minnesota and Michigan urged statewide elimination of racially derogatory symbology. Nebraska, Wisconsin, and Kentucky soon followed suit, along with the city of

Dallas, Texas. New York State is investigating the matter. The Los Angeles County school district decided to stop using native names and motifs in their schools in 1997. The decision was challenged in federal court on free-speech grounds, but the mascots' fans lost in 1998 (Harjo 1999). In August 2005 the NCAA banned the use of Native American mascots by sports teams during its postseason tournaments.

Efforts to end race-based mockery in sports exist in most states. Some are calm and reasoned; others are heated and rife with racial epithets. After a century of offenses and three decades of victories, many Americans are aware of antinative racism in sports and want to end it.

Native American Women Are Not Squaws

Native Americans reject the use of the word *squaw* in reference to Native American women. The word was imposed on Native Americans by European Americans and appears on hundreds of geographic place-names across the United States and Canada. The issue affected my own family in 1993 when my youngest daughter, Fawn, decided to go to local, state, and federal officials to change the name of Squaw Creek in central Iowa. She saw the use of the term both degrading to Native American women and causing ignorance to be taught to her classmates in high school (Norden 1996).

Maria Pearson, Iowa's government liaison for Native American affairs, stated in response to Fawn's efforts that "What makes this a misrepresentation to other people is that when it's used, people should know what that word means. If you're going to use that word, use it accurately. Don't hide behind it" (Norden 1996). Johnathan Buffalo, the historical coordinator of the Mesquakie Settlement near Toledo, Iowa, supports Fawn's efforts. He says, "Personally, I think it's a bad name. It degrades our females. We've been degraded for 500 years and to the general public they're walking around thinking that they did something great by naming a creek or river *Squaw*. It stings a little. It'd be like if a shopping mall were called Holocaust Mall. We're not angry, we know what it means. But we have to educate the general public first" (Norden 1996).

Despite Fawn's hard work and support by many Native Americans, non-Indians, public officials, and even AIM, Squaw Creek remains in central Iowa and in several other parts of our nation. It would take an act of Congress to get the U.S. Board of Geographic Names in Virginia to change the name. Fawn's efforts were honored by her elders, as Maria Pearson stated that "I think it is great. We are preparing another generation (of Native Americans) to understand racism. She should be commended for her courage. The older generation should appreciate her effort" (Norden 1996).

We can educate each other that names like squaw and redskins and the misuse of tribal names is offensive, not only to Native Americans but to all the people of the world. When people argue that the word *squaw* appears in the dictionary, remind them that the word is also identified as derogatory. The *Thesaurus of Slang* lists the term *squaw* as a synonym for prostitute, harlot, hussy, and floozy. Note that in Algonquin and Mohawk languages, the word *squaw* means vagina or female genitalia. The word has different meanings or may not exist at all in hundreds of other Native American Indian languages.

Derogatory words or statements about a race or ethnic group are often attributed to attitudes of white supremacy, which fosters the labeling of groups with dehumanizing terms. The term *squaw* is not only derogatory toward Native American women, it is derogatory toward all women. Worse, organizations such as the National Organization for Women (NOW) and the League of Women Voters do not view this as a major women's issue.

Columbus Day or Native American Month

"In school the history teachers did not tell us that Columbus cut off the hands of Indians who failed to bring him gold" (Kipp 1997).

There are two conflicting views of Christopher Columbus, the Euro-American view of Columbus the discoverer and the Native American view of Columbus the initiator of genocide. In the process of Columbus's conquest it was necessary to convince the monarchical governments of the time that there were no intellectuals or philosophers among these "barbarians." Those Spanish who followed Columbus to America burned the manuscripts of the great libraries of the Aztec and Maya, destroying forever the scholarship of Native Americans, and then called them "barbarians and savages." The destruction of such Native American masterpieces are one reason why Native American history has remained mostly an oral history (Mohawk 1988).

During the Columbus Day weekend of October 10–12, 1992, while modern nontribal peoples celebrated the five hundredth anniversary of Christopher Columbus's inauguration of "The Age of Discovery,"

Native American and other indigenous tribal peoples celebrated "500 Years of Resistance." On Saturday, October 10, in Denver, Colorado, the city where Columbus Day was first proclaimed an official holiday, Native Americans were joined by African Americans, Hispanic Americans, Korean Americans, and others in protesting the annual Columbus Day parade, and quincentenary activities were stopped in their tracks (Churchill 1997).

The Associated Press reported that the day marking the five hundredth anniversary of Christopher Columbus's landing in the Americas got as much attention from Indians who were mourning Europe's conquest of the New World as it did for traditional celebrations of the voyage. Thousands of people crowded into a huge communal Indian gathering in Boston to watch a dance exhibition, eat raccoon stew and corn bread, and mingle with descendants of the people who lived in Massachusetts nine thousand years before the Pilgrims landed. In Columbus, Ohio, the largest city in the world named for the explorer, only about two blocks separated the opposing viewpoints. An afternoon ceremony celebrating the explorer's arrival was planned aboard a full-scale replica of the *Santa Maria*, one of Columbus's three ships, docked on the Scioto River. Nearby in a park, about a hundred people showed up for a memorial service held by American Indian groups for those victimized by the European arrival in the Americas.

Only a few blocks also separated the two sides in Chicago, where Native Americans were invited to join the downtown parade, but an anti-Columbus group planned an alternative march. In San Francisco, chanting demonstrators gathered on Sunday at the waterfront and anchored five sailboats offshore to block a reenactment of Columbus's arrival. The reenactment never took place (*Dallas Morning News,* October 12, 1992, 1). Also on Sunday, according to the Prodigy computer service, Philadelphia police said protesters dressed in traditional Native American garb tossed red paint at a new monument honoring Christopher Columbus, just hours before the monument was to be dedicated at the close of the city's Columbus Day observance.

Since 1992, the Columbus Day celebration has continued to be criticized by Native American groups for glorifying the event that led to Europe's bloody conquest of the New World. Although Columbus Day continues to be celebrated in many communities, others have changed it to Native American Day, which acknowledges both historical events and the differences between the two worldviews. Congress has made November "Native American Month," leading to comments among Native Americans that Columbus only gets one day; we get a whole month of recognition.

The Protection and Proper Use of Native American Knowledge

Native Americans are by far the most researched group of Americans. Non-Indian academics have made their reputations and millions of dollars studying Native Americans. Unfortunately, such research has led to the misunderstanding of Native American history and culture and conflict between tribal and Western-based knowledge. Native American tribes and researchers have become more active in both protecting and ensuring the proper use of Native American knowledge in the twenty-first century.

The literature on conducting research among American Indians has increased greatly over the past five years but mainly focuses on the lack of knowledge and understanding within the academic community about the diverse beliefs, practices, history, and values across American Indian communities (Stubben 2001). One such issue is the use of culturally competent surveys and measurements, because objective empirical measures, tools, and techniques that work well with the society at large may not be valid or reliable in the evaluation of American Indian communities (May 1992). In order to develop culturally competent surveys, measures, and research practices, collaborative efforts between tribal communities and universities have increased greatly (Stubben 1997 and 2001; Fisher and Ball 2003), and such collaborative efforts dominate the literature on research among American Indians.

Although research in Native American communities has increased in the last ten years, nearly all such research is externally controlled by non-Indian researchers and universities (Fisher and Ball 2003). Few, if any, academic research projects have been fully directed by American Indian or Alaska Native researchers, communities, or tribal colleges, and the evolution of tribally controlled research centers remains only a theory.

This lack of Native American academic and community control limits the credibility of academic research among American Indians and their communities (Flute et al. 1985; Stubben 2001; Beardslee 2004). Even more disturbing is the fact that the academic community considers as suspect the academic accomplishments of Native Americans (Beardslee 2004) and often limits American Indian faculty to positions in ethnic studies programs (e.g., American Indian Studies) that are generally poorly funded or held in low esteem by other tenured faculty (Glazer 2001). American Indian knowledge continues to be marginalized and plagiarized, and foundational philosophical concepts in democracy are still credited to European philosophers long after it has been clearly established that they originated from Native American political thought (Stubben 2000 and 2001). American Indians have been conducting research in America for thousands of years longer than any other ethnic or racial group. In fact, American Indians invented most of the foods (corn, potatoes), drugs (aspirin), and social and governmental structures (socialism and democracy) that presently exist in America.

In "an American Indian controlled and reviewed journal," Vine Deloria, Jr. (1990) observes that

> the knowledge and technology of tribal peoples, primitive peoples and the ancient ones does not really appear in the modern scientific scheme unless it is to be found with the minor articulations of the concept of cultural evolution hidden in the backwaters of anthropology, sociology, and history. This knowledge, which served our ancestors so well emerges from time to time when modern scientists advocate a novel interpretation of data and, in order to claim some historical roots for their ideas, since new ideas are forbidden in academia, ancient or tribal peoples are cited as societies that once used certain practices or held certain beliefs. But the presentation of the ideas is usually accompanied by the patronizing view that although tribal people did originate the idea or the practice, they could not have possibly understood its significance.

Deloria's words are reinforced by the fact that the author has yet to find a research project among American Indians that was not based on non-Indian knowledge and control to a degree much higher than that of the American Indians themselves. In the vast majority of research projects in American Indian communities, the principal investigator is non-Indian, the majority of evaluation tools are non-Indian, the grant application is reviewed by non-Indians, the funding agency is controlled by non-Indians, and non-Indian universities receive the funding for such projects, not the tribal government or college. Even more amazing is the fact that the non-Indians and many Indian researchers involved in research on American Indians continue to perpetuate policies of assimilation and integration of those under study into the non-Indian America (Beardslee 2004).

Due to the aforementioned problems, some tribes are no longer allowing academic researchers on their lands, and others just ignore the researchers who approach them. The dilemma that arises from this is that many tribes need the information generated from such research in order to offer evidence to funding agencies at both the state and federal levels that a problem exists in the community and that specific tribal methods of dealing with such problems are effective. Other tribes are requiring direct research contracts and utilizing Indian academics as gatekeepers and overseers of such research (Stubben 1997 and 2001), and some are setting up their own research institutes or offices of research.

American Indians have always sought knowledge. In conducting over one hundred talking circles (similar to focus groups, see Krueger 1988) over the past six years among both reservation and urban Indians, most of the American Indian participants expressed a willingness to help non-Indians learn about Indian culture and traditions. They would like non-Indians to learn about the history, culture, spirituality, and morality of American Indian people. Some of the American Indian participants taught courses in American Indian Studies programs at universities and colleges where nearly all of their students were non-Indians and several spoke on tribal culture and affairs to non-Indian groups and schools in their areas. Some expressed concern that non-Indians did not respect Indian knowledge; others were concerned that (especially in terms of spiritual knowledge) non-Indians seek Indian knowledge in order to profit from it. Nevertheless, many in the American Indian world appear willing to share their knowledge, if it is sought in a respectful manner.

> White people have always tried to make us (Indians) like them.
> And we have always fought to remain Indian.
> I think we (Indians) have won this war for we still practice the ways of our ancestors and the white people don't. They now come to us to learn our ways. (Black Elk and Lyon 1990)

American Indian research is in a state of chaotic change, and until educational institutions incorporate Native American researchers as role models on equal academic and socioeconomic status with non-Indian academics, Native American communities, researchers, and people will restrict both the access and the knowledge given to non-Indian researchers. American institutions of higher education continue to model for its citizens a "Jim Crow" cultural pattern of discrimination and segregation that remains unsurpassed in other fields of employment for Native Americans (Beardslee 2004) and a pattern of paternalism that restricts research in a manner that does not benefit the people being studied, the Native American people.

Conclusion

Native American protest movements remain viable, although changing tactics are necessary, and sometimes very independent depending on the issue and geographic location. In the international community, tribal movements have evolved and become more political and militant in some instances. The Zapitistasin Mexico and the recent alliance between the U.S. government and tribal coalitions in Afghanistan add evidence to the fact that after five hundred years of Western domination and nationalism, tribal interests still exist and are being reborn, even within the borders of the United States.

What the future holds for Native Americans and their tribal governments is unclear. Much will depend on the willingness of the United States to uphold its historic promises and upon the vigilance of tribal people to maintain their rights and their culture. But it is clear that Native Americans have maintained their governments and their identity despite five hundred years of attempts by non-Indians to end their existence. This tenacity remains today and will continue, through both nonviolent and violent means, in increased interest group activity within the American and international political arena (O'Brien 1989).

References

Abrams, Philip. 1967. *John Locke: Two Tracts of Government.* Cambridge, UK: Cambridge University Press.

Andrus, Cecil D. 1979. *American Indian Religious Freedom Act Report.* Washington, D.C.: Government Printing Office.

Avery, Elroy M. 1905. *A History of the United States and Its People.* 15 vols. Cleveland: Burrows Brothers.

Axtell, James. 1981. *The European and the Indian: Essays in the Ethnology of Colonial North America.* New York: Oxford University Press.

Beardslee, L. 2004. "Arguments for Integrations in the Field of Education in Northern Michigan," *Multicultural Education,* Spring.

Beauvais, F., and S. LaBoueff. 1985. "Drug and Alcohol Abuse Intervention in American Indian Communities," *International Journal of Addictions* 20: 139–171.

Black Elk, Wallace H., and William S. Lyon. 1990. *Black Elk: The Sacred Ways of the Lakota.* San Francisco: Harper and Row.

Brockunier, Samuel H. 1940. *The Irrepressible Democrat: Roger Williams.* New York: Ronald Press.

Brownell, Charles De Wolf. 1865. *The Indian Races of North and South America.* Hartford, Conn.: Scranton, Hurlbut.

Burnette, Robert, and John Koster. 1974. *The Road to Wounded Knee.* New York: Bantam Books.

Chicago Tribune. April 18, 1990.

Churchill, Ward. 1997. "The Bloody Wake of Alcatraz." In *American Indian Activism: Alcatraz to the Longest Walk.* Edited by Troy Johnson, Joane Nagel, and Duane Champagne. Urbana and Chicago: University of Illinois Press.

Covey, Cyclone. 1966. *The Gentle Radical: A Biography of Roger Williams.* New York: Macmillan.

Dallas Morning News. 1992. "Indian Events Add Facet to Columbus Day Ceremonies," October 13, 14A.

De Montaigne, Michel. 1575. *Essais (Essays).* Translated by John Cotton, edited by W. Carew Hazlitt. Chicago: Encyclopedia Britannica, 1955.

De Tocqueville, Alexis. 1969. *Democracy in America.* Translated by George Lawrence. Garden City, N.Y.: Doubleday Anchor.

Deloria, Vine, Jr. 1990. "Traditional Technology," *Winds of Change—A Magazine of American Indians,* Spring.

Dewing, Rolland, 1985. *Wounded Knee: The Meaning and Significance of the Second Incident.* New York: Irvington.

Ernst, James. 1932. *Roger Williams: New England Firebrand.* New York: Macmillan.

Fisher, P. A., and T. J. Ball. 2003. "Tribal Participatory Research: Mechanisms of a Collaborative Model," *American Journal of Community Psychology* 32 (3/4).

Flute, J., E. Grobsmith, and M. Revenaugh. 1985. *A Generation at Risk: American Indian Youth in the Great Plains: A Report from 15 Reservations.* New York: Association of American Indian Affairs.

Gaustad, Edwin S. 1991. *Liberty of Conscience: Roger Williams in America.* Grand Rapids, Mich.: William B. Eerdmans.

Giddings, James L. 1957. *Roger Williams and the Indians.* Typescript. Providence: Rhode Island Historical Society.

Glazer, N. 2001. "The Future of Race in the United States." In *Race in 21st Century America,* edited by Curtis Stokes et al. East Lansing: Michigan State University Press, pp. 73–78.

Granston, Maurice. 1957. *John Locke: A Biography.* New York: Macmillan.

Green, Norma Kidd. 1969. *Iron Eye's Family: The Children of Joseph La Flesche.* Lincoln, Nebr.: Johnson.

Grinde, Donald A., Jr., and Bruce E. Johansen. 1991. *Exemplar of Liberty: Native America and the Evolution of Democracy.* Los Angeles: American Indian Studies, UCLA Press.

Hand, Floyd. 1992. Oral presentation. "The Red Road." 2nd Annual American Indian Substance Abuse Conference, Des Moines, Iowa, October 7.

Harjo, Susan. 1999. "Honoring? 'Name Calling Instills Racism,'" *Native Peoples Magazine,* Summer.

Hauptman, Laurence. 1992. "Congress, Plenary Power, and the American Indian 1870 to 1992." In *Exiled in the Land of the Free,* edited by Oren Lyons. Santa Fe, N.Mex.: Clear Light Books.

Howard, James H. 1965. *The Ponca Tribe.* Smithsonian Institute Bureau of American Ethnology Bulletin 195. Washington, D.C.: Government Printing Office.

Hutchinson, Thomas. 1764. *History of the Colony and Province of Massachusetts Bay: 1628–91.* Boston: Harvard University Press.

Johnson, Troy, Joane Nagel, and Duane Champagne. 1997. *American Indian Activism: Alcatraz to the Longest Walk.* Urbana and Chicago: University of Illinois Press.

Jumper-Thurman, P. 1992. "Native American Community Alcohol Prevention Research." Paper delivered at the NIAAA Working Group on Alcohol Prevention Research in Minority Communities, Washington, D.C., May.

King, James T. 1969. "'A Better Way': General George Crook and the Ponca Indians," *Nebraska History* 50 (Fall): 239–256.

Kipp, Woody. 1997. "The Eagles I Fed Who Did Not Love Me." In *American Indian Activism: Alcatraz to the Longest Walk,* edited by Troy Johnson, Joane Nagel, and Duane Champagne. Urbana and Chicago: University of Illinois Press.

Krueger, R. A. 1988. *Focus Groups: A Practical Guide for Applied Research.* Newport, CA: Sage Publications.

Lake Mohonk Proceedings. 1914. Washington, D.C.: U.S. Department of the Interior.

Lesser, A. 1933. *Cultural Significance of the Ghost Dance.* New York: Columbia University Press.

Locke, John. 1824. "Second Treatise on Civil Government." In *The Works of John Locke.* London: C. and J. Rivington.

———. 1979 [1690]. "Second Treatise on Civil Government." In *The Development of the Democratic Idea,* edited by Charles Sherover. New York: New American Library.

Mardock, Robert Winston. 1971. *The Reformers and the American Indian.* Columbia: University of Missouri Press, pp. 168–191.

———. 1979. "Standing Bear and the Reformers." In *Indian Leaders: Oklahoma's First Statesmen,* edited by H. Glenn Jordan and Thomas M. Holm. Oklahoma City: Oklahoma Historical Society, pp. 101–113.

Matthisessen, Peter. 1991. *In the Spirit of Crazy Horse.* New York: Viking Penguin.

Means, Russell. 1995. *Where White Men Fear to Tread.* New York: St. Martin's Griffin.

Mohawk, John. 1988. "The Indian Way Is a Thinking Tradition," *Northeast Indian Quarterly* 4(4) 1987 and 5(1) 1988.

Nabokov, Peter. 1991. *Native American Testimony: A Chronicle of Indian-White Relations from Prophecy to the Present, 1492–1992.* New York: Viking.

Norden, Todd. 1996. "Fawn Stubben: Heritage Hero," *Goldfinch* 18 (1): 5–7.

Northern Cheyenne Tribe and Reservation. 1988. Tribal government information packet. Lame Deer, Mont.: Northern Cheyenne Tribe.

O'Brien, Sharon. 1989. *American Indian Tribal Governments.* Norman: University of Oklahoma Press.

Orme, William. 1826. *Memoirs of the Life, Writings, and Religious Connections of John Owen, D.D.* London: Oxford University Press.

Parker, Arthur C. 1916. "The Constitution of the Five Nations," reprinted from the New York State Museum Bulletin, Albany, New York, April 1, 1916. In *The Iroquois and the Founding of the American Nation,* edited by Donald A. Grinde, Jr. Washington, D.C.: Indian Historian Press, 1977.

Pearson, Maria. 1992. Conversation between author and Maria Pearson, Iowa governor's Indian liaison. Ames, Iowa, September.

Ponca Agency. "Letters and Other Documents." Washington, D.C. National Archives of the United States. Microcopy No. 234. Rolls No. 674, 1876–1877, and 676, 1878–1879.

Pueblo De Acoma. 1989. *The Pueblos: History.* Tribal Government Survey and information packet. Received December 18.

Rider, Sidney S. 1904. *The Lands of Rhode Island as They Were Known to Caunonicus and Miantunnomu When Roger Williams Came in 1626.* Providence, R.I.: Sidney Rider.

Rousseau, Jean Jacques. 1950. "A Discourse on the Origin of Inequality." In *The Social Contract.* New York: E. P. Dutton.

Schmidt, Robert. 1994. "Indians' Beliefs: Separate, Unequal," *Des Moines Register,* 11A.

Stoffle, Richard W., David B. Halmo, John E. Olmsted, and Michael J. Evans. 1990. *Native American Cultural Resource Studies at Yucca Mountain, Nevada.* Ann Arbor: University of Michigan Press.

Stubben, J. 1997. "Culturally Competent Substance Abuse Prevention among Rural American Indians." In *Rural Substance Abuse: State of Knowledge and Issues.* Washington D.C.: U.S. Department of Health and Human Services, National Institute on Drug Abuse (NIDA) Monograph Series 168.

———. 2000. "The Indigenous Influence Theory of American Democracy," *Social Science Quarterly* 81 (3): 716–731.

———. 2001. "Working with and Conducting Research among American Indian Families," *American Behavioral Scientist* 44 (9): 1466–1481.

Tibbles, Thomas Henry. 1972. *The Ponca Chiefs: An Account of the Trial of Standing Bear.* Lincoln: University of Nebraska Press.

United States Commission on Civil Rights. 1980. *American Indian Civil Rights Handbook.* Washington, D.C.: Government Printing Office.

Voltaire. 1940. "The Huron, or Pupil of Nature." In *The Best Known Works of Voltaire.* New York: Literary Classics of the U.S.

Wilkins, David. 2002. *Nations within States: American Indian Politics and the American Political System.* Boulder, CO: Rowman and Littlefield.

Wilson, Mona, and Saunie Wilson. 2001. Personal correspondence with the author.

Wishart, David J. 1994. *An Unspeakable Sadness: The Dispossession of the Nebraska Indians.* Lincoln: University of Nebraska Press.

Yerington Paiute Tribe. 1985. *Introduction to Tribal Government.* Yerington, Nev.: Yerington Piaute Tribe.

3

Participation in Social Movements and Interest Groups

cClain and Stewart (1998) note that "interest groups that focus on issues of importance to blacks, Latinos, Asians, and American Indians have been essential to the progress made toward the incorporation of these groups into the American political system." While this statement is broadly accurate for most of the groups, the situation of indigenous nations is much more complicated.

The general thrust of most racial and ethnic groups and their members has been to seek inclusion (to become constitutionally incorporated) into the American social contract, whereas the general thrust of most Native American nations and their citizens (notwithstanding their American citizenship) has been to retain their political and cultural exclusion from absorption or incorporation in the American polity. American colonialism, which includes the imposition of Western religious beliefs, social norms and values, and capitalism, has attempted to incorporate Indian lands, resources, and citizens into mainstream America.

Background

The imposition of Western culture caused conflict in many areas of American Indian society. Two major issues that led to war and continue to be major cultural conflicts today are spirituality and land ownership. American Indian societies did not separate religion from government. In fact, they made little distinction between the political and religious worlds. Political wisdom was synonymous with religious power. All political actions were undertaken "with spiritual guidance and oriented toward spiritual as well as political fulfillment" (O'Brien 1989). Tribal leaders sought spiritual advice in nearly every decision they made.

Western cultural concepts, such as individual ownership and exploitation of land, conflicted with American Indian values of tribal/communal ownership and respect for nature. Individual ownership of land did exist among some tribes. Land disputes began when Columbus first landed. Later, the movement of tribes off their ancestral lands created a treaty-making process between European and U.S. governments that provided the legal foundation of the relationship that presently exists between tribal governments and other governments (state, local, federal, and international). This treaty relationship is also the reason that American Indians are not simply an ethnic or racial group; they are a political entity with rights and responsibilities that other such groups do not possess.

During the last thirty years, there has been an increase in action by the U.S. government toward respecting Indian treaty rights, attempting to restore some tribal lands and providing some protection for Indian religious beliefs and sacred sites, and reducing government efforts toward total assimilation in the society at large.

Assimilation policies, combined with high interracial and intertribal marriage rates, the urbanization of Indians, and the influence of the media, have contributed to a Native American world that is more diversified than ever before. Native Americans can be from reservations or urban areas, may be full blood or of mixed blood, and may be recognized as belonging to a tribe or not. Many tribes may be operating under treaty rights, and some continue to practice traditional spiritual beliefs while others have adopted Christianity. In his 1962 essay, Frell M. Owl wrote about who is an American Indian: "So many Indians have moved from reservations to integrate into the general population that accurate record keeping is an impossibility. Tribal rolls keep fairly accurate records of enrolled Indians. Reservations' census records and Bureau of Census records contain valuable statistics concerning American Indians. The number of non-enrolled Indians is probably larger than records indicate" (Owl 1962, 270).

Yet even with this increasing and seemingly inexorable diversification among indigenous peoples, maintaining and reaffirming Indian political, economic, and cultural identity is a central issue for Native American nations and people at this point in history. Nearly 100 percent of native people identify themselves by their tribal affiliation before American citizenship, and more than half never identify themselves as American citizens at all (McClain and Stewart 1998; Wilkins 2002). Being Native American and preserving that identity remains a key part of Native American social and political activism (Duran and Duran 1995; Deloria 1999).

Native American Political Organization

Native Americans have politically organized on five levels in pursuing their various goals: intratribal, tribal, intertribal coalitions and alliances, alliances of like-minded individuals, and extratribal coalitions and alliances (Wilkins 2002).

Intratribal Political Organization

Intratribal political organization occurs when segments of specific tribes, frustrated by the direction of tribal leadership, organize to challenge or confront the existing tribal power structure. A number of intratribal interest groups have been formed over the years, bent on lobbying or pressing their government to create or block policies deemed important to the group's membership.

These intratribal interest groups promote a variety of intratribal issues, ranging from the peaceful efforts of the Northern (Osni) Ponca Heduska Society in promoting spiritual and cultural issues within the Northern Ponca Tribe to the more political and often controversial groups, such as in the Orange County Pechanga Tribe, where one side is fighting the other in an attempt to disenroll groups of tribal members. Some, such as the Dine Coalition, work toward environmental causes. It was made up of Navajo individuals opposed to coal gasification in the 1970s. Similarly, the Dine C.A.R.E. (Citizens Against Ruining the Environment) organized in 1988 to oppose the dumping of toxic waste and other environmental degradation of Navajo lands (Wilkins 2002).

On February 1, 2000, a lawsuit between the Hopi and Navajos over the partitioning of land in New Mexico ended with both Hopis and Navajos considered trespassers on the other's reservations. The two groups were forced to share reservation land beginning in the 1800s. By the 1860s, the Navajos had grown and spread herds across both tribes' land. In 1958 the U.S. federal court ruled in *Healing v. Jones* that the Hopi would continue to have control over 631,194 acres known as District 6, but 1.8 million acres would be controlled by both tribes (Rowe 2001, 26). By 1974, the Hopis had requested that the acreage be split between the two tribes, leaving each tribe in charge of 911,000 acres. Nearly a hundred Hopi families had to move because of the 1974 ruling, and nearly four hundred Navajo families were forced to relocate to their side of the land. Both tribes have historical and spiritual roots in the land, and many families refuse to move because of their connection to the land. Others have been unable to afford the move. The dispute remains embroiled in court proceedings, and many fear some type of forced relocation will be required.

Tribal Political Organization

Tribal mobilization involves organization and action by members of a single tribe in pursuit of tribe-specific goals. Examples include the Northern Ponca Restoration Committee, Inc., which successfully lobbied the federal government for reinstatement of the Northern Ponca Tribe during the 1980s and early 1990s (Ritter 1994) or tribal landowners associations that lobby the tribal council and Bureau of Indian Affairs land offices.

In 1988, the Pueblo of Sandia began a systematic process to save their local waterways (Swift 2000a). In 1991, the tribe became the first Indian nation to apply water quality standards under the Clean Water Act. The tribe went on to create their water quality standards, which were approved by the Environmental Protection Agency in 1993. A Water Quality Management Program was established that year as well. The Pueblo of the Sandia Tribe has since acquired equipment to test and maintain their standards. Harvard University's "Best Practices" council awarded the movement $10,000 in 2000 to build a water quality classroom.

On November 29, 2000, tribal leaders of the Pyramid Lake Paiute Tribe of Nevada were the first in history to gain control of a federal waterway not incorporated within a reservation. The Paiute signed an agreement with the U.S. government granting the tribe the right to manage the Trukee River (Swift 2000b). As part of the agreement several agencies—the U.S. Fish and Wildlife Service, the Bureau of Reclamation, and the Bureau of Indian Affairs—joined in a four-part team led by the Paiute Tribe. This agreement was reached after more than forty years of court battles, negotiations, and federal guidelines.

Similarly, in the early 1990s, the Nez Perce Tribe of Lapwai, Idaho, began working with state and federal officials to be included in part of a recovery program for gray wolves in the area. Finally, after years of negotiation with the U.S. Fish and Wildlife Service, the Nez Perce were granted responsibility for overseeing the restoration of the gray wolf. "I learned early on that there's a mirror between what the wolf went through and what the Nez Perce people went through," tribe member Jaime Pinkham said. "The wolves were a barrier, and so were the Indian people. The Indians were eventually confined to a reservation through wars and epidemics, and the wolves were run out by hunters." The Nez Perce view this success not only as a way to reestablish spiritual and cultural connections to the gray wolf but also as a means of strengthening the tribe (Swift 2000b).

Intertribal Coalitions and Alliances

Intertribal coalitions and alliances involve action by the members of multiple tribes united on the basis of tribal affiliations in pursuit of common political or economic goals. Contemporary examples of intertribal coalitions and alliances, both regional and national (some now defunct), include the United South and Eastern Tribes, Inc. (USET); the Great Lakes Intertribal Council; the Intertribal Council of California; the Alaska Native Brotherhood and Sisterhood (ANB/S); Coalition of Eastern Native Americans (CENA) (defunct); the Northwest Indian Fisheries Commission (NIFC); the Columbia River Intertribal Fish Commission; the National Congress of American Indians (NCAI); the National Tribal Chairmen's Association (NTCA) (defunct); and the Council of Energy Resource Tribes (CERT) (Wilkins 2002).

State-sponsored Native American coalitions and alliances also exist. In some states, this includes state Indian commissions made up of tribal and urban members. Such commissions—the Nebraska Indian Commission and Iowa's Governor's Indian Advisory Council are two examples—advise the legislative, executive, and even judicial branches of state government. Normally, however, tribal councils negotiate with and lobby their state officials either individually or intertribally (O'Brien 1989).

In 2000, the California Rural Indian Health Board (CRIHB) prepared to present forty tribes with an opportunity to create the nation's first Indian-controlled health maintenance organization (HMO). CRIHB created the HMO in response to the inadequacy of federal insurance programs and Indian Health Service facilities, which have been woefully underfunded and geographically inaccessible (Capozza 2000). On January 15, 2000, the group voted to move ahead with their HMO plans in response to studies showing California, Arizona, and Oklahoma receive the least funding from Indian Health Service for health care (Capozza 2000).

Alliances of Like-Minded Individuals

Alliances of like-minded Indian individuals (also known as pan-Indian or supratribal organizations) involve organizations and action by individual Indians on the basis of Indianness and in pursuit of pan-Indian goals. A host of "American Indian" and "Native American" organizations testify to the numerous cooperative political efforts by Indian groups and organizations on behalf of both tribal and supratribal interests.

On August 24, 1996, a group of Indian pipe makers and spiritual leaders from several tribes joined together in Pipestone, Minnesota, to form a spiritual organization to protect the Great Pipestone Quarries in Minnesota. The group called itself "Keepers of the Sacred Tradition of Pipemaking." Prior to the group's formation, anyone was free to visit the quarries and collect the stone, catlinite, for pipe-making purposes. However, no one was charged with caring for the quarries. The group works to raise awareness of pipe making and is converting the former Pipestone Indian Boarding School superintendent's home into a museum. The group is an intertribal collection of pipe makers and spiritual leaders (Ceriano 2000, 28).

In 2000, Alexander J. Pires, Jr. and Phillip L. Fraas brought suit against the U.S. Department of Agriculture claiming that Native Americans had been discriminated against in the USDA's lending policies. The suit represents three hundred native farmers and charges that "the government wrongfully denied them loans, provided them late, or loaned less money than they needed to farm" (Fogarty 2000, 22). The suit follows a similar action brought by African American farmers, which settled with 18,000 African American farmers for around $1.1 billion.

Staff at the Nebraska Urban Indian Medical Center began teaching expectant and new mothers to carry infants in traditional styles. The tradition of carrying infants in a cradle board was introduced to the facility in early 2001. Most health practitioners there are Caucasians who had never seen a cradle board, but the use of cradle boards is an ancient tradition that can prevent colic in infants and can support an infant's need for security. "They hadn't seen a cradle board until we brought patients in with them. They saw the benefit right away" claimed Andrea Cranby ("Age-Old Tradition" 2001, 6).

Extratribal Coalitions and Alliances

Pan-Indian or supratribal interest groups generally espouse a political identity rather than a cultural identity and, importantly, are the result of Indian–non-Indian interaction. Extratribal coalitions and alliances arose from the civil rights movement of the 1960s. Prior to the 1960s, tribes and urban Indians did not collaborate with non-Indian coalitions and alliances. But in 1964, a group of young Native Americans adopted some of the tactics and ideas of the civil rights movement by holding a "fish-in" in the Pacific Northwest aimed at publicizing the problems the Puyallup and other tribes were having exercising their treaty right to fish (Wilkins 2002).

From that beginning, the so-called Red Power movement became a national movement in 1969. Richard Oakes, along with several students from San Francisco State University, landed on Alcatraz Island in San Francisco Bay. Calling themselves "Indians of all tribes," the group claimed they had "discovered" the island and claimed right to it. The group began negotiating with local and state authorities during the next nineteen months. Eventually, in 1971, the group was forced to leave the island, but not without first highlighting native grievances and waking the spirit of the nation's native people (Nagel 1995).

A partial list of these political interest organizations (and their founding dates) includes the National Indian Youth Council (NIYC) (1961), the Alaska Federation of Natives (1966), United Native Americans (1967), American Indian Movement (1968), Native American Rights Fund (1970), International Indian Treaty Council (1974), Women of All Red Nations (1975), Indian Law Resource Center (1977), and the Institute for the Development of Indian Law (1971) (Wilkins 2002).

More recently, in 1998, the forty-two Indian member tribes of the Inter Tribal Bison Cooperative (ITBC), with a collective herd of over eight thousand bison, joined in an unsuccessful lawsuit. *Intertribal Bison Cooperative et al. v. Babbitt* sought to enjoin the Department of the Interior's buffalo control plan, reached in agreement with the state of Montana, to slaughter some of Yellowstone National Park's bison herd. The bison allegedly were a threat to cattle herds. Ranchers feared the buffalo might infect their herds with brucellosis, a bacterial disease that affects cattle and causes undulant fever in humans. ITBC's coalition partners included the Earth Justice Legal Defense Fund, the Greater Yellowstone Coalition, the Jackson Hole Alliance for Responsible Planning, Defenders of Wildlife, and Gallatin Wildlife Association, among others. The coalition partners appealed this decision to the Ninth Circuit Court of Appeals in May 1999, and that court affirmed the district court's ruling (LaRose 2000; Wilkins 2002).

Tillie Black Bear founded the White Buffalo Calf Women's Shelter on the Rosebud Reservation in Mission, South Dakota. After the shelter sent her to Washington, D.C., to attend a conference on domestic violence and rape, she became a founding member of the National Coalition against Domestic Violence (Rowe 2001). In 1978, she started a South Dakota affiliate of the national group. The first workshop was open to any South Dakotan who wished to attend, and seventy-seven women attended the workshop. Since then, the women's shelter has grown to a forty-five-bed facility that houses around 250 women and 500 children per year. The board of supervisors has grown to seven members.

Currently, two of the best-known Native American political organizations are the National Congress of American Indians (NCAI) and the Native American Rights Fund (NARF).

The National Congress of American Indians

The oldest and most representative national Indian organization is the National Congress of American Indians (NCAI), which was founded in 1944 in response to termination and assimilation policies of the U.S. government. The NCAI stressed the need for unity and cooperation among tribal governments for the protection of their treaty and sovereign rights. The National Congress of American Indians has been working for over fifty years to inform the public and Congress of the rights of American Indians and Alaska Natives (O'Brien 1989).

The NCAI has grown over the years from its modest beginnings of one hundred people to include 250 member tribes from throughout the United States. Now serving as the major national tribal government organization, the NCAI is positioned to monitor federal policy and coordinate efforts to inform tribes of federal decisions that affect tribal government interests.

Now as in the past, the NCAI works to secure for natives and their descendants the rights and benefits to which they are entitled, to enlighten the public toward the better understanding of the Indian people, to preserve rights under Indian treaties or agreements with the United States, and to promote the common welfare of the American Indians and Alaska Natives. The current issues and activities of the NCAI include protection of programs and services that benefit Indian families, specifically those targeting Indian youth and elders. Also included are promotion and support of Indian education, including Head Start, elementary, postsecondary, and adult education. The NCAI also works to enhance Indian health care, including prevention of juvenile substance abuse, HIV-AIDS, and other major diseases. Support of environmental protection and natural resources management as well as protection of Indian cultural resources and religious freedom rights are also recognized activities of the NCAI. It works to promote the rights of Indians to economic opportunity both on and off reservations, including securing programs to provide incentives for economic development and the attraction of private capital to Indian country. Finally, the NCAI works to protect the rights of all Indian people to decent, safe, and affordable housing (http://www.ncai.org/).

Native American Rights Fund (NARF)

This section is dedicated to a staff member, friend, and Omaha brother, Kenneth (Ken) Wayne Springer, who joined our ancestors in 1981. Ken worked at NARF in a variety of capacities, mainly as the printer of all the legal and scholarly materials that NARF produced. NARF and those who worked there were a major part of the Ken Springer Memorial Basketball Tournament, which brought in teams from all over Indian country for an annual tournament and social gathering for Ken. His spirit touched many at NARF and continues to watch over his NARF brothers and sisters as they work, not for themselves but for the people.

As part of the War on Poverty launched in the mid-1960s under the Office of Economic Opportunity, federally funded legal services programs were established around the country to assist poor and disadvantaged people. Many of these programs were located on or near Indian reservations (http://www.narf.org/). As these programs began working with their Indian clients, a common realization developed. Program aides and policy directors realized that Indians had special legal problems that were, for the most part, governed and controlled by a specialized and little-known area of the law known as "Indian law." Indian law is a complex body of law comprising hundreds of Indian treaties and court decisions and thousands of federal Indian statutes, executive orders, and administrative rulings. As legal services lawyers and organizations, such as the Association of American Indian Affairs, contended with Indian law, they became more aware of its relevance and applicability to the problems of their Indian clients.

The relevance of Indian law significantly impacted legal services located on reservations, where trust land, tribal resources, and tribal government institutions necessarily involved the basic tenets of Indian law. Legal services lawyers soon became involved in various matters with national implications. It became clear to those working in legal services and to others working for Indian rights that cases involving major national issues of Indian law must be handled with the greatest consideration. A national organization was needed—one staffed by Indian advocates with experience and expertise in Indian law and with a strong enough financial foundation that important Indian cases were not lost or abandoned for lack of funds (Hauptman 1995).

In 1970, with funding from the Ford Foundation, California Indian Legal Services (one of the federally funded legal services programs serving California Indians) implemented a pilot project to provide legal services to Indians on a national level. That project became known as the Native American Rights Fund. One year later, the Native American Rights Fund separated from California Indian Legal Services and relocated in a more central location, Boulder, Colorado. NARF incorporated separately with an all-Indian board of directors, and in a few short years, the Native American Rights Fund grew from a three-lawyer staff to a firm of forty full-time staff members and fifteen attorneys. That same year, with start-up funding from the Carnegie Corporation, NARF established the National Indian Law Library (NILL) to be located at NARF's main office in Boulder.

The National Indian Law Library
at the Native American Rights Fund

The Native American Rights Fund maintains one of the most comprehension Native American law libraries in the world. The National Indian Law Library functions as a department of the Native American Rights Fund and serves both NARF and the public. The collection is devoted exclusively to Native American law. The mission of NILL is to develop and make accessible a unique and valuable collection of Native American legal resources and to assist people with their research needs. Special emphasis is placed on helping individuals and organizations who are working on behalf of Native Americans and have the greatest potential to positively influence their lives. Reference and research assistance is provided by a professional staff, and copies of documents are provided at a nominal charge. Native American Rights Fund publications are sold and distributed at NILL, and referrals to other libraries and organizations are also provided.

The collection of the National Indian Law Library Collection includes tribal self-governance documents such as tribal constitutions, codes, ordinances, charters, and bylaws; selected legal pleadings from important Native American law cases; Native American law-related reporters, handbooks, manuals, and guides; Native American treaties; federal administrative documents relating to Native American law; and a basic collection of general reference and historical/cultural books on Native Americans.

John E. Echohawk

I first met John E. Echohawk in 1973 when I worked for the Nebraska Indian Commission and was visiting NARF in regard to the rights of Native American inmates in Nebraska to practice their tribal religions. This quiet but direct, mild-mannered but vigilant, and very respectful man has always struck me as what a traditional representative in a dispute between tribal members or clans would have been like. John is not one to beat another attorney and gloat; instead, he shows the opposing side their mistake and wins in a good way. He has helped my family maintain our children's right to their tribal heritage, and he and his cousin Walter (Bunky) are two Native American attorneys who have shown other Native Americans that courts are an honorable arena in which one can help one's people. He is truly one of Laurence Hauptman's (1995) "Warriors with Attaché Cases."

The following comes from the NARF web page bibliography of the one person who has been with NARF since the beginning.

John E. Echohawk, a Pawnee, is the Executive Director of the Native American Rights Fund. He was the first graduate of the University of New Mexico's special program to train Indian lawyers, and was a founding member of the American Indian Law Students Association while in law school. John has been with NARF since its inception, having served continuously as Executive Director since 1977. He has been recognized as one of the 100 most influential lawyers in America by the National Law Journal since 1988 and has received numerous service awards and other recognition for his leadership in the Indian law field. He serves on the Boards of the American Indian Resources Institute, the Association on American Indian Affairs, the National Committee for Responsive Philanthropy, Natural Resources Defense Council, and the National Center for American Indian Enterprise Development. B.A., University of New Mexico (1967); J.D., University of New Mexico (1970); Reginald Heber Smith Fellow (1970–72); Native American Rights Fund (August 1970 to present); admitted to practice law in Colorado. (NARF Website)

Bureau of Indian Affairs

The Bureau of Indian Affairs (BIA) has had a greater impact on Native American politics and people than any other factor. Some see the BIA as the trustee of Native American interests, while others view it as the enemy. Most are unsure about how Native American tribes and people would operate without it. Since its inception on March 11, 1824, the Bureau of Indian Affairs has been involved, either directly or indirectly, in every social and political movement that has affected Native Americans.

The Bureau of Indian Affairs has always been a political issue among Native Americans. Its role has changed from one of domination over Indian affairs to that of partnership based on the government-to-government relationship between the United States and tribal nations. The mission of the Bureau of Indian Affairs is to act as the principal agent of the United States in carrying out the government-to-government relationship that exists between the United States and the federally recognized American Indian tribes and to act as principal agent of the United States in carrying out the responsibilities of the United States as a trustee for property it holds for federally recognized tribes and individual American Indians.

The twin cornerstones of the mission of the Bureau of Indian Affairs—the government-to-government relationship with American Indian tribes and Alaska Natives, and the responsibilities—are the results of more than two centuries of interaction between the United States and tribal groups. Virtually everything the bureau does stems from these two concepts, and both are inextricably bound to the past. A historical perspective, then, is necessary in understanding the role performed by the Bureau of Indian Affairs.

The Spanish, French, Dutch, and British were the first Europeans to settle this continent, and they each brought with them their own ideas on how to deal with the inhabitants of the new lands. These early concepts eventually became the basis of the U.S. Indian policy:

1. Tribes were to be thought of as separate sovereign nations to be dealt with on a government-to-government basis.
2. As separate nations, the internal affairs of tribes were the responsibility of the tribal entity and were not to be tampered with.
3. Relations with tribes were considered to be between two nations and were to be handled by the central (U.S.) government.

Acceptance of these concepts was necessary before treaties could be made with Indian tribes, since treaties can be made only between sovereigns, and only by the central government, and they affirm, rather that deny, the mutual right of self-government.

The government-to-government aspect of federal-tribal relations has suffered some serious assaults through the years. There are currently 556 federally recognized tribes in the United States. In 1978, the Department of the Interior enacted an acknowledgment process for federal-tribal recognition. Since then, the BIA has recognized an additional fourteen tribes, while denying thirteen tribes acknowledgement. In 2000, there were sixteen tribes awaiting approval of their recognition petitions (DuBrule 2000).

Recently, however, tribes have adopted measures to strengthen their tribal governments and take control of their own affairs. The bureau is supportive of the tribes in this endeavor. Also, capabilities of the Bureau of Indian Affairs are being expanded to improve and strengthen the technical support provided the tribal governments and tribal court systems. Special initiatives are directed at formal training, specialized guidance, improvement of tribal governing document codes, and other regulations that enhance a tribe's capacity to govern itself.

History of the Bureau of Indian Affairs

In 1778, the first treaty was signed between an Indian tribe, the Delaware, and the U.S. government. In signing this treaty, the United States was affirming the English and European tradition of dealing with tribes as political entities. Early U.S. policy was consistent with the European practice of recognizing tribes as governments with full internal sovereignty. By 1832, however, tribal sovereignty had been limited, after the tribes had agreed to regard themselves as under the protection of the United States. Tribes began to consent to extinguish their external sovereignty and to recognize the legislative powers of Congress over them through treaties with the U.S. government. This agreement did not do away with tribal sovereignty altogether. A tribe's sovereign powers can only be extinguished by an act of Congress.

One of the first actions taken by the Continental Congress in 1775 was to name a Committee on Indian Affairs. The committee established three departments of Indian Affairs and called upon such prominent Americans as Benjamin Franklin and Patrick Henry to assume leadership roles in the operation of these offices. Henry Knox, secretary of war, assumed responsibility for Indian affairs with the ordinance of August 7, 1786 (O'Brien 1989).

The first Congress continued administration of Indian affairs within the War Department, established in 1789, with direction to the secretary to place armed militia at the disposal of Indian commissioners "for negotiating treaties with the Indians." Trading houses were maintained from 1786 to 1822 to supply Indians with necessary goods and, in exchange, to offer them a fair price for their furs. This was a matter of importance and concern for the government. As a result, the office of superintendent of trade was created in 1806 to place some controls on the practice of trading with Indians (O'Brien 1989).

Without authorization from Congress, Secretary of War John C. Calhoun on March 11, 1824, created what he called the Bureau of Indian Affairs. The logical choice to head this office was Thomas

McKenny, who had been superintendent of trade when that post was abolished two years prior. Congress fiercely debated whether to approve the creation of this post. But before such a measure was passed, the lawmakers created the position of commissioner of Indian Affairs. On July 9, 1832, Congress authorized the president "to appoint by and with the advice and consent of the Senate, a Commissioner of Indian affairs, who shall, under the direction of the Secretary of War, and agreeable to such regulations as the President may, from time to time, prescribe, have the direction and management of all Indian affairs, and of all matters arising out of Indian relations."

The first presidentially appointed commissioner was Elbert Herring. His salary was set at $3,000 per year. In the first session of the 23rd Congress in 1834, the Committee on Indian Affairs of the House of Representatives produced three bills dealing with Indian affairs. These included measures to (1) organize a Department of Indian Affairs, (2) regulate trade with Indians, and (3) provide for the establishment of a Western territory in which the Indians should be separated. The third measure did not pass, but the other two were enacted into law.

BIA: Structure and Work in the 1800s to Present

On June 30, 1834, the Bureau of Indian Affairs came into being through what has since become known as the organic law of the Indian office. The organizational structure of Indian affairs during the 1800s primarily included two types of field jurisdictions: superintendents and agents. Superintendents were generally responsible for Indian affairs within a geographical area, usually a territory. Agents, who reported to superintendents or directly to the Indian affairs office, were concerned with the affairs of one or more tribes. The Bureau of Indian Affairs was to remain in the War Department for fifteen years after its creation by Congress. The Department of the Interior was established on March 3, 1849, and Indian affairs passed from military to civilian control.

Development of the reservation system gained momentum in the mid-1850s after experimentation with reservation policy in California. The role of the BIA changed in the last quarter of the 1800s, and it began specializing in activities such as irrigation, forestry, Indian employment, law enforcement, health, and construction. Education of young Indians came to the forefront in 1879, when the first off-reservation boarding school was established at Carlisle, Pennsylvania. Chemwa Indian School in Oregon, Haskell Institute in Kansas, and Chilocco Indian School in Oklahoma were opened within the next five years. Other schools followed.

After World War II, a system of area offices was established and area directors were made responsible for administering all Indian programs within their geographical locations. This three-tier structure continues today, with organizational lines extending from Washington, D.C., to the area offices to the agencies at the reservation level. Until 1973, the Bureau of Indian Affairs was under an Interior Department assistant secretary whose principal responsibilities revolved around land and water resources or other Interior programs. Indian affairs were a secondary concern of this official, and frequently Indian goals and objectives were opposed by other Interior agencies. This situation was partially corrected when Morris Thompson became commissioner in 1973 and was made directly responsible to the secretary of the Interior.

Finally, in 1977, the post of assistant secretary of Indian affairs was created, thereby assuring the bureau of a voice in policy matters within the Interior Department. Forrest Gerard, a member of the Blackfeet Indian Tribe, became the first to fill this office.

Bureau of Indian Affairs: Trust (Ir)responsibility

Title to land is held in trust for American Indian tribes by the United States through the Bureau of Indian Affairs. The trust itself consists of a series of laws passed by Congress and federal administrative practice. There is also a separate body of Indian trust law developed by the decisions of the federal courts (*American Indians Today* 1987). In some cases, the Bureau of Indian Affairs also holds land in trust for individual American Indians. The same applies to tribal funds derived from lease agreements and sales of natural resources.

The trust responsibility is extensive regarding land. It encompasses anything connected with the land, such as the minerals under the ground, the water flowing over it, the trees that grow on it, and all other natural resources. The Bureau of Indian Affairs has a responsibility to manage and protect these resources.

The trust relationship between the Bureau of Indian Affairs and the American Indian tribes and the Alaska Natives has been difficult to define. For this reason, misunderstandings sometimes arise, and often parties will disagree on the extent of the trust. The trust agreement is not written out in any document. Rather, the trust has evolved throughout the years to accommodate changing times and situations. This does not mean that the trust is not important or significant. It is an established legal and moral obligation requiring the United States to protect and enhance the property and resources of American Indian tribes. The trust responsibility of the United States is a direct outgrowth of English law, which held that title to newly discovered lands was in the Crown or government but subject to a compensable right of occupancy by the native people (*American Indians Today* 1987; O'Brien 1989).

In 1996, Elouise Pepion Cobell filed suit against Secretary of the Interior Babbitt in order to receive a proper accounting of the funds held in trust for herself and thousands of other Native Americans. The Native American Rights Fund provided legal services for the *Cobell* case. The Interior Department spent over $1 billion to fight the case. The Native American plaintiffs have won almost every federal district court ruling and all but one appeal court ruling. When President George W. Bush took office in 2000, the case was refiled against the new secretary of the Interior, Gale Norton (*Cobell v. Norton*). At present, it is estimated that the government owes over 500,000 Native Americans nationwide over $1 billion (Blackfeet Reservation Development Fund, Inc. 2004). The *Cobell* case continues to highlight the history of mismanagement of Native American trust funds by the federal trustee/guardian, the United States of America.

On February 4, 2000, the U.S. Court of Federal Claims, under Judge Lawrence M. Baskir, ruled that the Department of the Interior (DOI) had violated its trust obligations and breached fiduciary responsibilities to the Navajo Nation (Tirado 2000). The court ruled Donald Hodel, former Interior secretary, had been swayed by lobbyists to change a coal royalty rate. However, the court ruled that while the DOI had failed to uphold its legal trust responsibilities, the violations did not mandate a monetary compensation. The Navajo had asked for $600 million in compensation (Tirado 2000). Judge Baskir ruled that the Navajo must be able to demonstrate that the Indian Mineral Leasing Act (IMLA) of 1938 had placed specific fiduciary duties on the federal government. The act has quite extensive provisions for oil and gas but only one provision for coal. The Navajo will be unable to prove their case under current law.

Traditional Interests

Throughout the history of Native American political participation there has been one major issue that no other minority group has so strongly recognized and fought for. That issue is the preservation of traditional interests—traditional food, language, and politics. Tribal nations and peoples have utilized the courts, Congress, and their own tribal sovereign powers to maintain tradition aspects of their tribal cultures. The following are examples of recent political actions to preserve and expand traditional interests.

The Rebirth of Native American Languages

On October 30, 1990, Congress passed Public Law 101–477, commonly referred to as the "Native American Languages Act" (Sec. 101, 104 Stat. 1153). It declares that it is

> the policy of the United States to protect the rights of Native Americans to use and develop their languages, and prohibits restrictions of the right of Native Americans to express themselves in their native language during public proceedings, including publicly supported education programs . . . recognizes the right of Native American governing bodies to use their languages as a medium of instruction in BIA-funded schools . . . and the right of Native American governing bodies to give official status to Native American languages for conducting their own business and establishes as U.S. policy the encouragement of elementary, secondary, and higher education institutions to include Native American languages in their curricula as foreign languages.

When tribes were confined to reservations, they fought desperately to preserve their traditions. But as Native Americans have moved from reservations to local towns and cities, reservation populations have shrunk, and since the 1940s increased and better communications have brought more Anglo culture to the reservation (White 1974). As early as the 1900s, writers commented on the lost language of the tribes. White (1974) wrote: "Many of the younger people today are not very familiar with tribal language, rituals and cultural norms; they do not 'dance Indian,' and they know little of the oral tradition. Yet they feel very deeply that they are Native Americans, and they feel alienated from Anglo American society."

There are over two hundred Indian languages in America today, and they are often used in separate regions throughout the United States (Leap 1981). These languages vary widely and often have little in common—there is wide diversity of language even among tribes and on reservations. A history of understanding other native languages is based in marriage, political alliances, trade relationships, and ceremonial ties bringing different nations together (Leap 1981). When factoring in the boarding schools and reservation system created as part of America's so-called Manifest Destiny, it is easy to see how tribal languages have been scattered throughout the nation (Leap 1981).

In response to the loss of culture and language, many tribes have worked to bring back their heritage. This movement has led to serious changes in the Indian community. Some tribes have made sure that schools taught in tribal languages. Others work within English-as-first-language programs to bring back languages to the people. Groups like the Indian Language Program at Mary College in North Dakota serve the Mandan-, Hidatsa-, and Arikara-speaking tribes. The northern Indian California Education Project serves the Yurok, Karok, Hupa, and Talowa speakers in the region (Leap 1981).

Studies in the late quarter of the twentieth century have revealed important facts about language acquisition in tribal communities. These studies have shown there are several factors in the success of attaining and maintaining a strong cultural language. Studies have shown geographical isolation to be an important factor in the development of native language. Those students living larger distances from Anglo culture showed higher rates of tribal language fluency (Canfield, as in Leap 1981).

Other studies have revealed other factors. A student's comprehension of English impacts their success in tribal languages, since the ability to use and respond to a language reflects a student's ability to use the same skills in a different language. Also, family size and how the family participates in "traditional" activities can impact language use. The number of adult language speakers is also a recognized factor. In general, the more people are exposed and participate in language use, the better they are at learning the language (Leap 1981).

Traditional Protection of the Dead and the Unborn

There is a traditional view among most tribes that the living must honor their ancestors by protecting their places of burial and by protecting the next generation to come, the unborn. It is also thought that one must pass the earth on to the next generation in better shape than the previous generations received it. Both the federal government and specific tribes have passed laws in an attempt to do this.

In 1990 President George Bush, Sr. signed into law Public Law 101–601, the Native American Graves Protection and Repatriation Act, or NAGPRA. It forced an examination of all Native American and Native Hawaiian remains in museums, schools, and state and federal repositories and strengthened tribal and state laws regarding grave desecration and reburial (Pearson 2000).

For Native Americans repatriation has always been an issue, since non-Indians, especially European Americans, have consistently attempted to take or destroy everything in the name of progress. It appears that a double standard was part of our emerging nation in regard to human rights. In respect to grave goods and human remains in burials, laws were initiated in 1788 for European American burials but not extended to include Native Americans. Even Thomas Jefferson had his slaves dig a trench through a burial mound on his Monticello plantation.

Dr. Samuel Morton, a Philadelphia doctor, collected over one thousand human skulls in the mid-nineteenth century to measure cranial capacities and determine brain size, which was viewed as the criteria for human intelligence. Many of the skulls were of Native Americans recently dispossessed by the 1830 Indian Removal Act, which caused the removal of most of the Eastern Woodland people west of the Mississippi. Morton has been discredited, but in his day his conclusions that African Americans and Native Americans were "inferior races" influenced attitude and policies regarding slavery, human remains, and religion.

After 1868, the Army Medical Museum in Washington, D.C., embarked on its own study of Native American skulls from battlefields and even from recently buried individuals on reservations. These were collected by army surgeons, Indian agents, anthropologists, and locals. An 1892 letter by army surgeon Z. T. Daniel reveals how he obtained skulls from the Blackfeet:

> I collected them in a way somewhat unusual: the burial place is in plain sight of many Indian houses and very near frequented roads. I had to visit the country at night when not even the dogs were stirring. . . . The greatest fear I had was that some Indian would miss the heads, see my tracks & ambush me, but they didn't.

There are a number of documents indicating that skulls were taken not only from battlefields but from fresh graves and from bodies of Native Americans who died at the hands of government agents. This became a common concern for Native American people. Often bodies had to be forcibly taken away from non-Indian authorities because of such rampant desecration. Famous remains could even be sold to carnivals for exhibit. Native Americans were forced to bury their dead in secret to prevent them from being dug up for "scientific research" as universities and museums sent out their own expeditions to plunder Indian burials.

The displacement of many Native American people and the general nineteenth-century perception that Native Americans would eventually disappear led to many prehistoric sites being pillaged or used as tourist attractions, including burial mounds. The Antiquities Act of 1906 protected federal lands from being looted by pot hunters but did not prevent desecration of graves and repatriation of human remains by public and private museums. In the early part of the twentieth century, Native American populations, especially in North America, reached their lowest numbers (approximately 200,000 in the U.S.) but steadily increased to two million by the 1990s.

After World War II, the civil rights movement and the war in Vietnam, along with Native American cultural revitalization, led to increasing challenges to the erosion of Native American sovereignty. The questioning of ethics in the academic community brought on a number of changes leading to the Repatriation Movement. During the 1970s a number of cases concerning Native American burials and human remains were brought to the courts, resulting in reburial and even in changing the law, after two hundred years, to finally protect the graves of Native Americans.

Since the federal government would not defend Native American civil rights, many Native American groups formed to advocate such issues. One organization called American Indians Against Desecration (AID) has worked in conjunction with the National Congress of American Indians (NCAI), Native American Rights Fund (NARF), and others to repatriate Indian remains. According to NARF attorney, Walter Echo Hawk, well over five hundred thousand Indian bodies have been dug up and carried away, making this "the paramount human rights problem for American Indians today" (Nabokov 1991).

At the state level, individual Indians took protecting their ancestors' remains into their own hands. In the mid-1970s, Maria Pearson was informed by her husband John, an engineer for the Iowa Department of Transportation, that a highway construction crew had moved eight graves. Seven were non-Indians, who were reburied in a nearby cemetery. The eighth was an Indian woman whose body was sent to the state archeologist. That night her deceased grandmother came to her in a vision and told her "to speak for those who could not, her ancestors." Maria, dressed in her finest buckskin and beaded dress, went to the governor's office in Des Moines, Iowa. Governor Robert Ray was informed by his secretary that an Indian woman was sitting in the lobby, and she had come to get her ancestor's bones. Maria was invited into his office, and within a few days the remains of the Indian woman were reburied. This action by the late Maria Pearson led to the first burial protection and repatriation laws at the state level and the model for NAGPRA. Maria was instrumental in the reburial of thousands of ancestors' remains over thirty years and was honored by tribes, states, and nations for living her grandmother's message (Pearson 2000). Maria joined the ancestors in May 2003.

Many anthropologists opposed the actions of the Native American groups, arguing that science has precedence over religious beliefs and that living Native Americans did not always have claim to prehistoric remains thousands of years old that are difficult to trace. An organization known as the American Committee for Preservation of Archaeological Collections (ACPAC) has become a strong advocate for combating the reburial movement.

The federal government has enacted a number of pieces of legislation allowing for repatriation, protecting burials and cultural resources, and protecting sacred sites.

NAGPRA has had the most sweeping effects and set into motion a process that requires public institutions to report their holdings of human remains, grave goods, and other sacred objects. Native Americans have gotten some resolution to the recovery of human remains and objects that hold religious or sacred import. Unfortunately, some scholars, mainly anthropologists, use such legislation purely as a political tool to argue against any cultural interference with scientific research and do not seem to be willing to communicate or empathize with those who hold differing points of view. Non-Indian scholars continue to fiercely debate the topic. Physical anthropologists, who chemically analyze bones to discover ancient diseases and evolutionary linkages, stood with many archaeologists who resisted returning "cultural materials."

Native American groups have led both peaceful and violent demonstrations against universities and museums. In some cases these actions have led to the destruction of property and ancestral

TABLE 3.1
Federal American Indian
Burial and Religious Freedom Laws

Legislation	Passed	Notes
Antiquities Act	1906	Protection of archaeological resources for archaeological science
National Historical Preservation Act (NHPA)	1966	Provides for consultation with Native Americans and the public in reference to national registry sites
National Environmental Policy Act (NEPA)	1969	Mandates assessments of natural and cultural resources
Archaeological Resource Protection Act (ARPA)	1979	Requires consultation with tribal governments or their representatives and confidentiality about archaeological resources that require federal permits
American Indian Religious Freedom Act (ARFA)	1979	Not well enforced, especially in courts; protects the rights of Native Americans to practice their religious ceremonies without local, state, or federal interference (e.g., peyote in Native American Church ceremonies)
Native American Graves Protection and Repatriation Act (NAGPRA)	1990	In reference to human remains, funeral objects, and sacred objects in public agency control, provides for consultation and repatriation with Native Americans

artifacts. Some Native American groups have sincere traditional beliefs and some scientists sincerely seek knowledge and scientific inquiry. Furthermore, this legislation is not a means to recovering all valuable art and cultural resources, as some opponents claim. Native American cultures have different beliefs about human remains, mortuary customs, and sacred objects. Some Native American groups, nations, and communities have and continue to work cooperatively with anthropologists in studying their past (Nabokov 1991).

In terms of the unborn, the Cheyenne River Sioux Tribe in South Dakota in 1994 "reinforced the tribal relationship with the people when it won a case in the 8th U.S. Circuit Court of Appeals in which the tribe may incarcerate a pregnant woman in a tribal substance abuse treatment program for the term of her pregnancy if she is found using alcohol, drugs or other substances which may harm the fetus" (Emery 1994).

Tribal Traditional Justice: Banishment or Public Humiliation

Although particular tribes have always maintained certain forms of punishment for tribal members who violate tribal or external laws, ancestral tribal justice, or what some identify as such, has come to the attention of the outside world recently.

During the summer of 1994 two young men from the Tlingit Nation in Alaska were sentenced by a Washington State judge to "banishment for one year on uninhabited islands with only hand tools and a little food." The two had robbed and beaten a pizza delivery driver in the summer of 1993, causing the victim partial paralysis. Under Washington law, they faced from three to five and a half years in prison. Tlingit Judge Rudy James convinced Superior Court Judge James Allendoerfer that the prison sentence would not have as much impact on the two seventeen-year-olds as banishment to uninhabited islands. "When Columbus came, one thing he didn't find here was prisons," James explained (*Des Moines Register* 1994, 5A).

In the 1990s a wave of drug-related crimes, many violent and deadly, swept across many reservations. In some cases, elders were beaten to death by young tribal members who sought money or other valuables for the purchase of methamphetamine, crack, or other illegal drugs. Elders were also beaten as a gang initiation. Tribal governments began implementing laws that banished tribal members who used or sold drugs on tribal lands. And in some cases, the offending persons were removed from the tribal rolls and identified as non-Indians (Mille Lacs 2003).

Indian Gaming Regulatory Act

In the mid-1970s, some California tribes opened bingo halls in order to bring jobs and revenue to their poverty-stricken people and tribes. After more than ten years of state raids, tribal protest movements, lawsuits, and lobbying by the tribes and their non-Indian financial partners, the Indian Gaming Regulatory Act was enacted in 1988 as Public Law 100–497 and now codified at 25 U.S.C. §2701. It established the jurisdictional framework that presently governs Indian gaming. By 2000, Indian gaming had spread across the country to nearly two hundred facilities, most tribally managed (National Indian Gaming Commission 2004).

The act establishes three classes of games with a different regulatory scheme for each. Class I gaming is defined as traditional Indian gaming and social gaming for minimal prizes. Regulatory authority over Class I gaming is vested exclusively in tribal governments. Class II gaming is defined as the game of chance commonly known as bingo (whether or not electronic, computer, or other technological aids are used in connection therewith) and if played in the same location as the bingo, pull tabs, punch board, tip jars, instant bingo, and other games similar to bingo. Class II gaming also includes nonbanked card games, that is, games that are played exclusively against other players rather than against the house or a player acting as a bank.

The act specifically excludes slot machines or electronic facsimiles of any game of chance from the definition of Class II games. Tribes retain their authority to conduct, license, and regulate Class II gaming. As long as the state in which the tribe is located permits such gaming for any purpose and the tribal government adopts a gaming ordinance approved by the commission, tribal governments are responsible for regulating Class II gaming with commission oversight.

The definition of Class III gaming is extremely broad. It includes all forms of gaming that are neither Class I nor II. Games commonly played at casinos, such as slot machines, black jack, craps, and roulette, would clearly fall in the Class III category, as well as wagering games and electronic facsimiles of any game of chance. Generally Class III is referred to as casino-style gaming. As a compromise, the act restricts tribal authority to conduct Class III gaming.

Before a tribe may lawfully conduct Class III gaming, the following conditions must be met: (1) the particular form of Class III gaming that the tribe wants to conduct must be permitted in the state in which the tribe is located; (2) the tribe and the state must have negotiated a compact that has been approved by the secretary of the Interior, or the secretary must have approved regulatory procedures; and (3) the tribe must have adopted a tribal gaming ordinance that has been approved by the chairman of the commission.

The regulatory scheme for Class III gaming is more complex than a casual reading of the statute might suggest. Although Congress clearly intended regulatory issues to be addressed in tribal-state compacts, it left a number of key functions in federal hands, including approval authority over compacts, management contracts, and tribal gaming ordinances. Congress also vested in the commission broad authority to issue regulations in furtherance of the purposes of the act. Accordingly, the commission plays a key role in the regulation of Class II and III gaming (National Indian Gaming Commission 2004).

Gaming has created large amounts of revenue for several tribes, and some have used these revenues to lobby for preservation and expansion of the Indian Gaming Act and to influence elected officials at both the state and federal levels. Campaign donations in the 2000 presidential and congressional elections from tribal governments were estimated to be between $10 and $100 million. Yet the debate over Native American rights to gaming continues, especially between state and tribal governments. In March 2004, two Republican lawmakers in Minnesota introduced a bill to force tribes to renegotiate their gaming compacts or lose their right to operate slot machines. According to Rep. Jim Knoblach and Sen. Tom Neuville, tribes should share revenues with the state. "The point is that either of these, getting rid of the slots or renegotiation, is better than what we've got now" (*Minneapolis Star Tribune* 2004; *St. Paul Pioneer Press* 2004). The bill also attempts to stop tribes from seeking off-reservation trust lands. The state governor is usually required to approve these types of acquisitions.

More than a thousand Native Americans turned out at the Minnesota state capitol on March 9, 2004, to protest this bill that threatens to ban slot machines. Tribal leaders and tribal members criticized the bill, which calls on tribes to renegotiate their gaming compacts or lose their slot machines. "We created 14,000 jobs in the state of Minnesota. We don't want to lose them," Melanie Benjamin, chief executive of the Mille Lacs Band of Ojibwe, was quoted as saying. Several lawmakers addressed the crowd and said they would vote against the Republican-sponsored bill. "I'm telling you that they're going to take Indian gaming away from Indians only if they can pry my cold, dead finger off my 'no' button because I will vote 'no' every time," one was quoted as saying *(Minneapolis Star Tribune* 2004; *St. Paul Pioneer Press* 2004).

Indian gaming revenues are seen by many tribal leaders and members as the salvation of tribal sovereignty and culture, since such funds revitalize the ability of tribes to decide their own political future without federal intervention or funds. As one tribal leader stated in an anonymous interview, "The white man's government is based on money and now the Indian has the money to buy out that government." According to the National Indian Gaming Commission, tribes brought in $14.5 billion in 2002, a growth of 13 percent from the prior year. In 2005, Indian casinos are projected to take in $18 billion. The amount of money flowing into Indian country has concerned some members of Congress, who are trying to put limits on the development of new casinos, especially those built on off-reservation lands (*Hartford Courant* 2004).

Conclusion

Native American interest groups operate in nearly every political and legal arena in the United States and often in the international arena as well. Native American interest group activism has become more focused on the influence of nontribal political systems; more selective lawsuits in state and federal courts based on the ideological bent of the nation; education of the general public in regard to sovereign and cultural rights; and the use of economic influence, which previously was unavailable but now exists because of gambling revenues for some tribes (Wilkins 2002). The rise in Native American lobbying and interest groups has also led to a rise in Native American voting and electoral participation.

References

"Age-Old Tradition Gains New Life." 2001. *American Indian Report,* March, 6.

American Indians Today. 1987. "Answers to Your Questions," Washington, D.C.: United States Department of the Interior, Bureau of Indian Affairs, Government Printing Office, 0-179-782.

Banks, Dennis. 1994. "Foreword." In *Native America: Portrait of the Peoples.* Detroit: Visible Ink Press.

Capozza, Koren L. 2000. "Health Board Plans First Native HMO," *American Indian Report,* April, 23.

Ceriano, Valerie. 2000. "Pipemakers' Smokedream: A Boarding School Museum," *American Indian Report,* March, 28.

Deloria, Vine, Jr. 1999. *Spirit & Reason.* Golden, Colo.: Fulcrum.

Des Moines Register. 1994. "Tribal Justice," October 25, 5A.

DuBrule, Deborah. 2000. "Feds Change Recognition Procedure," *American Indian Report,* April 2000, 10–11.

Duran, Eduardo, and Bernita Duran. 1995. *Native American Postcolonial Psychology.* Albany: State University of New York Press.

Emery, Steve. 1994. Attorney General and Tribal Member of Cheyenne River Sioux Tribe of South Dakota. Harvard Law School Graduate, Lakota Speaker and Singer, and Family Friend. Telephone interviews by author, summer and fall.

Fogarty, Mark. 2000. "Bitter Harvest: Indian Farmers Seek Billions as Redress for Alleged USDA Discrimination," *American Indian Report,* February, 22–23.

Hartford Courant. 2004. "Tribal Casino Boom Stirs Congress," July 25.

Hauptman, Laurence M. 1995. *Tribes & Tribulations: Misconceptions about American Indians and Their Histories.* Albuquerque: University of New Mexico Press.

LaRose, Louis. 2000. Winnebago Bison Project director, Winnebago Reservation, Nebr. Personal Interview with author, August.

Leap, William, L. 1981. "American Indian Language Maintenance," *Annual Review of Anthropology* 10: 209–236.

McClain, Paula D., and Joseph Stewart, Jr. 1998. *Can We All Get Along? Racial and Ethnic Minorities in American Politics.* Boulder, Colo.: Westview Press.

Mille Lacs Band of Ojibwe. 2003. Tribal Drug Abuse Policy. Onamia, Minn.

Minneapolis Star Tribune. 2004. "Bills Would Threaten Casinos' Video Slot," March, 4.

Muscogee Creek Nation. 1990. "Cultural Characteristics," tribal information packet. Received January 24.

Nabokov, Peter. 1991. *Native American Testimony: A Chronicle of Indian-White Relations from Prophecy to the Present, 1492–1992.* New York: Viking.

Nagel, Joane. 1995. "American Indian Ethnic Renewal: Politics and the Resurgence of Identity," *American Sociological Review* 60 (6): 947–965.

Native American Rights Fund. http://www.narf.org/.

O'Brien, Sharon. 1989. *American Indian Tribal Governments.* Norman: University of Oklahoma Press.

Owl, Frell M. 1962. "Who and What Is an American Indian?" *Ethnohistory* 9 (3): 265–284.

Pearson, Maria. 2000. Iowa Department of Transportation NAGPRA director. Personal interview with the author. Ames, Iowa, November.

Ritter, Beth R. 1994. "The Politics of Retribalization: The Northern Ponca Case," *Great Plains Research,* August.

Rowe, Randi Hicks. 2000. "Land Dispute Nears an End: Evictions Loom for Navajo and Hopi on Partionland," *American Indian Report,* March, 26–27.

———. 2001. "A Survivor's Tale," *American Indian Report,* February, 28.

St. Paul Pioneer Press. "Bill Aims to Unplug Slot Machines," March, 4.

———. 2004. "Of the People Minnesota Gaming: Tribes Protest Casino Proposal," March, 10.

Swift, Shelley. 2000a. "Making the Rivers Grand Again," *American Indian Report,* April, 24–25.

———. 2000b. "The Flow of Power: Paiute's Control of the Truckee River Bodes Well for Fish and Waterways, *American Indian Report,* February, 24–25.

Tirado, Michelle. 2000. "Raked over Coal," *American Indian Report,* April, 8–9.

White, Robert, A. 1974. "Value Themes of the Native American Tribalistic Movement among the South Dakota Sioux," *Current Anthropology* 15 (3): 284–303.

Wilkins, David. 2002. *Nations within States: American Indian Politics and the American Political System.* Boulder, Colo.: Rowman and Littlefield.

4

Native American Participation in Electoral Politics

Native Americans have participated in their own tribal politics and institutions since the beginning of time. As independent and sovereign nations, their participation in external politics was initially based on nation-to-nation status between individual tribes or confederacies and the European invaders, mainly England, Spain, France, and the Dutch. The nation-to-nation relationship continues today, and a new individual basis developed in the 1920s, when all Native Americans were "granted" U.S. citizenship. The nation-to-nation relationship was explained in chapter 1, and the individual relationship continues to evolve.

In terms of the individual Native American's relationship with the U.S. government, Native Americans were counted as "full" citizens if they paid taxes, as defined by the U.S. Constitution. Prior to the Indian Citizenship Act of 1924, many Indians were denied basic political rights, including the right to vote in federal and state elections. The citizenship act granted Native Americans all the rights granted to other U.S. citizens, but these rights have been and still are denied. Arizona Indians were denied the right to vote in state elections until 1948. Utah did not allow Native Americans living on the reservations to vote until the late 1950s, and New Mexico lifted its ban only in 1962. In 1982 legislation to prohibit reservation Indians from voting in New Mexico state and local elections was introduced in the state legislature but died in committee, probably because it would have been ruled unconstitutional in federal court (O'Brien 1989).

Since the 1980s, Native Americans have had few legal challenges to their right to vote in local, state, and federal elections, except for the normal registration laws that impact all Americans. Table 4.1 offers insight into the participation rates for both voter registration and voting in nontribal elections during the 1990s.

Table 4.1 identifies that nearly 53 percent of Native Americans, on average, were registered to vote in nontribal elections and that nearly 42 percent did vote during elections in the 1990s. In surveys of over four hundred tribal officials and citizens, the author found that, on average, 77 percent voted in tribal elections. So it would appear that tribal elections, which in most cases require registration and tribal membership, are more popular with Native Americans than nontribal elections.

In comparison with other ethnic/racial groups in America, Native Americans (42 percent) voted in nontribal elections at a slightly higher rate than Latino (40 percent) and black (40 percent) populations but at a slightly lower rate than Asian (43 percent) and a much lower rate than white (56 percent) Americans. These data often may reflect the fact that the only candidates for president in the 1990s were white, and the majority of local, state, and federal candidates were white. A growing body of research demonstrates that ethnic and racial minorities feel alienated from the general election process because they do not feel represented by the white candidates offered to them for selection. In the 1992 and 1996 presidential elections, Native Americans (50 percent) voted at lower rates than whites (67 percent), blacks (58 percent), and Asian-Americans (57 percent) but at a slightly higher rate than Latino Americans (49 percent) (Lien 2001). The next section offers further insight into intratribal electoral participation.

Navajo Voter Turnout

Coauthored with Kaye Tatro (Lakota/Navajo)

To assess Navajo voter turnout, data were collected from three types of elections: state, local, and general elections; U.S. presidential general elections; and tribal elections. Election returns for 1986–1994 comprised the data set (see table 4.2).

TABLE 4.1
Percentage Distribution of Voting and Registration
in the Elections of 1990–1998 by Race

	Asian	Latino	Indian	Black	White
November 1990 Election					
U.S. Citizenship	51%	59%	96%	93%	96%
Registration	28(56)	32(55)	52(55)	59(64)	67(70)
Voting	20(40)	21(36)	35(36)	39(43)	49(51)
Among registered	72	65	66	67	74
November 1992 Election					
U.S. Citizenship	53%	58%	99%	95%	98%
Registration	31(62)	35(63)	61(63)	64(70)	74(77)
Voting	27(56)	29(54)	51(55)	55(63)	67(72)
Among Registered	88	83	84	85	91
November 1994 Election					
U.S. Citizenship	55%	59%	99%	96%	98%
Registration	29(52)	31(53)	56(56)	59(61)	68(69)
Voting	22(40)	20(34)	37(37)	37(39)	50(51)
Among registered	76	64	66	64	74
November 1996 Election					
U.S. Citizenship	57%	61%	99%	96%	98%
Registration	33(58)	36(59)	61(62)	64(67)	72(73)
Voting	26(46)	27(44)	45(46)	51(53)	60(61)
Among registered	79	75	73	80	83
November 1998 Election					
U.S. Citizenship	59%	61%	98%	96%	98%
Registration	29(49)	34(55)	57(58)	61(64)	68(69)
Voting	19(32)	20(33)	35(35)	40(42)	47(47)
Among registered	66	60	61	66	68

Source: Pei-te Lien. *The Making of Asian America through Political Participation.* Philadelphia: Temple University Press, 2001. Based on author's analysis of the U.S. Department of Commerce, Bureau of the Census data. Current Population Survey: Voter Supplement File 1990, 1992, 1994, 1996, 1998 [Computer files]. ICPSR version.

Navajo tribal data were reported by each region district on the Navajo reservation, called Chapters, but such was not the case for county election returns or other elections under the jurisdiction of the state and county boards of elections, which tend to be reported by precincts. While state election officials reported that their county

TABLE 4.2
Elections Used in Study

Year	Election Type
1986	November 4, general state, local, tribal council, and tribal president. Slate included governor, U.S. Congress, county and local offices, and state questions. No issues on tribal ballot.
1988	November 8, U.S. presidential and state general elections. Slate included U.S. state legislators, other state offices, county and local offices.
1990	November 6, state general election and tribal council. Slate included governor, U.S. Congress, county and local offices, and state questions. No issues on tribal ballot.
	November 20, tribal president only.
1992	November 3, U.S. presidential and state general elections. Slate included state legislators, county and local offices, and state questions.
	August 13, tribal Chapter officers only. No issues on tribal ballot.
1994	November 8, tribal president only. No issues on tribal ballot.

Note: Election returns and registration data were obtained from the following county election boards: (1) New Mexico—San Juan, Rio Arriba, Sandoval, and McKinley; (2) Arizona—Coconino, Apache, and Navajo; (3) Utah—San Juan. Navajo tribal election returns and registration data were obtained from the Navajo Board of Election Supervisors in Window Rock, Arizona.

precincts attempted to follow Chapter boundaries, the match between the two was often difficult to determine, especially in New Mexico. In many instances, a Navajo Chapter straddled two precincts, or even two different counties. For example, Naschitti, White Rock, and Lake Valley Chapters are divided nearly down the middle between two New Mexico counties, McKinley and San Juan. There was also a problem with Chapters that were divided by state boundaries. There were nine Chapters having portions in both Arizona and New Mexico and eight Chapters with portions in Arizona and Utah. Those nine Chapters that straddled both county and state lines presented particular difficulties. To assign voter activity in divided precincts and Chapters required using precinct and Chapter maps, population cluster maps, and personal knowledge of the area. In the end, the data approximated Chapter boundaries as nearly as possible.

The dependent variables for the analysis were voter turnout by Chapter and were computed as the percent of registered voters who actually cast ballots in each election. This method was used for two reasons. First, at the time this study began, neither the 1980 census nor the Navajo Nation had tabulated voting-age population by Chapter. It was not until 1993 that data were available, but data had already been collected for seven elections. Second, an effort was made to figure voter turnout as a percentage of voting-age population, but intrinsic problems soon became apparent because of the nature of Chapter membership. The 1990 census counted numbers of persons who actually lived in the Chapter full-time, while Navajo law and practice allows a person to vote in the Chapter while they live and/or work somewhere else.

For example, the Shiprock, New Mexico, Chapter is only thirty miles via an excellent four-lane highway from the more urban area of Farmington, New Mexico, where many Navajos work and live during the week. On weekends they come home to stay with relatives, and unless they change their registration to another Chapter, they are still qualified to vote at Shiprock. The same is true of many other Chapters on the reservation, especially those near large urban areas surrounding the reservation. Thus, when figuring turnout percentages using voting-age population, it was not at all uncommon to find a Chapter with 112 percent turnout! For each Chapter there are

TABLE 4.3
Comparison of Socioeconomic Indicators
among Different Voting Populations

	White	*Black*	*Hispanic*	*Indian*	*Navajo*
Percent high school graduates	78	63	50	65	41
Percent bachelor's degree or more	21	11	9	6	3
Percent living in poverty	13	19	21	31	58
Median family income (dollars)	35,225	22,400	25,064	21,750	11,880
Median age	33	25	25	26	22

Note: Turnout was tabulated for all U.S. Indians (Navajo included) and then for the Navajo separately.

Source: U.S. Department of Commerce. *We the Americans* (September 1993). (From the Economics and Statistics Administration, Bureau of the Census). Washington, D.C.: Government Printing Office and Navajo Board of Election Administration.

seven measures of turnout, one for each of the seven elections held during the time period from 1986 to 1994, and all are based on registration figures, not on census data.

Analytic Framework

Based on existing literature on turnout (Nie, Verba, and Petrocik 1979; Wolfinger and Rosenstone 1980), one would expect the Navajo to have relatively low voter turnout. They are a largely rural, minority population with lower levels of education and lower incomes than average. Yet examination of turnout date shows Navajo turnout is, in fact, higher for the Navajo tribe taken as a whole (see table 4.4) than for any other ethnic group, including whites.

As a first step in identifying possible patterns of turnout, correlation between the dependent variables was created (see table 4.5). As can be seen, the tribal elections are generally highly correlated with each other. However, the pattern suggests that there are likely to be generic underlying factors as well as election-specific factors that explain voter turnout across Chapters and elections.

The 1986 election included, besides Navajo tribal president, such offices as governor, U.S. senators and representatives, state constitutional officers, and local school board members. State questions on that ballot included such matters as phone deregulation, limits on state campaign contributions, and a proposed increase in state legislative salaries but no issues specific to the Navajo people.

The context of the 1990 election was particularly salient to the Navajo because of conflict surrounding the criminal indictment of the tribal president, Peter McDonald. McDonald had been a candidate for reelection when, on October 17, he was indicted for bribery and conspiracy in tribal courts. On October 18, the Navajo Nation Board of Election Supervisors disqualified McDonald as a candidate, and on October 19 the Navajo Tribal Council (NTC) voted to delay the election for tribal president for two weeks to "give the candidates time to campaign" (*Navajo Times,* October 23, 1990, 1). Thus, Navajo voters went to the polls with the general Anglo population on November 8 to cast ballots for federal, state, and local offices and candidates and to choose members of the NTC. Then they again went to the polls on November 20' when only tribal members voted for tribal president.

Turnout for the 1990 tribal presidential election was five percentage points higher than turnout for the 1990 general and tribal coun-

TABLE 4.4
Turnout Average (Percentages) for Navajo,
White, Black, and Hispanic, 1986–1994

Group	Election Year and Turnout			
	1986G	*1988G*	*1990G*	*1992G*
Navajo	69	69	48	67
White	47	59	47	64
Black	43	51	39	54
Hispanic	24	29	21	29

Average Turnout (Percentage) for Navajo Tribal Elections Only

1990T	*1992T*	*1994T*
53	38	53

Note: Percentages were tabulated using the number of registered voters versus those who actually voted. G indicates an inclusive general election; T indicates a tribal election only.

Source: Information Please Almanac. 1995. Boston: Houghton Mifflin and the Navajo Board of Election Supervisors, Window Rock, Arizona.

TABLE 4.5
Intercorrelation Coefficients of Seven Elections

(R equals .15 or above)

	1986G	*1988G*	*1990G*	*1990T*	*1992G*	*1992T*	*1994T*
1986G	–	.252*	.513**	.514**	.280*	.342**	.468**
1988G	.252*	–	.205	.301**	.163	.403**	.394**
1990G	.513**	.205	–	.636**	.284*	.439**	.578**
1990T	.514**	.301**	.636*	–	.214	.399**	.633**
1992G	.280*	.163	.284*	.214	–	.395**	.278*
1992T	.342**	.403**	.439**	.399**	.395**	–	.515**
1994T	.468**	.394**	.578**	.633**	.278*	.515**	–

*P = .01
**P < .001

Note: G indicates an inclusive general election; T indicates a tribal election only. P = significance level (The lower this number, the higher the level of significance. .001 identifies a higher level of correlation between the two variables than .01. Most studies identify any P score below .05 as significant.)

cil election. This could be explained in part by voter anger at the NTC for postponing the tribal presidential election for two weeks. Area and tribal newspapers such as the *Gallup Independent,* in Gallup, New Mexico (October 23, 1990, 1), ran editorials denouncing the decision. A one-page memo distributed by the Zah-Plummer candidacy denounced the illegality of the decision (Zah-Plummer Campaign Release, October 21, 1990). The Zah campaign ran radio ads every hour for two days decrying the action by the NTC, but in that same week the Navajo supreme court upheld the decision.

There was also open conflict between McDonald supporters and interim president Leonard Haskie, who was also a candidate for the presidency. When McDonald was indicted and disqualified, Haskie assumed the presidency until the election. McDonald supporters barricaded tribal headquarters in an attempt to stop him. The conflict turned ugly, with shots fired and one person killed (*Gallup Independent,* October 20, 1990, 1). Since this type of activity flies in the face of traditional Navajo behavior, which relies on harmony with all around you and consensus agreements, it undoubtedly affected turnout. In the 1986 election Navajo voters went to the polls with the general public and also elected a tribal president and tribal council. Table 4.4 points out that turnout was twenty-one percentage points higher than was the case for the 1990 contentious tribal presidential election. Apparently voter anger was directed at the NTC (and indirectly at the state general election), not at the office of the tribal president, though here, too, turnout was lower than for the previous (1986) election. Nonetheless, 1990 turnout for the presidential election was higher than 1990 turnout for the election to fill state and federal offices, suggesting the importance of tribal government to the Navajo people even in times of trouble and nontraditional behavior.

While voter turnout, on average, was higher among the Navajo, table 4.4 shows that turnout was higher for U.S. presidential elections and lower for federal off-year elections, or for purely tribal elections. At the same time, when looking at voter turnout by Chapter for each election, we find great variations among the Chapters, even those situated within the same geographic region. To illustrate this anomaly, table 4.6 shows voter turnout percentages for five Chapters within the same geographic area in the northeastern corner of the reservation. Four of the Chapters—Beclabeto, Sanostee, Red Valley, and Cove—were in the top twentieth percentile for all seven elections when the Chapters were ranked from highest to lowest turnout percentages, and Shiprock Chapter was consistently in the lower

TABLE 4.6
Comparison of Voter Turnout of Chapters in
Same Geographic Region on Navajo Reservation in Arizona

	High Turnout for Seven Elections (Percentages)						
	1986G	1988G	1990G	1990T	1992G	1992T	1994T
Beclabeto	79	76	62	63	76	52	60
Sanostee	75	80	58	73	73	49	58
Red Valley	79	80	59	66	73	45	62
Cove	74	74	57	57	68	50	58
	Low Turnout for Seven Elections (Percentages)						
Shiprock	59	54	47	48	53	30	44

Note: G indicates an inclusive general election; T indicates a tribal election only.

twentieth percentile for the seven elections measured. What could account for these differences in voter turnout among Chapters within the same region?

A theoretical question that has driven this study concerns the relationship between community (which includes size, degree of urbanization and/or economic development, opportunities for social networking, and the degree of penetration or influence by non-Indians) and voter turnout. Nie, Verba, and Petrocik (1979) found little correlation between community size and participation. They did find, however, that a significant relationship existed between political participation and what they called "boundedness"—the extent to which a community (in this case a Chapter) is well defined or identified. But they were unable to find any community that actually fit their "boundedness" category, noting that "of course none of the communities in our study approaches [is] a completely autonomous community; all are embedded in American Society" (Nie, Verba, and Petrocik 1979). While the Navajo reservation and the Chapters comprising it are not perfectly autonomous, some Chapters are possibly better examples of the "boundedness" characteristic.

Conclusion

With the "boundedness" characteristic in mind, this analysis of Navajo voting turnout finds that the more integrated or assimilated the Chapter into the Anglo world, the lower voter turnout is for all elections.

Federal Indian policy and traditional Anglo wisdom has always assumed that if the Indians were "Christianized and civilized," they would become better citizens. Conventional political science research has also shown that higher socioeconomic status is correlated with an increase in voter turnout (Nie, Verba, and Petrocik 1979; Wolfinger and Rosenstone 1980; Rosenstone and Hansen 1993). In Chapters more economically assimilated, it would seem logical to expect that there would be more exposure to educational opportunities, media information, jobs, and an increase in incomes. This exposure, according to the Anglo models, is then expected to increase the likelihood of voting. This study argues the opposite—that this very economic assimilation is what breaks down the traditional fabric of Navajo culture that encouraged voter turnout in the first place. Furthermore, the more integrated or assimilated the Navajo Chapters, the higher voter turnout is in those elections not specifically tribal. Psychological motivation such as interest in politics and/or campaigns has been shown to contribute to participation in elections (Conway 2000). The more Navajos become like Anglos, the less interest they have in tribal elections and the more interest they have in federal elections.

Conversely, the more traditional Chapters—those less assimilated into mainstream American life—have higher turnouts in tribal elections. Those Chapters perceived as rural or "backward" have less contact with outsiders and retain the more traditional Navajo behavior, which emphasized participation in political decision making.

It also appears that the greater the employment by government entities within the Chapter, the greater the turnout in federal and state elections. Persons in occupational categories such as governmental employment are more likely to vote than would be predicted from other sociodemographic characteristics. Job security and income of government employees are directly and significantly affected by governmental activities. Therefore, those who work for the government tend to have more interest in politics, more access to political information, and higher rates of voting turnout (Lewis-Beck 1977; Wolfinger and Rosenstone 1980). The federal government has some measure of control over nearly all economic aspects of Navajo life. In 1990, governmental employment (federal, state, and tribal) accounted for 27 percent of the employment on the whole Navajo Reservation (Rodgers 1995), but in some Chapters government employment rates are as high as 100 percent.

Another finding is that Chapters with the greatest opportunities for internal social networking have higher turnouts. Social networks reduce the costs of obtaining political information, thus reducing the costs of voting (Huckfeldt and Sprague 1995). In those Chapters where there are opportunities to meet and mingle with others, such as at churches, schools, convenience stores, traditional fairs, dances, and powwows, the exchange of political information should be expedited and/or made easier.

Tribal Officials' Political Opinion Survey

> Tribal Government must never get away from the grassroots people, their voices must be heard, they must be allowed to participate in all decisions that affect them. (Elected Tribal Council Member from South Dakota)

The author has conducted several political surveys of tribal elected officials since 1989. The following analysis is from data collected from the 1994 survey of 480 randomly selected present or past tribal council members in the continental United States and Alaska. The home or office addresses of the tribal officials were provided by the regional offices of the Bureau of Indian Affairs (BIA). (Similar to Julnes's [1994] findings, the author found that the BIA did not have accurate records concerning many tribal officials. Addresses were incorrect for 35 percent [169] of the tribal officials.)

Of the 480 sent out, 157 survey forms were returned from the initial and follow-up mailings as of January 1994, a return rate of 33 percent. Those who sent back the survey forms represented 59 different tribes. Of these, 118 questionnaires were filled out by elected tribal council persons, and the other 39 were filled out by nonelected tribal officials or were missing necessary responses.

Tribal Officials' Opinions

Life on the Reservations

In terms of how things are going on each respondent's reservation or in their particular community, most (53 percent) felt things were going fairly well. Only 11 percent felt that things were not going too well, and 18.5 percent felt that things were going very well. One could surmise from these data that the majority of tribal leaders, 71.5 percent, see their communities in a fairly positive situation at the present time. Other comments made by the participants in this survey indicate that increased revenue from gaming and other economic ventures, more local control through self-determination and self-governance, and a rebirth of traditional tribal cultures and lifestyles have improved their reservation communities.

The 11 percent who felt things were not going well in their communities said that the continued dependency on federal funds, the lack of land base and revenue from tribal land, the factions in the tribal government that used their power to control everything and to oppress the people, the breakdown of traditional family structure and values, and basic disrespect for the community, especially among the young, were the reasons that their community was not doing well. They felt that holding families responsible for the actions of their kids, increased roles for the elders in tribal government, more tribal employment and businesses, and a return to old ways were needed to make their communities a better place to live.

Governmental Relations and Trust

The federal government has had the most influence over tribal sovereignty due to its trust responsibility over tribal lands. Tribal elected officials were asked which branch of the federal government protected their sovereign rights. Forty-one percent felt that Congress best protected their sovereign rights, while 23 percent felt that the Supreme Court did, and only 6 percent saw the president as the best protector of their sovereign rights. Thirty-one percent felt that none of these branches protected their sovereign rights. This group felt that "Congress's support is based upon how well Congress gets it's way." They felt that the traditional structure of sovereign nations best protects the indigenous people, since "Congress, the president, and the Supreme Court are working hard against Indian people because they still want tribal lands." Many felt that the tribes are in constant battles with the states over sovereignty and that the federal government often supports the states over the tribes. One example given was the Indian Gaming Act, whereby Congress violated their own Constitution by allowing a compact between sovereign nations and states. There was a general feeling that tribes can govern themselves best.

Similarly, many non-Indians have expressed the view that they feel more connection to their local governments (city, county, school) than to the state or federal governments. In the 1970s this phenomenon was identified as "New Federalism" and was promoted in the Reagan administration's view that the government closest to the people served them best. Billions of dollars of federal funds were transferred to local governments for programming and services delivered to local people by local government officials.

Even though Congress was chosen by the majority of respondents as the branch of the federal government that best protects the sovereign rights of Native Americans, the vast majority of respondents did not approve of how the U.S. Congress had been handling Indian affairs. Seventy-five percent disapproved, 16.5 percent approved, and 8.5 percent had other comments that mainly focused on the fact that none of the three branches of the federal government handles Indian affairs very well. It appears from the comments on Congress that "although Congress could do a great deal to assist Indian nations and protect the rights of Indian people, they have chose not to." As one respondent put it, "How far can I go back, I disapprove of Congress's dealings with our tribes for over 200 years." Another view of the future of tribal political participation in Congress is that "money runs the Congress, the tribes need to unite and use our gambling and other revenues to buy the votes in Congress necessary to get what our people need."

The handling of tribal sovereignty by presidents Bush and Clinton was viewed mostly in the negative. Eighty percent of the respondents disapproved, 14 percent approved, and 6 percent had other comments that once again focused on the lack of support of any of the three branches of government for Indian affairs and tribal sovereignty. Several commented that Bush really never gave much consideration to, knew very little about, and just wasn't interested in Indian affairs. Some commented more favorably on Clinton, but most felt that the improvement of tribal-federal relations needed more than just a favorable president.

The trust level of the federal government by Indian tribal leaders appears to be moderate to low. None of the respondents felt that they could trust the federal government to always handle Indian trust responsibilities, 11 percent felt they could trust the government most of the time, 54 percent felt that they could trust them some of the time, and 32 percent felt that they could never trust the federal government. Three percent had other comments. Many of the respondents appeared to feel that overall the federal government and its major overseer of Indian affairs, the Bureau of Indian Affairs, were very incompetent in the handling of trust responsibilities. The following comment is evidence of this: "The federal government and the BIA mismanage our funds and programs and won't let us manage our own affairs. They need to be educated about tribal affairs."

State governments are viewed in an even more negative manner than the federal government. Only one (.8 percent) tribal official felt that state governments were working very hard to help American Indians, 9.2 percent felt that they were working fairly hard, 50.5 percent not very hard, 31 percent not hard at all, and 8.5 percent felt that state officials were working against American Indians. State-tribal relations appear to be very strained, as the following opinions from survey respondents indicate:

"They (states) are in the process of finalizing termination of Indigenous people in Alaska. State government is all over the reservation in social services, education requirements, police force certification to our gaming compact. The states want to tax us and put us under their laws. South Dakota is the most prejudice state in the union. South Dakota officials are the most prejudice in the union. State officials are trying to control Indians, just like they control everyone else. They are working hard against Indians."

A final point that needs further research was expressed by nearly a dozen respondents—that states do not work with American Indians because of a view by state officials and their non-Indian citizens that Indian people do not pay state taxes. Thus, as one respondent stated, "no taxes, no representation."

In terms of party affiliation, like the other minority populations in the United States, the vast majority of American Indian tribal officials in this survey were Democrats (61 percent), while only 10 percent were Republicans, 13 percent were Independents, and 6 percent had other party affiliations. Ten percent had no party affiliation.

Most comments about party differences focused on Democratic candidates being more knowledgeable of and receptive to tribal concerns than their Republican counterparts. A favorable reference was made to Nixon's and Reagan's policies of self-determination and self-governance. Another tribal official stated that "in traditional structures there is no need for parties, because everything is done by a true consensus of the people and the party system has only under-mined and separated the people of America."

Tribal Government

The most important government on the reservation is the tribal gov-ernment. The attributes of candidates that are important to tribal voters when they select their tribal leaders are vastly understudied. I found that only 1.5 percent of tribal leaders vote for their tribal can-didates based on party, 78 percent on individual platform, 6 percent on whether the candidate is a relative, 4 percent on the age of the candidate, 2 percent on the gender of the candidate, and 8.5 percent for other reasons. The vast majority felt that a candidate should be judged on his or her viewpoints and way of life. One respondent probably stated this feeling best: "The candidate who tells the people the truth will represent all his family, elders, and people."

Of all the federal, state, and local government officials, tribal gov-ernment officials have the greatest influence on the people on their reservations, from jobs to housing. The people determine who serves them and by doing so determine what issues are most impor-tant to them. The majority of respondents (27 percent) felt that their main duty as a tribal elected leader was to protect tribal sovereignty. Three percent felt that their main duty was to get tribal ordinances passed. Twenty-five percent felt that providing services to their tribal constituents and 23 percent felt that aiding in the economic development of the tribe were their main duties. Twenty-two percent felt that all of the aforementioned were their main du-ties as tribal officials. And 3 percent felt that most tribal officials feel that their main duty is to personally gain from their position. It is safe to say they these 3 percent are very skeptical of their individual tribal councils. Another tribal official viewed his main duty as "all of the above—to fulfill each of the above while protecting and as-serting tribal sovereignty."

There are many issues that demand the attention of tribal offi-cials. Table 4.7 identifies that education, the elderly, and employ-ment are very important issues among the respondents.

Most of the other issues, except gambling, appeared to be of some importance to the respondents. Although Indian gambling is the most visible Indian issue to most Americans, gambling is not a very important issue to most of the respondents and is not of interest to

TABLE 4.7
Tribal Government Surveys from 1992 and 1996

	Very Important	Somewhat Important	Not Very Important	Not of Interest
Elderly	105 (89%)	13 (11%)	0	0
Business	90 (76%)	25 (21%)	3 (2.5%)	0
Employment	104 (88%)	14 (12%)	0	0
Family services	90 (76.5%)	26 (22%)	2 (1.5%)	0
Environment	72 (61%)	42 (36%)	4 (3%)	0
Civil rights	73 (62%)	35 (30%)	9 (7.5%)	1 (.5%)
Tribal jurisdiction	88 (75%)	25 (21%)	5 (4%)	0
Substance abuse	89 (75.5%)	26 (22%)	3 (2.5%)	0
Education	113 (96%)	5 (4%)	0	0
Tribal traditions	92 (78%)	22 (19%)	4 (3%)	0
Gambling	24 (20%)	47 (40%)	26 (22%)	21 (18%)

18 percent. No other interests or issues were identified by the respondents.

The tribal leaders identified the following as the accomplishments that they are proudest of during their tenure as a tribal elected official:

TABLE 4.8
Proudest Accomplishments While on Tribal Council

Minutes of tribal meetings are published	Brought business to the reservation
Roll call votes	Strengthened/reorganized IRA government
Obtaining indirect costs from federal grants	Dissolved state-chartered municipality
Creating a water commission	Tribal police force
HUD grant (housing and business)	Health care programs and facilities
Tenacity and determination of our tribe	Jobs
Gymnasium	Water tank and system
Education (schools and colleges)	Pride and accountability to tribe
Increased tribal assets and resources	Creating an "open" policy of government
First ever tribal feast and dance	New motel and truck firm
P. L. 638 contracts from BIA and IHS	Bingo
Revising tribal constitution and bylaws	Library

Casino and management contract

Dividend payment to tribal members

Industry

Long-term planning

Keeping tribal kids in school

CDBG block grant

Elderly programs

Tribal newspaper

Tribal tax bill

ICWA programs

Speaking in D.C. on behalf of my people

Smoke shop

Financial accountability for programs

Funding students for extracurricular activities

Fought for our lands, even though we lost in court

Straightened out tribal land subleases

Tax commission and gaming commission

Protected our ancestors' graves

IHS clinic in the community

Legislation against Crazy Horse alcohol

Substantially reduced tribal debt

Creation of separation of powers

Kept job corps

Fair election process

Grant writing

ANA grant

Decreased unemployment rate by 40%

Enrolled 500 new tribal members

Campgrounds

Housing

Got rid of waste dump on reservation

Stopped loans for political favors

Restoration

Settled some knotty problems successfully

Three branches of government work together

Reestablishing village corporation

Vote as I understand I should

Burial expenses

Day care

Tribal law enforcement code

Salmon hatchery activities

Initiated and won effective lawsuit for land claims, which reestablished our reservation

Got women on council

Alcoholism programs on reservation

Tribe was broke, took two years to resolve

Black Hills claims

Demonstrated abilities as a young leader

Social services programs

Obtained highest bid on tribal land leases

Electronics company

Turned failing farm business into profit-making business for tribe

New tribal management system

Established tribal offices and positions

Protected people from power-seeking tribal council

Unified and harmonized our people

In terms of gender of the respondents there were thirty-eight female and eighty male respondents. The percentage of women (32 percent) is consistent with tribal official records from the area offices of the Bureau of Indian Affairs that identify the percentage of female tribal council members between 1988 and 1994 as averaging 34 percent. The percentage of female tribal elected officials is much higher than the average percentage of women in local, state, or national female elected offices, which varies between 12 and 20 percent at the municipal, county, state, and federal governmental levels. In the majority of tribes, women have traditionally sought and achieved leadership roles.

We then asked how each respondent would rate the effectiveness of women members compared to their male counterparts. The majority (47 percent) felt that women and men were equally effective on tribal councils. Thirteen percent did not answer this question and commented that it was not an appropriate question to ask. Although the vast majority of the respondents were men, many (27 percent) felt that women were more effective than men. Twenty-two women and ten men felt that women were more effective than men, whereas sixteen men and no women felt that men were more effective than women. One respondent seemed to sum up the feelings of the majority—that both are effective to the same degree—in the following statement: "Human soul is the same. We all go to happy hunting ground when we die."

The average number of years that the respondents had served as tribal council members was six years and six months. The longest service was forty years, and the shortest was one month. The average age of the respondents was forty-five years old. Age and experience appear to be key elements in selecting tribal leaders. The average age at which the respondents were first elected was thirty. The oldest tribal council person was seventy-two, and the youngest was eighteen when first elected.

Nineteen percent had high school diplomas. The majority (36 percent) had some college, and 8 percent had attended technical school. Twenty percent had college degrees, and 16 percent had graduate degrees.

Forty-five percent of the respondents were grandparents. Since grandparents are often considered to be elders by tribal communities, it appears that gaining this status is important in nearly half of the tribal elections.

Blood quantum is an important issue for Native Americans that does not affect other minorities. The percentage of one's tribal blood

TABLE 4.9
Percentage of Indian Blood

Blood Quantum %	Count	Blood Quantum %	Count
Would not report	3	56	2
6	3	59	2
13	3	63	3
19	1	66	1
20	1	69	1
22	1	75	16
25	12	81	1
31	1	85	1
33	1	86	3
38	6	88	2
44	2	93	3
50	20	100	28
53	1	1	

determines one's tribal membership status, ability to participate in tribal elections, ability to serve on tribal council, and ones' access to tribal employment. The blood quantum mean for the respondents was 61.75 percent. The number of respondents for each blood quantum percentage identified is listed above.

Further analysis showed that those with one-half or less blood quantum were far more likely to hold elected or appointed offices outside of tribal government and/or administration than those with over one-half blood quantum or more.

There are a number of reasons for the influence of the degree of blood quantum. One is that those who have the least amount of Native American blood also have fewer physical racial attributes (look more white) and are subjected less to racism and discrimination. They also have more interaction with their white relatives and acquaintances. Another is that those with a higher blood quantum tend to have more physical racial attributes, which subjects them to a higher degree of racism and discrimination and limits their interactions with whites. This is definitely an area open to study among all races of Americans.

Forty-two percent of the respondents held a political office, other than tribal council, such as school board, state legislator, etc. The following are the offices that they held:

Mayor of city; city council member; vice-mayor; Title V Indian education committee; secretary of intertribal wilderness council; Nebraska Intertribal Corporation—chairman; Head Start board; tribal parks and wildlife board; land management board; school board; gaming commission; housing commission; state human rights commission; native corporation board member; health board; planning commission; tribal college board of trustees; personnel board; state Democratic Party affirmative action committee; Johnson O'Malley (JOM) Committee; state Indian commission; PTA; tribal stewardship in construction committee; state historical society board; Native American Church; tribal industrial development commission; tribal judge; youth council; state board of regents; Indian legal services board; utility board; enrollment committee; child protection team member; county clerk; county commissioner; university minority student affairs council; and National Congress of American Indians.

Politics at any level requires compromise and negotiation, and tribal elected officials, like other elected legislators, are required to secure a majority of votes on any law or policy they are promoting. This often requires bargaining for votes from other tribal council members. However, 60 percent of the respondents stated that they never bargain with other tribal officials for their votes. Tribal council members, in terms of their legislative duties, appear to use several techniques in securing votes, some different (such as nepotism) from those used by their counterparts in local, state, or federal government, where bargaining for votes is commonplace. Eleven percent bargained for votes most of the time, 7 percent frequently, and 22 percent occasionally.

In terms of the most important issues that tribal governments and Indian people are confronting, the following were identified by the respondents.

The following issues received less than ten responses: self-governance, land acquisition, employment/job training, environment/waste dumps, and tribal courts/jurisdiction received 9 responses; identity as Indian people/cultural maintenance, 8; religious freedom, 7; tax litigation against states and intergovernmental relations with states, 6; get rid of the BIA and IHS, having tribal role models for the youth, housing, elderly programs, and treaty rights, 5; blood quantum/enrollment and fetal alcohol syndrome, 4; smoke shops, 2; and tribal taxation, tribal governments unite, elitism among tribal offi-

TABLE 4.10
The Key Issues from the Tribal Leaders Survey

Most Important Issue	Number of Respondents	Percentage of Respondents
Protection of tribal sovereignty	48	41%
Gambling and state compacts	22	19%
Economic development	21	18%
Health care and facilities	21	18%
Each other/individual greed	18	15%
Alcohol and drug abuse	15	13%
Education	12	10%
Lack of federal funding	12	10%
Tribal self-sufficiency	10	9%

cials, parental responsibility, and development of tribal natural resources had 1 response each.

Environmental Issues

There was strong disapproval of tribal economic development programs that might have a negative effect on the local environment, such as a solid waste dump. Seventy-eight percent of the respondents disapproved, and only 11 percent approved. Eleven percent had other comments that strongly disapproved of any type of negative use of local land. One respondent stated his disapproval in a strong manner: "Indigenous people have been at the bottom of the shit pile long enough. If you should shit in your bed long enough, pretty soon you will have to lay in it. Make the people who create the waste sleep with it."

Those that approved commented that oftentimes because of the poverty of their people they were forced to look at such extreme economic development strategies. Over half of those that approved placed restrictions on such ventures as solid waste and ruled out any type of nuclear waste disposal on their lands.

For the vast majority that disapproved, their comments mainly focused on the importance of protecting the environment for future generations. And most felt that if anyone was going to protect the environment, it would be Indian people. As one respondent stated, "An Indian person would never allow the destruction of Mother Earth."

Indian Preference and Tribal Management

Indian preference in hiring at both the federal and tribal levels was first initiated in 1934 with the passage of the Indian Reorganization Act. In 1972, Louis Bruce, the first Indian commissioner of Indian affairs, instituted Indian preference in hiring and promotions at the Bureau of Indian Affairs. Non-Indian employees sued based on the Equal Employment Act of 1972 and lost. In *Morton v. Mancari* the U.S. Supreme Court, in a unanimous decision, reversed the lower court verdict and remanded the case to a lower court, stating that the federal policy of hiring preference to Indians in the Indian service dates back at least to an 1834 congressional act (Stubben 1994).

Seventy-two percent of the participants favored Indian preference in hiring on their reservations and in the Bureau of Indian Affairs, Indian Health Service, and other Native American agencies and organizations. Less than 8 percent were against such hiring and promotion policies, and 20.5 percent favored Indian preference with some restrictions, such as making sure the person was qualified for the job, not basing such employment on nepotism, and the person's motivation to work for the people.

Comments from those who favored Indian preference centered around the right of Indian tribes through their sovereign status to determine their own hiring practices and the importance of having Indian employees working with the tribal people due to their cultural knowledge. Basically the person best qualified to understand Indian people is an Indian person. Nearly a third of the participants felt that the tribes must hire the most qualified person for any job regardless of whether they are Indian or not. One example given was the hiring of non-Indian casino managers who then trained tribal members to take over the job.

Oftentimes the true power in tribal government lies in the administration. Tribal officials were asked what specific qualifications are necessary for a tribal administrator or manager.

The following qualifications were offered with the number of respondents selecting them in parentheses:

> College degree (37)
> Commitment to the people and not to self (28)

Knowledge of local customs (21)
Fair and honest (21)
Indian/tribal traditional knowledge (16)
Successful experience working with Indians (16)
Knowledge of federal Indian law (15)
American Indian or enrolled tribal member (11)
Business background (10)
Grant writer (9)
Budget knowledge (9)
Writing and communication skills (7)
Supervisory skills (5)
Reliable—shows up at office (5)
Speaks tribal language (4)
Leader (4)
Elder (4)
Sober (3)
Objective (3)
Good judgment (2)
Non-Indian world experience (2)
Computer skills (1)
Elected by the people (1)
Compassion (1)

The key qualifications respondents identified for a tribal manager were a college degree, preferably in law or administration, a strong sense of group rather than individual commitment, and fairness and honesty, along with both knowledge of and experience in tribal traditional customs and local norms. Sufficient knowledge of both the Indian and non-Indian worlds, labeled as bicultural competence by LaFromboise and Rowe (1983), is also important for an Indian person to cope with the world around them. The respondents recognize that they walk in two worlds and take assets from both.

Many tribal colleges (see tribal college list) and some non-Indian universities that are geographically close to major Indian populations or reservations offer tribal management courses for those seeking such employment. With the advent of tribal casinos, management courses such as those offered at Turtle Mountain Community College in North Dakota have become mandatory for casino staff, which has increased the number of tribal members with management and financial training.

The respondents also appear to prefer that persons who manage tribal concerns are either an enrolled member of the tribe for which they work or at least an Indian person enrolled in another federally recognized Indian nation. This view further supports Indian and tribal preference laws and ordinances and the need to have Indian people working with Indian people.

Abortion, Death Penalty, and Adulthood

The abortion issue appeared to be as controversial among tribal leaders as it is among the American public in general. Even though 54 percent of the respondents wanted to keep abortion legal, nearly half of them identified restrictions. Twenty-six percent wanted to make abortion illegal, and 20 percent had other comments, which mainly focused on restrictions.

The restrictions centered around parental or grandparental notification (namely mothers or grandmothers), the age of the mother, and reason for abortion. Most of those who placed restrictions on abortions felt that the health of the mother was an important issue; if giving birth would threaten the life of the mother, then an abortion was all right. Likewise, abortions due to rape and incest appeared to be permissible among the group that favored continued legalization of abortions. Several felt that it was not the baby's fault that he or she was conceived by rape or incest and that someone in the tribe would appreciate and raise the baby when it was born.

Some felt that abortion should not be used as a form of birth control, while most felt that it was a decision that should be left up to the mother and her family. Respondents made comments such as, "Such things must be left up to the mother and her mother and grandmother." "Only the woman's family knows what is best." "The woman's family must be consulted."

One male respondent stated that "as a man, I personally feel that this is an issue I have no right to commit on." Another respondent pointed out that "Indian people have always practiced abortion through the use of herbs or other medicine."

Those who wanted to make abortions illegal focused "on the importance of all life, including the animals and land, to Indian people and that a traditional Indian person would never harm the unborn. Indian people would never believe in such genocide of their own or another people."

Some of the respondents shifted their opinion on abortion when it came to allowing abortions in Indian Health Service (IHS) hospitals. Although the majority (53 percent) still favored abortions when they were performed in IHS facilities, 35 percent were opposed and 12 percent would place strict restrictions. Likewise, over half of the 53 percent who favored abortions in IHS facilities placed restrictions on allowing such abortions. Most favored restricting abortions in IHS facilities unless the life of the mother was threatened or in the case of rape or incest.

Fourteen of the respondents felt that "IHS facilities might use abortion to sterilize Indian women, as had occurred in the 1960s and 1970s, mostly during gynecological exams." One respondent felt that "federal and state governments might use IHS abortions to get rid of tribes."

Overall, the drop in support for abortions in IHS facilities as compared to support for legal abortions in general may lie in the fact that abortion for the public at large does not impact Indian societies to the degree that abortion within IHS facilities does. In offering evidence of this, a female respondent stated that "abortions in IHS hospitals directly affect Indian people, because it is Indian people who will have the abortions and Indian people that will be aborted in these hospitals." Or as another female respondent put it, "Let white and black people have abortions, us Indian people don't need it."

The tribal officials had a conservative stand on the death penalty, with 62 percent favoring the death penalty for off-reservation murders; 18.5 percent were against the death penalty, and 19.5 percent felt that use of the death penalty depended on the situation under which the murder occurred. Likewise, the majority of respondents (69 percent) favored the death penalty for persons who commit murder on the reservation, 17.8 percent were against the use of the death penalty for on-reservation murderers, and 13.2 percent felt that use of the death penalty depended on the situation under which the murder occurred. Intent to kill and self-defense were often cited as reasons that might mitigate against or for the use of the death penalty.

Many stated that the use of the death penalty, especially when the victim was killed without just cause, was the norm in traditional Indian societies before the coming of the non-Indians. The following comments from the tribal leaders offer evidence of this belief: "Indigenous people have always practiced capital punishment." "The victim's family used to decide the murderer's punishment." "It should be up to the victim's mother or father to choose punishment." "They have taken a life away from the parents and family, so parents and family must decide if murderer should die."

There also appears to be some evidence of the influence of Christian moral views in the comments of some of the respondents, such as "an eye for an eye and a life for a life." Other interesting comments regarding the use of the death penalty, whether on or off tribal lands, were "Hang them high." "Indian people accused of murder should only be tried in tribal court, so they can get a fair trial; too many minorities get the death penalty because white judges set the penalties." "Depends on circumstances." "I heard a story from my elders that if you murder someone then someone will murder you as punishment. Murder is murder, no matter what color you are."

Thus, it would appear that American Indians may be slightly more conservative in their views toward the use of the death penalty than other minority groups, especially African Americans. They also favor the use of the death penalty more strongly than Democrats and liberal whites.

Tribal officials felt that a child becomes an adult at 18.5 years, which is similar to local, state, and national voter-age laws.

Gaming

Forty-seven percent of the tribes in this survey had gaming operations on their tribal lands and 53 percent did not. Most of those tribes that did not have gaming operations were looking into building such a facility in the future. Only two respondents commented that gambling should never be allowed on their tribal lands.

Six percent felt that the main reason for gaming was to increase tribal sovereignty, 17 percent felt that it was to provide employment for tribal members, only 1 percent felt that its purpose was to provide funds for tribal land purchases, while the vast majority (42 percent) felt that gaming should provide funds for tribal services and 34 percent chose the "other" category. Within the "other" category, three-fourths of the respondents felt that all of the above were reasons for having tribal gambling enterprises. Thus, 24 percent of all respondents felt that gaming was an expression of tribal sovereignty and provided funds for employment of tribal members, tribal land purchases, and tribal services. Some of the other main reasons for gaming were "funding for tribal council pay, education, tribal schools and scholarships," "a way to get back some of the money that white people have stolen from us," "economic development," and "builds a strong sense of pride in tribal ownership of such a successful business."

The negative reponses about gaming on tribal lands stated that gaming was "a senseless pasttime," "an infringement on tribal sovereignty," "allowed for state control on tribal land," "ruined families who become addicted to gambling," and "was not the tribal way." Many felt that tribal governments "should not offer per capita gaming payments but rather use the money to buy back tribal land, develop long-term economic development projects, bring back the culture and language and improve educational and employment opportunities."

Business Ownership

We asked the tribal officials to rank five types of business ownership based on how each would best serve Indian people on reservation lands. The dependent variables utilized in the following analysis are individual tribal member ownership, individual non-Indian ownership, tribal ownership, individual Indian nontribal member ownership, and another tribal ownership. A Likert scale outcome on each of the dependent variables determined the type of business ownership preferred by the survey participants in regard to which type would best serve the needs of the people on their reservation. The Likert scale was 1 to 10, with 1 being "not serve the people at all" and 10 being "serving the people the best." The mean scores obtained from the likert scale are presented in table 4.11.

Similar to previous findings (Stubben 1991), data in table 4.11 show that the elected tribal officials greatly preferred tribal ownership of businesses (82 percent favorability rating) on tribal land over the other four forms of ownership. Individual tribal member ownership ranked second with a nearly 71 percent favorability rating. Ownership by an individual Indian nontribal member (44.7 percent), another tribe (44.3 percent), or an individual non-Indian (33.9 percent) are preferred at much lower levels.

These findings are significant for several reasons. First, tribal ownership is both allowed and promoted by tribal sovereign status. Second, the intergovernmental relationship between the U.S. government and sovereign Indian nations promotes federal financial support for such enterprises. Johnson (1986) illuminates the role of federal funding when he notes that "adequate federal funding is the

TABLE 4.11
Business Ownership Best Serving "Tribal" People

	0	1	2	3	4	5	6	7	8	9	10
Tribal Ownership											8.20
Individual Indian Tribal Member Ownership											7.085
Individual Indian Nontribal Member Ownership											4.47
Another Tribal Ownership											4.43
Individual Non-Indian Ownership											3.19

Note: The Likert scale was 1 to 10, with 1 being "not serve the people at all" and 10 being "serving the people the best."

key to Indian control of Indian resources." Third, expectations are affirmed regarding the importance of pride of self-determination through tribal ownership or individual tribal member ownership and, by extension, tribal control of efforts relating to development policies. The latter finding lends support to the importance of American Indian values, especially communal ownership of property, in economic development, according to Lorrie Kirst (1987). Kirst argued that the historical economic exploitation of Indians by the broader culture has left Indians with bitter feelings toward off-reservation investors. This accounts for the lower rating of individual Indian nonmember, another tribal, and especially individual non-Indian ownership of businesses and other economic enterprises on tribal land.

For Indians, tribal ownership could further guarantee that their citizens and tribal resources would not become conduits for exploitation-bent nonreservation investors. It is conceivable, however, that such ownership also increases the sense of cohesion and trust within the tribe and offers the group both a reason and the forum to discuss necessary strategies for sustaining business activities.

Concluding Statements by the Tribal Leaders on a Variety of Issues

In conclusion, the following statements are the political concerns of tribal officials and peoples, in their own words, that will need to be addressed in the twenty-first century:

Tribal leaders are selected from a group who know nothing about what they are supposed to be doing until they leave office.
For the first year every councilman is incompetent.
For the second year it's a learning process.
For the third year it's establishing a working order.
For the fourth year they're looked at as incompetent.
"End of office" (Nebraska).

Let us not be blinded by self-importance and the power that is delegated to us (Oklahoma).

The totally inadequate trust management of the federal government will probably never improve. The tribes must sophisticate their operations to compete with major businesses. We must also become more and more vocal and active in local, state and national legislative areas (Oklahoma).

WATER will be what the next world war will be fought over (Oklahoma).

Make parents responsible for their off-spring and rebuilding families and build a consensus that reservations will go no where economically, socially, and educationally without developing human resources (Nebraska).

Substance Abuse, Public Law 280 and equitable funding for small tribes (California).

You got volcanoes on the earth that you could throw the waste in and it will burn up or recycle itself (Nebraska).

If you can prove Indian descent by tribal records then the tribe should set its own blood degree. Who can justify that a three-fourths is better than a half, etc. If Blood Quantum is important then only full Bloods should get the benefits (Oklahoma).

1. Tribal language is very, very important, our tribe has only 12 speaking elders that are still with us. We need more help in preserving our culture.
2. More help in getting us off the government payrolls, with business other than gambling.
3. Government is creating a welfare system with Indian people, we want jobs, not handouts (California).

What can we do to change the situation we are currently living in? Restructure our Tribal Government!!! (California).

Government to Government relations with States.
Establishing better role models and guidance for our young People.
Learning to diversify our economic base and not rely on "Gambling" (Oklahoma).

I think that business ventures should be conducted as such, business. No political involvement. And any political or tribal council duties are to be based upon the issues, ideals, motives and not upon personal conflicts. When this does occur we defeat ourselves and most of all we defeat our duties toward the band members & tribal members. Now I say this at this time. I am a born again Christian believer and think that this would help in our priorities concerning tribal business. Whether political or business. However, if this action doesn't occur then to be alcohol and drug free. This would most definitely make the difference. No matter what tribe you belong to. It's been said that a people without vision will perish. A nation without set goals and clear vision, nor walking in wisdom will perish. That determination must be alcohol & drug free. Hopefully a godly one. At least the leaders! If the head is sick the body will be sick. Thank you the chance to express my thoughts & views. I pray they help (Oklahoma).

Bureau of Indian Affairs is *very ineffective* (Oklahoma).

Indian Gaming is a social experiment in America—It has allowed tribes to provide for themselves—opportunities that the Federal Government has not been able to accomplish for 500 years. The real question is how does (gaming) voluntarily assimilate us into American capitalistic mainstream without losing our social/cultural ethnocentric soul (South Dakota).

I don't think white man's God is perfect. He created too many people in the whole world. And they fight too much. For example George Bush & Saddim Hussein. Too wild (Alaska).

We must recover the family ties of close relationship. And we must protect the blessings of human nature, the land, the water, the air, and our religious beliefs, and finally all animals and vegetation for our future generations (Alaska).

Maybe you should solicit information on minimum qualifications for tribal council membership (Nebraska).

State & Federal Governments are continuously working to terminate the Federal Trust that Indian Tribes have. We must always be on guard to Protect Our Governmental Powers. We must be united with other Tribes as well as within our own Tribe. We must be strong and have accountability within our management systems (Oklahoma).

Age doesn't make you an adult or mature. Life and all of its adventures does that (Alaska).

How tribes feel about balancing traditional & cultural ways of running their communities with modern day knowledge of influences (social-political-economic).
How tribes feel about Tribal Religion.
How tribes feel about Tourism.
The Status of Indian Housing (Alaska).

I think your survey should have focused on my opinions for *my* tribe. I have no right to take a position on what Indians in general decide is appropriate for their communities. I do support the rights of tribes to decide for themselves (Location Unknown).

Indian Re-Organization Act—Tribes, Reservations, etc. do not have any legal authority to involve its self in matters that affect the survival of Indian people unless the Traditional Tribal Laws are adhered to and/or obeyed by that Federal or State corporation (Alaska).

Tribal Government is very complex & you are always learning. Being on the Council is a full time job & you give up alot of your time being there. Its very difficult to be on the council & work, also (California).

Learning to forget the prefix in front of Americans. Take our responsible place in our country. Too late to change the old, the younger members must learn to stand without assistance (Oklahoma).

The most important thing is to find a way to bring back the buffalo (South Dakota).

More Elderly on the Council. Tribes must make own decisions directly to Washington. Tribes develop their own court systems (Nebraska).

Letting the younger generation become involved in tribal government affairs because decisions made today will affect them tomorrow (Location Unknown).

Tribal Governments should be working nationally to ensure tribal future in these areas: economics, environment, education, housing, medical needs, culture while leading their way to an alcohol and drug free youthful future!!! (North Dakota).

Better relationship and understanding of Indian people amongst Governors, Legislatures, and the Citizens of each State. Everyone mentioned above have misconceptions of Indian people—for example Indian people receive Gov't checks every month, we're lazy savages, alcoholics and don't pay taxes (Nebraska).

Being a council member for five (5) terms I have observed that we, as Native Americans, sometimes are our own worst enemy. In-fighting by different "factions" within the council is responsible for clouding the issues on important legislation and instead of voting on the merits of the legislation, the legislation is decided by personal conflicts that some members may have with the author of the proposed legislation (South Dakota).

WE, as Native Americans have an obvious "jealousy" streak within us that prevents us from progressing as we could, and should be doing. The Federal Government in ten (10) years couldn't do to us what we do to ourselves in five (5) (Location Unknown).

One of the major obstacles to effective leadership in the Central California Area is a lack of funding to support Tribal Council members' efforts. For example, if TC positions had an allowance for stipends and travel, I believe that more tribal members would participate in the process. As it now stands, many members must work and cannot afford to donate the time required to carry out tribal operations. As a direct result of this barrier tribes are limited in the number and quality of people who serve (California).

Any leader, whatever the title or position, must have no other goals or motives than to serve their tribal members in particular and Indian people as a whole in general and not lose sight of those goals and dreams of greatness of their people (Oklahoma).

We need more of a voice in Washington, D.C. Tribes should all be Federally recognized (California).

Integration equals assimilation equals annihilation of our Indian people (South Dakota).

Are there any Indians left? I sometimes wonder because tribal officials seem to be more interested in their positions than in the people. We need to become Indians again and then our tribes will be great once more (Location Unknown).

Conclusion

American Indians demand full participation in political decisions and activities that affect them, at the tribal level and beyond, including political parties and lobbying. The involvement of the people in all decision making is evident throughout this chapter. Tribal people and their leaders support self-governance and sovereignty, along with the restoration of cultural norms and values. Ironically, with the passage of the Indian Gaming Regulatory Act by Congress in 1988, the economic resources necessary to influence political venues have become available to many tribes.

Gaming revenues have allowed Native Americans to assert an array of issues in courts and in front of other policy makers. These revenues have made tribes serious lobbying groups within national and state political systems in order to assure that legislation and regulations pertaining to them do not diminish "the integrity and rights of tribes to be governed by their own laws, exclusive of state jurisdiction" (Thompson and Dever 1998).

Native American Election Information Program

Native American leaders understand the importance of their opinions to themselves and their people, and they further understand that American politics is decided by the number of votes one receives and not their opinions. In New Mexico, Native Americans and state officials have come together to increase the number of Native American voters by removing the barriers that have prevented them from voting in the past and providing electoral information to Native Americans across the state.

Starting in 1978, the Office of the Secretary of State in New Mexico established an avenue to assist Native Americans in the electoral process. Native American interpreters were hired to interpret state election documents in various New Mexico tribal language dialects. These interpreters also informed tribal members about voter information and candidate requirements needed during an election. In 1988, the Department of Justice took legal action in New Mexico to extend greater election information to Native Americans based on the minority language assistance amendments to the Federal Voting Rights Act of 1965. As a result of these actions, the Native American Election Information Program (NAEIP) was established in the Office of the Secretary of State, within the Bureau of Elections, to assist in developing voter education projects for eleven New Mexico counties with substantial Native American populations: Bernalillo, Cibola, McKinley, Otero, Rio Arriba, Sandoval, San Juan, Santa Fe, Socorro, Taos, and Valencia. Over the years, NAEIP has served New Mexico tribes and its tribal members. The program's goals are to provide voter education and to ensure compliance with the minority language assistance amendments of the Federal Voting Rights Act of 1965. To accomplish these goals, the program is designed to communicate with Native American voters on a wide range of information: voter and candidacy requirements, electoral process, and participation. The program has representatives from both the Navajo and Pueblo who are responsible for the overall coordination of the oral assistance and voter education programs. Voter registration among Native Americans has increased, and table 4.12 presents the voter registration report for the three tribes that participated in this program.

TABLE 4.12
Voter Registration Report for
Native Americans in New Mexico as of March 23, 2001

Tribes	Democrats	Republicans	Greens	Other	DTS	Total
Apaches	1,224	244	4	41	192	1,705
Pueblos	9,310	1,157	130	429	1,674	12,700
Navajos	24,304	6,336	73	258	3,672	34,643
Total	**34,838**	**7,737**	**207**	**728**	**5,538**	**49,048**

Source: Native American Education Information Program,
NAEIP Coordinators, 325 Don Gaspar, Suite 300, Santa Fe,
NM 87503; Toll-Free: (800) 477-3632; Tel: (505) 827-3600;
Fax: (505) 827-8403.

The Native American Vote Does Count

U.S. Senator Tim Johnson (D-SD) owes his reelection in 2002 to the Native American people of his state. Senator Johnson defeated Republican congressman John Thune by a 528-vote margin. The returns from the Pine Ridge Reservation in Shannon County that erased Thune's lead graphically illustrated the importance of the Native American vote to Democrats. On the state's reservations, whose residents had largely ignored state and federal politics in the past, a concerted voter registration drive by Democrats had registered four thousand new Indian voters since July. Voter turnout reached 44.6 percent in Shannon County; 51.8 percent in Todd County, where the Rosebud Sioux Tribe is concentrated; and 56.7 percent in Dewey County, home of the Cheyenne River Sioux Tribe. Participation by Indian voters in the general election was up 20 percent or more over historic averages (Harriman 2002).

Senator Johnson serves on the Senate Indian Affairs Committee and is a strong supporter of tribal colleges and the development of Native American political leaders. He has also been involved in the struggle to protect tribal sovereignty, which is being eroded by federal legislation and the court rulings. Johnson stated that "they [tribal governments] are asking that the government-to-government relationship that is supposed to exist between the tribes be honored and that the federal government not try to impose Washington solutions that are contrary to what the Native people themselves want." He also noted as an example the effort to correct a century of mismanagement of federally administered Indian trusts in which the federal government has refused to allow the tribes to participate in seeking a solution—and as a result of which Secretary of the Interior Gale Norton was held in contempt of court by a federal judge. "Some of the greatest frustration and anger I sense in Indian Country comes from this paternalistic attitude that has so often dominated federal and state relationships with the tribes," says Johnson (Harriman 2002).

South Dakota's senior U.S. senator and fellow Democrat Tom Daschle points out that in his race in 1986 and in Johnson's first Senate bid in 1996, "It would be accurate to say we would not have won without the Indian vote." But the Indian vote was not nearly as extensively courted then. Johnson's dramatic comeback, however, signals a new era for Indians in South Dakota politics. "I believe this election proved beyond a doubt they are a powerful voting bloc in South Dakota, and they will continue to grow in power and clout as future elections go forward," daschle said (Harriman 2002).

Attorney Steve Emery, director of the Policy Institute at Sinte Gleska College on the Rosebud Reservation, feels that "the Indian vote has always been there for the Democrats but finally has been recognized in this close race. But now Johnson and the Democrats must prove to the Indian people that they can deliver the policies of those who elected them" (Harriman 2002). In 2003, Oglala Sioux political activist Russell Means announced his support of Representative Thune over Senator Daschle in the November 2004 election.

References

Bureau of Indian Affairs. 1987. *American Indians Today.* Washington, D.C.: Government Printing Office.

Conway, Margaret M. 2000. *Political Participation in the United States.* Washington, D.C.: CQ Press.

Harriman, Peter. 2002. "Johnson Pledges to Repay Indians," *Sioux Falls Argus Leader,* 1A.

Huckfeldt, Robert R., and John Sprague. 1995. *Citizens, Politics, and Social Communication: Information and Influence in an Election Campaign.* Cambridge, England, and New York: Cambridge University Press.

Johnson, Edward C. 1986. "Indian Control of Indian Resources." In *Indian Self-Rule,* edited by Kenneth R. Philp. Salt Lake City, Utah: Howe Brothers.

Julnes, T. 1994. "Economic Development as the Foundation for Self-Determination." In *American Indian Policy,* edited by Lyman Legters and Fremont Lyden. Westport, Conn.: Greenwood Press.

Kirst, Lorrie. 1987. *Journal of Planning Literature* 2 (1).

LaFromboise, T. D., and W. Rowe. 1983. "Skills Training for Bicultural Competence: Rationale and Application," *Journal of Counseling Psychology* 30: 589–595.

Nie, Norman H., Sidney Verba, and John R. Petrocik. 1979. *The Changing American Voter.* Cambridge, Mass.: Harvard University Press.

Rosenstone, Steven J. 1993. *Mobilization, Participation and Democracy in America.* New York: Macmillan.

Stubben, Jerry. 1991. "American Indian Values and Their Impact on Tribal Economic Development," *Agriculture and Human Values* 8 (3).

———. 1994. "Indian Preference: Racial Discrimination or a Political Right?" In *American Indian Policy: Self-Governance and Economic Development,* edited by Lyman H. Legters and Fremont J. Lyden. Westport, Conn.: Greenwood.

Thompson, William, and Diana R. Dever. 1998. "Indian Gaming Promotes Native American Sovereignty." In *Native American Rights,* edited by Bruno Leone. San Diego: Greenhaven Press, pp. 88–92.

Wolfinger, Raymond E., and Steven J. Rosenstone. 1980. *Who Votes?* New Haven, Conn.: Yale University Press.

5

Native American Participation in Political Officeholding

Native Americans are citizens of two separate nations, the United States and their own individual tribal nation. And they, like African Americans, have only recently been incorporated into the legal participation of the former. The 1924 Indian Citizenship Act offered Native Americans "full" citizenship and the legal right to participate (vote, run for office, and hold office) in the federal, state, and local political arenas, an offer that many Native Americans did not want or accept. So Native American participation in federal, state, and local elections has been sporadic at best (O'Brien 1989).

Tribal nations are sovereign and separate political bodies not beholden to either federal or state constitutions for their existence. Thus Native Americans can choose to participate in two separate political arenas, one of which is not open to other citizens of the United States. Tribal elections normally have a much higher turnout by tribal members than federal, state, or local elections. A Democratic county committee member in Nebraska pointed out that in the 2000 elections, over 75 percent of the on-reservation tribal members voted in tribal elections, but less than 30 percent voted in the county, state, and federal elections, even though there was a presidential contest (Anonymous source interview, 2000). Perhaps this is due to several factors: the belief that tribal politics affects them more than federal, state, or local elections; direct family ties to those running; the desire by some to protect their tribal employment; or the belief that federal, state, and local elections only affect "non-Indian" government, whereas tribal elections have a direct effect on Native American government.

The disenfranchisement from the American political system by Native Americans is based on a long history of cultural conflicts that have created an intergenerational feeling of distrust toward government in general (Deloria 1985 and 1999).

Native American Electoral Partisanship

Native Americans do engage in some partisan politics outside tribal elections, and their party identification and political orientation have been remarkably stable (McClain and Stewart 1998). The majority of Native Americans, like African Americans and Hispanics, identify themselves as and voted as Democrats. According to the tribal officials survey mentioned in the previous chapter, the ratio is about 61 percent Democrats and 10 percent Republicans (Tribal Officials Surveys, 1992 and 1996). But on many issues, such as the death penalty, limiting federal control, and abortion, Native American elected leaders are conservative. This might explain how the lone Indian congressman, Ben Nighthorse Campbell (Colorado), made the switch from the Democratic to the Republican Party with relative ease during the 104th Congress. Campbell asserts that the core Republican principles of loosening federal government control and championing the free enterprise system are in keeping with tribal philosophies. On the other hand, Navajos, over the last forty years or so, "have shifted from Republican to Democratic and, during the Reagan years, slightly back to the Republican, at least in national elections" (McClain and Stewart 1998).

Besides tribe-specific differences, evidence of generational differences has been recently shown as well. Over one thousand Indian high school and college-age students were surveyed by the Solidarity Foundation, an Indian research group. Their responses were then compared with an equivalent sample of Indians over the age of thirty-five. The preliminary results indicated that "the coming generation is more inclined and better equipped than ever to assume leadership positions in their communities." The survey found that "the

Indian youth of today are more aware, more involved, and more concerned about Native issues than ever before" (Wilkins 2002). This could be due to higher education levels or to the increase in political activism since the 1970s that has created more interest in politics in Indian country and more informed young voters. The survey's results also show that Indian youth are moving away from clear partisan affiliation, preferring to identify as independent or nonaffiliated. When asked, "With which political party do you most closely associate your own beliefs and values?" only 37 percent of those under twenty-six years of age replied that they identified as Democrat. This compared with 54 percent of those over twenty-six who identified as Democrat.

Native Americans, regardless of their views on partisanship, appear to view state, county, and local politics as more important than they did in the past, especially as more and more Native Americans seek offices at the nonfederal levels of government. In the period from 1997 to 1999, twenty-eight Native American and Alaska Natives served in eight state legislatures, balancing their membership in their tribal nation with service to the state. As McClain and Stewart (1998) show in table 5.1, only three of the twenty-eight Native American and Alaskan Native state legislators in the 1997–1999 legislative sessions were Republican.

Native Americans have also served at the federal level in the U.S. House, Senate and in the vice presidency. Charles Curtis, Kaw-Osage from Kansas, served in both the U.S. House and Senate and as vice president to Herbert Hoover from 1929 to 1933. Former president Bill Clinton acknowledged some Native American heritage, but which tribe or tribes his ancestors belonged to is not clear. Table 5.2 identifies those who have served in the House and Senate.

However, the Indian heritage of some of the Congress members listed in table 5.2 is suspect. Bibliographies identify Hiram Rhoades Revels "as chaplain of a Negro regiment and organizer of African American churches in Mississippi [who] served in the U.S. Senate from February 23, 1870 until March 3, 1871 as the first African American U.S. Senator" (Thompson 1982). Matthew Stanley Quay is identified as a longtime political boss in Pennsylvania whose "skill in organization and manipulation of patronage kept Pennsylvania thoroughly Republican in the 1800s." But there is no mention of his tribal or Indian background (Kehl 1981). But the Native American and tribal background of the rest of those listed in table 5.2 has been recognized in bibliographic writings. Will Rogers, Jr. was the son of the world-famous humorist–journalist–movie star Will Rogers.

TABLE 5.1
American Indian and Alaskan
Native State Legislators, 1972–1999

State	Body	Name	Tribe	Party	First Year in Office
Arizona	House	Jack Jackson	Navajo	Democrat	1985
		Ben Hamley	Navajo	Democrat	1972
	Senate	James Henderson	Navajo	Democrat	1982
Alaska	House	Irene Nicolal	Athabascan	Democrat	1992
		Bill Williams	Tlingit	Democrat	1980
		Albert Kookesh	Tlingit	Democrat	1996
		Beverly Masek	Athabascan	Republican	1994
		Reggie Joule	Inupiat Eskimo	Democrat	1996
		Ivan Ivan	Yupiit	Democrat	1990
	Senate	Lyman Hoffman	Yupic-Eskimo	Democrat	1994
		Al Adams	Inupait	Democrat	1980
		Georgina Lincoln	Athabascan	Democrat	1992
Montana	House	Jay Stovall	Crow	Republican	1993
		George Heavy Runner	Blackfoot	Democrat	1994
		George Pease	Crow	Democrat	1996
		Bill Whitehead	Assiniboine	Democrat	1996
New Mexico	House	Leo Watchman	Navajo	Democrat	1993
		James Madalena	Jemez Pueblo	Democrat	1985
		Lynda Lovejoy	Navajo	Republican	1996
	Senate	John Pinto	Navajo	Democrat	1989
		Leo Tsosie	Navajo	Democrat	1977
North Carolina	House	Ronnie Sutton	Lumbee	Democrat	1993
Oklahoma	Senate	Kelly Haney	Seminole Creek	Democrat	1991
South Dakota	House	Ron Volesky	Standing Rock Sioux	Democrat	1987
		Richard Hagen	Oglala Sioux	Democrat	1980
	Senate	Paul Valandra	Rosebud Sioux	Democrat	1982
North Dakota	Senate	Les FaFountain	Chippewa	Democrat	1990

Source: Paula D. McClain and Joseph Stewart, Jr. *"Can We All Get Along?" Racial and Ethnic Minorities in American Politics,* 2d. edition (Boulder, Colo.: Westview, 1998): pp. 124–125.

TABLE 5.2
American Indians Who Have Served in
the U.S. Senate and House of Representatives

Name	Tribe	State	Service Years
Senate			
Hiram R. Revels	Lumbee	Mississippi	1870–1871
Matthew Stanley Quay	Abenaki or Delaware	Pennsylvania	1887–1899, 1901–1904
Charles Curtis[a]	Kaw-Osage	Kansas	1907–1913, 1915–1929
Robert L. Owen	Cherokee	Oklahoma	1907–1925
B. Nighthorse Campbell	Northern Cheyenne	Colorado	1992–2000
House of Representatives			
Charles Curtis	Kaw-Osage	Kansas	1893–1907
Charles D. Carter	Choctow	Oklahoma	1907–1927
W. W. Hastings	Cherokee	Oklahoma	1915–1921, 1923–1935
Will Rogers, Jr.	Cherokee	California	1942–1944
William G. Stigler	Choctaw	Oklahoma	1944–1952
Benjamin Reifel	Rosebud Sioux	South Dakota	1961–1971
Nicholas Joseph Begich	Alaska Native	Alaska	1971–1972
Clem Rogers McSpadden	Cherokee	Oklahoma	1972–1975
B. Nighthorse Campbell	Northern Cheyenne	Colorado	1987–1992

[a] Charles Curtis served as Herbert Hoover's vice president for the period 1929–1933 and thus served as president of the Senate during that time.

Source: Paula D. McClain and Joseph Stewart, Jr. *"Can We All Get Along?" Racial and Ethnic Minorities in American Politics* (Boulder, Colo.: Westview, 1988).

Elected and National Native American Leaders

Benjamin Reifel: U.S. Congressman from Rosebud Also Known as Wiyaka Wanjila, "Lone Feather"

Benjamin Reifel was born on September 19, 1906, in a log cabin near Parmelee, South Dakota, on the Rosebud Reservation. He was the son of a German American father, William Reifel, and a full-blooded Lakota Sioux, Lucy Burning Breast. Ben Reifel was an enrolled member of the Rosebud Sioux Tribe; his Indian name was Lone Feather.

He attended both a Rosebud Reservation boarding school and a county school. He graduated from the eighth grade at age sixteen and spoke both the Lakota and the English languages. After working on his parents' farm for three years, he entered the School of Agriculture in Brookings, South Dakota. Upon completion of this high school program in 1928, he enrolled as a special student at South Dakota State College. He paid his own way through four years of college, with the aid of one of the first loans made available to college students. In his senior year he was elected president of the students' association. He graduated in 1932 with a bachelor of science degree in agriculture. Ben Reifel married a college classmate, Alice Janet Johnson of Erwin, South Dakota, on December 26, 1933. They had only one child, Loyce Nadine.

After graduation, Reifel was hired as boy's adviser on his reservation at Hare's School in Mission, South Dakota. In 1933 he began a long, distinguished career with the Bureau of Indian Affairs (BIA), when he was appointed "farm agent" at Oglala, on the Pine Ridge Reservation. That first appointment lasted only a year before he was promoted to field agent at the headquarters in Pierre. He was assigned to promote the new programs under the Indian Reorganization Act signed by President Roosevelt in 1934. This was a period of drought and intense hardship on the reservations, but young Ben, who ordinarily met with resistance from some members of the tribes, was extraordinarily successful in winning support for the Reorganization Act, first at Pine Ridge and later on other reservations across South Dakota. He is credited with the major responsibility for making the programs of the Bureau of Indian Affairs effective on South Dakota reservations.

World War II interrupted Reifel's career in the BIA. He had been commissioned as second lieutenant in the U.S. Army Reserve in 1931, and in March 1942 Reifel was ordered to active duty. He served in the army until July 1946, achieving distinction in France and

Germany and earning the rank of lieutenant colonel. After his discharge, Reifel continued his work with the BIA. He was appointed tribal relations officer and later served as superintendent of the Fort Berthold Reservation in North Dakota.

In 1949, Mr. Reifel felt the need to continue his education, and he was awarded a scholarship in public administration at Harvard University, where he received his master's degree in 1950. A John Hay Whitney Foundation Opportunity Fellowship enabled him to further his education. He completed his doctorate in public administration in 1952. After graduating from Harvard, Dr. Reifel returned once more to the BIA, then returned to Fort Berthold as reservation superintendent. He then served at the Pine Ridge Reservation and in 1955 was appointed area director of the Aberdeen Area Office in Aberdeen, South Dakota. Now responsible for more than a thousand employees, and for the application of federal policies and programs among the Indians of South Dakota, North Dakota, and Nebraska, he served as superintendent until his retirement.

During this period and immediately following, the distinction of Dr. Reifel's career was marked by several awards. He received the Outstanding American Indian Award in 1956 and was awarded the Annual Indian Achievement Award by the Indian Council Fire in 1960. That same year he received the Silver Antelope Award from the Boy Scouts, also the Silver Beaver, Silver Buffalo, and Gray Wolf awards in Scouting. In addition, he received the Department of the Interior's Distinguished Service Award in 1961 for an outstanding career with the Bureau of Indian Affairs.

In 1960, Dr. Reifel resigned from the bureau to run for Congress from the first district, South Dakota. He was elected by a substantial margin and served for five terms as representative from South Dakota. His political popularity was reflected in the solid support he received in every election. He was regarded as a "conservative Republican" and a thinker who prepared himself well on legislative matters, always able to give a substantial and thoughtful basis for his stand on issues. He was the first person of Sioux ancestry to serve in the Congress and the only Native American in Congress throughout the 1960s.

While a member of Congress, Dr. Reifel held several important committee assignments. In his first term he was appointed to the House Agricultural Committee and in only his second term to the House Committee on Appropriations. Thereafter, he served as ranking Republican on the House Appropriations Subcommittee on Interior Department Affairs, which oversees the Bureau of Indian Affairs.

Using these important posts, Congressman Reifel gave distinguished service on behalf of his constituents. He worked hard for farming interests in South Dakota and the Plains states in general, opposing cuts in farm support programs and pushing the Oahe irrigation project.

At the same time, he continued to work vigorously for Indian education, and his accomplishments were significant. A stern opponent of segregation, he believed that the key to the plight of the Indian people lay in educational programs enrolling Indian and non-Indian students together in modern progressive facilities. While in Congress, Dr. Reifel gave his support to the Civil Rights Act of 1966 and to the act increasing the minimum wage. Reifel was instrumental in getting the Earth Resources Observation Systems center (EROS) located in South Dakota and in keeping Ellsworth Air Force Base an active military base in the state. On a broader national level, he was instrumental in securing passage of legislation that created the National Arts Council and the National Endowment for the Humanities.

Despite his popularity and success, Congressman Reifel decided not to seek reelection in 1970. Although he had intended to retire in 1971, he remained very active. He accepted an appointment by President Nixon as chairman of the National Capital Planning Commission and served as special assistant for Indian programs to the director of the National Park Service in the Department of the Interior. He also served as interim commissioner of Indian affairs during the last two months of the Ford administration. Reifel gave many speeches at community events, speaking at Memorial Day and July 4th celebrations and several high school and university commencement exercises.

Throughout the 1960s and 1970s, Reifel was a member of several organizations. He was a member of the Masons, Rotarians, and Elks. He also served on the National Council of the Protestant Episcopal Church and the National Council of the Boy Scouts of America. He also served as national president of Arrow, Inc., an Indian service organization. In 1977, Ben became a trustee of the South Dakota Art Museum in Brookings and served terms as their board president in 1982–1983. He established the first Native American collection at the art museum in 1977, donating most of his personal collection.

Ben's first wife, Alice Johnson Reifel, died of pneumonia on February 8, 1972. Ben remarried on August 14, 1972, to Frances U. Colby of De Smet, South Dakota. Reifel died of cancer on January 2, 1990.

Sources: (*Biographical Dictionary of Indians of the Americas* 1983; *Biographical Directory of the United States Congress 1774–1989* 1989;

Champagne 1994; Fielder 1975; Paulson 1982; Paulson and Moses 1988).

In 1964, Congressman Ben Reifel recruited the author and several other youth from Niobrara, Nebraska (Santee-Sioux and Ponca reservations) to place "Goldwater for President" signs in Yankton, South Dakota. The author's interest in politics was greatly enhanced by this event and meeting Ben Reifel.

U.S. Senator Ben Nighthorse Campbell

U.S. Senator Ben Nighthorse Campbell was born in Auburn, California, on April 13, 1933. His parents were Mary Vierra, a Portuguese immigrant, and Albert Campbell, a Northern Cheyenne Indian. In 2004, Campbell remains the only American Indian serving in either the U.S. House of Representatives or Senate.

He received a bachelor's degree in physical education and fine arts from San Jose State University in 1957 and later attended Meiji University in Tokyo in 1960 as a special research student. Before entering college, Campbell served in the U.S. Air Force from 1951 to 1953. He was stationed in Korea, where he attainined the rank of airman second class. Campbell is a self-employed jewelry designer, rancher, and was at one time a trainer of champion quarter horses. He is married to the former Linda Price and the father of two grown children, Colin Campbell and Shanan Longfellow, and grandfather to Luke and Saylor Longfellow.

He was elected to the Colorado state legislature in 1982, where he served for four years. He served from 1987 to 1992 in the U.S. House of Representatives, representing Colorado's third district. He was elected to the U.S. Senate on November 3, 1992, and again on November 3, 1998. Senator Campbell is the first American Indian to serve in the Senate in more than sixty years and the first American Indian to chair the Indian Affairs Committee. He was also on four key Senate committees: Indian Affairs Committee (chair), the Appropriations Committee, the Interior, and the Veterans' Affairs Committee.

He has consistently fought to balance the federal budget by reducing spending, supporting a balanced budget amendment, and reducing the tax rate for families. He is a leader in public lands and natural resources policy and is recognized for his role in the passage of legislation to settle Indian water rights and the protection of America's natural resources.

In 1991, Campbell sponsored the legislation that changed the name of the Custer Battlefield Monument in Montana to the Little Bighorn Battlefield National Monument. He also introduced and passed legislation to establish the National Museum of the American Indian within the Smithsonian Institution and is a leader in the battle against fetal alcohol syndrome. In 1996 he secured funding through legislation to create the first ever Rocky Mountain High Intensity Drug Trafficking Area (HIDTA). In 1998 Senator Campbell sponsored legislation to recognize the victims of the Sand Creek Massacre in Colorado. In 1999 he sponsored legislation that created the Black Canyon of the Gunnison National Park in Colorado.

Senator Campbell was the 1998 recipient of the Watchdogs of the Treasury "Golden Bulldog" award for his efforts to cut federal spending, eliminate government waste, and reduce the deficit. He was voted Senator of the Year for 1997 by the National Association of Police Organizations and recognized by the National Federation of Independent Businesses for his work on behalf of Small Businesses in America. *Newsweek* magazine designated him as one of twenty "people to watch for policy and the future of the American West." Campbell also received the U.S. Capitol Police Service Award for coming to the aid of an officer struggling with a violent felon; was inducted into Council of 44 Chiefs, Northern Cheyenne Tribe, Lame Deer, Montana; is an All-American in Judo, three-time U.S. Judo champion; was captain of the U.S. Olympic Judo Team at the Tokyo Games in 1964; was a gold medalist in the Pan-American Games of 1963; coached the U.S. International Judo Team; and has received more than two hundred first-place and best-of-show awards for jewelry design.

In February 2004, Senator Campbell announced that he would not seek a third term in the Senate. His decision to step down was influenced by health concerns.

Sources: www.senate.gov/~campbell.

Ada E. Deer: Tribal Leader and Assistant Secretary of the Interior

Ada Deer was born on the Menominee Reservation in northern Wisconsin in 1935 and was the first member of her tribe to graduate from the University of Wisconsin in Madison and the first American Indian to receive a master's degree from the School of Social Work at Columbia University in New York. In the early 1970s, she returned to the reservation to help her tribe overturn its termination as a federally recognized tribe. She built coalitions, lobbied members of the House and the Senate, and rallied supporters around the country. On December 22, 1973, President Nixon signed the Menominee Restoration Act, the first time Congress reversed itself in a specific matter of Indian policy. She then became tribal chair.

Ms. Deer soon became a lecturer at the University of Wisconsin in Madison and continued her advocacy work by serving on many national boards of directors and running for political office. She served on such boards as the Native American Rights Fund, Independent Sector, Council on Foundations, the President's Commission on White House Fellowships, Common Cause, and Girl Scouts U.S.A. She ran unsuccessfully for secretary of state and for the U.S. House of Representatives from the second district. She was a delegate to the Democratic convention in 1984 and worked tirelessly in many campaigns.

Ada E. Deer was the first female assistant secretary for Indian affairs in the history of the Department of the Interior. President Clinton announced his intention to nominate Ms. Deer on May 11, 1993. She was confirmed by the U.S. Senate on July 16, 1993.

When Ada Deer testified before the Senate Committee on Indian Affairs on July 15, 1993, she said, "Personally, you should know that forty years ago, my tribe, the Menominee, was terminated; twenty years ago we were restored; and today I come before you as a true survivor of Indian policy." Her vision of the Bureau of Indian Affairs was to create a progressive federal-tribal partnership, a partnership to fulfill long-held promises and to address long-smoldering injustices. She stated that the heart of Indian policy must be strong, effective tribal sovereignty. The role of the federal government should be to support and to implement tribally inspired solutions to tribally defined problems without the interference of the entrenched BIA bureaucracy (including herself) or other higher-ranking federal officials.

There were many achievements during Ada Deer's tenure as assistant secretary, including the recognition of over 220 Alaska Native villages, the increasing number of self-governance tribes and tribes who contract for programs previously administered by the federal government, and the reorganization of the bureau.

Deer was also active in many of the initiatives undertaken by the Clinton administration. She was a member of the President's Inter-Agency Council on Women, which is charged with the implementation of the Platform for Action agreed upon at the UN's Fourth

Conference on Women. She has testified before the UN Human Rights Committee and has led the domestic activities in conjunction with the Decade of the World's Indigenous Peoples, working closely with the State Department.

Deer credits her non-Indian mother with instilling within her the drive to work for her people (Deer 2001).

Wilma Mankiller: Former Principal Chief of the Cherokee Nation

Wilma Mankiller, former principal chief of the Cherokee Nation of Oklahoma, lives on the land that was allotted to her paternal grand-father, John Mankiller, just after Oklahoma became a state in 1907. Surrounded by the Cherokee Hills and the Cookson Hills, she lives in an area rich in Cherokee history, where people's worth is not deter-mined by the size of their bank account or stock portfolio. Her fam-ily name, Mankiller, appears to be an old military title that was given to the person in charge of protecting the village. As the leader of the Cherokee people she represented the second-largest tribe in the United States, the Dine (Navajo) Tribe. Mankiller was the first female in modern history to lead a major Native American tribe. With an enrolled population of over 140,000, an annual budget of more than $75 million, and more than 1,200 employees spread over 7,000 square miles, her task equaled that of a chief executive officer of a major corporation (Mankiller 1993).

Initially, Wilma's candidacy for principal chief was opposed by those not wishing to be led by a woman. Her tires were slashed and her life was threatened during her campaign. But now she has won the respect of the Cherokee Nation and made an impact on the cul-ture as she focused on her mission—to bring self-sufficiency to her people.

In 1975 Mankiller had been asked by Ross Swimmer, then presi-dent of a small bank, who assumed leadership of the Cherokee Na-tion in 1975, to run as his deputy chief. They won. In 1985, Swim-mer resigned as chief to head the Bureau of Indian Affairs, and Cherokee law mandated that the deputy chief assume the duties of the former chief. In the historic tribal elections of 1987, Mankiller won the post outright (by 56 percent of the vote) and brought un-precedented attention to the tribe as a result. "Prior to my election," says Mankiller, "young Cherokee girls would never have thought that they might grow up and become chief." The effect of her election was remarkable. "We are a revitalized tribe," said Mankiller. "After every major upheaval, we have been able to gather together as a people and rebuild a community and a government. Individually and collectively, Cherokee people possess an extraordinary ability to face down adversity and continue moving forward. We are able to do that because our culture, though certainly diminished, has sustained us since time immemorial. This Cherokee culture is a well-kept secret."

Mankiller attibutes her understanding of her people's history partially to her own family's forced removal to California when she was a young girl, part of the government's Indian relocation policy. Her concern for Native American issues was ignited in 1969 when a group of university students occupied Alcatraz Island in order to attract attention to the issues affecting their tribes. Shortly afterward, she began working in preschool and adult education programs in the Pit River Tribe of California.

In 1974, she divorced her husband after eleven years of marriage when the rift over her role continued to widen. She moved back to her ancestral lands outside of Tahlequah and immediately began helping her people by procuring grants enabling them to launch critical rural programs. In 1979 she enrolled in the nearby University of Arkansas. Upon returning home from class one night she was almost killed in a head-on collision in which one of her best friends, who had been driving the other car, was killed. After barely avoiding the amputation of her right leg, she endured another seventeen operations. Mankiller says that it was during that long process that she really began reevaluating her life, and it proved to be a time of deep spiritual awakening.

Then in 1980, just a year after the accident, she was diagnosed with myasthenia gravis, a chronic neuromuscular disease that causes varying degrees of weakness in the voluntary muscles of the body. It was the realization of how precious life is, she maintains, that spurred her to begin projects for her people, such as the Bell project, where members of the community revitalized a whole community themselves. It was the success of the Bell project that thrust Mankiller into national recognition as an expert in community development.

Her election to deputy chief did not come until two years later. In 1986, Wilma married longtime friend and former director of tribal development, Charlie Soap. Mankiller's love of family and community became a source of strength when again a life-threatening illness struck. Recurring kidney problems forced Mankiller to have a kidney transplant, and her brother Don Mankiller served as the donor. During her convalescence, she had many long talks with her family, and it was decided that she would run again for chief in order to complete the many community projects she had begun (Mankiller 1993; http://www.powersource.com/gallery/people/wilma.html).

In *A Chief and Her People* (1993), Mankiller tells her family's story of leaving Oklahoma for California in 1956 as part of the Bureau of Indian Affairs Relocation Program set up to urbanize poor, rural Native Americans. She details her social and political involvement in American Indian and women's issues and her return to her northeast Oklahoma roots in 1974. Since then, Mankiller worked on many community development programs designed to provide jobs and/or homes to Native American people. In 1991, she was reelected as chief. In 1994, Oklahoma's Institute of Indian Heritage honored Chief Wilma Mankiller during their annual Spirit of the People fall festival. She left her position as chief in 1995 because of poor health. During her tenure as chief, she was an effective spokesperson in Washington, worked for health care programs, and fought for the rights of children. Mankiller holds an honorary doctorate in humane letters from Yale University (http://www.uic.edu/depts/owa/history_month_97/mankiller.html).

She has shown in her typically exuberant way that not only can Native Americans learn a lot from the whites, but that whites can learn from native people. Understanding the interconnectedness of all things, many whites are beginning to understand the value of native wisdom, culture, and spirituality. Spirituality, then, is the key to the public and private life of Wilma Mankiller, who has become known not only for her community leadership but also for her spiritual presence (http://www.powersource.com/gallery/people/wilma.html).

Native American Lobbying

Tribes have been lobbying non-Indian governments at all levels since the British, mainly to protect their sovereign status as separate nations. During the mid- to late 1800s, hundreds of Native American tribal leaders made the long trip to Washington, D.C., to lobby on their peoples' behalf, especially in negotiating treaties and then seeking out the rights and resources promised to them under such treaties. As the treaty era ended, Native American leaders continued to lobby presidents and other federal officials. After the Indian Reorganization Act of 1924, tribes continued to lobby for sovereign rights, but like many other Americans, they also lobbied for civil rights and resources. In the thirties they lobbied for economic and public works projects. In the fifties, many tribes were forced to defend their own existence by lobbying against the termination policies of the federal government. Some tried to prevent the taking of their already diminished land base for massive public works projects, such as the Pick-Sloan Project, which flooded millions of acres of productive tribal land.

During the 1950s organizations like the National Congress of American Indians and certain tribal leaders recognized that influencing non-Indian governments took more than votes—it took money. The era of the Indian lobbyist began in earnest. Since then it has grown geometrically, largely due to gambling revenues (Deloria 1999).

Since the 1970s Native Americans have become more active in influencing non-Indian governments through lobbyists and campaign contributions. Due to the fact that Native Americans make up less than 2 percent of the total population in the United States, their voting influence is limited. But there remains a romantic tie to the past that has promoted Native American issues among non-Indian voters and elected officials. As a Nebraska state legislator commented to the author regarding a proposed state law authorizing gambling on tribal trust land, "It is hard to vote against a law that benefits Indians, due to past atrocities that we have brought upon them." On the other side, another legislator stated, "Giving Indians the sole right to own casinos in our state is discrimination against all other citizens in the state. I will not support such discrimination."

Today, lobbying and campaign funds are big business in Indian country. The Pequot, who operate the Foxwoods Casino in Ledyard, Connecticut, gave more in political contributions from 1988 to 1996 than any other gaming donor, a total of $974,625. This exceeded the $569,250 donated by the Interface Group—Sands Hotel; the $554,000 of the Mirage Resorts; and the $470,905 given by Bally Entertainment (*New York Times* 1997).

In 1998, eighty-eight tribes in California, representing 96 percent of the state's reservation-based Indians, fought for and secured (with a lot of nontribal support) passage of an initiative, Proposition 5, that requires that the tribes be granted a gaming compact, upon request, to continue their existing gaming activities on their reservation lands. This was the most expensive state initiative ever, with the pro– and anti–Proposition 5 sides having raised nearly $86 million combined. The tribes raised more than two-thirds of that amount. Proposition 5 was declared invalid by the Supreme Court of California in August 1999, but the tribes and their allies lobbied the public, the governor, and the state legislature, and an amendment to the California constitution was approved in March 2000 that allows tribes to operate Nevada-style casinos if a compact is signed with the governor and ratified by the state legislature (Wilkins 2002).

The California tribes had previously been deeply involved in state gubernatorial campaigns, when in 1994 they contributed more than $800,000 to unsuccessful campaigns to unseat Governor Pete Wilson and Attorney General Dan Lungren. The California Indian Nation Political Action Committee contributed almost $1.1 million to California candidates and political parties between 1994 and 1996 (Garrity 1998).

On the national level but also centered around Indian gaming and campaign finances was Attorney General Janet Reno's probe of Secretary of the Interior Bruce Babbitt's alleged involvement in the 1995 rejection of an application by Ojibwe Indians to build a casino off their reservation at a failing dog track in Wisconsin. The fiercest opposition to this project came from other tribes in Minnesota whose established casinos would face competition from the new one. Those tribes hired legal counsel with strong connections to the Democratic Party and White House. Their lawyers got the ear of the president and close aides, and the Wisconsin tribe's gaming application was rejected. Soon afterward, the opposing tribes made a nearly $300,000 donation to the reelection effort for Clinton-Gore (Lardner and Suro 1998). Babbitt was eventually cleared of all charges.

Clearly, Indian gaming has increased the lobbying efforts of some tribes in state and federal politics on an unprecedented scale. Such lobbying efforts will need to continue and perhaps increase as tribal leaders protect sovereign rights and economic prosperity. Since the budgets of the Bureau of Indian Affairs, Indian Health Service, and other federal agencies have been reduced, tribes are likely to experience increased dependence on gaming revenues as a major source of their financial security (Layng 1998). Some in Congress want to impose federal taxes on Indian gaming revenues and want to deny money to tribes if their income is above a certain level. These and other measures have arisen, tribes say, "because of a perception that Indian reservations are prospering with casino gambling, disregarding the fact that most of them remain among the poorest places in the nation" (Egan 1997). Tension between some states and tribal governments will most likely increase, as tribes strive for continued increases in sovereign powers in such areas as taxation, law enforcement, and burial rights (Wilkins 2002).

Some tribal leaders from indigenous nations, like the Iroquois Confederacy, consider the act of voting in a non-Indian election of any kind to be almost an act of treason, a betrayal of one's own indigenous nationality. And yet, many tribal leaders do not feel that their tribal sovereignty is negatively affected by active participation in local, state, and federal elections. Many of these tribes argue that from their perspective, voting may be the best and possibly only realistic way to protect their remaining land rights, economic rights to conduct gaming operations, and cultural rights, such as bilingual education (Wilkins, 2002).

The issue of Native American political participation in non-Indian politics is of tremendous interest to those intent on invigorating tribal sovereignty, not solely because greater participation necessarily produces better policy decisions but because of the educational and social value of participation. It enhances the meaning of their lives as well as the value of their relationships to one another and their respective indigenous communities. The overriding goal of the African American civil rights movement was to achieve individual equality and individual rights as promised within the philosophy of liberalism. Native American leaders, on the other hand, have historically demanded recognition of their tribal—that is, national—rights as guaranteed by treaties, executive agreements, and statutes (Wilkins 2002).

Why Do Native Americans Participate in Politics?

Political scientists have conducted few studies of Native America politics, particularly in regard to officeholding and voting patterns. Part of the reason for the reluctance of political scientists to examine indigenous political participation rests in that tribal nations generally do not consider themselves to be part of the pluralistic mosaic that predominates in political science literature. Vine Deloria, Jr. explains that the primary difference between African Americans and Indians is that African Americans are pursuing equality of acceptance and equal opportunity in American society while Indians pursue justice. By "justice," Deloria means Indians' right to maintain their sovereign integrity and to rest assured that their treaty and trust rights will be protected. These goals are evidenced in the tribes' focus on tribal sovereignty and maintaining and enhancing their separate land base—goals dissimilar to those of America's other racial and ethnic minority groups (Deloria 1985 and 1999; Wilkins 2002).

In the mid-1990s, my colleague and fellow political scientist Diane Duffy conducted research on the issue of Native American views of patriotism. She interviewed tribal leaders in Nebraska, Iowa, and Wisconsin and based on these interview data described the following categories of Native American patriotism:

1. Indigenous (traditional) patriotism: the tribal nation is the sole allegiance for Native Americans. This allegiance is expressed in positive Indian, not antiwhite, language.
2. Measured-separatism patriotism: primary allegiance is to the tribe, but also there is some (measured) support for the United States and willingness to "serve" as "allies" with the United States in the armed services in battles with foreign nations.
3. Anti-American patriotism: against the U.S. (rather than for their tribe). Adherents would under no circumstances "serve" in the U.S. military because they would consider it treasonous.
4. Environmental patriotism: similar to the first category, but allegiance is explicitly tied to all of the creation and not simply human society.
5. Assimilative patriotism: the United States is perceived as the superior power and the tribal nation is subordinate.
6. Cooptive or colonized patriotism: adherents refuse to conceive of a separate tribal political consciousness that has merit and is deserving of allegiance.
7. Apatriotic: believe that patriotism is an irrelevant concept for Native Americans (Duffy 1997).

As Duffy's categories show, the subject of patriotism is far more complicated than many might imagine. A number of Native Americans support tribal sovereignty, but they also believe that in order to protect their sovereign rights they must participate in the American electoral process. And policies such as the allotment of tribal lands; forced boarding school policies; destruction of tribal traditional governing values, structures, and institutions; U.S. citizenship; federal policies of Christianization; relocation; termination; federal housing; public health; and even gambling have promoted assimilation into American culture and politics.

In other words, while most racial/ethnic groups and women faced a forced exclusion from the American social contract, Indians, since the

1880s, faced a forced inclusion into American society. But it was an inconsistent and ambivalent inclusion at best. Most of the actions by federal policy makers from the 1800s to the 1970s were aimed at "Americanizing" and "civilizing" Indians. However, there were occasionally opposite actions by lawmakers and justices that insisted that Indians were "alien peoples" or were not quite up to or deserving of complete American citizenship (Deloria 1985 and 1999; Wilkins 2002).

McCool (1985) found that states have devised a number of strategies to keep Indians from holding office and voting. He grouped them in three categories: constitutional ambiguity, political and economic factors, and cultural and racial discrimination. Evidence of constitutional ambiguity is found in several states—Idaho, New Mexico, and Washington—that denied Indians the vote because of a specific provision in their constitutions regarding the disenfranchisement of "Indians not taxed." Such Indians, according to the Idaho constitution, could not vote or serve as jurors if they were considered to be nontaxable, because they had not "severed their tribal relations and adopted the habits of civilization" (Margold 1937).

Political scientist Glenn Phelps finds an ongoing constitutional tension in American electoral politics regarding Indians as citizens/voters that is unique to the tribal-federal relationship. The tension is this: "Claims of tribal sovereignty and immunity from state and local processes cannot, in principle, coexist with the responsibilities incumbent upon citizenship and suffrage in state and local governments." Put another way: "Indians living within Indian Country are immune from state and local taxes and are largely immune from state and local laws. Yet they claim the right to vote for representatives who can levy taxes and make rules and regulations for non-Indians—taxes and rules from which reservation Indians themselves are immune" (Phelps 1991). This status suits tribal citizens fine and is clearly rooted in the treaty and trust relationship. But some non-Indians take offense at this political arrangement, arguing that it is a violation of the rule of law. Nevertheless, it is a tension that remains part of both the American and Native American landscape.

Conclusion

The subject matter of Indian political participation, or lack thereof, in non-Indian political affairs is made up of an extremely complicated set of historical, sociological, and political/legal processes. As a result of Indian gaming revenues, it promises to be an exceedingly volatile and unpredictable area, because tribes continue to exist as distinctive sovereigns with, in many cases, fiercely loyal citizens, yet an increasing number of Native Americans and tribal governments are becoming more actively engaged in local, state, and federal political matters.

How these seemingly contradictory forces will affect the future of intergovernmental relations is impossible to predict. What will become of tribal sovereignty if tribal participatory rates in non-Indian politics continues to escalate? Will federal forces set about to revive the terminationist sentiment of the 1950s and 1960s because of a perception that indigenous participation in non-Indian politics means that Indians have become so assimilated that their own governing structures and institutions are no longer necessary? Or will they strive to make tribes more self-sufficient through self-governance policies of the 1980s and 1990s? How will tribes respond? It is a state of affairs that promises to remain dynamic (Wilkins 2002), especially with the shift to a Republican ex-governor living in the White House, the home of the Great White Father.

References

Biographical Dictionary of Indians of the Americas. 1983. Newport Beach, Calif.: American Indian Publishers, pp. 403–406.

Biographical Directory of the United States Congress 1774–1989. Washington D.C.: Government Printing Office, 1989, p. 1705.

Brownell, Charles De Wolf. 1865. *The Indian Races of North and South America.* Hartford, Conn.: Hurlbut, Scranton.

Champagne, Duane, ed. 1994. *Native North American Almanac.* Detroit: Gale Research, pp. 1142–1143.

Deer, Ada. 2001. "Indigenous America—Poised at the Threshold of the Next Seven Generations." Speech given at the Iowa State University American Indian Symposium, April 6.

Deloria, Vine, Jr. 1999. *Spirit and Reason.* Golden, Colo.: Fulcrum.

Deloria, Vine, Jr., ed. 1985. *American Indian Policy in the Twentieth Century.* Norman: University of Oklahoma Press.

Duffy, Diane. 1997. "An Attitudinal Study of Native American Patriotism." Unpublished paper presented at the International Society for Political Psychology Scientific Services, Krakov, Poland, July.

Egan, Timothy. 1997. "Senate Measures Would Deal Blow to Indian Rights," *New York Times,* August 27, A1.

Fielder, Mildred. 1975. *Sioux Indian Leaders.* Seattle: Superior, pp. 127–148, 155.

Garrity, Michael. 1998. "California Gaming: Las Vegas Lines Up against Tribes on November Initiative," *Native Americas* 15 (3).

Grinde, Donald A., Jr., and Bruce E. Johansen. 1991. *Exemplar of Liberty: Native America and the Evolution of Democracy.* Los Angeles: American Indian Studies, UCLA Press.

Kehl, James. 1981. "Boss Rule in the Gilded Age: Matt Quay of Pennsylvania." In *Dictionary of American Biography.* Pittsburgh: University of Pittsburgh Press.

Lardner, George, Jr., and Roberto Suro. 1998. "Investigation of Casino Decision Would Reach beyond Babbit Officials Say," *Washington Post,* February 11, A12.

Layng, Anthony. 1998. "Indian Gaming: An Overview." In *Native American Rights.* San Diego: Greenwood Press.

Mankiller, Wilma. 1993. *A Chief and Her People.* New York: St. Martin's Press.

Margold, Nathan R. 1937. "Suffrage-Discrimination against Indians." In *Opinions of the Solicitors of the Department of Interior, Relating to Indian Affairs: 1917–1974.* Vol. 1.

Matthisessen, Peter. 1991. *In the Spirit of Crazy Horse.* New York: Viking Penguin.

McClain, Paula D., and Joseph Stewart, Jr. 1998. *Can We All Get Along? Racial and Ethnic Minorities in American Politics.* Boulder, Colo.: Westview.

McCool, Daniel. 1985. "Indian Voting." In *American Indian Policy in the Twentieth Century,* edited by Vine Deloria, Jr. Norman: University of Oklahoma Press.

New York Times. 1997. "Pequot Tribe Tops List of Political Donors," June 29, 26N.

O'Brien, Sharon. 1989. *American Indian Tribal Governments.* Norman: University of Oklahoma Press.

Painter, John S. 1989. "Transitional Sioux Leader: Benjamin Reifel." In *South Dakota Leaders,* edited by Herbert T. Hoover and Larry J. Zimmerman. Vermillion: University of South Dakota Press, pp. 331–354.

Parker, Arthur C. 1916. "The Constitution of the Five Nations," reprinted from the New York State Museum Bulletin, Albany, April 1. In *The Iroquois and the Founding of the American Nation,* by Donald A. Grinde, Jr. Washington, D.C.: Indian Historian Press, 1977.

Paulson, T. Emogene. 1982. *Sioux Collections.* Vermillion: University of South Dakota Press, pp. 131–132.

Paulson, T. Emogene, and Lloyd R. Moses. 1988. *Who's Who among the Sioux.* Vermillion: Institute of Indian Studies, University of South Dakota Press, pp. 196–197.

Phelps, Glenn A. 1991. "Mr. Gerry Goes to Arizona: Electoral Geography and Voting Rights," *American Indian Culture and Research Journal* 15 (2).

Thompson, Julius. 1982. *Hiram R. Revels, 1827–1901: A Biography.* New York: Arno Press.

Wilkins, David. 2002. *Nations within States: American Indian Politics and the American Political System.* Boston: Rowman and Littlefield.

Documents

The Constitution of the Iroquois Nations:
The Great Binding Law, Gayanashagowa

Among the political and spiritual leaders of the nations that formed the Iroquois Confederacy in 1390 C.E. was a holy man whose name, the Grand Chiefs decided, can no longer be written by human hands or even whispered by human lips. Today, he is remembered as the Great Peacemaker and the founder of the Iroquois Great Law of Peace, which predates the Magna Carta and is viewed as the first democratic constitution in both America and the world.

1. I am Dekanawidah and with the Five Nations' Confederate Lords I plant the Tree of Great Peace. I plant it in your territory, Adodarhoh, and the Onondaga Nation, in the territory of you who are Firekeepers. I name the tree the Tree of the Great Long Leaves. Under the shade of this Tree of the Great Peace we spread the soft white feathery down of the globe thistle as seats for you, Adodarhoh, and your cousin Lords. We place you upon those seats, spread soft with the feathery down of the globe thistle, there beneath the shade of the spreading branches of the Tree of Peace. There shall you sit and watch the Council Fire of the Confederacy of the Five Nations, and all the affairs of the Five Nations shall be transacted at this place before you, Adodarhoh, and your cousin Lords, by the Confederate Lords of the Five Nations.

2. Roots have spread out from the Tree of the Great Peace, one to the north, one to the east, one to the south and one to the west. The

name of these roots is The Great White Roots and their nature is Peace and Strength. If any man or any nation outside the Five Nations shall obey the laws of the Great Peace and make known their disposition to the Lords of the Confederacy, they may trace the Roots to the Tree and if their minds are clean and they are obedient and promise to obey the wishes of the Confederate Council, they shall be welcomed to take shelter beneath the Tree of the Long Leaves. We place at the top of the Tree of the Long Leaves an Eagle who is able to see afar. If he sees in the distance any evil approaching or any danger threatening he will at once warn the people of the Confederacy.

3. To you Adodarhoh, the Onondaga cousin Lords, I and the other Confederate Lords have entrusted the caretaking and the watching of the Five Nations Council Fire. When there is any business to be transacted and the Confederate Council is not in session, a messenger shall be dispatched either to Adodarhoh, Hononwirehtonh or Skanawatih, Fire Keepers, or to their War Chiefs with a full statement of the case desired to be considered. Then shall Adodarhoh call his cousin (associate) Lords together and consider whether or not the case is of sufficient importance to demand the attention of the Confederate Council. If so, Adodarhoh shall dispatch messengers to summon all the Confederate Lords to assemble beneath the Tree of the Long Leaves. When the Lords are assembled the Council Fire shall be kindled, but not with chestnut wood, and Adodarhoh shall formally open the Council. [Ed. note: chestnut wood throws out sparks in burning, thereby creating a disturbance in the council.] Then shall Adodarhoh and his cousin Lords, the Fire Keepers, announce the subject for discussion. The Smoke of the Confederate Council Fire shall ever ascend and pierce the sky so that other nations who may be allies may see the Council Fire of the Great Peace. Adodarhoh and his cousin Lords are entrusted with the Keeping of the Council Fire.

4. You, Adodarhoh, and your thirteen cousin Lords, shall faithfully keep the space about the Council Fire clean and you shall allow neither dust nor dirt to accumulate. I lay a Long Wing before you as a broom. As a weapon against a crawling creature I lay a staff with you so that you may thrust it away from the Council Fire. If you fail to cast it out then call the rest of the United Lords to your aid.

5. The Council of the Mohawk shall be divided into three parties as follows: Tekarihoken, Ayonhwhathah and Shadekariwade are the first party; Sharenhowaneh, Deyoenhegwenh and Oghrenghrehgowah are the second party, and Dehennakrineh, Aghstawenserenthah and Shoskoharowaneh are the third party. The third party is to listen only

to the discussion of the first and second parties and if an error is made or the proceeding is irregular they are to call attention to it, and when the case is right and properly decided by the two parties they shall confirm the decision of the two parties and refer the case to the Seneca Lords for their decision. When the Seneca Lords have decided in accord with the Mohawk Lords, the case or question shall be referred to the Cayuga and Oneida Lords on the opposite side of the house.

6. I, Dekanawidah, appoint the Mohawk Lords the heads and the leaders of the Five Nations Confederacy. The Mohawk Lords are the foundation of the Great Peace and it shall, therefore, be against the Great Binding Law to pass measures in the Confederate Council after the Mohawk Lords have protested against them. No council of the Confederate Lords shall be legal unless all the Mohawk Lords are present.

7. Whenever the Confederate Lords shall assemble for the purpose of holding a council, the Onondaga Lords shall open it by expressing their gratitude to their cousin Lords and greeting them, and they shall make an address and offer thanks to the earth where men dwell, to the streams of water, the pools, the springs and the lakes, to the maize and the fruits, to the medicinal herbs and trees, to the forest trees for their usefulness, to the animals that serve as food and give their pelts for clothing, to the great winds and the lesser winds, to the Thunderers, to the Sun, the mighty warrior, to the moon, to the messengers of the Creator who reveal his wishes and to the Great Creator who dwells in the heavens above, who gives all the things useful to men, and who is the source and the ruler of health and life. Then shall the Onondaga Lords declare the council open. The council shall not sit after darkness has set in.

8. The Firekeepers shall formally open and close all councils of the Confederate Lords, and they shall pass upon all matters deliberated upon by the two sides and render their decision. Every Onondaga Lord (or his deputy) must be present at every Confederate Council and must agree with the majority without unwarrantable dissent, so that a unanimous decision may be rendered. If Adodarhoh or any of his cousin Lords are absent from a Confederate Council, any other Firekeeper may open and close the Council, but the Firekeepers present may not give any decisions, unless the matter is of small importance.

9. All the business of the Five Nations Confederate Council shall be conducted by the two combined bodies of Confederate Lords. First the question shall be passed upon by the Mohawk and Seneca Lords, then it shall be discussed and passed by the Oneida and

Cayuga Lords. Their decisions shall then be referred to the Onondaga Lords (Fire Keepers) for final judgement. The same process shall obtain when a question is brought before the council by an individual or a War Chief.

10. In all cases the procedure must be as follows: when the Mohawk and Seneca Lords have unanimously agreed upon a question, they shall report their decision to the Cayuga and Oneida Lords who shall deliberate upon the question and report a unanimous decision to the Mohawk Lords. The Mohawk Lords will then report the standing of the case to the Firekeepers, who shall render a decision as they see fit in case of a disagreement by the two bodies, or confirm the decisions of the two bodies if they are identical. The Fire Keepers shall then report their decision to the Mohawk Lords who shall announce it to the open council.

11. If through any misunderstanding or obstinacy on the part of the Fire Keepers, they render a decision at variance with that of the Two Sides, the Two Sides shall reconsider the matter and if their decisions are jointly the same as before they shall report to the Fire Keepers who are then compelled to confirm their joint decision.

12. When a case comes before the Onondaga Lords (Fire Keepers) for discussion and decision, Adodarhoh shall introduce the matter to his comrade Lords who shall then discuss it in their two bodies. Every Onondaga Lord except Hononwiretonh shall deliberate and he shall listen only. When a unanimous decision shall have been reached by the two bodies of Fire Keepers, Adodarhoh shall notify Hononwiretonh of the fact when he shall confirm it. He shall refuse to confirm a decision if it is not unanimously agreed upon by both sides of the Fire Keepers.

13. No Lord shall ask a question of the body of Confederate Lords when they are discussing a case, question or proposition. He may only deliberate in a low tone with the separate body of which he is a member.

14. When the Council of the Five Nation Lords shall convene they shall appoint a speaker for the day. He shall be a Lord of either the Mohawk, Onondaga or Seneca Nation. The next day the Council shall appoint another speaker, but the first speaker may be reappointed if there is no objection, but a speaker's term shall not be regarded more than for the day.

15. No individual or foreign nation interested in a case, question or proposition shall have any voice in the Confederate Council except to answer a question put to him or them by the speaker for the Lords.

16. If the conditions which shall arise at any future time call for an addition to or change of this law, the case shall be carefully considered and if a new beam seems necessary or beneficial, the proposed change shall be voted upon and if adopted it shall be called, "Added to the Rafters."

Rights, Duties and Qualifications of Lords

17. A bunch of a certain number of shell (wampum) strings each two spans in length shall be given to each of the female families in which the Lordship titles are vested. The right of bestowing the title shall be hereditary in the family of the females legally possessing the bunch of shell strings and the strings shall be the token that the females of the family have the proprietary right to the Lordship title for all time to come, subject to certain restrictions hereinafter mentioned.

18. If any Confederate Lord neglects or refuses to attend the Confederate Council, the other Lords of the Nation of which he is a member shall require their War Chief to request the female sponsors of the Lord so guilty of defection to demand his attendance of the Council. If he refuses, the women holding the title shall immediately select another candidate for the title. No Lord shall be asked more than once to attend the Confederate Council.

19. If at any time it shall be manifest that a Confederate Lord has not in mind the welfare of the people or disobeys the rules of this Great Law, the men or women of the Confederacy, or both jointly, shall come to the Council and upbraid the erring Lord through his War Chief. If the complaint of the people through the War Chief is not heeded the first time it shall be uttered again and then if no attention is given a third complaint and warning shall be given. If the Lord is contumacious the matter shall go to the council of War Chiefs. The War Chiefs shall then divest the erring Lord of his title by order of the women in whom the titleship is vested. When the Lord is deposed the women shall notify the Confederate Lords through their War Chief, and the Confederate Lords shall sanction the act. The women will then select another of their sons as a candidate and the Lords shall elect him. Then shall the chosen one be installed by the Installation Ceremony. When a Lord is to be deposed, his War Chief shall address him as follows: "So you, _____, disregard and set at naught the warnings of your women relatives. So you fling the warnings over your shoulder to cast them behind you. Behold the brightness of the Sun and in the brightness of the Sun's light I depose you of your title and remove the sacred emblem of

your Lordship title. I remove from your brow the deer's antlers, which was the emblem of your position and token of your nobility. I now depose you and return the antlers to the women whose heritage they are." The War Chief shall now address the women of the deposed Lord and say: "Mothers, as I have now deposed your Lord, I now return to you the emblem and the title of Lordship, therefore repossess them." Again addressing himself to the deposed Lord he shall say: "As I have now deposed and discharged you so you are now no longer Lord. You shall now go your way alone, the rest of the people of the Confederacy will not go with you, for we know not the kind of mind that possesses you. As the Creator has nothing to do with wrong so he will not come to rescue you from the precipice of destruction in which you have cast yourself. You shall never be restored to the position which you once occupied." Then shall the War Chief address himself to the Lords of the Nation to which the deposed Lord belongs and say: "Know you, my Lords, that I have taken the deer's antlers from the brow of _____, the emblem of his position and token of his greatness." The Lords of the Confederacy shall then have no other alternative than to sanction the discharge of the offending Lord.

20. If a Lord of the Confederacy of the Five Nations should commit murder the other Lords of the Nation shall assemble at the place where the corpse lies and prepare to depose the criminal Lord. If it is impossible to meet at the scene of the crime the Lords shall discuss the matter at the next Council of their Nation and request their War Chief to depose the Lord guilty of crime, to "bury" his women relatives and to transfer the Lordship title to a sister family. The War Chief shall address the Lord guilty of murder and say: "So you, _____ (giving his name) did kill _____ (naming the slain man), with your own hands! You have committed a grave sin in the eyes of the Creator. Behold the bright light of the Sun, and in the brightness of the Sun's light I depose you of your title and remove the horns, the sacred emblems of your Lordship title. I remove from your brow the deer's antlers, which was the emblem of your position and token of your nobility. I now depose you and expel you and you shall depart at once from the territory of the Five Nations Confederacy and nevermore return again. We, the Five Nations Confederacy, moreover, bury your women relatives because the ancient Lordship title was never intended to have any union with bloodshed. Henceforth it shall not be their heritage. By the evil deed that you have done they have forfeited it forever." The War Chief shall then hand the title to a sister family and he shall address it and say: "Our moth-

ers, _____, listen attentively while I address you on a solemn and important subject. I hereby transfer to you an ancient Lordship title for a great calamity has befallen it in the hands of the family of a former Lord. We trust that you, our mothers, will always guard it, and that you will warn your Lord always to be dutiful and to advise his people to ever live in love, peace and harmony that a great calamity may never happen again."

21. Certain physical defects in a Confederate Lord make him ineligible to sit in the Confederate Council. Such defects are infancy, idiocy, blindness, deafness, dumbness and impotency. When a Confederate Lord is restricted by any of these conditions, a deputy shall be appointed by his sponsors to act for him, but in case of extreme necessity the restricted Lord may exercise his rights.

22. If a Confederate Lord desires to resign his title he shall notify the Lords of the Nation of which he is a member of his intention. If his coactive Lords refuse to accept his resignation he may not resign his title. A Lord in proposing to resign may recommend any proper candidate which recommendation shall be received by the Lords, but unless confirmed and nominated by the women who hold the title the candidate so named shall not be considered.

23. Any Lord of the Five Nations Confederacy may construct shell strings (or wampum belts) of any size or length as pledges or records of matters of national or international importance. When it is necessary to dispatch a shell string by a War Chief or other messenger as the token of a summons, the messenger shall recite the contents of the string to the party to whom it is sent. That party shall repeat the message and return the shell string and if there has been a summons he shall make ready for the journey. Any of the people of the Five Nations may use shells (or wampum) as the record of a pledge, contract or an agreement entered into and the same shall be binding as soon as shell strings shall have been exchanged by both parties.

24. The Lords of the Confederacy of the Five Nations shall be mentors of the people for all time. The thickness of their skin shall be seven spans—which is to say that they shall be proof against anger, offensive actions and criticism. Their hearts shall be full of peace and good will and their minds filled with a yearning for the welfare of the people of the Confederacy. With endless patience they shall carry out their duty and their firmness shall be tempered with a tenderness for their people. Neither anger nor fury shall find lodgement in their minds and all their words and actions shall be marked by calm deliberation.

25. If a Lord of the Confederacy should seek to establish any authority independent of the jurisdiction of the Confederacy of the Great Peace, which is the Five Nations, he shall be warned three times in open council, first by the women relatives, second by the men relatives and finally by the Lords of the Confederacy of the Nation to which he belongs. If the offending Lord is still obdurate he shall be dismissed by the War Chief of his nation for refusing to conform to the laws of the Great Peace. His nation shall then install the candidate nominated by the female name holders of his family.

26. It shall be the duty of all of the Five Nations Confederate Lords, from time to time as occasion demands, to act as mentors and spiritual guides of their people and remind them of their Creator's will and words. They shall say: "Hearken, that peace may continue unto future days! Always listen to the words of the Great Creator, for he has spoken. United people, let not evil find lodging in your minds. For the Great Creator has spoken and the cause of Peace shall not become old. The cause of peace shall not die if you remember the Great Creator." Every Confederate Lord shall speak words such as these to promote peace.

27. All Lords of the Five Nations Confederacy must be honest in all things. They must not idle or gossip, but be men possessing those honorable qualities that make true royaneh. It shall be a serious wrong for anyone to lead a Lord into trivial affairs, for the people must ever hold their Lords high in estimation out of respect to their honorable positions.

28. When a candidate Lord is to be installed he shall furnish four strings of shells (or wampum) one span in length bound together at one end. Such will constitute the evidence of his pledge to the Confederate Lords that he will live according to the constitution of the Great Peace and exercise justice in all affairs. When the pledge is furnished the Speaker of the Council must hold the shell strings in his hand and address the opposite side of the Council Fire and he shall commence his address saying: "Now behold him. He has now become a Confederate Lord. See how splendid he looks." An address may then follow. At the end of it he shall send the bunch of shell strings to the opposite side and they shall be received as evidence of the pledge. Then shall the opposite side say: "We now do crown you with the sacred emblem of the deer's antlers, the emblem of your Lordship. You shall now become a mentor of the people of the Five Nations. The thickness of your skin shall be seven spans—which is to say that you shall be proof against anger, offensive actions and criticism. Your heart shall be filled with peace and good will and your

mind filled with a yearning for the welfare of the people of the Confederacy. With endless patience you shall carry out your duty and your firmness shall be tempered with tenderness for your people. Neither anger nor fury shall find lodgement in your mind and all your words and actions shall be marked with calm deliberation. In all of your deliberations in the Confederate Council, in your efforts at law making, in all your official acts, self interest shall be cast into oblivion. Cast not over your shoulder behind you the warnings of the nephews and nieces should they chide you for any error or wrong you may do, but return to the way of the Great Law which is just and right. Look and listen for the welfare of the whole people and have always in view not only the present but also the coming generations, even those whose faces are yet beneath the surface of the ground—the unborn of the future Nation."

29. When a Lordship title is to be conferred, the candidate Lord shall furnish the cooked venison, the corn bread and the corn soup, together with other necessary things and the labor for the Conferring of Titles Festival.

30. The Lords of the Confederacy may confer the Lordship title upon a candidate whenever the Great Law is recited, if there be a candidate, for the Great Law speaks all the rules.

31. If a Lord of the Confederacy should become seriously ill and be thought near death, the women who are heirs of his title shall go to his house and lift his crown of deer antlers, the emblem of his Lordship, and place them at one side. If the Creator spares him and he rises from his bed of sickness he may rise with the antlers on his brow. The following words shall be used to temporarily remove the antlers: "Now our comrade Lord (or our relative Lord) the time has come when we must approach you in your illness. We remove for a time the deer's antlers from your brow, we remove the emblem of your Lordship title. The Great Law has decreed that no Lord should end his life with the antlers on his brow. We therefore lay them aside in the room. If the Creator spares you and you recover from your illness you shall rise from your bed with the antlers on your brow as before and you shall resume your duties as Lord of the Confederacy and you may labor again for the Confederate people."

32. If a Lord of the Confederacy should die while the Council of the Five Nations is in session the Council shall adjourn for ten days. No Confederate Council shall sit within ten days of the death of a Lord of the Confederacy. If the Three Brothers (the Mohawk, the Onondaga and the Seneca) should lose one of their Lords by death, the Younger Brothers (the Oneida and the Cayuga) shall come to the

surviving Lords of the Three Brothers on the tenth day and console them. If the Younger Brothers lose one of their Lords then the Three Brothers shall come to them and console them. And the consolation shall be the reading of the contents of the thirteen shell (wampum) strings of Ayonhwhathah. At the termination of this rite a successor shall be appointed, to be appointed by the women heirs of the Lordship title. If the women are not yet ready to place their nominee before the Lords the Speaker shall say, "Come let us go out." All shall leave the Council or the place of gathering. The installation shall then wait until such a time as the women are ready. The Speaker shall lead the way from the house by saying, "Let us depart to the edge of the woods and lie in waiting on our bellies." When the women title holders shall have chosen one of their sons the Confederate Lords will assemble in two places, the Younger Brothers in one place and the Three Older Brothers in another. The Lords who are to console the mourning Lords shall choose one of their number to sing the Pacification Hymn as they journey to the sorrowing Lords. The singer shall lead the way and the Lords and the people shall follow. When they reach the sorrowing Lords they shall hail the candidate Lord and perform the rite of Conferring the Lordship Title.

33. When a Confederate Lord dies, the surviving relatives shall immediately dispatch a messenger, a member of another clan, to the Lords in another locality. When the runner comes within hailing distance of the locality he shall utter a sad wail, thus: "Kwa-ah, Kwa-ah, Kwa-ah!" The sound shall be repeated three times and then again and again at intervals as many times as the distance may require. When the runner arrives at the settlement the people shall assemble and one must ask him the nature of his sad message. He shall then say, "Let us consider." Then he shall tell them of the death of the Lord. He shall deliver to them a string of shells (wampum) and say "Here is the testimony, you have heard the message." He may then return home. It now becomes the duty of the Lords of the locality to send runners to other localities and each locality shall send other messengers until all Lords are notified. Runners shall travel day and night.

34. If a Lord dies and there is no candidate qualified for the office in the family of the women title holders, the Lords of the Nation shall give the title into the hands of a sister family in the clan until such a time as the original family produces a candidate, when the title shall be restored to the rightful owners. No Lordship title may be carried into the grave. The Lords of the Confederacy may dispossess a dead Lord of his title even at the grave.

Election of Pine Tree Chiefs

35. Should any man of the Nation assist with special ability or show great interest in the affairs of the Nation, if he proves himself wise, honest and worthy of confidence, the Confederate Lords may elect him to a seat with them and he may sit in the Confederate Council. He shall be proclaimed a "Pine Tree sprung up for the Nation" and shall be installed as such at the next assembly for the installation of Lords. Should he ever do anything contrary to the rules of the Great Peace, he may not be deposed from office—no one shall cut him down—but thereafter everyone shall be deaf to his voice and his advice. Should he resign his seat and title no one shall prevent him. A Pine Tree chief has no authority to name a successor nor is his title hereditary.

Names, Duties and Rights of War Chiefs

36. The title names of the Chief Confederate Lords' War Chiefs shall be: Ayonwaehs, War Chief under Lord Takarihoken (Mohawk) Kahonwahdironh, War Chief under Lord Odatshedeh (Oneida) Ayendes, War Chief under Lord Adodarhoh (Onondaga) Wenenhs, War Chief under Lord Dekaenyonh (Cayuga) Shoneradowaneh, War Chief under Lord Skanyadariyo (Seneca). The women heirs of each head Lord's title shall be the heirs of the War Chief's title of their respective Lord. The War Chiefs shall be selected from the eligible sons of the female families holding the head Lordship titles.

37. There shall be one War Chief for each Nation and their duties shall be to carry messages for their Lords and to take up the arms of war in case of emergency. They shall not participate in the proceedings of the Confederate Council but shall watch its progress and in case of an erroneous action by a Lord they shall receive the complaints of the people and convey the warnings of the women to him. The people who wish to convey messages to the Lords in the Confederate Council shall do so through the War Chief of their Nation. It shall ever be his duty to lay the cases, questions and propositions of the people before the Confederate Council.

38. When a War Chief dies another shall be installed by the same rite as that by which a Lord is installed.

39. If a War Chief acts contrary to instructions or against the provisions of the Laws of the Great Peace, doing so in the capacity of his office, he shall be deposed by his women relatives and by his men relatives. Either the women or the men alone or jointly may act in such a case. The women title holders shall then choose another candidate.

40. When the Lords of the Confederacy take occasion to dispatch a messenger in behalf of the Confederate Council, they shall wrap up any matter they may send and instruct the messenger to remember his errand, to turn not aside but to proceed faithfully to his destination and deliver his message according to every instruction.

41. If a message borne by a runner is the warning of an invasion he shall whoop, "Kwa-ah, Kwa-ah," twice and repeat at short intervals; then again at a longer interval. If a human being is found dead, the finder shall not touch the body but return home immediately shouting at short intervals, "Koo-weh!"

Clans and Consanguinity

42. Among the Five Nations and their posterity there shall be the following original clans: Great Name Bearer, Ancient Name Bearer, Great Bear, Ancient Bear, Turtle, Painted Turtle, Standing Rock, Large Plover, Deer, Pigeon Hawk, Eel, Ball, Opposite-Side-of-the-Hand, and Wild Potatoes. These clans distributed through their respective Nations, shall be the sole owners and holders of the soil of the country and in them is it vested as a birthright.

43. People of the Five Nations members of a certain clan shall recognize every other member of that clan, irrespective of the Nation, as relatives. Men and women, therefore, members of the same clan are forbidden to marry.

44. The lineal descent of the people of the Five Nations shall run in the female line. Women shall be considered the progenitors of the Nation. They shall own the land and the soil. Men and women shall follow the status of the mother.

45. The women heirs of the Confederated Lordship titles shall be called Royaneh (Noble) for all time to come.

46. The women of the Forty Eight (now fifty) Royaneh families shall be the heirs of the Authorized Names for all time to come. When an infant of the Five Nations is given an Authorized Name at the Midwinter Festival or at the Ripe Corn Festival, one in the cousinhood of which the infant is a member shall be appointed a speaker. He shall then announce to the opposite cousinhood the names of the father and the mother of the child together with the clan of the mother. Then the speaker shall announce the child's name twice. The uncle of the child shall then take the child in his arms and walking up and down the room shall sing: "My head is firm, I am of the Confederacy." As he sings the opposite cousinhood shall respond by chanting, "Hyenh, Hyenh, Hyenh, Hyenh," until the song is ended.

47. If the female heirs of a Confederate Lord's title become extinct, the title right shall be given by the Lords of the Confederacy to the sister family whom they shall elect and that family shall hold the name and transmit it to their (female) heirs, but they shall not appoint any of their sons as a candidate for a title until all the eligible men of the former family shall have died or otherwise have become ineligible.

48. If all the heirs of a Lordship title become extinct, and all the families in the clan, then the title shall be given by the Lords of the Confederacy to the family in a sister clan whom they shall elect.

49. If any of the Royaneh women, heirs of a titleship, shall wilfully withhold a Lordship or other title and refuse to bestow it, or if such heirs abandon, forsake or despise their heritage, then shall such women be deemed buried and their family extinct. The titleship shall then revert to a sister family or clan upon application and complaint. The Lords of the Confederacy shall elect the family or clan which shall in future hold the title.

50. The Royaneh women of the Confederacy heirs of the Lordship titles shall elect two women of their family as cooks for the Lord when the people shall assemble at his house for business or other purposes. It is not good nor honorable for a Confederate Lord to allow his people whom he has called to go hungry.

51. When a Lord holds a conference in his home, his wife, if she wishes, may prepare the food for the Union Lords who assemble with him. This is an honorable right which she may exercise and an expression of her esteem.

52. The Royaneh women, heirs of the Lordship titles, shall, should it be necessary, correct and admonish the holders of their titles. Those only who attend the Council may do this and those who do not shall not object to what has been said nor strive to undo the action.

53. When the Royaneh women, holders of a Lordship title, select one of their sons as a candidate, they shall select one who is trustworthy, of good character, of honest disposition, one who manages his own affairs, supports his own family, if any, and who has proven a faithful man to his Nation.

54. When a Lordship title becomes vacant through death or other cause, the Royaneh women of the clan in which the title is hereditary shall hold a council and shall choose one from among their sons to fill the office made vacant. Such a candidate shall not be the father of any Confederate Lord. If the choice is unanimous the name is referred to the men relatives of the clan. If they should disapprove

it shall be their duty to select a candidate from among their own number. If then the men and women are unable to decide which of the two candidates shall be named, then the matter shall be referred to the Confederate Lords in the Clan. They shall decide which candidate shall be named. If the men and the women agree to a candidate his name shall be referred to the sister clans for confirmation. If the sister clans confirm the choice, they shall refer their action to their Confederate Lords who shall ratify the choice and present it to their cousin Lords, and if the cousin Lords confirm the name then the candidate shall be installed by the proper ceremony for the conferring of Lordship titles.

Official Symbolism

55. A large bunch of shell strings, in the making of which the Five Nations Confederate Lords have equally contributed, shall symbolize the completeness of the union and certify the pledge of the nations represented by the Confederate Lords of the Mohawk, the Oneida, the Onondaga, the Cayuga and the Senecca, that all are united and formed into one body or union called the Union of the Great Law, which they have established. A bunch of shell strings is to be the symbol of the council fire of the Five Nations Confederacy. And the Lord whom the council of Fire Keepers shall appoint to speak for them in opening the council shall hold the strands of shells in his hands when speaking. When he finishes speaking he shall deposit the strings on an elevated place (or pole) so that all the assembled Lords and the people may see it and know that the council is open and in progress. When the council adjourns the Lord who has been appointed by his comrade Lords to close it shall take the strands of shells in his hands and address the assembled Lords. Thus will the council adjourn until such time and place as appointed by the council. Then shall the shell strings be placed in a place for safekeeping. Every five years the Five Nations Confederate Lords and the people shall assemble together and shall ask one another if their minds are still in the same spirit of unity for the Great Binding Law and if any of the Five Nations shall not pledge continuance and steadfastness to the pledge of unity then the Great Binding Law shall dissolve.

56. Five strings of shell tied together as one shall represent the Five Nations. Each string shall represent one territory and the whole a completely united territory known as the Five Nations Confederate territory.

57. Five arrows shall be bound together very strong and each arrow shall represent one nation. As the five arrows are strongly bound

this shall symbolize the complete union of the nations. Thus are the Five Nations united completely and enfolded together, united into one head, one body and one mind. Therefore they shall labor, legislate and council together for the interest of future generations. The Lords of the Confederacy shall eat together from one bowl the feast of cooked beaver's tail. While they are eating they are to use no sharp utensils for if they should they might accidentally cut one another and bloodshed would follow. All measures must be taken to prevent the spilling of blood in any way.

58. There are now the Five Nations Confederate Lords standing with joined hands in a circle. This signifies and provides that should any one of the Confederate Lords leave the council and this Confederacy his crown of deer's horns, the emblem of his Lordship title, together with his birthright, shall lodge on the arms of the Union Lords whose hands are so joined. He forfeits his title and the crown falls from his brow but it shall remain in the Confederacy. A further meaning of this is that if any time any one of the Confederate Lords choose to submit to the law of a foreign people he is no longer in but out of the Confederacy, and persons of this class shall be called "They have alienated themselves." Likewise such persons who submit to laws of foreign nations shall forfeit all birthrights and claims on the Five Nations Confederacy and territory. You, the Five Nations Confederate Lords, be firm so that if a tree falls on your joined arms it shall not separate or weaken your hold. So shall the strength of the union be preserved.

59. A bunch of wampum shells on strings, three spans of the hand in length, the upper half of the bunch being white and the lower half black, and formed from equal contributions of the men of the Five Nations, shall be a token that the men have combined themselves into one head, one body and one thought, and it shall also symbolize their ratification of the peace pact of the Confederacy, whereby the Lords of the Five Nations have established the Great Peace. The white portion of the shell strings represent the women and the black portion the men. The black portion, furthermore, is a token of power and authority vested in the men of the Five Nations. This string of wampum vests the people with the right to correct their erring Lords. In case a part or all the Lords pursue a course not vouched for by the people and heed not the third warning of their women relatives, then the matter shall be taken to the General Council of the women of the Five Nations. If the Lords notified and warned three times fail to heed, then the case falls into the hands of the men of the Five Nations. The War Chiefs shall then, by right of

such power and authority, enter the open council to warn the Lord or Lords to return from the wrong course. If the Lords heed the warning they shall say, "we will reply tomorrow." If then an answer is returned in favor of justice and in accord with this Great Law, then the Lords shall individualy pledge themselves again by again furnishing the necessary shells for the pledge. Then shall the War Chief or Chiefs exhort the Lords urging them to be just and true. Should it happen that the Lords refuse to heed the third warning, then two courses are open: either the men may decide in their council to depose the Lord or Lords or to club them to death with war clubs. Should they in their council decide to take the first course the War Chief shall address the Lord or Lords, saying: "Since you the Lords of the Five Nations have refused to return to the procedure of the Constitution, we now declare your seats vacant, we take off your horns, the token of your Lordship, and others shall be chosen and installed in your seats, therefore vacate your seats." Should the men in their council adopt the second course, the War Chief shall order his men to enter the council, to take positions beside the Lords, sitting between them wherever possible. When this is accomplished the War Chief holding in his outstretched hand a bunch of black wampum strings shall say to the erring Lords: "So now, Lords of the Five United Nations, harken to these last words from your men. You have not heeded the warnings of the women relatives, you have not heeded the warnings of the General Council of women and you have not heeded the warnings of the men of the nations, all urging you to return to the right course of action. Since you are determined to resist and to withhold justice from your people there is only one course for us to adopt." At this point the War Chief shall let drop the bunch of black wampum and the men shall spring to their feet and club the erring Lords to death. Any erring Lord may submit before the War Chief lets fall the black wampum. Then his execution is withheld. The black wampum here used symbolizes that the power to execute is buried but that it may be raised up again by the men. It is buried but when occasion arises they may pull it up and derive their power and authority to act as here described.

60. A broad dark belt of wampum of thirty-eight rows, having a white heart in the center, on either side of which are two white squares all connected with the heart by white rows of beads shall be the emblem of the unity of the Five Nations. [Ed. note: This is the Hiawatha Belt, now in the Congressional Library.] The first of the squares on the left represents the Mohawk nation and its territory; the second square on the left and the one near the heart, represents

the Oneida nation and its territory; the white heart in the middle represents the Onondaga nation and its territory, and it also means that the heart of the Five Nations is single in its loyalty to the Great Peace, that the Great Peace is lodged in the heart (meaning the Onondaga Lords), and that the Council Fire is to burn there for the Five Nations, and further, it means that the authority is given to advance the cause of peace whereby hostile nations out of the Confederacy shall cease warfare; the white square to the right of the heart represents the Cayuga nation and its territory and the fourth and last white square represents the Seneca nation and its territory. White shall here symbolize that no evil or jealous thoughts shall creep into the minds of the Lords while in Council under the Great Peace. White, the emblem of peace, love, charity and equity surrounds and guards the Five Nations.

61. Should a great calamity threaten the generations rising and living of the Five United Nations, then he who is able to climb to the top of the Tree of the Great Long Leaves may do so. When, then, he reaches the top of the tree he shall look about in all directions, and, should he see that evil things indeed are approaching, then he shall call to the people of the Five United Nations assembled beneath the Tree of the Great Long Leaves and say: "A calamity threatens your happiness." Then shall the Lords convene in council and discuss the impending evil. When all the truths relating to the trouble shall be fully known and found to be truths, then shall the people seek out a Tree of Ka-hon-ka-ah-go-nah, [a great swamp Elm], and when they shall find it they shall assemble their heads together and lodge for a time between its roots. Then, their labors being finished, they may hope for happiness for many days after.

62. When the Confederate Council of the Five Nations declares for a reading of the belts of shell calling to mind these laws, they shall provide for the reader a specially made mat woven of the fibers of wild hemp. The mat shall not be used again, for such formality is called the honoring of the importance of the law.

63. Should two sons of opposite sides of the council fire agree in a desire to hear the reciting of the laws of the Great Peace and so refresh their memories in the way ordained by the founder of the Confederacy, they shall notify Adodarhoh. He then shall consult with five of his coactive Lords and they in turn shall consult with their eight brethren. Then should they decide to accede to the request of the two sons from opposite sides of the Council Fire, Adodarhoh shall send messengers to notify the Chief Lords of each of the Five Nations. Then they shall despatch their War Chiefs to notify their

brother and cousin Lords of the meeting and its time and place. When all have come and have assembled, Adodarhoh, in conjunction with his cousin Lords, shall appoint one Lord who shall repeat the laws of the Great Peace. Then shall they announce who they have chosen to repeat the laws of the Great Peace to the two sons. Then shall the chosen one repeat the laws of the Great Peace.

64. At the ceremony of the installation of Lords if there is only one expert speaker and singer of the law and the Pacification Hymn to stand at the council fire, then when this speaker and singer has finished addressing one side of the fire he shall go to the opposite side and reply to his own speech and song. He shall thus act for both sides of the fire until the entire ceremony has been completed. Such a speaker and singer shall be termed the "Two Faced" because he speaks and sings for both sides of the fire.

65. I, Dekanawida, and the Union Lords, now uproot the tallest pine tree and into the cavity thereby made we cast all weapons of war. Into the depths of the earth, down into the deep underearth currents of water flowing to unknown regions we cast all the weapons of strife. We bury them from sight and we plant again the tree. Thus shall the Great Peace be established and hostilities shall no longer be known between the Five Nations but peace to the United People.

Laws of Adoption

66. The father of a child of great comliness, learning, ability or specially loved because of some circumstance may, at the will of the child's clan, select a name from his own (the father's) clan and bestow it by ceremony, such as is provided. This naming shall be only temporary and shall be called, "A name hung about the neck."

67. Should any person, a member of the Five Nations' Confederacy, specially esteem a man or woman of another clan or of a foreign nation, he may choose a name and bestow it upon that person so esteemed. The naming shall be in accord with the ceremony of bestowing names. Such a name is only a temporary one and shall be called "A name hung about the neck." A short string of shells shall be delivered with the name as a record and a pledge.

68. Should any member of the Five Nations, a family or person belonging to a foreign nation submit a proposal for adoption into a clan of one of the Five Nations, he or they shall furnish a string of shells, a span in length, as a pledge to the clan into which he or they wish to be adopted. The Lords of the nation shall then consider the proposal and submit a decision.

69. Any member of the Five Nations who through esteem or other feeling wishes to adopt an individual, a family or number of families may offer adoption to him or them and if accepted the matter shall be brought to the attention of the Lords for confirmation and the Lords must confirm adoption.

70. When the adoption of anyone shall have been confirmed by the Lords of the Nation, the Lords shall address the people of their nation and say: "Now you of our nation, be informed that such a person, such a family or such families have ceased forever to bear their birth nation's name and have buried it in the depths of the earth. Henceforth let no one of our nation ever mention the original name or nation of their birth. To do so will be to hasten the end of our peace.

Laws of Emigration

71. When any person or family belonging to the Five Nations desires to abandon their birth nation and the territory of the Five Nations, they shall inform the Lords of their nation and the Confederate Council of the Five Nations shall take cognizance of it.

72. When any person or any of the people of the Five Nations emigrate and reside in a region distant from the territory of the Five Nations Confederacy, the Lords of the Five Nations at will may send a messenger carrying a broad belt of black shells and when the messenger arrives he shall call the people together or address them personally displaying the belt of shells and they shall know that this is an order for them to return to their original homes and to their council fires.

Rights of Foreign Nations

73. The soil of the earth from one end of the land to the other is the property of the people who inhabit it. By birthright the Ongwehonweh (Original beings) are the owners of the soil which they own and occupy and none other may hold it. The same law has been held from the oldest times. The Great Creator has made us of the one blood and of the same soil he made us and as only different tongues constitute different nations he established different hunting grounds and territories and made boundary lines between them.

74. When any alien nation or individual is admitted into the Five Nations the admission shall be understood only to be a temporary one. Should the person or nation create loss, do wrong or cause suffering of any kind to endanger the peace of the Confederacy, the Confederate Lords shall order one of their war chiefs to reprimand

him or them and if a similar offence is again committed the offending party or parties shall be expelled from the territory of the Five United Nations.

75. When a member of an alien nation comes to the territory of the Five Nations and seeks refuge and permanent residence, the Lords of the Nation to which he comes shall extend hospitality and make him a member of the nation. Then shall he be accorded equal rights and privileges in all matters except as after mentioned.

76. No body of alien people who have been adopted temporarily shall have a vote in the council of the Lords of the Confederacy, for only they who have been invested with Lordship titles may vote in the Council. Aliens have nothing by blood to make claim to a vote and should they have it, not knowing all the traditions of the Confederacy, might go against its Great Peace. In this manner the Great Peace would be endangered and perhaps be destroyed.

77. When the Lords of the Confederacy decide to admit a foreign nation and an adoption is made, the Lords shall inform the adopted nation that its admission is only temporary. They shall also say to the nation that it must never try to control, to interfere with or to injure the Five Nations nor disregard the Great Peace or any of its rules or customs. That in no way should they cause disturbance or injury. Then should the adopted nation disregard these injunctions, their adoption shall be annuled and they shall be expelled. The expulsion shall be in the following manner: The council shall appoint one of their War Chiefs to convey the message of annulment and he shall say, "You (naming the nation) listen to me while I speak. I am here to inform you again of the will of the Five Nations' Council. It was clearly made known to you at a former time. Now the Lords of the Five Nations have decided to expel you and cast you out. We disown you now and annul your adoption. Therefore you must look for a path in which to go and lead away all your people. It was you, not we, who committed wrong and caused this sentence of annulment. So then go your way and depart from the territory of the Five Nations and from the Confederacy."

78. Whenever a foreign nation enters the Confederacy or accepts the Great Peace, the Five Nations and the foreign nation shall enter into an agreement and compact by which the foreign nation shall endeavor to pursuade other nations to accept the Great Peace.

Rights and Powers of War

79. Skanawatih shall be vested with a double office, duty and with double authority. One-half of his being shall hold the Lordship title

and the other half shall hold the title of War Chief. In the event of war he shall notify the five War Chiefs of the Confederacy and command them to prepare for war and have their men ready at the appointed time and place for engagement with the enemy of the Great Peace.

80. When the Confederate Council of the Five Nations has for its object the establishment of the Great Peace among the people of an outside nation and that nation refuses to accept the Great Peace, then by such refusal they bring a declaration of war upon themselves from the Five Nations. Then shall the Five Nations seek to establish the Great Peace by a conquest of the rebellious nation.

81. When the men of the Five Nations, now called forth to become warriors, are ready for battle with an obstinate opposing nation that has refused to accept the Great Peace, then one of the five War Chiefs shall be chosen by the warriors of the Five Nations to lead the army into battle. It shall be the duty of the War Chief so chosen to come before his warriors and address them. His aim shall be to impress upon them the necessity of good behavior and strict obedience to all the commands of the War Chiefs. He shall deliver an oration exhorting them with great zeal to be brave and courageous and never to be guilty of cowardice. At the conclusion of his oration he shall march forward and commence the War Song and he shall sing:

> *Now I am greatly surprised*
> *And, therefore I shall use it—*
> *The power of my War Song.*
> *I am of the Five Nations*
> *And I shall make supplication*
> *To the Almighty Creator.*
> *He has furnished this army.*
> *My warriors shall be mighty*
> *In the strength of the Creator.*
> *Between him and my song they are*
> *For it was he who gave the song*
> *This war song that I sing!*

82. When the warriors of the Five Nations are on an expedition against an enemy, the War Chief shall sing the War Song as he approaches the country of the enemy and not cease until his scouts have reported that the army is near the enemies' lines when the War Chief shall approach with great caution and prepare for the attack.

83. When peace shall have been established by the termination of the war against a foreign nation, then the War Chief shall cause all the weapons of war to be taken from the nation. Then shall the Great Peace be established and that nation shall observe all the rules of the Great Peace for all time to come.

84. Whenever a foreign nation is conquered or has by their own will accepted the Great Peace their own system of internal government may continue, but they must cease all warfare against other nations.

85. Whenever a war against a foreign nation is pushed until that nation is about exterminated because of its refusal to accept the Great Peace and if that nation shall by its obstinacy become exterminated, all their rights, property and territory shall become the property of the Five Nations.

86. Whenever a foreign nation is conquered and the survivors are brought into the territory of the Five Nations' Confederacy and placed under the Great Peace the two shall be known as the Conqueror and the Conquered. A symbolic relationship shall be devised and be placed in some symbolic position. The conquered nation shall have no voice in the councils of the Confederacy in the body of the Lords.

87. When the War of the Five Nations on a foreign rebellious nation is ended, peace shall be restored to that nation by a withdrawal of all their weapons of war by the War Chief of the Five Nations. When all the terms of peace shall have been agreed upon a state of friendship shall be established.

88. When the proposition to establish the Great Peace is made to a foreign nation it shall be done in mutual council. The foreign nation is to be persuaded by reason and urged to come into the Great Peace. If the Five Nations fail to obtain the consent of the nation at the first council a second council shall be held and upon a second failure a third council shall be held and this third council shall end the peaceful methods of persuasion. At the third council the War Chief of the Five nations shall address the Chief of the foreign nation and request him three times to accept the Great Peace. If refusal steadfastly follows the War Chief shall let the bunch of white lake shells drop from his outstretched hand to the ground and shall bound quickly forward and club the offending chief to death. War shall thereby be declared and the War Chief shall have his warriors at his back to meet any emergency. War must continue until the contest is won by the Five Nations.

89. When the Lords of the Five Nations propose to meet in conference with a foreign nation with proposals for an acceptance of the

Great Peace, a large band of warriors shall conceal themselves in a secure place safe from the espionage of the foreign nation but as near at hand as possible. Two warriors shall accompany the Union Lord who carries the proposals and these warriors shall be especially cunning. Should the Lord be attacked, these warriors shall hasten back to the army of warriors with the news of the calamity which fell through the treachery of the foreign nation.

90. When the Five Nations' Council declares war any Lord of the Confederacy may enlist with the warriors by temporarily renouncing his sacred Lordship title which he holds through the election of his women relatives. The title then reverts to them and they may bestow it upon another temporarily until the war is over when the Lord, if living, may resume his title and seat in the Council.

91. A certain wampum belt of black beads shall be the emblem of the authority of the Five War Chiefs to take up the weapons of war and with their men to resist invasion. This shall be called a war in defense of the territory.

Treason or Secession of a Nation

92. If a nation, part of a nation, or more than one nation within the Five Nations should in any way endeavor to destroy the Great Peace by neglect or violating its laws and resolve to dissolve the Confederacy, such a nation or such nations shall be deemed guilty of treason and called enemies of the Confederacy and the Great Peace. It shall then be the duty of the Lords of the Confederacy who remain faithful to resolve to warn the offending people. They shall be warned once and if a second warning is necessary they shall be driven from the territory of the Confederacy by the War Chiefs and his men.

Rights of the People of the Five Nations

93. Whenever a specially important matter or a great emergency is presented before the Confederate Council and the nature of the matter affects the entire body of the Five Nations, threatening their utter ruin, then the Lords of the Confederacy must submit the matter to the decision of their people and the decision of the people shall affect the decision of the Confederate Council. This decision shall be a confirmation of the voice of the people.

94. The men of every clan of the Five Nations shall have a Council Fire ever burning in readiness for a council of the clan. When it seems necessary for a council to be held to discuss the welfare of the clans, then the men may gather about the fire. This council shall have the same rights as the council of the women.

95. The women of every clan of the Five Nations shall have a Council Fire ever burning in readiness for a council of the clan. When in their opinion it seems necessary for the interest of the people they shall hold a council and their decisions and recommendations shall be introduced before the Council of the Lords by the War Chief for its consideration.

96. All the Clan council fires of a nation or of the Five Nations may unite into one general council fire, or delegates from all the council fires may be appointed to unite in a general council for discussing the interests of the people. The people shall have the right to make appointments and to delegate their power to others of their number. When their council shall have come to a conclusion on any matter, their decision shall be reported to the Council of the Nation or to the Confederate Council (as the case may require) by the War Chief or the War Chiefs.

97. Before the real people united their nations, each nation had its council fires. Before the Great Peace their councils were held. The five Council Fires shall continue to burn as before and they are not quenched. The Lords of each nation in future shall settle their nation's affairs at this council fire governed always by the laws and rules of the council of the Confederacy and by the Great Peace.

98. If either a nephew or a niece see an irregularity in the performance of the functions of the Great Peace and its laws, in the Confederate Council or in the conferring of Lordship titles in an improper way, through their War Chief they may demand that such actions become subject to correction and that the matter conform to the ways prescribed by the laws of the Great Peace.

Religious Ceremonies Protected

99. The rites and festivals of each nation shall remain undisturbed and shall continue as before because they were given by the people of old times as useful and necessary for the good of men.

100. It shall be the duty of the Lords of each brotherhood to confer at the approach of the time of the Midwinter Thanksgiving and to notify their people of the approaching festival. They shall hold a council over the matter and arrange its details and begin the Thanksgiving five days after the moon of Dis-ko-nah is new. The people shall assemble at the appointed place and the nephews shall notify the people of the time and place. From the beginning to the end the Lords shall preside over the Thanksgiving and address the people from time to time.

101. It shall be the duty of the appointed managers of the Thanksgiving festivals to do all that is needed for carrying out the duties of the occasions. The recognized festivals of Thanksgiving shall be the Midwinter Thanksgiving, the Maple or Sugar-making Thanksgiving, the Raspberry Thanksgiving, the Strawberry Thanksgiving, the Corn-planting Thanksgiving, the Corn Hoeing Thanksgiving, the Little Festival of Green Corn, the Great Festival of Ripe Corn and the complete Thanksgiving for the Harvest. Each nation's festivals shall be held in their Long Houses.

102. When the Thanksgiving for the Green Corn comes the special managers, both the men and women, shall give it careful attention and do their duties properly.

103. When the Ripe Corn Thanksgiving is celebrated the Lords of the Nation must give it the same attention as they give to the Midwinter Thanksgiving.

104. Whenever any man proves himself by his good life and his knowledge of good things, naturally fitted as a teacher of good things, he shall be recognized by the Lords as a teacher of peace and religion and the people shall hear him.

The Installation Song

105. The song used in installing the new Lord of the Confederacy shall be sung by Adodarhoh and it shall be:

> *Haii, haii Agwah wi-yoh*
> *A-kon-he-watha*
> *Ska-we-ye-se-go-wah*
> *Yon-gwa-wih*
> *Ya-kon-he-wa-tha*
> *Haii, haii*

> *It is good indeed*
> *(That) a broom,*
> *A great wing,*
> *It is given me*
> *For a sweeping instrument.*

106. Whenever a person properly entitled desires to learn the Pacification Song he is privileged to do so but he must prepare a feast at which his teachers may sit with him and sing. The feast is provided that no misfortune may befall them for singing the song on an occasion when no chief is installed.

Protection of the House

107. A certain sign shall be known to all the people of the Five Nations which shall denote that the owner or occupant of a house is absent. A stick or pole in a slanting or leaning position shall indicate this and be the sign. Every person not entitled to enter the house by right of living within it upon seeing such a sign shall not approach the house either by day or by night but shall keep as far away as his business will permit.

Funeral Addresses

108. At the funeral of a Lord of the Confederacy, say: "Now we become reconciled as you start away. You were once a Lord of the Five Nations' Confederacy and the United People trusted you. Now we release you for it is true that it is no longer possible for us to walk about together on the earth. Now, therefore, we lay it (the body) here. Here we lay it away. Now then we say to you, 'Persevere onward to the place where the Creator dwells in peace. Let not the things of the earth hinder you. Let nothing that transpired while yet you lived hinder you. In hunting you once took delight; in the game of Lacrosse you once took delight and in the feasts and pleasant occasions your mind was amused, but now do not allow thoughts of these things to give you trouble. Let not your relatives hinder you and also let not your friends and associates trouble your mind. Regard none of these things.' Now then, in turn, you here present who were related to this man and you who were his friends and associates, behold the path that is yours also! Soon we ourselves will be left in that place. For this reason hold yourselves in restraint as you go from place to place. In your actions and in your conversation do no idle thing. Speak not idle talk neither gossip. Be careful of this and speak not and do not give way to evil behavior. One year is the time that you must abstain from unseemly levity but if you can not do this for ceremony, ten days is the time to regard these things for respect."

109. At the funeral of a War Chief, say: "Now we become reconciled as you start away. You were once a War Chief of the Five Nations' Confederacy and the United People trusted you as their guard from the enemy." (The remainder is the same as the address at the funeral of a Lord).

110. At the funeral of a Warrior, say: "Now we become reconciled as you start away. Once you were a devoted provider and protector of your family and you were ever ready to take part in battles for the Five Nations' Confederacy. The United People trusted you." (The remainder is the same as the address at the funeral of a Lord).

111. At the funeral of a young man, say: "Now we become reconciled as you start away. In the beginning of your career you are taken away and the flower of your life is withered away." (The remainder is the same as the address at the funeral of a Lord).

112. At the funeral of a chief woman, say: "Now we become reconciled as you start away. You were once a chief woman in the Five Nations' Confederacy. You once were a mother of the nations. Now we release you for it is true that it is no longer possible for us to walk about together on the earth. Now, therefore, we lay it (the body) here. Here we lay it away. Now then we say to you, 'Persevere onward to the place where the Creator dwells in peace. Let not the things of the earth hinder you. Let nothing that transpired while you lived hinder you. Looking after your family was a sacred duty and you were faithful. You were one of the many joint heirs of the Lordship titles. Feastings were yours and you had pleasant occasions . . ." (The remainder is the same as the address at the funeral of a Lord).

113. At the funeral of a woman of the people, say: "Now we become reconciled as you start away. You were once a woman in the flower of life and the bloom is now withered away. You once held a sacred position as a mother of the nation. (Etc.) Looking after your family was a sacred duty and you were faithful. Feastings . . . (etc.)" (The remainder is the same as the address at the funeral of a Lord).

114. At the funeral of an infant or young woman, say: "Now we become reconciled as you start away. You were a tender bud and gladdened our hearts for only a few days. Now the bloom has withered away . . . (etc.) Let none of the things that transpired on earth hinder you. Let nothing that happened while you lived hinder you." (The remainder is the same as the address at the funeral of a Lord). [Ed. note: the above ellipses and "etc." remarks are transcribed directly from the text I copied.]

115. When an infant dies within three days, mourning shall continue only five days. Then shall you gather the little boys and girls at the house of mourning and at the funeral feast a speaker shall address the children and bid them be happy once more, though by a death, gloom has been cast over them. Then shall the black clouds roll away and the sky shall show blue once more. Then shall the children be again in sunshine.

116. When a dead person is brought to the burial place, the speaker on the opposite side of the Council Fire shall bid the bereaved family cheer their minds once again and rekindle their hearth fires in peace, to put their house in order and once again be in

brightness for darkness has covered them. He shall say that the black clouds shall roll away and that the bright blue sky is visible once more. Therefore shall they be in peace in the sunshine again.

117. Three strings of shell one span in length shall be employed in addressing the assemblage at the burial of the dead. The speaker shall say: "Hearken you who are here, this body is to be covered. Assemble in this place again ten days hence for it is the decree of the Creator that mourning shall cease when ten days have expired. Then shall a feast be made." Then at the expiration of ten days the speaker shall say: "Continue to listen you who are here. The ten days of mourning have expired and your minds must now be freed of sorrow as before the loss of a relative. The relatives have decided to make a little compensation to those who have assisted at the funeral. It is a mere expression of thanks. This is to the one who did the cooking while the body was lying in the house. Let her come forward and receive this gift and be dismissed from the task." In substance this shall be repeated for every one who assisted in any way until all have been remembered.

Source: Prepared by Gerald Murphy (The Cleveland Free-Net - aa300) Distributed by the Cybercasting Services Division of the National Public Telecomputing Network (NPTN). Permission is hereby granted to download, reprint, and/or otherwise redistribute this file, provided appropriate point of origin credit is given to the preparer(s) and the National Public Telecomputing Network.

The Northwest Ordinance (1787)

Because the Articles of Confederation, adopted by the states in 1781 as the country's first constitution, have often been considered a failure, it is all too easy to overlook the significant accomplishments of the American government under the articles. The confederation negotiated a peace treaty ending the war with Great Britain, carried on diplomatic relations with foreign countries, settled land disputes with the Indian tribes, and, in two brilliant pieces of legislation, established a far-reaching policy for the settlement and incorporation of western lands.

After first providing for the survey of the land west of the Appalachian Mountains, the so-called Northwest Territory, Congress enacted the Northwest Ordinance of 1787, the single most important piece of legislation in the confederation period. The ordinance provided the means by which new states would be created out of the western lands and then admitted into the Union. Governors and judges appointed by Congress would rule a terri-

tory until it contained five thousand free male inhabitants of voting age; then the inhabitants would elect a territorial legislature, which would send a nonvoting delegate to Congress. When the population reached sixty thousand, the legislature would submit a state constitution to Congress, and, upon its approval, the state would enter the Union.

The importance of the statute, aside from providing for orderly westerly settlement, is that it made clear that the new states would be equal to the old; there would be no inferior or superior states in the Union. Moreover, it guaranteed the settlers of the territories that they would be equal citizens of the United States and would enjoy all of the rights that had been fought for in the Revolution. Where the Articles of Confederation lacked a bill of rights, the ordinance provided one that included many of the basic liberties the colonists had considered essential, such as trial by jury, habeas corpus, and religious freedom. Nevertheless, property ownership still played an important role in government, a holdover from British theory that only those with a tangible stake in society should partake in its governance.

The Northwest Ordinance would, with minor adjustments, remain the guiding policy for the admission of all future states into the Union.

For further reading: Merrill Jensen, *The New Nation: A History of the United States during the Confederation, 1781–1789* (1950); John Porter Bloom, ed. (1974); T. C. Pease, "The Ordinance of 1787," *Mississippi Valley Historical Review* 25 (1938): 167.

The Northwest Ordinance

Be it ordained by the authority aforesaid, That there shall be appointed from time to time by Congress, a governor, whose commission shall continue in force for the term of three years, unless sooner revoked by Congress; he shall reside in the district, and have a freehold estate therein in 1,000 acres of land, while in the exercise of his office.

There shall be appointed from time to time by Congress, a secretary, whose commission shall continue in force for four years unless sooner revoked; he shall reside in the district, and have a freehold estate therein in 500 acres of land, while in the exercise of his office. It shall be his duty to keep and preserve the acts and laws passed by the legislature, and the public records of the district, and the proceedings of the governor in his executive department, and transmit authentic copies of such acts and proceedings, every six months, to the Secretary of Congress: There shall also be appointed a court to consist of three judges, any two of whom to form a court, who shall have a common law jurisdiction, and reside in the district, and have each therein a freehold estate in 500 acres of land while in the exercise of their offices; and their commissions shall continue in force during good behavior.

The governor and judges, or a majority of them, shall adopt and publish in the district such laws of the original States, criminal and civil, as may be necessary and best suited to the circumstances of the district, and report them to Congress from time to time: which laws shall be in force in the district until the organization of the General Assembly therein, unless disapproved of by Congress; but afterwards the Legislature shall have authority to alter them as they shall think fit.

The governor, for the time being, shall be commander-in-chief of the militia, appoint and commission all officers in the same below the rank of general officers; all general officers shall be appointed and commissioned by Congress.

Previous to the organization of the general assembly, the governor shall appoint such magistrates and other civil officers in each county or township, as he shall find necessary for the preservation of the peace and good order in the same: After the general assembly shall be organized, the powers and duties of the magistrates and other civil officers shall be regulated and defined by the said assembly; but all magistrates and other civil officers not herein otherwise directed, shall, during the continuance of this temporary government, be appointed by the governor.

For the prevention of crimes and injuries, the laws to be adopted or made shall have force in all parts of the district, and for the execution of process, criminal and civil, the governor shall make proper divisions thereof; and he shall proceed from time to time as circumstances may require, to lay out the parts of the district in which the Indian titles shall have been extinguished, into counties and townships, subject however to such alterations as may thereafter be made by the legislature.

So soon as there shall be five thousand free male inhabitants of full age in the district, upon giving proof thereof to the governor, they shall receive authority, with time and place, to elect representatives from their counties or townships to represent them in the general assembly:

Provided, That, for every five hundred free male inhabitants, there shall be one representative, and so on progressively with the number of free male inhabitants shall the right of representation increase, until the number of representatives shall amount to twenty-five; after which, the number and proportion of representatives shall be regulated by the legislature:

Provided, That no person be eligible or qualified to act as a representative unless he shall have been a citizen of one of the United States three years, and be a resident in the district, or unless he shall have resided in the district three years; and, in either case, shall likewise hold in his own right, in fee simple, two hundred acres of land within the same;

Provided, also, That a freehold in fifty acres of land in the district, having been a citizen of one of the states, and being resident in the district, or the like freehold and two years residence in the district, shall be necessary to qualify a man as an elector of a representative.

The representatives thus elected, shall serve for the term of two years; and, in case of the death of a representative, or removal from office, the governor shall issue a writ to the county or township for which he was a member, to elect another in his stead, to serve for the residue of the term.

The general assembly or legislature shall consist of the governor, legislative council, and a house of representatives. The Legislative Council shall consist of five members, to continue in office five years, unless sooner removed by Congress; any three of whom to be a quorum: and the members of the Council shall be nominated and appointed in the following manner, to wit: As soon as representatives shall be elected, the Governor shall appoint a time and place for them to meet together; and, when met, they shall nominate ten persons, residents in the district, and each possessed of a freehold in five hundred acres of land, and return their names to Congress; five of whom Congress shall appoint and commission to serve as aforesaid; and, whenever a vacancy shall happen in the council, by death or removal from office, the house of representatives shall nominate two persons, qualified as aforesaid, for each vacancy, and return their names to Congress; one of whom Congress shall appoint and commission for the residue of the term. And every five years, four months at least before the expiration of the time of service of the members of council, the said house shall nominate ten persons, qualified as aforesaid, and return their names to Congress; five of whom Congress shall appoint and commission to serve as members of the council five years, unless sooner removed. And the governor, legislative council, and house of representatives, shall have authority to make laws in all cases, for the good government of the district, not repugnant to the principles and articles in this ordinance established and declared. And all bills, having passed by a majority in the house, and by a majority in the council, shall be referred to the governor for his assent; but no bill, or legislative act whatever, shall be of any force without his assent. The governor shall have power to convene, prorogue, and dissolve the general assembly, when, in his opinion, it shall be expedient.

The governor, judges, legislative council, secretary, and such other officers as Congress shall appoint in the district, shall take an oath or affirmation of fidelity and of office; the governor before the president of congress, and all other officers before the Governor. As soon as a legislature shall be formed in the district, the council and house assembled in one room, shall have authority, by joint ballot, to elect a delegate to Congress, who shall have a seat in Congress, with a right of debating but not of voting during this temporary government.

And, for extending the fundamental principles of civil and religious liberty, which form the basis whereon these republics, their laws and constitutions are erected; to fix and establish those principles as the basis of all laws, constitutions, and governments, which forever hereafter shall be formed in the said territory: to provide also for the establishment of States, and permanent government therein, and for their admission to a share in the federal councils on an equal footing with the original States, at as early periods as may be consistent with the general interest: It is hereby ordained and declared by the authority aforesaid, That the following articles shall be considered as articles of compact between the original States and the people and States in the said territory and forever remain unalterable, unless by common consent, to wit:

ART. 1. No person, demeaning himself in a peaceable and orderly manner, shall ever be molested on account of his mode of worship or religious sentiments, in the said territory.

ART. 2. The inhabitants of the said territory shall always be entitled to the benefits of the writ of habeas corpus, and of the trial by jury; of a proportionate representation of the people in the legislature; and of judicial proceedings according to the course of the common law. All persons shall be bailable, unless for capital offenses, where the proof shall be evident or the presumption great. All fines shall be moderate; and no cruel or unusual punishments shall be inflicted. No man shall be deprived of his liberty or property, but by the judgment of his peers or the law of the land; and, should the public exigencies make it necessary, for the common preservation, to take any person's property, or to demand his particular services, full compensation shall be made for the same. And, in the just preservation of rights and property, it is understood and declared, that no law ought ever to be made, or have force in the said territory, that shall, in any manner whatever, interfere with or affect private contracts or engagements, bona fide, and without fraud, previously formed.

ART. 3. Religion, morality, and knowledge, being necessary to good government and the happiness of mankind, schools and the means of education shall forever be encouraged. The utmost good faith shall always be observed towards the Indians; their lands and property shall never be taken from them without their consent; and, in their property, rights, and liberty, they shall never be invaded or disturbed, unless in just and lawful wars authorized by Congress; but laws founded in justice and humanity, shall from time to time be made for preventing wrongs being done to them, and for preserving peace and friendship with them. . . .

ART. 5. There shall be formed in the said territory, not less than three nor more than five States. . . . And, whenever any of the said States shall have sixty thousand free inhabitants therein, such State shall be admitted, by its delegates, into the Congress of the United States, on an equal footing with the original States in all respects whatever, and shall be at liberty to form a permanent constitution and State government: Provided, the constitution and government so to be formed, shall be republican, and in conformity to the principles contained in these articles; and, so far as it can be consistent with the general interest of the confederacy, such admission shall be allowed at an earlier period, and when there may be a less number of free inhabitants in the State than sixty thousand.

ART. 6. There shall be neither slavery nor involuntary servitude in the said territory, otherwise than in the punishment of crimes whereof the party shall have been duly convicted: Provided, always, That any person escaping into the same, from whom labor or service is lawfully claimed in any one of the original States, such fugitive may be lawfully reclaimed and conveyed to the person claiming his or her labor or service as aforesaid.

Source: F. N. Thorpe, ed., *Federal and State Constitutions,* vol. 2 (1909), 957.

The Indian Removal Act of 1830

This Jackson-era legislation authorized the president to transfer eastern Indian tribes to the western territories, falsely promising that they could remain there "forever secure." The actual relocation culminated in the 1838 Trail of Tears, the notorious forced march, one of the most shameful incidents in the history of U.S. governmental domestic policy.

CHAP. CXLVIII.—An Act to provide for an exchange of lands with the Indians residing in any of the states or territories, and for their removal west of the river Mississippi.

Be it enacted by the Senate and House of Representatives of the United States of America, in Congress assembled, That it shall and may be lawful for the President of the United States to cause so much of any territory belonging to the United States, west of the river Mississippi, not included in any state or organized territory, and to which the Indian title has been extinguished, as he may judge necessary, to be divided into a suitable number of districts, for the reception of such tribes or nations of Indians as may choose to exchange the lands where they now reside, and remove there; and to cause each of said districts to be so described by natural or artificial marks, as to be easily distinguished from every other.

SEC. 2. And be it further enacted, That it shall and may be lawful for the President to exchange any or all of such districts, so to be laid off and described, with any tribe or nation within the limits of any of the states or territories, and with which the United States have existing treaties, for the whole or any part or portion of the territory claimed and occupied by such tribe or nation, within the bounds of any one or more of the states or territories, where the land claimed and occupied by the Indians is owned by the United States, or the United States are bound to the state within which it lies to extinguish the Indian claim thereto.

SEC. 3. And be it further enacted, That in the making of any such exchange or exchanges, it shall and may be lawful for the President solemnly to assure the tribe or nation with which the exchange is made, that the United States will forever secure and guaranty to them, and their heirs or successors, the country so exchanged with them; and if they prefer it, that the United States will cause a patent or grant to be made and executed to them for the same: Provided always, That such lands shall revert to the United States, if the Indians become extinct, or abandon the same.

SEC. 4. And be it further enacted, That if, upon any of the lands now occupied by the Indians, and to be exchanged for, there should be such improvements as add value to the land claimed by any individual or individuals of such tribes or nations, it shall and may be lawful for the President to cause such value to be ascertained by appraisement or otherwise, and to cause such ascertained value to be paid to the person or persons rightfully claiming such improvements. And upon the payment of such valuation, the improvements so valued and paid for, shall pass to the United States, and possession shall not afterwards be permitted to any of the same tribe.

SEC. 5. And be it further enacted, That upon the making of any such exchange as is contemplated by this act, it shall and may be lawful for the President to cause such aid and assistance to be furnished to the emigrants as may be necessary and proper to enable them to remove to, and settle in, the country for which they may have exchanged; and also, to give them such aid and assistance as may be necessary for their support and subsistence for the first year after their removal.

SEC. 6. And be it further enacted, That it shall and may be lawful for the President to cause such tribe or nation to be protected, at their new residence, against all interruption or disturbance from any other tribe or nation of Indians, or from any other person or persons whatever.

SEC. 7. And be it further enacted, That it shall and may be lawful for the President to have the same superintendence and care over any tribe or nation in the country to which they may remove, as contemplated by this act, that he is now authorized to have over them at their present places of residence.

General Allotment Act (Dawes Act) of 1887

This congressional act authorized the president to allot portions of certain reservation land to individual Indians—160 acres to each head of family and 80 acres to others—to establish private farms and authorized the secretary of the Interior to negotiate with the tribes for purchasing "excess" lands for non-Indian settlement. Indians were to select their own lands, but if they failed to do so, the Indian agent would select land for them. The federal government was to hold title to the land in trust for twenty-five years, thus preventing its sale until allottees could learn to treat it as real estate. Allotment primarily sought to destroy Indian communities where property sharing encouraged "tribalism" and to open Indian lands for non-Indian purchase and settlement. The result was that from 1887 to 1934 (when the act was repealed), Indian landholdings decreased from 138 million acres to 48 million. The Cherokees, Creeks, Choctaws, Chickasaws, and Seminoles were excluded from the provisions of the Allotment Act.

Be it enacted by the Senate and House of Representatives of the United States of America in Congress assembled, That in all cases where any tribe or band of Indians has been, or shall hereafter be, located upon any reservation created for their use, either by treaty stipulation or by virtue of an act of Congress or executive order setting apart the same for their use, the President of the United States be, and he hereby is, authorized, whenever in his opinion any reservation or any part thereof of such Indians is advantageous for agricultural and grazing purposes, to cause said reservation, or any part thereof, to be surveyed, or resurveyed if necessary, and to allot the lands in said reservation in severalty to any Indian located thereon in quantities as follows: To each head of a family, one-quarter of a section; To each single person over eighteen years of age, one-eighth of a section; To each orphan child under eighteen years of age, one-eighth of a section; and To each other single person under eighteen years now living, or who may be born prior to the date of the order of the President directing an allotment of the lands embraced in any reservation, one-sixteenth of a section: *Provided,* That in case there is not sufficient land in any of said reservations to allot lands to each individual of the classes above named in quantities as above provided, the lands embraced in such reservation or reservations shall be allotted to each individual of each of said classes pro rata in accordance with the provisions of this act: *And provided further,* That where the treaty or act of Congress setting apart such reservation provides the allotment of lands in severalty in quantities in excess of those herein provided, the President, in making allotments upon such reservation, shall allot the lands to each individual Indian belonging thereon in quantity as specified in such treaty or act: *And provided further,* That when the lands allotted are only valuable for grazing purposes, an additional allotment of such grazing lands, in quantities as above provided, shall be made to each individual.

SEC. 2. That all allotments set apart under the provisions of this act shall be selected by the Indians, heads of families selecting for their minor children, and the agents shall select for each orphan child, and in such manner as to embrace the improvements of the Indians making the selection. Where the improvements of two or more Indians have been made on the same legal subdivision of land, unless they shall otherwise agree, a provisional line may be run dividing said lands between them, and the amount to which each is entitled shall be equalized in the assignment of the remainder of the land to which they are entitled under his act: *Provided,* That if any one entitled to an allotment shall fail to make a selection within four years after the President shall direct that allotments may be made on a particular reservation, the Secretary of the Interior may direct the agent of such tribe or band, if such there be, and if there be no agent, then a special agent appointed for that purpose, to make a selection for such Indian, which selection shall be allotted as in cases where selections are made by the Indians, and patents shall issue in like manner.

SEC. 3. That the allotments provided for in this act shall be made by special agents appointed by the President for such purpose, and the agents in charge of the respective reservations on which the allotments are directed to be made, under such rules and regulations as the Secretary of the Interior may from time to time prescribe, and shall be certified by such agents to the Commissioner of Indian Affairs, in duplicate, one copy to be retained in the Indian Office and the other to be transmitted to the Secretary of the Interior for his action, and to be deposited in the General Land Office.

SEC. 4. That where any Indian not residing upon a reservation, or for whose tribe no reservation has been provided by treaty, act of Congress, or executive order, shall make settlement upon any surveyed or unsurveyed lands of the United States not otherwise appropriated, he or she shall be entitled, upon application to the local land-office for the district in which the lands are located, to have the same allotted to him or her, and to his or her children, in quantities and manner as provided in this act for Indians residing upon reservations; and when such settlement is made upon unsurveyed lands, the grant to such Indians shall be adjusted upon the survey of the lands so as to conform thereto; and patents shall be issued to them for such lands in the manner and with the restrictions as herein provided. And the fees to which the officers of such local land-office would have been entitled had such lands been entered under the general laws for the disposition of the public lands shall be paid to them, from any moneys in the Treasury of the United States not otherwise appropriated, upon a statement of an account in their behalf for such fees by the Commissioner of the General Land Office, and a certification of such account to the Secretary of the Treasury by the Secretary of the Interior.

SEC. 5. That upon the approval of the allotments provided for in this act by the Secretary of the Interior, he shall cause patents to issue therefor in the name of the allottees, which patents shall be of the legal effect, and declare that the United States does and will hold the land thus allotted, for the period of twenty-five years, in trust for the sole use and benefit of the Indian to whom such allotment shall have been made, or, in case of his decease, of his heirs according to the laws of the State or Territory where such land is located, and that at the expiration of said period the United States will convey the same by patent to said Indian, or his heirs as aforesaid, in fee, discharged of said trust and free of all charge or encumbrance whatsoever: *Provided,* That the President of the United States may in any case in his discretion extend the period. And if any conveyance shall be made of the lands set apart and allotted as herein provided, or any contract made touching the same, before the expiration of the time above mentioned, such conveyance or contract shall be absolutely null and void: *Provided,* That the law of descent and partition in force in the State or Territory where such lands are situate shall apply thereto after patents therefor have been executed and delivered, except as herein otherwise provided; and the laws of the State of Kansas regulating the descent and partition of real estate shall, so far as practicable, apply to all lands in the Indian Territory which may be allotted in severalty under the provisions of this act: And provided further, That at any time after lands have been allotted to all the Indians of any tribe as herein provided, or sooner if in the opinion of the President it shall be for the best interests of said tribe, it shall be lawful for the Secretary of the Interior to negotiate with such Indian tribe for the purchase and release by said tribe, in conformity with the treaty or statute under which such reservation is held, of such portions of its reservation not allotted as such tribe shall, from time to time, consent to sell, on such terms and conditions as shall be considered just and equitable between the United States and said tribe of Indians, which purchase shall not be complete until ratified by Congress, and the form and manner of executing such release shall also be prescribed by Congress: *Provided however,* That all lands adapted to agriculture, with or without irrigation so sold or released to the United States by any Indian tribe shall be held by the United States for the sole purpose of securing homes to actual settlers and shall be disposed of by the United States to actual and bona fide settlers only tracts not exceeding one hundred and sixty acres to any one person, on such terms as Congress shall prescribe, subject to grants which Congress may make in aid of education: *And provided further,* That no patents shall issue therefor except to the person so taking the same as and homestead, or his heirs, and after the expiration of five years occupancy thereof as such homestead; and any conveyance of said lands taken as a homestead, or any contract touching the same, or lien thereon, created prior to the date of such patent, shall be null and void. And the sums agreed to be paid by the United States as purchase money for any portion of any such reservation shall be held in the Treasury of the United States for the sole use of the tribe or tribes Indians to whom such reservations belonged; and the same, with interest thereon at three per cent per annum, shall be at all times subject to appropriation by Congress for the education and civilization of such tribe or tribes of Indians or the members thereof. The patents aforesaid shall be recorded in the General Land Office, and afterward delivered, free of charge, to the allottee entitled thereto. And if any religious society or other organization is now occupying any of the public lands to which this act is applicable, for religious or educational work among the Indians, the Secretary of the Interior is hereby authorized to confirm such occupation to such society or organization, in quantity not exceeding one hundred and sixty acres in any one tract, so long as the same shall be so occupied, on such terms as he shall deem just; but nothing herein contained shall change or alter any claim of such society for religious or educational purposes heretofore granted by law. And hereafter in the employment of Indian police, or any other employees in the public service among any of the Indian tribes or bands affected by this act, and where Indians can perform the duties required, those Indians who have availed themselves of the provisions of this act and become citizens of the United States shall be preferred.

SEC. 6. That upon the completion of said allotments and the patenting of the lands to said allottees, each and every member of the respective bands or tribes of Indians to whom allotments have been made shall have the benefit of and be subject to the laws, both civil and criminal, of the State or Territory in which they may reside; and no Territory shall pass or enforce any law denying any such Indian within its jurisdiction the equal protection of the law. And every Indian born within the territorial limits of the United States to whom allotments shall have been made under the provisions of this act, or under any law or treaty, and every Indian born within the territorial limits of the United States who has voluntarily taken up, within said limits, his residence separate and apart from any tribe of Indians therein, and has adopted the habits of civilized life, is hereby declared to be a citizen of the United States, and is entitled to all the rights, privileges, and immunities of such citizens, whether said Indian has been or not, by birth or otherwise, a member of any tribe of Indians within the territorial limits of the United States without in any manner affecting the right of any such Indian to tribal or other property.

SEC. 7. That in cases where the use of water for irrigation is necessary to render the lands within any Indian reservation available for agricultural purposes, the Secretary of the Interior be, and he is hereby, authorized to prescribe such rules and regulations as he may deem necessary to secure a just and equal distribution thereof among the Indians residing upon any such reservation; and no other appropriation or grant of water by any riparian proprietor shall be permitted to the damage of any other riparian proprietor.

SEC. 8. That the provisions of this act shall not extend to the territory occupied by the Cherokees, Creeks, Choctaws, Chickasaws, Seminoles, and Osage, Miamies and Peorias, and Sacs and Foxes, in the Indian Territory, nor to any of the reservations of the Seneca Nation of New York Indians in the State of New York, nor to that strip of territory in the State of Nebraska adjoining the Sioux Nation on the south added by executive order.

SEC. 9. That for the purpose of making the surveys and resurveys mentioned in section two of this act, there be, and hereby is, appropriated, out of any moneys in the Treasury not otherwise appropriated, the sum of one hundred thousand dollars, to be repaid proportionately out of the proceeds of the sales of such land as may be acquired from the Indians under the provisions of this act.

SEC. 10. That nothing in this act contained shall be so construed to affect the right and power of Congress to grant the right of way through any lands granted to an Indian, or a tribe of Indians, for railroads or other highways, or telegraph lines, for the public use, or condemn such lands to public uses, upon making just compensation.

SEC. 11. That nothing in this act shall be so construed as to prevent the removal of the Southern Ute Indians from their present reservation in Southwestern Colorado to a new reservation by and with consent of a majority of the adult male members of said tribe.

Approved, February, 8, 1887.

Source: U.S. National Archives and Records Administration, 700 Pennsylvania Avenue NW, Washington DC 20408. Phone: (860) 272-6272.

United States Code Title 25— Indians Chapter 21—Indian Child Welfare

CONTENTS

CHAPTER 21—INDIAN CHILD WELFARE

SUBCHAPTER I—CHILD CUSTODY PROCEEDINGS

SUBCHAPTER II—INDIAN CHILD AND FAMILY PROGRAMS

SUBCHAPTER III—RECORDKEEPING, INFORMATION AVAILABILITY, AND TIMETABLES

SUBCHAPTER IV—MISCELLANEOUS PROVISIONS

§ 1901. Congressional findings

Recognizing the special relationship between the United States and the Indian tribes and their members and the Federal responsibility to Indian people, the Congress finds—

(1) that clause 3, section 8, article I of the United States Constitution provides that "The Congress shall have Power * * * To regulate Commerce * * * with Indian tribes; (2) that Congress, through statutes, treaties, and the general course of dealing with Indian tribes, has assumed the responsibility for the protection and preservation of Indian tribes and their resources; (3) that there is no resource that is more vital to the continued existence and integrity of Indian tribes than their children and that the United States has a direct interest, as trustee, in protecting Indian children who are members of or are eligible for membership in an Indian tribe; (4) that an alarmingly high percentage of Indian families are broken up by the removal, often unwarranted, of their children from them by nontribal public and private agencies and that an alarmingly high percentage of such children are placed in non-Indian foster and adoptive homes and institutions; and (5) that the States, exercising their recognized jurisdiction over Indian child custody proceedings through administrative and judicial bodies, have often failed to recognize the essential tribal relations of Indian people and the cultural and social standards prevailing in Indian communities and families.

§ 1902. Congressional declaration of policy

The Congress hereby declares that it is the policy of this Nation to protect the best interests of Indian children and to promote the stability and security of Indian tribes and families by the establishment of minimum Federal standards for the removal of Indian children from their families and the placement of such children in foster or adoptive homes which will reflect the unique values of Indian culture, and by providing for assistance to Indian tribes in the operation of child and family service programs.

§ 1903. Definitions

For the purposes of this chapter, except as may be specifically provided otherwise, the term—

(1) "child custody proceeding" shall mean and include—(i) "foster care placement" which shall mean any action removing an Indian child from its parent or Indian custodian for temporary placement in a foster home or institution or the home of a guardian or conservator where the parent or Indian custodian cannot have the child returned upon demand, but where parental rights have not been terminated; (ii) "termination of parental rights" which shall mean any action resulting in the termination of the parent-child relationship;

(iii) "preadoptive placement" which shall mean the temporary placement of an Indian child in a foster home or institution after the termination of parental rights, but prior to or in lieu of adoptive placement; and (iv) "adoptive placement" which shall mean the permanent placement of an Indian child for adoption, including any action resulting in a final decree of adoption. Such term or terms shall not include a placement based upon an act which, if committed by an adult, would be deemed a crime or upon an award, in a divorce proceeding, of custody to one of the parents.

(2) "extended family member" shall be as defined by the law or custom of the Indian child's tribe or, in the absence of such law or custom, shall be a person who has reached the age of eighteen and who is the Indian child's grandparent, aunt or uncle, brother or sister, brother-in-law or sister-in-law, niece or nephew, first or second cousin, or stepparent; (3) "Indian" means any person who is a member of an Indian tribe, or who is an Alaska Native and a member of a Regional Corporation as defined in 1606 of title 43; (4) "Indian child" means any unmarried person who is under age eighteen and is either (a) a member of an Indian tribe or (b) is eligible for membership in an Indian tribe and is the biological child of a member of an Indian tribe; (5) "Indian child's tribe" means (a) the Indian tribe in which an Indian child is a member or eligible for membership or (b), in the case of an Indian child who is a member of or eligible for membership in more than one tribe, the Indian tribe with which the Indian child has the more significant contacts; (6) "Indian custodian" means any Indian person who has legal custody of an Indian child under tribal law or custom or under State law or to whom temporary physical care, custody, and control has been transferred by the parent of such child; (7) "Indian organization" means any group, association, partnership, corporation, or other legal entity owned or controlled by Indians, or a majority of whose members are Indians; (8) "Indian tribe" means any Indian tribe, band, nation, or other organized group or community of Indians recognized as eligible for the services provided to Indians by the Secretary because of their status as Indians, including any Alaska Native village as defined in section 1602(c) of title 43; (9) "parent" means any biological parent or parents of an Indian child or any Indian person who has lawfully adopted an Indian child, including adoptions under tribal law or custom. It does not include the unwed father where paternity has not been acknowledged or established; (10) "reservation" means Indian country as defined in section 1151 of title 18 and any lands, not covered under such section, title to which is either held by the

United States in trust for the benefit of any Indian tribe or individual or held by any Indian tribe or individual subject to a restriction by the United States against alienation; (11) "Secretary" means the Secretary of the Interior; and (12) "tribal court" means a court with jurisdiction over child custody proceedings and which is either a Court of Indian Offenses, a court established and operated under the code or custom of an Indian tribe, or any other administrative body of a tribe which is vested with authority over child custody proceedings.

§ 1911. Indian tribe jurisdiction over Indian child custody proceedings

(a) Exclusive jurisdiction

An Indian tribe shall have jurisdiction exclusive as to any State over any child custody proceeding involving an Indian child who resides or is domiciled within the reservation of such tribe, except where such jurisdiction is otherwise vested in the State by existing Federal law. Where an Indian child is a ward of a tribal court, the Indian tribe shall retain exclusive jurisdiction, notwithstanding the residence or domicile of the child.

(b) Transfer of proceedings; declination by tribal court

In any State court proceeding for the foster care placement of, or termination of parental rights to, an Indian child not domiciled or residing within the reservation of the Indian child's tribe, the court, in the absence of good cause to the contrary, shall transfer such proceeding to the jurisdiction of the tribe, absent objection by either parent, upon the petition of either parent or the Indian custodian or the Indian child's tribe: Provided, That such transfer shall be subject to declination by the tribal court of such tribe.

(c) State court proceedings; intervention

In any State court proceeding for the foster care placement of, or termination of parental rights to, an Indian child, the Indian custodian of the child and the Indian child's tribe shall have a right to intervene at any point in the proceeding.

(d) Full faith and credit to public acts, records, and judicial proceedings of Indian tribes

The United States, every State, every territory or possession of the United States, and every Indian tribe shall give full faith and credit to the public acts, records, and judicial proceedings of any Indian tribe applicable to Indian child custody proceedings to the same extent that such entities give full faith and credit to the public acts, records, and judicial proceedings of any other entity.

§ 1912. Pending court proceedings

(a) Notice; time for commencement of proceedings; additional time for preparation in any involuntary proceeding in a State court, where the court knows or has reason to know that an Indian child is involved, the party seeking the foster care placement of, or termination of parental rights to, an Indian child shall notify the parent or Indian custodian and the Indian child's tribe, by registered mail with return receipt requested, of the pending proceedings and of their right of intervention. If the identity or location of the parent or Indian custodian and the tribe cannot be determined, such notice shall be given to the Secretary in like manner, who shall have fifteen days after receipt to provide the requisite notice to the parent or Indian custodian and the tribe. No foster care placement or termination of parental rights proceeding shall be held until at least ten days after receipt of notice by the parent or Indian custodian and the tribe or the Secretary: Provided, That the parent or Indian custodian or the tribe shall, upon request, be granted up to twenty additional days to prepare for such proceeding.

(b) Appointment of counsel

In any case in which the court determines indigency, the parent or Indian custodian shall have the right to court-appointed counsel in any removal, placement, or termination proceeding. The court may, in its discretion, appoint counsel for the child upon a finding that such appointment is in the best interest of the child. Where State law makes no provision for appointment of counsel in such proceedings, the court shall promptly notify the Secretary upon appointment of counsel, and the Secretary, upon certification of the presiding judge, shall pay reasonable fees and expenses out of funds which may be appropriated pursuant to section 13 of this title.

(c) Examination of reports or other documents

Each party to a foster care placement or termination of parental rights proceeding under State law involving an Indian child shall have the right to examine all reports or other documents filed with the court upon which any decision with respect to such action may be based.

(d) Remedial services and rehabilitative programs; preventive measures

Any party seeking to effect a foster care placement of, or termination of parental rights to, an Indian child under State law shall satisfy the court that active efforts have been made to provide remedial services and rehabilitative programs designed to prevent the breakup of the Indian family and that these efforts have proved unsuccessful.

(e) Foster care placement orders; evidence; determination of damage to child

No foster care placement may be ordered in such proceeding in the absence of a determination, supported by clear and convincing evidence, including testimony of qualified expert witnesses, that the continued custody of the child by the parent or Indian custodian is likely to result in serious emotional or physical damage to the child.

(f) Parental rights termination orders; evidence; determination of damage to child

No termination of parental rights may be ordered in such proceeding in the absence of a determination, supported by evidence beyond a reasonable doubt, including testimony of qualified expert witnesses, that the continued custody of the child by the parent or Indian custodian is likely to result in serious emotional or physical damage to the child.

§ 1913. Parental rights; voluntary termination

(a) Consent; record; certification matters; invalid consents

Where any parent or Indian custodian voluntarily consents to a foster care placement or to termination of parental rights, such consent shall not be valid unless executed in writing and recorded before a judge of a court of competent jurisdiction and accompanied by the presiding judge's certificate that the terms and consequences of the consent were fully explained in detail and were fully understood by the parent or Indian custodian. The court shall also certify that either the parent or Indian custodian fully understood the explanation in English or that it was interpreted into a language that the parent or Indian custodian understood. Any consent given prior to, or within ten days after, birth of the Indian child shall not be valid.

(b) Foster care placement; withdrawal of consent

Any parent or Indian custodian may withdraw consent to a foster care placement under State law at any time and, upon such withdrawal, the child shall be returned to the parent or Indian custodian.

(c) Voluntary termination of parental rights or adoptive placement; withdrawal of consent; return of custody

In any voluntary proceeding for termination of parental rights to, or adoptive placement of, an Indian child, the consent of the parent may be withdrawn for any reason at any time prior to the entry of a final decree of termination or adoption, as the case may be, and the child shall be returned to the parent.

(d) Collateral attack; vacation of decree and return of custody; limitations

After the entry of a final decree of adoption of an Indian child in any State court, the parent may withdraw consent thereto upon the grounds that consent was obtained through fraud or duress and may petition the court to vacate such decree. Upon a finding that such consent was obtained through fraud or duress, the court shall vacate such decree and return the child to the parent. No adoption which has been effective for at least two years may be invalidated under the provisions of this subsection unless otherwise permitted under State law.

§ 1914. Petition to court of competent jurisdiction to invalidate action upon showing of certain violations

Any Indian child who is the subject of any action for foster care placement or termination of parental rights under State law, any parent or Indian custodian from whose custody such child was removed, and the Indian child's tribe may petition any court of competent jurisdiction to invalidate such action upon a showing that such action violated any provision of sections 1911, 1912, and 1913 of this title.

§ 1915. Placement of Indian children

(a) Adoptive placements; preferences

In any adoptive placement of an Indian child under State law, a preference shall be given, in the absence of good cause to the contrary, to a placement with (1) a member of the child's extended family; (2) other members of the Indian child's tribe; or (3) other Indian families.

(b) Foster care or preadoptive placements; criteria; preferences

Any child accepted for foster care or preadoptive placement shall be placed in the least restrictive setting which most approximates a family and in which his special needs, if any, may be met. The child shall also be placed within reasonable proximity to his or her home, taking into account any special needs of the child. In any foster care or preadoptive placement, a preference shall be given, in the absence of good cause to the contrary, to a placement with—

(i) a member of the Indian child's extended family; (ii) a foster home licensed, approved, or specified by the Indian child's tribe; (iii) an Indian foster home licensed or approved by an authorized non-Indian licensing authority; or (iv) an institution for children approved by an Indian tribe or operated by an Indian organization which has a program suitable to meet the Indian child's needs.

(c) Tribal resolution for different order of preference; personal preference considered; anonymity in application of preferences

In the case of a placement under subsection (a) or (b) of this section, if the Indian child's tribe shall establish a different order of preference by resolution, the agency or court effecting the placement shall follow such order so long as the placement is the least restrictive setting appropriate to the particular needs of the child, as provided in subsection (b) of this section. Where appropriate, the preference of the Indian child or parent shall be considered: Provided, That where a consenting parent evidences a desire for anonymity, the court or agency shall give weight to such desire in applying the preferences.

(d) Social and cultural standards applicable

The standards to be applied in meeting the preference requirements of this section shall be the prevailing social and cultural standards of the Indian community in which the parent or extended family resides or with which the parent or extended family members maintain social and cultural ties.

(e) Record of placement; availability

A record of each such placement, under State law, of an Indian child shall be maintained by the State in which the placement was made, evidencing the efforts to comply with the order of preference specified in this section. Such record shall be made available at any time upon the request of the Secretary or the Indian child's tribe.

§ 1916. Return of custody

(a) Petition; best interests of child

Notwithstanding State law to the contrary, whenever a final decree of adoption of an Indian child has been vacated or set aside or the adoptive parents voluntarily consent to the termination of their parental rights to the child, a biological parent or prior Indian custodian may petition for return of custody and the court shall grant such petition unless there is a showing, in a proceeding subject to the provisions of section 1912 of this title, that such return of custody is not in the best interests of the child.

(b) Removal from foster care home; placement procedure

Whenever an Indian child is removed from a foster care home or institution for the purpose of further foster care, preadoptive, or adoptive placement, such placement shall be in accordance with the provisions of this chapter, except in the case where an Indian child is being returned to the parent or Indian custodian from whose custody the child was originally removed.

§ 1917. Tribal affiliation information and other information for protection of rights from tribal relationship; application of subject of adoptive placement; disclosure by court

Upon application by an Indian individual who has reached the age of eighteen and who was the subject of an adoptive placement, the court which entered the final decree shall inform such individual of the tribal affiliation, if any, of the individual's biological parents and provide such other information as may be necessary to protect any rights flowing from the individual's tribal relationship.

§ 1918. Reassumption of jurisdiction over child custody proceedings

(a) Petition; suitable plan; approval by Secretary

Any Indian tribe which became subject to State jurisdiction pursuant to the provisions of the Act of August 15, 1953 (67 Stat. 588), as amended by title IV of the Act of April 11, 1968 (82 Stat. 73, 78), or pursuant to any other Federal law, may reassume jurisdiction over child custody proceedings. Before any Indian tribe may reassume jurisdiction over Indian child custody proceedings, such tribe shall present to the Secretary for approval a petition to reassume such jurisdiction which includes a suitable plan to exercise such jurisdiction.

(b) Criteria applicable to consideration by Secretary; partial retrocession

(1) In considering the petition and feasibility of the plan of a tribe under subsection (a) of this section, the Secretary may consider, among other things: (i) whether or not the tribe maintains a membership roll or alternative provision for clearly identifying the persons who will be affected by the reassumption of jurisdiction by the tribe; (ii) the size of the reservation or former reservation area which will be affected by retrocession and reassumption of jurisdiction by the tribe; (iii) the population base of the tribe, or distribution of the population in homogeneous communities or geographic areas; and (iv) the feasibility of the plan in cases of multitribal occupation of a single reservation or geographic area. (2) In those cases where the Secretary determines that the jurisdictional provisions of section 1911(a) of this title are not feasible, he is authorized to accept partial retrocession which will enable tribes to exercise referral jurisdiction as provided in section 1911(b) of this title, or, where appropriate,

will allow them to exercise exclusive jurisdiction as provided in section 1911(a) of this title over limited community or geographic areas without regard for the reservation status of the area affected.

(c) Approval of petition; publication in Federal Register; notice; reassumption period; correction of causes for disapproval

If the Secretary approves any petition under subsection (a) of this section, the Secretary shall publish notice of such approval in the Federal Register and shall notify the affected State or States of such approval. The Indian tribe concerned shall reassume jurisdiction sixty days after publication in the Federal Register of notice of approval. If the Secretary disapproves any petition under subsection (a) of this section, the Secretary shall provide such technical assistance as may be necessary to enable the tribe to correct any deficiency which the Secretary identified as a cause for disapproval.

(d) Pending actions or proceedings unaffected

Assumption of jurisdiction under this section shall not affect any action or proceeding over which a court has already assumed jurisdiction, except as may be provided pursuant to any agreement under section 1919 of this title.

§ 1919. Agreements between States and Indian tribes

(a) Subject coverage

States and Indian tribes are authorized to enter into agreements with each other respecting care and custody of Indian children and jurisdiction over child custody proceedings, including agreements which may provide for orderly transfer of jurisdiction on a case-by-case basis and agreements which provide for concurrent jurisdiction between States and Indian tribes.

(b) Revocation; notice; actions or proceedings unaffected

Such agreements may be revoked by either party upon one hundred and eighty days' written notice to the other party. Such revocation shall not affect any action or proceeding over which a court has already assumed jurisdiction, unless the agreement provides otherwise.

§ 1920. Improper removal of child from custody; declination of jurisdiction; forthwith return of child: danger exception

Where any petitioner in an Indian child custody proceeding before a State court has improperly removed the child from custody of the parent or Indian custodian or has improperly retained custody after a visit or other temporary relinquishment of custody, the court shall decline jurisdiction over such petition and shall forthwith return the child to his parent or Indian custodian unless returning the child to his parent or custodian would subject the child to a substantial and immediate danger or threat of such danger.

§ 1921. Higher State or Federal standard applicable to protect rights of parent or Indian custodian of Indian child

In any case where State or Federal law applicable to a child custody proceeding under State or Federal law provides a higher standard of protection to the rights of the parent or Indian custodian of an Indian child than the rights provided under this subchapter, the State or Federal court shall apply the State or Federal standard.

§ 1922. Emergency removal or placement of child; termination; appropriate action

Nothing in this subchapter shall be construed to prevent the emergency removal of an Indian child who is a resident of or is domiciled on a reservation, but temporarily located off the reservation, from his parent or Indian custodian or the emergency placement of such child in a foster home or institution, under applicable State law, in order to prevent imminent physical damage or harm to the child. The State authority, official, or agency involved shall insure that the emergency removal or placement terminates immediately when such removal or placement is no longer necessary to prevent imminent physical damage or harm to the child and shall expeditiously initiate a child custody proceeding subject to the provisions of this subchapter, transfer the child to the jurisdiction of the appropriate Indian tribe, or restore the child to the parent or Indian custodian, as may be appropriate.

§ 1923. Effective date

None of the provisions of this subchapter, except sections 1911(a), 1918, and 1919 of this title, shall affect a proceeding under State law for foster care placement, termination of parental rights, preadoptive placement, or adoptive placement which was initiated or completed prior to one hundred and eighty days after November 8, 1978, but shall apply to any subsequent proceeding in the same matter or subsequent proceedings affecting the custody or placement of the same child.

§ 1931. Grants for on or near reservation programs and child welfare codes

(a) Statement of purpose; scope of programs

The Secretary is authorized to make grants to Indian tribes and organizations in the establishment and operation of Indian child and family service programs on or near reservations and in the preparation and implementation of child welfare codes. The objective of every Indian child and family service program shall be to prevent the breakup of Indian families and, in particular, to insure that the permanent removal of an Indian child from the custody of his parent or Indian custodian shall be a last resort. Such child and family service programs may include, but are not limited to—

(1) a system for licensing or otherwise regulating Indian foster and adoptive homes; (2) the operation and maintenance of facilities for the counseling and treatment of Indian families and for the temporary custody of Indian children; (3) family assistance, including homemaker and home counselors, day care, afterschool care, and employment, recreational activities, and respite care; (4) home improvement programs; (5) the employment of professional and other trained personnel to assist the tribal court in the disposition of domestic relations and child welfare matters; (6) education and training of Indians, including tribal court judges and staff, in skills relating to child and family assistance and service programs; (7) a subsidy program under which Indian adoptive children may be provided support comparable to that for which they would be eligible as foster children, taking into account the appropriate State standards of support for maintenance and medical needs; and (8) guidance, legal representation, and advice to Indian families involved in tribal, State, or Federal child custody proceedings.

(b) Non-Federal matching funds for related Social Security or other Federal financial assistance programs; assistance for such programs unaffected; State licensing or approval for qualification for assistance under federally assisted program

Funds appropriated for use by the Secretary in accordance with this section may be utilized as non-Federal matching share in connection with funds provided under titles IV-B and XX of the Social Security Act (42 U.S.C. 620 et seq., 1397 et seq.) or under any other Federal financial assistance programs which contribute to the purpose for which such funds are authorized to be appropriated for use under this chapter. The provision or possibility of assistance under this chapter shall not be a basis for the denial or reduction of any assistance otherwise authorized under titles IV-B and XX of the Social Security Act or any other federally assisted program.

For purposes of qualifying for assistance under a federally assisted program, licensing or approval of foster or adoptive homes or institutions by an Indian tribe shall be deemed equivalent to licensing or approval by a State.

§ 1932. Grants for off-reservation programs for additional services

The Secretary is also authorized to make grants to Indian organizations to establish and operate off-reservation Indian child and family service programs which may include, but are not limited to—(1) a system for regulating, maintaining, and supporting Indian foster and adoptive homes, including a subsidy program under which Indian adoptive children may be provided support comparable to that for which they would be eligible as Indian foster children, taking into account the appropriate State standards of support for maintenance and medical needs; (2) the operation and maintenance of facilities and services for counseling and treatment of Indian families and Indian foster and adoptive children; (3) family assistance, including homemaker and home counselors, day care, afterschool care, and employment, recreational activities, and respite care; and (4) guidance, legal representation, and advice to Indian families involved in child custody proceedings.

§ 1933. Funds for on and off reservation programs

(a) Appropriated funds for similar programs of Department of Health and Human Services; appropriation in advance for payments

In the establishment, operation, and funding of Indian child and family service programs, both on and off reservation, the Secretary may enter into agreements with the Secretary of Health and Human Services, and the latter Secretary is hereby authorized for such purposes to use funds appropriated for similar programs of the Department of Health and Human Services: Provided, That authority to make payments pursuant to such agreements shall be effective only to the extent and in such amounts as may be provided in advance by appropriation Acts.

(b) Appropriation authorization under section 13 of this title

Funds for the purposes of this chapter may be appropriated pursuant to the provisions of section 13 of this title.

§ 1934. "Indian" defined for certain purposes

For the purposes of sections 1932 and 1933 of this title, the term "Indian" shall include persons defined in section 1603(c) of this title.

§ 1951. Information availability to and disclosure by Secretary

(a) Copy of final decree or order; other information; anonymity affidavit; exemption from Freedom of Information Act

Any State court entering a final decree or order in any Indian child adoptive placement after November 8, 1978, shall provide the Secretary with a copy of such decree or order together with such other information as may be necessary to show—

(1) the name and tribal affiliation of the child; (2) the names and addresses of the biological parents; (3) the names and addresses of the adoptive parents; and (4) the identity of any agency having files or information relating to such adoptive placement. Where the court records contain an affidavit of the biological parent or parents that their identity remain confidential, the court shall include such affidavit with the other information. The Secretary shall insure that the confidentiality of such information is maintained and such information shall not be subject to the Freedom of Information Act (5 U.S.C. 552), as amended.

(b) Disclosure of information for enrollment of Indian child in tribe or for determination of member rights or benefits; certification of entitlement to enrollment

Upon the request of the adopted Indian child over the age of eighteen, the adoptive or foster parents of an Indian child, or an Indian tribe, the Secretary shall disclose such information as may be necessary for the enrollment of an Indian child in the tribe in which the child may be eligible for enrollment or for determining any rights or benefits associated with that membership. Where the documents relating to such child contain an affidavit from the biological parent or parents requesting anonymity, the Secretary shall certify to the Indian child's tribe, where the information warrants, that the child's parentage and other circumstances of birth entitle the child to enrollment under the criteria established by such tribe.

§ 1952. Rules and regulations

Within one hundred and eighty days after November 8, 1978, the Secretary shall promulgate such rules and regulations as may be necessary to carry out the provisions of this chapter.

§ 1961. Locally convenient day schools

(a) Sense of Congress

It is the sense of Congress that the absence of locally convenient day schools may contribute to the breakup of Indian families.

(b) Report to Congress; contents, etc.

The Secretary is authorized and directed to prepare, in consultation with appropriate agencies in the Department of Health and Human Services, a report on the feasibility of providing Indian children with schools located near their homes, and to submit such report to the Select Committee on Indian Affairs of the United States Senate and the Committee on Interior and Insular Affairs of the United States House of Representatives within two years from November 8, 1978. In developing this report the Secretary shall give particular consideration to the provision of educational facilities for children in the elementary grades.

§ 1962. Copies to the States

Within sixty days after November 8, 1978, the Secretary shall send to the Governor, chief justice of the highest court of appeal, and the attorney general of each State a copy of this chapter, together with committee reports and an explanation of the provisions of this chapter.

§ 1963. Severability

If any provision of this chapter or the applicability thereof is held invalid, the remaining provisions of this chapter shall not be affected thereby.

For more information on public policy issues, contact NICWA staff member David Simmons by e-mail: desimmons@nicwa.org or by phone at (503) 222-4044, ext. 19.

Indian Gaming Regulatory Act (IGRA) of 1988

This congressional act affirmed the right of tribes to conduct gaming on Indian lands but made it subject to tribal-state compact negotiations for certain types of gaming.

1. Class I gaming includes social games played solely for prizes of minimal value or traditional forms of Indian gaming engaged in by individuals. The tribe has exclusive regulatory jurisdiction over Class I gaming.
2. Class II gaming includes all forms of bingo and similar games (pull-tabs and punch-boards) as long as they are played in the same location as bingo games; non-banking games that are either expressly allowed or not expressly prohibited by state law; and banking card games in existence in Michigan,

North Dakota, Montana, and Washington on or before May 1, 1988. Class II gaming is subject to tribal regulatory jurisdiction with extensive oversight by the National Indian Gaming Commission (NIGC).

3. Class III gaming includes all forms of gaming not mentioned in Class I or II, and includes slots, casino games, banking card games, horse and dog racing, pari-mutuel wagering, and jai-alai. Such gaming is lawful on Indian lands *only* (1) if it has been authorized by a tribal ordinance approved by the chairperson of the NIGC *and* (2) if such gaming is permitted by the state for any purpose by any person, organization, or entity, *and* (3) it is conducted in a way that conforms to the tribal-state compact in effect. Regulation of Class III gaming is left to the tribal-state compact negotiation process.

Under IGRA, a tribe must request that a state enter into compact negotiations. After such a request is made, the state is obligated to negotiate in good faith to enter into a compact, which must also be approved by the secretary of the Interior. Because some states have failed to live up to IGRA and good-faith negotiations, a number of lawsuits have arisen.

Indian Entities Recognized and Eligible to Receive Services from the United States Bureau of Indian Affairs

AGENCY: Bureau of Indian Affairs.

SUMMARY: Notice is hereby given of the current list of tribal entities recognized and eligible for funding and services from the Bureau of Indian Affairs by virtue of their status as Indian tribes. This notice is published pursuant to Section 104 of the Act of November 2, 1994 (Pub. L. 103–454; 108 Stat. 4791, 4792).

FOR FURTHER INFORMATION CONTACT: Daisy West, Bureau of Indian Affairs, Division of Tribal Government Services, MS-4631-MIB, 1849 C Street, NW, Washington, D.C. 20240. Telephone number: (202) 208-2475.

SUPPLEMENTARY INFORMATION: This notice is published in exercise of authority delegated to the Assistant Secretary—Indian Affairs under 25 U.S.C. 2 and 9 and 209 DM 8.

Published below are lists of federally acknowledged tribes in the contiguous forty-eight states and in Alaska. The list is updated from the last such list published in October 23, 1997 (62 FR 55270), to include name changes or corrections. There have been no new tribal entities added to the list. The listed entities are acknowledged to have the immunities and privileges available to other federally acknowledged Indian tribes by virtue of their government-to-government relationship with the United States as well as the responsibilities, powers, limitations, and obligations of such tribes.

INDIAN TRIBAL ENTITIES WITHIN THE CONTIGUOUS 48 STATES RECOGNIZED AND ELIGIBLE TO RECEIVE SERVICES FROM THE UNITED STATES BUREAU OF INDIAN AFFAIRS

A

Absentee-Shawnee Tribe of Indians of Oklahoma

Agua Caliente Band of Cahuilla Indians of the Agua Caliente Indian Reservation, California

Ak Chin Indian Community of the Maricopa (Ak Chin) Indian Reservation, Arizona

Alabama-Coushatta Tribes of Texas

Alabama-Quassarte Tribal Town, Oklahoma

Alturas Indian Rancheria, California

Apache Tribe of Oklahoma

Arapahoe Tribe of the Wind River Reservation, Wyoming

Aroostook Band of Micmac Indians of Maine

Assiniboine and Sioux Tribes of the Fort Peck Indian Reservation, Montana

Augustine Band of Cahuilla Mission Indians of the Augustine Reservation, California

B

Bad River Band of the Lake Superior Tribe of Chippewa Indians of the Bad River Reservation, Wisconsin

Bay Mills Indian Community of the Sault Ste. Marie Band of Chippewa Indians, Bay Mills Reservation, Michigan

Bear River Band of the Rohnerville Rancheria, California

Berry Creek Rancheria of Maidu Indians of California

Big Lagoon Rancheria, California

Big Pine Band of Owens Valley Paiute Shoshone Indians of the Big Pine Reservation, California

Big Sandy Rancheria of Mono Indians of California
Big Valley Rancheria of Pomo & Pit River Indians of California
Blackfeet Tribe of the Blackfeet Indian Reservation of Montana
Blue Lake Rancheria, California
Bridgeport Paiute Indian Colony of California
Buena Vista Rancheria of Me-Wuk Indians of California
Burns Paiute Tribe of the Burns Paiute Indian Colony of Oregon

C

Cabazon Band of Cahuilla Mission Indians of the Cabazon
    Reservation, California
Cachil DeHe Band of Wintun Indians of the Colusa Indian
    Community of the Colusa Rancheria, California
Caddo Indian Tribe of Oklahoma
Cahto Indian Tribe of the Laytonville Rancheria, California
Cahuilla Band of Mission Indians of the Cahuilla Reservation,
    California
Campo Band of Diegueno Mission Indians of the Campo Indian
    Reservation, California
Capitan Grande Band of Diegueno Mission Indians of California:
    Barona Group of Capitan Grande Band of Mission Indians of the
        Barona Reservation, California
    Viejas (Baron Long) Group of Capitan Grande Band of Mission
        Indians of the Viejas Reservation, California
Catawba Indian Nation (aka Catawba Tribe of South Carolina)
Cayuga Nation of New York
Cedarville Rancheria, California
Chemehuevi Indian Tribe of the Chemehuevi Reservation, California
Cher-Ae Heights Indian Community of the Trinidad Rancheria,
    California
Cherokee Nation of Oklahoma
Cheyenne-Arapaho Tribes of Oklahoma
Cheyenne River Sioux Tribe of the Cheyenne River Reservation,
    South Dakota
Chickasaw Nation, Oklahoma
Chicken Ranch Rancheria of Me-Wuk Indians of California
Chippewa-Cree Indians of the Rocky Boy's Reservation, Montana
Chitimacha Tribe of Louisiana
Choctaw Nation of Oklahoma

Citizen Potawatomi Nation, Oklahoma
Cloverdale Rancheria of Pomo Indians of California
Cocopah Tribe of Arizona
Coeur D'Alene Tribe of the Coeur D'Alene Reservation, Idaho
Cold Springs Rancheria of Mono Indians of California
Colorado River Indian Tribes of the Colorado River Indian
   Reservation, Arizona and California
Comanche Indian Tribe, Oklahoma
Confederated Salish & Kootenai Tribes of the Flathead Reservation,
   Montana
Confederated Tribes and Bands of the Yakama Indian Nation of the
   Yakama Reservation, Washington
Confederated Tribes of the Chehalis Reservation, Washington
Confederated Tribes of the Colville Reservation, Washington
Confederated Tribes of the Coos, Lower Umpqua and Siuslaw
   Indians of Oregon
Confederated Tribes of the Goshute Reservation, Nevada
   and Utah
Confederated Tribes of the Grand Ronde Community of Oregon
Confederated Tribes of the Siletz Reservation, Oregon
Confederated Tribes of the Umatilla Reservation, Oregon
Confederated Tribes of the Warm Springs Reservation of Oregon
Coquille Tribe of Oregon
Cortina Indian Rancheria of Wintun Indians of California
Coushatta Tribe of Louisiana
Cow Creek Band of Umpqua Indians of Oregon
Coyote Valley Band of Pomo Indians of California
Crow Creek Sioux Tribe of the Crow Creek Reservation, South
   Dakota
Crow Tribe of Montana
Cuyapaipe Community of Diegueno Mission Indians of the
   Cuyapaipe Reservation, California

D

Death Valley Timbi-Sha Shoshone Band of California
Delaware Tribe of Indians, Oklahoma
Delaware Tribe of Western Oklahoma
Dry Creek Rancheria of Pomo Indians of California
Duckwater Shoshone Tribe of the Duckwater Reservation, Nevada

E

Eastern Band of Cherokee Indians of North Carolina
Eastern Shawnee Tribe of Oklahoma
Elem Indian Colony of Pomo Indians of the Sulphur Bank
  Rancheria, California
Elk Valley Rancheria, California
Ely Shoshone Tribe of Nevada
Enterprise Rancheria of Maidu Indians of California

F

Fort Belknap Indian Community of the Fort Belknap Reservation of
  Montana
Fort Bidwell Indian Community of the Fort Bidwell Reservation of
  California
Fort Independence Indian Community of Paiute Indians of the Fort
  Independence Reservation, California
Fort McDermitt Paiute and Shoshone Tribes of the Fort McDermitt
  Indian Reservation, Nevada and Oregon
Fort McDowell Mohave-Apache Community of the Fort McDowell
  Indian Reservation, Arizona
Fort Mojave Indian Tribe of Arizona, California & Nevada
Fort Sill Apache Tribe of Oklahoma

G

Gila River Indian Community of the Gila River Indian Reservation,
  Arizona
Grand Traverse Band of Ottawa & Chippewa Indians of Michigan
Greenville Rancheria of Maidu Indians of California
Grindstone Indian Rancheria of Wintun-Wailaki Indians of
  California
Guidiville Rancheria of California

H

Hannahville Indian Community of Wisconsin Potawatomie Indians
  of Michigan
Havasupai Tribe of the Havasupai Reservation, Arizona

Ho-Chunk Nation of Wisconsin (formerly known as the Wisconsin
   Winnebago Tribe)
Hoh Indian Tribe of the Hoh Indian Reservation, Washington
Hoopa Valley Tribe, California
Hopi Tribe of Arizona
Hopland Band of Pomo Indians of the Hopland Rancheria,
   California
Houlton Band of Maliseet Indians of Maine
Hualapai Indian Tribe of the Hualapai Indian Reservation, Arizona
Huron Potawatomi, Inc., Michigan

I

Inaja Band of Diegueno Mission Indians of the Inaja and Cosmit
   Reservation, California
Ione Band of Miwok Indians of California
Iowa Tribe of Kansas and Nebraska
Iowa Tribe of Oklahoma

J

Jackson Rancheria of Me-Wuk Indians of California
Jamestown S'Klallam Tribe of Washington
Jamul Indian Village of California
Jena Band of Choctaw Indians, Louisiana
Jicarilla Apache Tribe of the Jicarilla Apache Indian Reservation,
   New Mexico

K

Kaibab Band of Paiute Indians of the Kaibab Indian Reservation,
   Arizona
Kalispel Indian Community of the Kalispel Reservation, Washington
Karuk Tribe of California
Kashia Band of Pomo Indians of the Stewarts Point Rancheria,
   California
Kaw Nation, Oklahoma
Keweenaw Bay Indian Community of L'Anse and Ontonagon Bands
   of Chippewa Indians of the L'Anse Reservation, Michigan
Kialegee Tribal Town, Oklahoma

Kickapoo Traditional Tribe of Texas
Kickapoo Tribe of Indians of the Kickapoo Reservation in Kansas
Kickapoo Tribe of Oklahoma
Kiowa Indian Tribe of Oklahoma
Klamath Indian Tribe of Oregon
Kootenai Tribe of Idaho

L

La Jolla Band of Luiseno Mission Indians of the La Jolla Reservation,
    California
La Posta Band of Diegueno Mission Indians of the La Posta Indian
    Reservation, California
Lac Courte Oreilles Band of Lake Superior Chippewa Indians of the
    Lac Courte Oreilles Reservation of Wisconsin
Lac du Flambeau Band of Lake Superior Chippewa Indians of the Lac
    du Flambeau Reservation of Wisconsin
Lac Vieux Desert Band of Lake Superior Chippewa Indians of
    Michigan
Las Vegas Tribe of Paiute Indians of the Las Vegas Indian Colony,
    Nevada
Little River Band of Ottawa Indians of Michigan
Little Traverse Bay Bands of Odawa Indians of Michigan
Los Coyotes Band of Cahuilla Mission Indians of the Los Coyotes
    Reservation, California
Lovelock Paiute Tribe of the Lovelock Indian Colony, Nevada
Lower Brule Sioux Tribe of the Lower Brule Reservation, South
    Dakota
Lower Elwha Tribal Community of the Lower Elwha Reservation,
    Washington
Lower Sioux Indian Community of Minnesota Mdewakanton Sioux
    Indians of the Lower Sioux Reservation in Minnesota
Lummi Tribe of the Lummi Reservation, Washington
Lytton Rancheria of California

M

Makah Indian Tribe of the Makah Indian Reservation, Washington
Manchester Band of Pomo Indians of the Manchester-Point Arena
    Rancheria, California

Manzanita Band of Diegueno Mission Indians of the Manzanita
Reservation, California
Mashantucket Pequot Tribe of Connecticut
Mechoopda Indian Tribe of Chico Rancheria, California
Menominee Indian Tribe of Wisconsin
Mesa Grande Band of Diegueno Mission Indians of the Mesa Grande
Reservation, California
Mescalero Apache Tribe of the Mescalero Reservation, New Mexico
Miami Tribe of Oklahoma
Miccosukee Tribe of Indians of Florida
Middletown Rancheria of Pomo Indians of California
Minnesota Chippewa Tribe, Minnesota (Six component reservations:
Bois Forte Band (Nett Lake); Fond du Lac Band; Grand Portage
Band; Leech Lake Band; Mille Lacs Band; White Earth Band)
Mississippi Band of Choctaw Indians, Mississippi
Moapa Band of Paiute Indians of the Moapa River Indian
Reservation, Nevada
Modoc Tribe of Oklahoma
Mohegan Indian Tribe of Connecticut
Mooretown Rancheria of Maidu Indians of California
Morongo Band of Cahuilla Mission Indians of the Morongo
Reservation, California
Muckleshoot Indian Tribe of the Muckleshoot Reservation, Washington
Muscogee (Creek) Nation, Oklahoma

N

Narragansett Indian Tribe of Rhode Island
Navajo Nation of Arizona, New Mexico & Utah
Nez Perce Tribe of Idaho
Nisqually Indian Tribe of the Nisqually Reservation, Washington
Nooksack Indian Tribe of Washington
Northern Cheyenne Tribe of the Northern Cheyenne Indian
Reservation, Montana
Northfork Rancheria of Mono Indians of California
Northwestern Band of Shoshoni Nation of Utah (Washakie)

O

Oglala Sioux Tribe of the Pine Ridge Reservation, South Dakota
Omaha Tribe of Nebraska

Oneida Nation of New York
Oneida Tribe of Wisconsin
Onondaga Nation of New York
Osage Tribe, Oklahoma
Otoe-Missouria Tribe of Indians, Oklahoma
Ottawa Tribe of Oklahoma

P

Paiute Indian Tribe of Utah
Paiute-Shoshone Indians of the Bishop Community of the Bishop Colony, California
Paiute-Shoshone Indians of the Lone Pine Community of the Lone Pine Reservation, California
Paiute-Shoshone Tribe of the Fallon Reservation and Colony, Nevada
Pala Band of Luiseno Mission Indians of the Pala Reservation, California
Pascua Yaqui Tribe of Arizona
Paskenta Band of Nomlaki Indians of California
Passamaquoddy Tribe of Maine
Pauma Band of Luiseno Mission Indians of the Pauma & Yuima Reservation, California
Pawnee Indian Tribe of Oklahoma
Pechanga Band of Luiseno Mission Indians of the Pechanga Reservation, California
Penobscot Tribe of Maine
Peoria Tribe of Indians of Oklahoma
Picayune Rancheria of Chukchansi Indians of California
Pinoleville Rancheria of Pomo Indians of California
Pit River Tribe, California (includes Big Bend, Lookout, Montgomery Creek & Roaring Creek Rancherias & XL Ranch)
Poarch Band of Creek Indians of Alabama
Pokagon Band of Potawatomi Indians of Michigan
Ponca Tribe of Indians of Oklahoma
Ponca Tribe of Nebraska
Port Gamble Indian Community of the Port Gamble Reservation, Washington
Potter Valley Rancheria of Pomo Indians of California
Prairie Band of Potawatomi Indians, Kansas

Prairie Island Indian Community of Minnesota Mdewakanton Sioux
Indians of the Prairie Island Reservation, Minnesota
Pueblo of Acoma, New Mexico
Pueblo of Cochiti, New Mexico
Pueblo of Isleta, New Mexico
Pueblo of Jemez, New Mexico
Pueblo of Laguna, New Mexico
Pueblo of Nambe, New Mexico
Pueblo of Picuris, New Mexico
Pueblo of Pojoaque, New Mexico
Pueblo of San Felipe, New Mexico
Pueblo of San Ildefonso, New Mexico
Pueblo of San Juan, New Mexico
Pueblo of Sandia, New Mexico
Pueblo of Santa Ana, New Mexico
Pueblo of Santa Clara, New Mexico
Pueblo of Santo Domingo, New Mexico
Pueblo of Taos, New Mexico
Pueblo of Tesuque, New Mexico
Pueblo of Zia, New Mexico
Puyallup Tribe of the Puyallup Reservation, Washington
Pyramid Lake Paiute Tribe of the Pyramid Lake Reservation, Nevada

Q

Quapaw Tribe of Indians, Oklahoma
Quartz Valley Indian Community of the Quartz Valley Reservation
of California
Quechan Tribe of the Fort Yuma Indian Reservation, California &
Arizona
Quileute Tribe of the Quileute Reservation, Washington
Quinault Tribe of the Quinault Reservation, Washington

R

Ramona Band or Village of Cahuilla Mission Indians of California
Red Cliff Band of Lake Superior Chippewa Indians of Wisconsin
Red Lake Band of Chippewa Indians of the Red Lake Reservation,
Minnesota
Redding Rancheria, California

Redwood Valley Rancheria of Pomo Indians of California
Reno-Sparks Indian Colony, Nevada
Resighini Rancheria, California (formerly known as the Coast Indian Community of Yurok Indians of the Resighini Rancheria)
Rincon Band of Luiseno Mission Indians of the Rincon Reservation, California
Robinson Rancheria of Pomo Indians of California
Rosebud Sioux Tribe of the Rosebud Indian Reservation, South Dakota
Round Valley Indian Tribes of the Round Valley Reservation, California (formerly known as the Covelo Indian Community)
Rumsey Indian Rancheria of Wintun Indians of California

S

Sac & Fox Tribe of the Mississippi in Iowa
Sac & Fox Nation of Missouri in Kansas and Nebraska
Sac & Fox Nation, Oklahoma
Saginaw Chippewa Indian Tribe of Michigan, Isabella Reservation
Salt River Pima-Maricopa Indian Community of the Salt River Reservation, Arizona
Samish Indian Tribe, Washington
San Carlos Apache Tribe of the San Carlos Reservation, Arizona
San Juan Southern Paiute Tribe of Arizona
San Manuel Band of Serrano Mission Indians of the San Manuel Reservation, California
San Pasqual Band of Diegueno Mission Indians of California
Santa Rosa Band of Cahuilla Mission Indians of the Santa Rosa Reservation, California
Santa Rosa Indian Community of the Santa Rosa Rancheria, California
Santa Ynez Band of Chumash Mission Indians of the Santa Ynez Reservation, California
Santa Ysabel Band of Diegueno Mission Indians of the Santa Ysabel Reservation, California
Santee Sioux Tribe of the Santee Reservation of Nebraska
Sauk-Suiattle Indian Tribe of Washington
Sault Ste. Marie Tribe of Chippewa Indians of Michigan
Scotts Valley Band of Pomo Indians of California
Seminole Nation of Oklahoma

Seminole Tribe of Florida, Dania, Big Cypress, Brighton, Hollywood & Tampa Reservations
Seneca-Cayuga Tribe of Oklahoma
Seneca Nation of New York
Shakopee Mdewakanton Sioux Community of Minnesota (Prior Lake)
Sheep Ranch Rancheria of Me-Wuk Indians of California
Sherwood Valley Rancheria of Pomo Indians of California
Shingle Springs Band of Miwok Indians, Shingle Springs Rancheria (Verona Tract), California
Shoalwater Bay Tribe of the Shoalwater Bay Indian Reservation, Washington
Shoshone-Bannock Tribes of the Fort Hall Reservation of Idaho
Shoshone-Paiute Tribes of the Duck Valley Reservation, Nevada
Shoshone Tribe of the Wind River Reservation, Wyoming
Sisseton-Wahpeton Sioux Tribe of the Lake Traverse Reservation, South Dakota
Skokomish Indian Tribe of the Skokomish Reservation, Washington
Skull Valley Band of Goshute Indians of Utah
Smith River Rancheria, California
Soboba Band of Luiseno Mission Indians of the Soboba Reservation, California
Sokaogon Chippewa Community of the Mole Lake Band of Chippewa Indians, Wisconsin
Southern Ute Indian Tribe of the Southern Ute Reservation, Colorado
Spirit Lake Tribe, North Dakota (formerly known as the Devils Lake Sioux Tribe)
Spokane Tribe of the Spokane Reservation, Washington
Squaxin Island Tribe of the Squaxin Island Reservation, Washington
St. Croix Chippewa Indians of Wisconsin, St. Croix Reservation
St. Regis Band of Mohawk Indians of New York
Standing Rock Sioux Tribe of North & South Dakota
Stillaguamish Tribe of Washington
Stockbridge-Munsee Community of Mohican Indians of Wisconsin
Summit Lake Paiute Tribe of Nevada
Suquamish Indian Tribe of the Port Madison Reservation, Washington
Susanville Indian Rancheria, California
Swinomish Indians of the Swinomish Reservation, Washington
Sycuan Band of Diegueno Mission Indians of California

T

Table Bluff Reservation–Wiyot Tribe, California
Table Mountain Rancheria of California
Te-Moak Tribes of Western Shoshone Indians of Nevada (Four
 constituent bands: Battle Mountain Band; Elko Band; South Fork
 Band and Wells Band)
Thlopthlocco Tribal Town, Oklahoma
Three Affiliated Tribes of the Fort Berthold Reservation, North
 Dakota
Tohono O'odham Nation of Arizona
Tonawanda Band of Seneca Indians of New York
Tonkawa Tribe of Indians of Oklahoma
Tonto Apache Tribe of Arizona
Torres-Martinez Band of Cahuilla Mission Indians of California
Tulalip Tribes of the Tulalip Reservation, Washington
Tule River Indian Tribe of the Tule River Reservation, California
Tunica-Biloxi Indian Tribe of Louisiana
Tuolumne Band of Me-Wuk Indians of the Tuolumne Rancheria of
 California
Turtle Mountain Band of Chippewa Indians of North Dakota
Tuscarora Nation of New York
Twenty-Nine Palms Band of Luiseno Mission Indians of California

U

United Auburn Indian Community of the Auburn Rancheria of
 California
United Keetoowah Band of Cherokee Indians of Oklahoma
Upper Lake Band of Pomo Indians of Upper Lake Rancheria of
 California
Upper Sioux Indian Community of the Upper Sioux Reservation,
 Minnesota
Upper Skagit Indian Tribe of Washington
Ute Indian Tribe of the Uintah & Ouray Reservation, Utah
Ute Mountain Tribe of the Ute Mountain Reservation, Colorado,
 New Mexico & Utah
Utu Utu Gwaitu Paiute Tribe of the Benton Paiute Reservation,
 California

W

Walker River Paiute Tribe of the Walker River Reservation, Nevada

Wampanoag Tribe of Gay Head (Aquinnah) of Massachusetts

Washoe Tribe of Nevada & California (Carson Colony, Dresslerville Colony, Woodfords Community, Stewart Community, & Washoe Ranches)

White Mountain Apache Tribe of the Fort Apache Reservation, Arizona

Wichita and Affiliated Tribes (Wichita, Keechi, Waco & Tawakonie), Oklahoma

Winnebago Tribe of Nebraska

Winnemucca Indian Colony of Nevada

Wyandotte Tribe of Oklahoma

Y

Yankton Sioux Tribe of South Dakota

Yavapai-Apache Nation of the Camp Verde Indian Reservation, Arizona

Yavapai-Prescott Tribe of the Yavapai Reservation, Arizona

Yerington Paiute Tribe of the Yerington Colony & Campbell Ranch, Nevada

Yomba Shoshone Tribe of the Yomba Reservation, Nevada

Ysleta Del Sur Pueblo of Texas

Yurok Tribe of the Yurok Reservation, California

Z

Zuni Tribe of the Zuni Reservation, New Mexico

Source: U.S. Department of the Interior. Bureau of Indian Affairs.

Key Terms and Events

aboriginal: Original; indigenous; native to a particular region.

abrogation: The action of terminating a treaty or international agreement.

Akicitas: Fraternal societies of the Plains tribes responsible for policing camp.

Alaskan Native Claims Settlement Act: A 1971 act extinguishing Alaskan land claims.

Algonkian: A language family of the midwestern and eastern United States, spoken by the Shawnees, Kickapoos, Delawares, Cheyennes, Potawatomis, and other tribes.

All-Indian Pueblo Council: Mutual alliance of Pueblo Indians. The first recorded meeting was in 1598, and the group was formally organized in 1965 with a constitution and bylaws.

allotment: Surveyed reservation land distributed by the government to individual Indians under the provisions of the Dawes Allotment Act. Generally, 160 acres were allotted to heads of families, 80 acres to single persons, and 40 acres to other family members.

Allotment Policy (also know as the General Allotment of the Dawes Act): Federal Indian policy initiated in 1887. Designed to break up tribal governments, abolish Indian reservations by the allotment of communally held reservation lands to individual Indians for private ownership, and force Indians to assimilate into Euro-American cultural society.

American Indian Chicago Conference: A conference of Indian persons held in 1961 on the University of Chicago campus. Indian leaders in attendance issued a declaration that emphasized the goal of self-determination.

American Indian Movement (AIM): Militant Indian organization established in Minneapolis, Minnesota, in 1968. Originally founded to assist urban Indians, the organization broadened its purpose to include protesting the denial of Indian treaty rights, land rights, and social welfare.

Anasazi: Prehistoric southwestern culture that flourished in the Colorado River basin. The Anasazi excelled as basket makers, builders, and farmers.

appeal: Complaint to a higher court or authority that a decision at a lower level was in error.

Articles of Confederation: Document adopted by the Second Continental Congress on November 15, 1777, and ratified by all states in 1781. Modeled on the structure of the Iroquois League, the articles served as the framework of the U.S. government until the Constitution was adopted in 1789.

assimilation: The absorption of a minority culture group into the main culture body.

at-large election: Election of government officials from among members of the entire territory instead of from smaller districts.

band: Part of a tribe.

Black Drink: A purgative beverage made from the *cussena* plant and used in ceremonies by southeastern tribes as a means of cleansing and preparing worshippers.

blood quantum: An administrative measure of Indian ancestry, whether defined by a tribal government, Congress, or various federal agencies, in which, for example, a person considered to be a "full-blooded" Navajo is alleged to be entirely descended from Navajo ancestors; one-half blood quantum typically denotes someone who has one non-Indian parent and one "full-blooded" parent.

Bureau of Indian Affairs (BIA): Agency within the U.S. Department of the Interior responsible for administering the U.S. government's relationships with Indian governments and for overseeing Congress's trust responsibility for Indian lands and existence.

Busk: Annual renewal rite celebrated by southeastern tribes; also known as the Green Corn Ceremony.

bylaws: Set of rules adopted by an organization or assembly for governing its own meetings or affairs.

cacique: A word of Arawakan (Caribbean Indian) origin applied by Spanish explorers and colonists to indigenous religious leaders. Among traditional Pueblos the term designated the supreme village or town priest. The Pueblo cacique is considered the primary authority in all matters religious and secular.

calumet: Pipe used by eastern, midwestern, and Plains tribes in ceremonies of religious and diplomatic importance.

cession: The ceding or yielding of rights, property, or territory from one group or person to another.

clan: Individuals sharing the same lineage; American Indian clans are usually represented by an animal totem.

clan mother: Eldest female member of a clan; serves as the clan leader in a matriarchal society.

colonialism: The policy and practice of a strong power extending its control territorially, materially, and psychologically over a weaker nation or people. Often thought of as the product of the late nineteenth-century imperialists who conquered large tracts of the globe; usually used pejoratively to denote an unwarranted sense of racial superiority and the set of attitudes, beliefs, and practices that sprang from this sense.

communal: Belonging to or shared by the community.

communal ownership: Land ownership as practiced by American Indian tribes; title was vested in the tribe rather than in individuals.

confederacy: A league or alliance for mutual support, aid, and common action.

consensus: An agreement or opinion held by all.

constitution: Written or unwritten fundamental laws and principles that prescribe the nature, functions, and limits of a government and guarantee certain rights to the people.

council: A group elected or appointed as an advisory or legislative body; council members are usually equal in power and authority.

Council of Energy Resource Tribes (CERT): Special-interest organization formed by tribes in 1975 to assist in the preservation and management of their natural resources.

coups: Plains Indian custom of "touching" the enemy. Getting close enough to the enemy to touch but not kill was regarded as an act of bravery. Warriors recorded their coups by carving marks for such deeds on the coup stick.

culture: The ideas, customs, skills, arts, etc., of a given people in a given period.

Dawes Allotment Act: Also known as the General Allotment act of 1887, this act required that communally held reservation lands be allotted to individuals for ownership.

Deganwidah: Iroquois leader who created the Iroquois League approximately one thousand years ago.

democracy: Government by the people; a government in which the supreme power is vested in the people and exercised by them either directly (pure democracy) or indirectly through a system of representation (republicanism).

discovery, doctrine of: First fully articulated in U.S law in the seminal Supreme Court case *Johnson v. McIntosh* in 1823. The Court held that European explorers' "discovery" of land occupied by Indian tribes gave the discovering European nation (and the United State as successor) "an exclusive right to extinguish the Indian titles of occupancy, either by purchase or conquest." This meant that the "discovering" nation had preempted other European powers' involvement with the tribes in a particular geographic area. More importantly, as interpreted by Western policy makers and legal scholars, this doctrine effectively excluded Indian tribes from direct participation as national entities in the process of international community development.

doctrinc of prior appropriation: Test by which water rights are determined in western states; whoever first used the water is given "primary rights" to its current usage.

domestic dependent nation: Term used by Chief Justice John Marshall in 1831 to characterize the legal status of the Indian nations.

Dreamer religion: Established by the Shaphaptian prophet Smohalla, the Dreamer religion stressed a return to Indian traditions and the use of meditation or dreaming to find guidance and truth.

economy: The collective material pursuits by which a community sustains itself.

encomienda: A system by which land and its Indian inhabitants were "given" to Spanish landowners by the Spanish Crown. The Indians were forced to work for the landowners, who, in turn, were to convert the Indians to Catholicism.

encroach: To gradually enter or force oneself upon another's property or rights.

endogamous: A tradition dictating that members of a group marry someone from within the group.

enumerated powers: Powers specifically listed in a constitution and granted to specific parts of a government.

ethnocentrism: The belief that one's own ethnic group and culture are superior to all others.

excise tax: A tax or duty on the manufacture, sale, or consumption of various commodities, such as liquor or tobacco.

exogamous: A tradition dictating that members of a group marry partners from outside the group.

extended family: Family membership that may include relatives other than the nuclear family.

extraconstitutional: Outside the constitutional framework. Tribes were preexisting and original sovereigns and did not participate in the creation of the U.S. Constitution, which focused on the establishment of the federal government and the relationship between the central government and the constituent states. Thus, tribal sovereign rights do not arise from and are not protected by the Constitution's provisions. The Indian Civil Rights Act of 1968 modified this relationship slightly because the U.S. Constitution's first ten amendments did not protect the rights of persons (Indian and non-Indian) within tribal jurisdiction.

extradition: Surrender of an alleged criminal by one government to another that has criminal jurisdiction.

federally recognized tribes: Tribes with whom the federal government maintains an official relationship, usually established by treaty, congressional legislation, or executive order.

fee-simple ownership: Private ownership of land, based largely on the traditional English common-law practice of land tenure.

Five Civilized Tribes: Name given by whites to the Cherokee, Choctaw, Chickasaw, Muscogee, and Seminole tribes from the Southeast because of their adoption of certain European practices, such as written language, written constitutions, and schools.

General Allotment Act: See Dawes Allotment Act.

general council: Supreme governing body of some tribes; traditionally composed of all adult members of the tribe.

Ghost Dance religion: Founded by Wovoka, a Paiute, in Nevada during the late nineteenth century, this religion stressed peace and special worship, including dancing, to restore tribal ways.

government: An organization responsible for administering a group's public affairs.

government-to-government relationship: Relationship that exists between federally recognized tribes and the federal government. Implicit in the relationship is a recognition of tribal sovereignty and the U.S. government's obligation to protect tribal lands.

Green Corn ceremony: See Busk.

guardian: One who guards, protects, or takes care of another person and the person's property.

Haudenosaunee: Iroquois League; also known as the Five (and later Six) Nations.

Hotchkiss: Air-cooled, gas-operated machine gun developed in 1878.

Indian Civil Rights Act (IRCA): A federal law passed in 1968, the ICRA was the first legislation to impose many of the provisions of the U.S. Bill of Rights on the actions of tribal governments with regard to reservation residents; it set out a model code for courts of Indian offenses and required states to secure tribal consent before assuming legal jurisdiction in Indian country under P. L. 280.

Indian Claims Commission: Commission established in 1946 by Congress to hear suits from tribes suing for lands lost or illegally taken.

Indian country: Land on which Indian laws and customs and federal laws relating to Indians govern.

Indian removal: Federal policy enacted in 1830 and lasting into the 1850s that authorized the president to negotiate with a majority of eastern (and other) tribes for their relocation to lands west of the Mississippi River.

Indian Reorganization Act (IRA): Also called the Wheeler-Howard Act (1934), the IRA was formulated largely by John Collier, commissioner of Indian affairs, and was aimed at strengthening tribal government and restoring tribal lands.

indigenous: The United Nations Working Group on Indigenous Populations defines indigenous populations as those "composed of the existing descendants of peoples who inhabited the present territory of a country wholly or partially at the time when persons of a different culture or ethnic origin arrived there from other parts of the world, overcame them, and by conquest, settlement or other means, reduced them to a nondominant or colonial situation; who today live more in conformity with their particular social, economic and cultural customs and traditions than with the institutions of the country of which they now form a part, under a State structure which incorporates mainly the national, social and cultural characteristics of other segments of the population which are dominant."

individualism: Assumption that the individual, and not society, is paramount; that all values, rights, and duties originate in individuals and not in society; that individual initiative and action should be independent of government control.

initiative: Laws introduced directly by the people and subject to a popular vote.

injunction: A writ or court order either prohibiting a person from carrying out a given action or ordering a given action to be undertaken.

Inter Caetera: Papal proclamation of 1493 that drew a longitudinal (north/south) line through the Western Hemisphere. The New World to the left (west) was under Spanish control. The land to the right (east) was under Portuguese control.

interest-group activities: The actions of organized associations of individuals who share the same views on a particular issue or set of issues and attempt to influence related government policies.

Iroquois League: Government and military alliance originally formed more than one thousand years ago and originally composed of five Indian nations: the Mohawks, Oneidas, Onondagas, Cayugas, and Senecas. A sixth nation, the Tuscaroras, joined in the 1700s. The league is still in existence.

Johnson O'Malley Act (JOM): Passed in 1934, this act provided supplementary funds to local school districts for improvements in Indian education.

jurisdiction: The legal power a government has to govern its people and territory.

Kachina: A small, wooden, colorfully decorated effigy or icon figure representing a tribal deity; used by Pueblo Indians.

Kachina cult: Pueblo association, usually of all male village members above the age of early childhood but in some villages including female members as well. The cults are concerned with supernatural beings loosely connected with ancestral spirits and believed to have the power to bring rain. Kachina dances are spectacular ceremonies in which male members of the cult impersonate the Kachina by donning masks and colorful costumes.

kinship: One of the most hotly contested aspects of Indian culture, given the complexity and diversity evident throughout Indian country. Most Indians believe that kinship provides a social structure of cooperation and nonviolence that is also a means of maintaining political alliances and economic interaction for their societies. Kinship systems, although varied, also tend to determine the social position of the individual in a given society. Kinship ties also determine lines of descent, whether through the male (patrilineal) or the female (matrilineal) or through both males and females.

kiva: Pueblo ceremonial structure, circular or rectangular in shape, wholly or partly underground. These chambers are used almost exclusively by males for religious purposes and as a town forum. Leaders traditionally gathered there to discuss political, criminal, social, and military problems.

Laws of the Indies: Body of laws published by the Spanish Crown in 1681 to govern lands and natives in the New World.

litigation: Legal contest carried out through the judicial process.

Manifest Destiny: Popular view held during the nineteenth century that the American mission was to expand its territorial limits to the Pacific Coast.

mass media: All means of communication with the public, including television, newspapers, magazines, radio, books, recordings, motion pictures, and the Internet.

materialism: Belief that an individual's material well-being is of great importance and that to pursue it at the expense of social and spiritual well-being is acceptable.

matrilineal: System of social organization in which families are mother-centered, and descent and property devolve through the female line.

matrilocal: Requirement in some societies that a married couple live with the wife's mother.

medicine: In American Indian societies, power derived from a supernatural source.

Meriam Report: A survey of Indian affairs commissioned by Congress and issued in 1928. The report detailed the deplorable conditions in which many Indians lived and called for reforms.

Micco: Highest traditional office of the Muscogee towns.

moiety: A French word meaning "half" and referring to the division of a tribe into two halves; a moiety usually comprises a cluster of clans.

Muskhogean: A language family of the Southeast, spoken by tribes including the Natchez, Choctaws, Chickasaws, Muscogees, and Seminoles.

Nacas: Traditional Lakota societies that directed the civil affairs of the tribes.

nation: A stable, historically developed community of people who share territory, economic life, distinctive culture, and language.

National Congress of American Indians (NCAI): Organization of tribal leaders formed during the 1940s to lobby for the protection of Indian rights and culture.

National Indian Youth Conference: Organization formed by tribal youths in 1961 to provide Indian youths with a voice in policy reform.

Native American Church: Established in the early 1900s, this church's teachings combine traditional Indian beliefs and elements of Christianity with the sacramental use of peyote.

negotiation: Discussion between two or more parties in an effort to settle a dispute.

nomads: Groups of people who roam from place to place for particular reasons, such as to search for food.

nonrecognized tribe: Tribe that does not maintain a government-to-government and trust relationship with the federal government and does not, in general, receive government services or recognition of its land base or sovereignty.

nuclear family: Kinship group consisting of a father and mother and their children.

pan-Indian: Involving more than one tribe. Typically used in reference to organizations, activities, goals, and culture relevant to all Indian tribes.

party identification: The attachment a group or an individual feels to a particular political party. It measures the degree of an individual's inclination toward a particular party and the intensity of support. Party identification is usually a good predictor of voting behavior.

patrilineal: System of social organization in which families are father-centered, and descent and property devolve through the male line.

patrilocal: Social requirement that a married couple reside with the husband's father's clan.

Peace Policy: Policy formulated during the administration of President Ulysses S. Grant in the late 1860s and based on dealing with Indians peacefully in the hopes of speeding their assimilation. This policy lasted until 1877.

plenary doctrine: Doctrine stating that the federal government has unlimited governmental control and jurisdiction over Indian tribes.

plenary power: Complete in all aspects or essentials. However, in federal Indian policy and law, this term has three distinct meanings: (a) exclusive—Congress, under the Commerce Clause, is vested with sole authority to regulate the federal government's affairs with Indian tribes; (b) preemptive—Congress may enact legislation that effectively precludes state governments from acting in Indian-related matters; (c) unlimited or absolute—this judicially created definition maintains that the federal government has virtually boundless authority and jurisdiction over Indian tribes, their lands, and their resources.

polygamy: Plural marriages; marriage with more than one spouse.

potlatch: Winter ceremony held by some Pacific Coast tribes. By giving gifts to their guests, individuals increased their own status.

Proclamation of 1763: Declaration by the British government in 1763 to reserve the western portion of the previously claimed French areas for Indian use and to maintain control over the colonies.

protectorate: Relationship between two sovereigns in which the weaker state places itself under the protection of the more powerful state.

pueblo: Communal village built by some southwestern tribes and consisting of one or more flat-roofed structures of stone or adobe arranged in terraces and housing a number of families.

quorum: The minimum number (usually a majority) of officers or members of a group whose presence is required for a valid decision or transaction to be made.

rancheria: A Spanish term applied to small reservations in California.

ratify: To confirm a treaty or amendment.

recall: To remove an elected official from office by popular vote.

Red Power: Refers to the rise of Indian militancy and Pan-Indianism in the 1960s and 1970s.

referendum: Process of submitting an issue to popular vote.

reformative goals: Indian tribes and organizations are said to be pursuing reformative goals if they seek incremental or moderate change in the basic structure of Indian/non-Indian relations through redistribution of services, resources, and rewards within the existing framework.

religious revitalization movements: Indian social movements inspired by religious figures (that is, the Shawnee Prophet, the Ghost Dance of 1870 and 1890) that seek to bring back the old ways of living, prior to the arrival of the Europeans.

relocation: Federal policy formulated in 1952. Indians were relocated from rural and reservation areas to urban areas for job training and employment.

Requerimiento: Royal decree issued by the Spanish government and read by conquistadors to tribes informing them of their duty to the Spanish Crown and their obligation to convert to Chirstianity.

reservation: Lands reserved for tribal use.

reserved-rights doctrine: Doctrine enunciated by the courts that tribes retain all rights to their land, water, and resources unless they have expressly granted them to the federal government.

retrocession: Procedure by which states may return to tribes the jurisdictional powers they gained under Public Law 280.

rider: A provision that may have no relation to the basic subject matter of the bill it is "riding" on. Riders become law if the bills in which they are included become law. Riders on appropriations bills are outstanding examples, though technically they are banned by the U.S. House of Representatives, which, unlike the Senate, has a strict germaneness rule; thus riders are usually Senate devices.

sachem: Iroquois chieftain.

sales tax: Tax applied to the retail price of goods or services and collected by the retailer.

secular: Pertaining to everyday life; nonreligious.

sedentary: Refers to a people who establish permanent residence sites, usually to engage in agriculture rather than living a nomadic lifestyle.

self-determination: Decision-making control over one's own affairs and the policies that affect one's life.

severance tax: Tax applied to a resource at the time of its removal from the earth.

shaman: A priest and healer among some tribes.

smoke shops: Stores on reservations, usually tribally owned, where cigarettes are sold to tribal members and no state sales tax is applied.

social revitalization movements: Indian social movements designed to enable Indian tribes to accommodate the tremendous changes they endured in the wake of American expansionism; they included the Handsome Lake Church, the Kickapoo Prophet, the Shaker Church, and the Native American Church.

societies: Groups in which membership is determined by voluntary choice or recruitment rather than by kinship. Pueblo moieties are examples of such associations. Membership in Pueblo moieties is for life, and all members are recruited and confirmed by elaborate initiation rites.

sovereign: Supreme in power or authority.

sovereignty: The status, dominion, rule, or power of a sovereign.

state-recognized tribes: Tribes that usually are not federally recognized but maintain a special relationship with their state government and whose lands and rights are recognized by the state.

Sun Dance: An annual renewal ceremony observed by the Lakotas and other Plains tribes. The traditional Sun Dance included self-torture by warriors to benefit the nation's spiritual state.

syllabary: A list or table of syllables or characters representing syllables; a language whose written characters represent syllables instead of single sounds.

Talwa: Muscogee term for a political entity with attributes of both a tribe and a town.

taxation: Compulsory payment collected from individuals by the government and used for public purposes.

terminated tribes: Tribes whose government-to-government and trust relationship with the federal government has been terminated. Most of the more than one hundred terminations occurred between 1954 and 1961.

termination: Federal Indian policy during the 1950s that sought to end the federal government's relationship with Indian tribes as prescribed under House Concurrent Resolution 108.

theocracy: Government by religious authorities.

tradition: Cultural beliefs and customs handed down from ancestors.

transformative goals: Indian tribes or organizations are said to support transformative goals if they favor a fundamental, dramatic restructuring or transformation of the current structure of Indian/non-Indian relations. Such goals include calls to restart the treaty relationship or to end congressional plenary power.

treaty: Formal agreement between two or more nations, relating to peace, alliance, trade, etc.

tribal sovereignty: The spiritual, moral, and dynamic cultural force within a given tribal community empowering the group toward political, economic, and most importantly, cultural integrity; it also means maturity in the tribe's relationships with its own members, with other peoples and their governments, and with the environment.

tribe: A group of individuals bound together by ancestry, kinship, languages, culture, and political authority.

trust: Property held by one person for the benefit of another.

trustee: Person to whom another's property, or the management of that property, is entrusted.

trusteeship: The federal government's legal obligation to protect tribal land, resources, and existence.

values: Beliefs, standards, and moral precepts.

village: Term used to denote a community of Alaskan Natives.

wakan: Omnipotent, creative, directive force in Lakota belief.

wampum: Small beads made of shells; used by tribes of the Northeast as money and for ornament.

wampum belts: Red, white, purple, and black shells woven into belts and used by tribes of the Northeast as symbols of peace and war and for other international messages.

wardship: Refers to the federal government's responsibility as trustee over Indians as carried out primarily by the Bureau of Indian Affairs.

winter count: A tribal history drawn on buffalo hide and kept by the Lakota and Kiowa nations. Pictographs are drawn to represent an important event from each year.

writ of habeas corpus: A written order issued by a court or a judge to bring a person before a court or judge, thereby releasing that person from illegal custody.

zoning: The dividing of an area of land, such as a city, township, or reservation, by ordinance into sections reserved for different purposes, such as housing, business, manufacturing, and recreation.

References

Bureau of Indian Affairs. 1987. *American Indians Today.* Washington, D.C.: Government Printing Office.

O'Brien, Sharon. 1989. *American Indian Tribal Governments.* Norman: University of Oklahoma Press.

Yerington Paiute Tribe. 1985. *Introduction to Tribal Government.* Yerington, Nevada.

Resources

AMERICAN INDIAN ORGANIZATIONS*

American Indian Archaeological
  Institute (AIAI)
38 Curtis Rd.
P.O. Box 1260
Washington Green, CT 06793-0260
Phone: (203) 868-0518
Fax: (203) 868-1649

American Indian College Fund
217 E. 85th St., Suite 201
New York, NY 10028
Phone: (212) 988-4155 or
  (800) 776-3863
Fax: (212) 734-5118

American Indian Culture Research
  Center (AICRC)
P.O. Box 98
Blue Cloud Abbey
Marvin, SD 57251
Phone: (605) 432-5528

American Indian Higher Education
  Consortium (AIHEC)
513 Capitol Court NE., Suite 100
Washington, DC
Phone: (202) 544-9289
Fax: (202) 544-4084

American Indian Science and
  Engineering Society (AISES)
1085 14th St., Suite 1506
Boulder, CO 80302
Phone: (303) 492-8658
Fax: (303) 492-7090

Association on American Indian
  Affairs (AAIA)
245 Fifth Ave.
New York, NY 10016
Phone: (212) 689-8720

Council for Native Americans
  (CNAIP)
280 Broadway, Suite 316
New York, NY 10007
Phone: (212) 732-0485

Council of Energy Resource Tribes
  (CERT)
695 S. Colorado Blvd.,
  Suite 10
Denver, CO 80246
Phone: (303) 282-7576

First Nations Development
  Institute (FNDI)
69 Kelley Rd.
Falmouth, VA 22405
Phone: (703) 371-5615

Intertribal Buffalo Cooperative
1560 Concourse Dr.
Rapid City, SD 57703
Phone: (605) 394-9730
Fax: (605) 394-7742

Mni Sose Intertribal Water Rights
  Coalition, Inc.
P.O. Box 2890
Rapid City, SD 57709-2890
Phone: (605) 343-6054
Fax: (605) 343-4722

National American Indian Court
  Judges Association
4410 Arapahoe Ave., Suite 135
Boulder, CO 80303
Phone: (303) 245-0786
Fax: (303) 245-0785

National American Indian Housing
  Council
900 Second St. NE, Suite 305
Washington, DC 20002
Phone: (202) 789-1754 or
  (800) 284-9165
Fax: (202) 789-1758

National Congress of American
  Indians (NCAI)
1301 Connecticut Ave. NW,
  Suite 200
Washington, DC 20036
Phone: (202) 466-7767
Fax: (202) 466-7797

National Indian Education
700 North Fairfax St., Suite 210
Alexandria, VA 22314
Phone: (703) 838-2870
Fax: (703) 838-1620

Native American Journalist
  Association
Al Neuharth Media Center
555 Dakota St.
Vermillion, SD 57069

Phone: (605) 677-5282
Fax: (866) 694-4264

Native American Rights Fund
  (NARF)
1506 Broadway
Boulder, CO 80302
Phone: (303) 447-8760
Fax: (303) 443-7776

Northwest Indian Fisheries
  Commission
6730 Martin Way E
Olympia, WA 98516
Phone: (360) 438-1180
Fax: (360) 753-8659

United National Indian Tribal
  Youth, Inc. (UNITY)
500 N. Broadway, Suite 250
Oklahoma City, OK 73102
Mailing address:
P.O. Box 800
Oklahoma City, OK 73101
Phone: (405) 236-2800
Fax: (405) 971-1071

* These are a few of the mostly
national American Indian
organizations that exist presently.
To find the thousands of other
national, tribal, regional, state,
local, religious, and clan-based
American Indian organizations,
use Internet search engines.

STATE-RECOGNIZED TRIBES AND CONTACTS

Alabama (6)

Contact: Darla F. Graves,
  executive director
Alabama Indian Affairs
  Commission

One Court Sq., Suite 106
Montgomery, AL 36104
Phone: (334) 242-2831

Tribes: Echota Cherokee, MaChis
Lower Creek, Mowa Choctaw,
Northeast Alabama Cherokee,
Southeast Alabama Cherokee,
Star Muskogee Creek

Connecticut (3)

Contact: Ed Sarabia,
    Indian affairs coordinator
Office of Indian Affairs
79 Elm St.
Hartford, CT 06106-5127
Phone: (860) 424-3066

Tribes: Golden Hill Paugussett (R),
Paucatuck Eastern Pequot (R),
Schagticoke (R)

Georgia (3)

Contact: Robert Giacomini,
    director
State Data and Research Center
    250 14th St. NW, Room 543
Atlanta, GA 30318
Phone: (404) 894-9416

Tribes: Georgia Eastern Cherokee,
Cherokee of Georgia, Lower
Muskogee Creek (R), Tama Tribal
Town

Louisiana (5)

Contact: Pat Arnold, deputy director
    of Indian affairs for Louisiana
1885 Woodale Blvd., 12th Floor
Baton Rouge, LA 70806
Phone: (225) 922-2200

Tribes: Choctaw-Apache of Ebarb
(TDSA), Caddo Tribe, Clifton

Choctaw (TDSA), Four Winds
Cherokee, United Houma Nation
(TDSA)

Massachusetts (5)

Contact: Janice Falcon
Commission of North American
    Indian Center of Boston
10 South Huntington Ave.
Jamaica Plain, MA 02130
Phone: (617) 727-6394

Tribes: None. There is no
mechanism in place in this state for
Indian tribes to petition for state
recognition.

Michigan (3)

Contact: Karen Kay
Michigan Commission on Indian
    Affairs
Michigan Department of Civil
    Rights
Victor Bldg., Suite 700
201 N. Washington Sq.
Lansing, MI 48913
Phone: (517) 373-0654

Tribes: Burt Lake Band of Ottawa
and Chippewa Indians, Grand River
Band of Ottawa Indians, Swan
Creek Black River Confederate Tribe

Montana (1)

Contact: Wyman J. McDonald
Office of Indian Affairs
State Capital, Room 202
P.O. Box 200801
Helena, MT 59620-0801
Phone: (406) 444-3702

Tribe: Little Shell Chippewa Tribe

New Jersey (3)

Contact: Chief Roy Crazy Horse, chairman
New Jersey Commission on American Indian Affairs
Rankokus Indian Reservation
P.O. Box 225
Rancocas, NJ 08703
Phone: (609) 777-0883

Tribes: Nanticoke Lenni-Lenape, Powhatan Renape (R), Ramapough Mountain (TDSA)

New York (2)

Contact: Patrick Kehoe, assistant counsel
State of New York Executive Chambers, Room 214
Albany, NY 12224
Phone: (518) 474-2294

Tribes: Shinnecock (R), Poospatuck (R)

North Carolina (9)

Contact: Mr. Gregory Richardson, executive director
North Carolina Commission of Indian Affairs
217 West Jones St.
Raleigh, NC 27603
Phone: (919) 733-5998

Tribes: Coharie (TDSA), Haliwa-Saponi (TDSA), Lumbee (TDSA), Meherrin (TDSA), Indians of Person County, Waccamaw-Siouan (TDSA), Cumberland County Association for Indian People, Guilford Native American Association, Metrolina Native American Association

Oklahoma (1)

Contact: Barbara Warner
Oklahoma Indian Affairs Commission
Phone: (405) 521-3828

Virginia (8)

Contact: Thomasina Jordon, chair
Virginia Council of Indians
3008 Russell Rd.
Alexandria, VA 22305
Phone: (804) 786-7765

Tribes: Chickahominy Indian Tribe (TDSA), Chickahominy Eastern Band (TDSA), Monacan Indian Nation, Nansemond Indian Tribe, Rappahannock Indian Tribe, Upper Mattaponi Tribe, Mattaponi Indian Tribe (R), Pamunkey Indian Tribe (R)

West Virginia (1)

Contact: Joanna Wilsin
The Cultural Center
1900 Kanawha Blvd.
Charleston, WV 25305-0300
Phone: (304) 558-0220

Tribe: Appalachian American Indians of West Virginia

Source: U.S. Census Bureau, 2001.

TABLE 8.1
Census 2000 PHC-T-18. American Indian and Alaska Native Tribes in the United States: 2000

This table shows data for American Indian and Alaska Native tribes alone and alone or in combination for the United States.

Those respondents who reported as American Indian or Alaska Native only and one tribe are shown in column 1. Respondents who reported two or more American Indian or Alaska Native tribes but no other race are shown in column 2. Those respondents who reported as American Indian or Alaska Native and at least one other race and one tribe are shown in column 3. Respondents who reported as American Indian or Alaska Native and at least one other race and two or more tribes are shown in column 4. Those respondents who reported as American Indian or Alaska Native in any combination of race(s) or tribe(s) are shown in column 5 and is the sum of the numbers in columns 1 through 4. For an explanation of the alone and alone or in combination concepts used in this table, see "The American Indian and Alaska Native Population: 2000," U.S. Census Bureau, Census 2000 Brief, C2KBR/01-15 at www.census.gov/population/www/cen2000/briefs.html.

American Indian and Alaska Native Tribes	American Indian and Alaska Native alone		American Indian and Alaska Native in combination with one or more races	American Indian and Alaska tribe alone or in any combination	
	One tribe reported	Two or more tribes reported	One tribe reported	Two or more tribes reported	
(leading dot indicates subpart)	(1)	(2)	(3)	(4)	(5)
Total tribes tallied[1]	2,409,578	133,259	1,581,122	124,914	4,248,873
Total persons	2,416,410	59,546	1,582,860	60,485	4,119,301
Abenaki Nation of Missiquoi	2,385	137	2,686	264	5,472
Algonquian	1,107	191	2,314	502	4,114
Apache	57,060	7,917	24,947	6,909	96,833
.Apache	24,582	7,611	21,200	6,754	60,147
.Chiricahua	1,134	83	896	76	2,189
.Fort Sill Apache	253	10	45	3	311
.Jicarilla Apache	3,132	56	304	8	3,500
.Lipan Apache	131	7	65	5	208
.Mescalero Apache	5,374	135	1,459	59	7,027
.Oklahoma Apache	454	35	150	5	644
.Payson Tonto Apache	131	1	52	3	187
.San Carlos Apache	9,716	40	322	1	10,079
.White Mountain Apache	12,107	33	440	24	12,604

	One tribe reported	Two or more tribes reported	One tribe reported	Two or more tribes reported	
	(1)	(2)	(3)	(4)	(5)
Arapahoe	7,000	443	1,534	281	9,258
.Arapahoe	2,509	415	1,366	277	4,567
.Northern Arapahoe	4,410	26	142	4	4,582
.Southern Arapahoe	67	2	23	–	92
.Wind River Arapahoe	14	–	3	–	17
Arikara	775	254	245	42	1,316
Assiniboine	3,946	188	630	74	4,838
.Assiniboine	2,570	186	585	73	3,414
.Fort Peck Assiniboine	302	2	32	1	337
.Fort Belknap Assiniboine	1,074	–	13	–	1,087
Assiniboine Sioux	1,740	25	370	10	2,145
.Assiniboine Sioux	1,384	25	363	10	1,782
.Fort Peck Assiniboine and Sioux	356	–	7	–	363
Bannock	38	5	42	4	89
Blackfeet	27,104	4,358	41,389	12,899	85,750
Brotherton	622	19	646	26	1,313
Burt Lake Band	60	–	19	1	80
Caddo	2,675	326	1,191	170	4,362
.Caddo	2,302	319	1,124	162	3,907
.Caddo Indian Tribe of Oklahoma	72	5	21	3	101
.Caddo Adais Indians	301	2	46	5	354
Cahuilla	2,142	297	662	87	3,188
.Agua Caliente Band of Cahuilla Indians	55	2	13	1	71
.Augustine	1	–	4	–	5
.Cabazon Band of Cahuilla Mission Indians	33	–	1	–	34
.Cahuilla	1,109	179	420	44	1,752
.Los Coyotes Band of Cahuilla Mission Indians	117	7	16	–	140
.Morongo Band of Cahuilla Mission Indians	621	106	163	38	928
.Santa Rosa Cahuilla	10	13	8	4	35
.Torres Martinez Band of Cahuilla Mission Indians	183	8	23	–	214
.Ramona Band or Village of Cahuilla Mission Indians	4	–	14	–	18
California Tribes	900	400	392	129	1,821
.Cahto Indian Tribe of the Laytonville Rancheria	123	18	31	3	175

.Chimariko	23	5	12	5	45
.Coast Miwok	80	19	62	6	167
.Kawaiisu	4	2	2	–	8
.Kern River Paiute Council	25	9	12	5	51
.Mattole	27	20	43	7	97
.Red Wood	3	10	9	5	27
.Santa Rosa Indian Community	66	118	13	18	215
.Takelma	3	1	4	–	8
.Wappo	108	56	56	28	248
.Yana	42	22	21	15	100
.Yuki	311	116	106	32	565
.Bear River Band of Rohnerville Rancheria	73	28	19	9	129
Canadian and Latin American	**108,802**	**2,236**	**79,499**	**2,233**	**192,770**
.Canadian Indian	3,770	351	3,729	452	8,302
.Central American Indian	7,230	232	12,637	193	20,292
.French American Indian	672	50	2,714	118	3,554
.Mexican American Indian	76,992	1,728	39,938	1,430	120,088
.South American Indian	10,534	229	13,140	342	24,245
.Spanish American Indian	9,282	295	7,111	170	16,858
Catawba Indian Nation	**1,725**	**88**	**728**	**133**	**2,674**
Cayuse	**60**	**29**	**34**	**3**	**126**
Chehalis	**536**	**20**	**98**	**7**	**661**
Chemakuan	**593**	**16**	**138**	**2**	**749**
.Chemakuan	3	–	3	–	6
.Hoh Indian Tribe	124	–	31	1	156
.Quileute	466	16	104	1	587
Chemehuevi	**696**	**62**	**229**	**13**	**1,000**
Cherokee	**281,069**	**18,793**	**390,902**	**38,769**	**729,533**
.Cherokee	258,246	18,749	381,693	38,733	697,421
.Cherokee Alabama	93	–	57	4	154
.Cherokees of Northeast Alabama	674	1	188	4	867
.Cherokees of Southeast Alabama	612	3	133	3	751
.Eastern Cherokee	8,166	42	1,974	28	10,210
.Echota Cherokee	4,066	12	1,784	12	5,874
.Georgia Eastern Cherokee	192	3	86	–	281
.Northern Cherokee Nation of Missouri and Arkansas	1,605	11	1,106	2	2,724
.Tuscola	11	–	6	–	17
.United Keetoowah Band of Cherokee	528	8	65	2	603
.Western Cherokee	5,744	61	3,306	42	9,153
.Southeastern Cherokee Council	178	3	57	2	240
.Sac River Band of the Chickamauga Cherokee	11	–	13	3	27

	One tribe reported	Two or more tribes reported	One tribe reported	Two or more tribes reported	
	(1)	(2)	(3)	(4)	(5)
.White River Band of the Chickamauga Cherokee	223	5	216	4	448
.Four Winds Cherokee	605	2	158	2	767
.Cherokee of Georgia	62	1	24	1	88
Cherokee Shawnee	**587**	**12**	**561**	**22**	**1,182**
Cheyenne	**11,191**	**1,365**	**4,655**	**993**	**18,204**
.Cheyenne	5,310	1,266	3,914	979	11,469
.Northern Cheyenne	5,555	93	637	13	6,298
.Southern Cheyenne	323	12	104	1	440
Cheyenne Arapaho	**3,634**	**100**	**746**	**30**	**4,510**
Chickahominy	**1,007**	**23**	**303**	**25**	**1,358**
.Chickahominy Indian Tribe	980	23	299	23	1,325
.Chickahominy Eastern Band	27	–	4	2	33
Chickasaw	**20,887**	**3,014**	**12,025**	**2,425**	**38,351**
Chinook	**639**	**121**	**755**	**174**	**1,689**
.Chinook	611	123	716	170	1,620
.Clatsop	17	4	26	5	52
.Columbia River Chinook	–	–	2	1	3
.Kathlamet	2	–	–	–	2
.Upper Chinook	–	2	–	1	3
.Wakiakum Chinook	2	–	–	3	5
.Willapa Chinook	2	–	–	–	2
.Wishram	1	–	7	2	10
Chippewa	**105,907**	**2,730**	**38,635**	**2,397**	**149,669**
.Bad River Band of the Lake Superior Tribe	2,686	13	632	5	3,336
.Bay Mills Indian Community of the Sault Ste. Marie Band	891	10	91	5	997
.Bois Forte/Nett Lake Band of Chippewa	1,175	13	178	3	1,369
.Burt Lake Chippewa	13	8	5	2	28
.Chippewa	40,557	2,577	25,644	2,301	71,079
.Fond du Lac	1,483	12	406	4	1,905
.Grand Portage	422	2	118	4	546
.Grand Traverse Band of Ottawa and Chippewa Indians	2,615	21	554	9	3,199
.Keweenaw Bay Indian Community of the L'Anse and Ontonagon Bands	1,130	18	333	5	1,486
.Lac Courte Oreilles Band of Lake Superior Chippewa	3,210	9	668	7	3,894

.Lac du Flambeau	1,491	4	132	–	1,627
.Lac Vieux Desert Band of Lake Superior Chippewa	199	12	11	1	223
.Lake Superior	312	9	94	4	419
.Leech Lake	4,414	24	491	3	4,932
.Little Shell Chippewa	977	63	443	19	1,502
.Mille Lacs	2,121	18	204	2	2,345
.Minnesota Chippewa	2,225	9	691	8	2,933
.Ontonagon	–	–	–	–	–
.Red Cliff Band of Lake Superior Chippewa	1,609	6	307	4	1,926
.Red Lake Band of Chippewa Indians	7,525	19	469	8	8,021
.Saginaw Chippewa	2,186	24	663	14	2,887
.St. Croix Chippewa	1,008	6	190	–	1,204
.Sault Ste. Marie Chippewa	8,089	71	2,801	29	10,990
.Sokoagon Chippewa	462	1	60	1	524
.Turtle Mountain Band	13,104	130	1,638	75	14,947
.White Earth	5,763	42	1,710	15	7,530
.Swan Creek Black River Confederate Tribe	51	4	34	6	95
Rocky Boy's Chippewa Cree	**5,531**	**180**	**1,294**	**99**	**7,104**
Chitimacha Tribe of Louisiana	**1,001**	**409**	**410**	**58**	**1,878**
Choctaw	**87,349**	**9,552**	**50,123**	**11,750**	**158,774**
.Choctaw	66,287	9,381	46,303	11,677	133,648
.Clifton Choctaw	76	–	22	5	103
.Jena Band of Choctaw	84	2	22	–	108
.Mississippi Band of Choctaw	7,626	82	851	24	8,583
.Mowa Band of Choctaw	1,572	11	206	7	1,796
.Oklahoma Choctaw	11,690	108	2,713	49	14,560
Choctaw Apache Community of Ebarb	**364**	**6**	**96**	**6**	**472**
Chumash	**4,032**	**394**	**2,277**	**230**	**6,933**
.Chumash	3,851	369	2,187	220	6,627
.Santa Ynez	70	7	35	7	119
.San Luis Rey Mission Indian	107	26	55	3	191
Clear Lake	**4**	**–**	**8**	**–**	**12**
Coeur D'Alene	**1,392**	**19**	**242**	**5**	**1,658**
Coharie	**1,259**	**60**	**157**	**20**	**1,496**
Colorado River Indian	**1,719**	**45**	**153**	**10**	**1,927**
Colville	**7,833**	**193**	**1,308**	**59**	**9,393**
Comanche	**10,120**	**1,568**	**6,120**	**1,568**	**19,376**
.Comanche	10,050	1,563	6,105	1,564	19,282
.Oklahoma Comanche	70	5	15	4	94
Coos, Lower Umpqua, and Siuslaw	**63**	**2**	**16**	**–**	**81**

	One tribe reported	Two or more tribes reported	One tribe reported	Two or more tribes reported	
	(1)	(2)	(3)	(4)	(5)
Coos	211	27	94	42	374
Coquille	407	1	163	5	576
Costanoan	1,484	236	994	123	2,837
Coushatta	1,466	40	500	56	2,062
.Alabama Coushatta Tribes					
of Texas	882	1	202	3	1,088
.Coushatta	584	39	298	53	974
Cowlitz	1,182	42	660	39	1,923
Cree	2,488	724	3,577	945	7,734
Creek	40,223	5,495	21,652	3,940	71,310
.Alabama Creek	19	1	23	2	45
.Alabama Quassarte Tribal Town	103	1	83	3	190
.Muscogee (Creek) Nation	36,654	5,493	20,450	3,934	66,531
.Eastern Creek	954	9	410	5	1,378
.Eastern Muscogee	12	–	5	–	17
.Kialegee Tribal Town	28	8	4	6	46
.Lower Muscogee Creek					
Tama Tribal Town	854	4	197	3	1,058
.Machis Lower Creek Indian	302	2	83	–	387
.Poarch Creek	1,167	9	330	4	1,510
.Principal Creek Indian Nation	21	1	27	3	52
.Star Clan of Muskogee Creeks	67	4	26	–	97
.Thlopthlocco Tribal Town	18	3	–	3	24
.Tuckabachee	4	–	3	–	7
Croatan	77	18	281	19	395
Crow	9,117	574	2,812	891	13,394
Cupeno	417	60	86	5	568
.Agua Caliente	243	4	57	1	305
.Cupeno	174	56	29	4	263
Delaware	8,304	602	6,866	569	16,341
.Delaware	5,555	433	4,213	394	10,595
.Delaware Tribe of Indians,					
Oklahoma	102	2	25	–	129
.LenniLanape	1,558	284	2,017	291	4,150
.Munsee	124	12	94	15	245
.Delaware Tribe of					
Western Oklahoma	131	7	26	1	165
.Ramapough Mountain	719	81	379	47	1,226
.Sand Hill Band of					
Delaware Indians	6	1	22	2	31

Diegueno	2,660	111	717	29	3,517
.Barona Group of Capitan Grande Band	267	16	32	5	320
.Campo Band of Diegueno Mission Indians	99	2	29	1	131
.Capitan Grande Band of Diegueno Mission Indians	21	–	4	–	25
.Cuyapaipe	4	5	–	–	9
.Diegueno	1,086	133	346	37	1,602
.La Posta Band of Diegueno Mission Indians	19	–	5	–	24
.Manzanita	31	2	13	–	46
.Mesa Grande Band of Diegueno Mission Indians	254	10	51	2	317
.San Pasqual Band of Diegueno Mission Indians	440	6	128	8	582
.Santa Ysabel Band of Diegueno Mission Indians	193	3	33	2	231
.Sycuan Band of Diegueno Mission Indians	41	–	34	–	75
.Viejas (Baron Long) Group of Capitan Grande Band	119	9	20	–	148
.Inaja Band of Diegueno Mission Indians of the Inaja and Cosmit Reservation	3	–	1	–	4
.Jamul Indian Village	45	1	8	–	54
Eastern Tribes	4,969	539	2,689	347	8,544
.Attacapa	13	2	52	8	75
.Biloxi	42	373	14	37	466
.Georgetown	44	1	3	1	49
.Moor	27	8	45	21	101
.Nansemond Indian Tribe	146	5	114	7	272
.Natchez	87	113	156	30	386
.Nausu Waiwash	37	3	19	–	59
.Golden Hill Paugussett	74	3	101	12	190
.Pocomoke Acohonock	37	2	28	1	68
.Southeastern Indians	1,495	330	1,217	203	3,245
.Susquehanock	115	17	258	45	435
.Tunica Biloxi	472	6	158	12	648
.Waccamaw Siouan	1,536	165	170	35	1,906
.Wicomico	2	–	4	–	6
.Meherrin Indian Tribe	593	9	307	22	931
Esselen	117	19	64	15	215
Fort Belknap	141	191	9	1	342

	One tribe reported	Two or more tribes reported	One tribe reported	Two or more tribes reported	
	(1)	(2)	(3)	(4)	(5)
Three Affiliated Tribes of North Dakota (Fort Bethold)	3,508	25	269	5	3,807
Fort McDowell Mohave Apache Community	128	6	16	4	154
Shoshone Bannock Tribes of the Fort Hall Reservation	4,587	40	503	5	5,135
Gabrieleno	1,168	106	467	34	1,775
Grand Ronde	2,130	36	665	21	2,852
Gros Ventres	2,881	242	488	71	3,682
.Atsina	8	–	9	–	17
.Gros Ventres	1,573	236	477	71	2,357
.Fort Belknap Gros Ventres	1,300	6	2	–	1,308
Haliwa Saponi	3,452	48	739	66	4,305
Hidatsa	624	489	135	87	1,335
Hoopa	2,499	114	432	48	3,093
.Hoopa Valley Tribe	2,495	114	428	48	3,085
.Trinity	1	–	4	–	5
.Whilkut	3	–	–	–	3
Hoopa Extension	–	4	1	2	7
Houma United Nation	6,798	79	1,794	42	8,713
Iowa	1,451	76	688	43	2,258
.Iowa	1,000	73	464	43	1,580
.Iowa of Kansas and Nebraska	333	3	204	–	540
.Iowa of Oklahoma	118	–	20	–	138
Indians of Person County	352	–	41	–	393
Iroquois	45,212	2,318	29,763	3,529	80,822
.Cayuga Nation	964	69	349	17	1,399
.Iroquois	3,157	433	6,558	1,202	11,350
.Mohawk	13,940	792	10,652	1,467	26,851
.Oneida Nation of New York	11,057	407	3,685	212	15,361
.Onondaga	2,130	82	909	84	3,205
.Seneca	7,203	405	4,240	490	12,338
.Seneca Nation	614	84	296	26	1,020
.Seneca Cayuga	1,509	120	440	36	2,105
.Tonawanda Band of Seneca	266	4	47	1	318
.Tuscarora	2,308	211	1,063	123	3,705
.Wyandotte	1,850	139	1,380	162	3,531
Juaneno (Acjachemem)	2,373	71	850	36	3,330
Kalispel Indian Community	306	30	42	2	380
Karuk Tribe of California	3,164	272	1,329	136	4,901

Kaw	1,150	149	563	130	1,992
Kickapoo	3,525	307	1,092	192	5,116
.Kickapoo	3,384	308	1,083	192	4,967
.Oklahoma Kickapoo	137	1	7	–	145
.Texas Kickapoo	3	–	2	–	5
Kiowa	8,559	1,130	2,119	434	12,242
.Kiowa	8,263	1,127	2,085	429	11,904
.Oklahoma Kiowa	295	5	34	5	339
S'Klallam	1,779	37	445	17	2,278
.Jamestown S'Klallam	345	1	109	1	456
.Klallam	650	125	254	32	1,061
.Lower Elwha Tribal Community	247	100	33	18	398
.Port Gamble Klallam	442	1	31	2	476
Klamath	2,632	490	715	206	4,043
Konkow	205	330	102	133	770
Kootenai	618	21	163	13	815
Lassik	3	–	3	–	6
Long Island	655	40	469	47	1,211
.Matinecock	36	2	44	2	84
.Montauk	335	30	281	34	680
.Poospatuck	284	8	144	11	447
.Setauket	–	–	–	–	–
Luiseno	4,317	203	999	46	5,565
.La Jolla Band of Luiseno Mission Indians	310	5	53	2	370
.Luiseno	1,814	283	401	53	2,551
.Pala Band of Luiseno Mission Indians	580	34	202	9	825
.Pauma Band of Luiseno Mission Indians	111	7	8	2	128
.Pechanga Band of Luiseno Mission Indians	601	118	178	37	934
.Soboba	536	7	78	2	623
.Twenty-Nine Palms Band of Luiseno Mission Indians	4	–	–	–	4
.Temecula	14	8	6	–	28
.Rincon Band of Luiseno Mission Indians	205	25	40	7	277
Lumbee	51,913	642	4,934	379	57,868
Lummi	3,073	104	592	43	3,812
Maidu	2,368	621	904	202	4,095
.Mooretown Rancheria of Maidu Indians	88	5	12	–	105
.Maidu	1,939	644	816	203	3,602
.Mountain Maidu	9	–	4	–	13

	One tribe reported	Two or more tribes reported	One tribe reported	Two or more tribes reported	
	(1)	**(2)**	**(3)**	**(4)**	**(5)**
.Nisenen (Nishinam)	15	–	10	1	26
.Mechoopda Indian Tribe of					
Chico Rancheria, California	128	6	42	3	179
.Berry Creek Rancheria of					
Maidu Indians	95	24	7	3	129
.Enterprise Rancheria	26	6	8	–	40
.Greenville Rancheria	36	–	1	–	37
Makah	**2,005**	**58**	**413**	**12**	**2,488**
Maliseet	**905**	**45**	**345**	**29**	**1,324**
.Maliseet	872	45	342	29	1,288
.Houlton Band of Maliseet Indians	33	–	3	–	36
Mandan	**369**	**456**	**318**	**160**	**1,303**
Mattaponi	**512**	**15**	**272**	**13**	**812**
.Mattaponi Indian Tribe	384	15	217	13	629
.Upper Mattaponi Tribe	128	–	55	–	183
Menominee	**7,883**	**258**	**1,551**	**148**	**9,840**
Miami	**3,811**	**114**	**2,334**	**158**	**6,417**
.Illinois Miami	73	4	129	9	215
.Indiana Miami	557	1	157	1	716
.Miami	2,612	109	1,896	150	4,767
.Oklahoma Miami	569	–	151	–	720
Miccosukee	**103**	**18**	**57**	**11**	**189**
Micmac	**2,913**	**254**	**3,199**	**356**	**6,722**
.Aroostook Band	49	16	8	1	74
.Micmac	2,855	256	3,190	357	6,658
Mission Indians	**1,008**	**185**	**481**	**62**	**1,736**
.Mission Indians	897	182	445	61	1,585
.Cahuilla Band of Mission Indians	21	2	6	–	29
.Juaneno Band of Mission Indians	90	1	30	1	122
Miwok	**110**	**11**	**54**	**2**	**177**
.Ione Band of Miwok Indians	82	9	41	1	133
.Shingle Springs Band of					
Miwok Indians	28	2	13	1	44
MeWuk	**2,881**	**526**	**1,718**	**247**	**5,372**
.MeWuk	2,843	524	1,681	243	5,291
.Jackson Rancheria of MeWuk					
Indians of California	11	–	23	3	37
.Tuolumne Band of MeWuk					
Indians of California	21	–	8	–	29
.Buena Vista Rancheria of MeWuk					
Indians of California	–	1	–	–	1

.Chicken Ranch Rancheria of MeWuk Indians	5	–	6	1	12
.Sheep Ranch Rancheria of MeWuk Indians	1	1	–	–	2
Modoc	**478**	**438**	**280**	**242**	**1,438**
.Modoc	466	437	277	242	1,422
.Oklahoma Modoc	12	1	3	–	16
Mohegan	**1,180**	**93**	**1,000**	**155**	**2,428**
Monocan	**707**	**39**	**302**	**48**	**1,096**
Mono	**1,744**	**424**	**659**	**93**	**2,920**
.Mono	1,643	424	634	93	2,794
.North Fork Rancheria	41	–	13	–	54
.Cold Springs Rancheria	43	–	3	–	46
.Big Sandy Rancheria	17	–	9	–	26
Nanticoke	**860**	**44**	**642**	**55**	**1,601**
Nanticoke Lenni Lenape	**555**	**–**	**191**	**3**	**749**
Narragansett	**2,137**	**184**	**1,827**	**194**	**4,342**
Navajo	**269,202**	**6,789**	**19,491**	**2,715**	**298,197**
.Alamo Navajo	50	45	38	17	150
.Tohajiileehee Navajo (Canoncito)	4	–	–	–	4
.Navajo	269,133	6,747	19,443	2,700	298,023
.Ramah Navajo	12	3	9	–	24
Nez Perce	**3,983**	**300**	**1,965**	**287**	**6,535**
Nipmuc	**666**	**34**	**737**	**47**	**1,484**
.Hassanamisco Band of the Nipmuc Nation	11	–	12	–	23
.Chaubunagungameg Nipmuc	1	–	1	–	2
.Nipmuc	654	34	724	47	1,459
Nomlaki	**360**	**171**	**98**	**23**	**652**
.Nomlaki	330	171	87	23	611
.Paskenta Band of Nomlaki Indians	30	–	11	–	41
Northwest Tribes	**378**	**24**	**682**	**10**	**1,094**
.Alsea	5	–	6	–	11
.Celilo	4	2	8	–	14
.Columbia	264	5	575	1	845
.Kalapuya	47	5	40	3	95
.Molalla	11	1	7	2	21
.Talakamish	3	3	1	–	7
.Tenino	1	–	2	–	3
.Tillamook	23	3	34	2	62
.Wenatchee	20	5	9	2	36
Omaha	**4,239**	**289**	**687**	**83**	**5,298**
Oneida Tribe of Wisconsin	**704**	**13**	**192**	**11**	**920**
Oregon Athabascan	**234**	**31**	**116**	**7**	**388**
Osage	**7,658**	**1,354**	**5,491**	**1,394**	**15,897**

	One tribe reported	Two or more tribes reported	One tribe reported	Two or more tribes reported	
	(1)	(2)	(3)	(4)	(5)
Otoe Missouria	1,470	336	505	133	2,444
Ottawa	6,432	623	3,174	448	10,677
.Burt Lake Ottawa	23	–	20	–	43
.Little River Band of Ottawa Indians of Michigan	955	9	386	5	1,355
.Oklahoma Ottawa	92	–	27	–	119
.Ottawa	3,784	624	2,235	447	7,090
.Little Traverse Bay Bands of Ottawa Indians of Michigan	1,285	14	367	1	1,667
.Grand River Band of Ottawa Indians	280	2	136	1	419
Paiute	9,705	1,163	2,315	349	13,532
.Bridgeport Paiute Indian Colony	3	30	3	–	36
.Burns Paiute Tribe	155	–	7	–	162
.Cedarville Rancheria	7	–	–	–	7
.Fort Bidwell	45	–	6	–	51
.Fort Independence	4	–	3	1	8
.Kaibab Band of Paiute Indians	153	–	10	–	163
.Las Vegas Tribe of the Las Vegas Indian Colony	49	–	18	–	67
.Lovelock Paiute Tribe of the Lovelock Indian Colony	125	–	16	–	141
.Malheur Paiute	–	–	–	–	–
.Moapa Band of Paiute	103	2	18	4	127
.Northern Paiute	223	11	80	1	315
.Paiute	5,900	1,166	1,874	338	9,278
.Pyramid Lake	1,274	9	55	1	1,339
.San Juan Southern Paiute	10	–	–	–	10
.Southern Paiute	127	4	20	3	154
.Summit Lake	31	2	12	–	45
.Utu Utu Gwaitu Paiute	42	–	15	–	57
.Walker River	931	2	122	1	1,056
.Yerington Paiute	427	–	37	2	466
.Yahooskin Band of Snake	10	1	7	2	20
.Susanville	49	2	6	–	57
.Winnemucca	3	3	4	–	10
Pamunkey Indian Tribe	347	35	322	72	776
Passamaquoddy	2,398	63	995	67	3,523
.Indian Township	–	–	–	–	–
.Passamaquoddy	2,397	63	994	66	3,520
.Pleasant Point Passamaquoddy	1	–	1	1	3

Pawnee	**2,485**	**487**	**1,246**	**322**	**4,540**
.Oklahoma Pawnee	32	3	5	6	46
.Pawnee	2,453	484	1,241	316	4,494
Penobscot	**2,045**	**50**	**1,557**	**149**	**3,801**
Peoria	**1,133**	**94**	**510**	**58**	**1,795**
.Oklahoma Peoria	271	2	66	–	339
.Peoria	860	96	444	58	1,458
Pequot	**1,283**	**147**	**1,190**	**177**	**2,797**
.Mashantucket Pequot	511	–	202	3	716
.Pequot	726	145	962	176	2,009
.Paucatuck Eastern Pequot	46	2	25	–	73
Pima	**8,519**	**999**	**1,741**	**234**	**11,493**
.Gila River Indian Community	1,757	57	188	7	2,009
.Pima	4,121	913	1,365	224	6,623
.Salt River Pima Maricopa	2,621	72	186	7	2,886
Piscataway	**932**	**16**	**452**	**43**	**1,443**
Pit River	**1,656**	**284**	**487**	**111**	**2,538**
.Pit River Tribe of California	1,588	283	467	111	2,449
.Alturas Indian Rancheria	–	–	6	–	6
.Redding Rancheria	68	1	14	–	83
Big Valley Rancheria of Pomo and Pit River Indians	**79**	**1**	**10**	**–**	**90**
Pomo	**5,111**	**776**	**1,720**	**267**	**7,874**
.Central Pomo	25	4	5	–	34
.Dry Creek	113	8	32	–	153
.Eastern Pomo	–	–	–	–	–
.Kashia Band of Pomo Indians of the Stewarts Point Rancheria	159	36	29	4	228
.Northern Pomo	22	11	13	4	50
.Pomo	3,638	856	1,427	265	6,186
.Scotts Valley Band	29	–	1	–	30
.Stonyford	1	–	–	–	1
.Elem Indian Colony of the Sulphur Bank	27	12	5	1	45
.Sherwood Valley Rancheria of Pomo Indians of California	204	6	26	1	237
.Guidiville Rancheria of California	38	7	5	–	50
.Lytton Rancheria of California	59	26	19	–	104
.Cloverdale Rancheria	52	6	15	1	74
.Coyote Valley Band	67	13	16	–	96
.Hopland Band of Pomo Indians	194	1	20	2	217
.Manchester Band of Pomo Indians of the Manchester Point Arena Rancheria	108	2	30	–	140
.Middletown Rancheria of Pomo Indians	24	–	23	–	47

	One tribe reported	Two or more tribes reported	One tribe reported	Two or more tribes reported	
	(1)	**(2)**	**(3)**	**(4)**	**(5)**
.Pinoleville Rancheria of Pomo Indians	28	2	7	–	37
.Potter Valley Rancheria of Pomo Indians	13	2	10	–	25
.Redwood Valley Rancheria of Pomo Indians	70	1	7	–	78
.Robinson Rancheria of Pomo Indians	118	3	17	1	139
.Upper Lake Band of Pomo Indians of Upper Lake Rancheria	12	–	7	–	19
Ponca	**3,355**	**437**	**927**	**139**	**4,858**
.Nebraska Ponca	190	4	63	1	258
.Oklahoma Ponca	153	–	14	–	167
.Ponca	3,012	433	850	138	4,433
Potawatomi	**15,817**	**592**	**8,602**	**584**	**25,595**
.Citizen Potawatomi Nation	1,385	32	601	10	2,028
.Forest County Potowatomi Community	139	2	26	–	167
.Hannahville Indian Community of Wisconsin Potawatomi	137	6	21	–	164
.Huron Potawatomi	224	9	114	5	352
.Pokagon Band of Potawatomi Indians	756	6	260	5	1,027
.Potawatomi	11,903	563	7,390	567	20,423
.Prairie Band of Potawatomi Indians	1,255	5	188	1	1,449
.Wisconsin Potawatomi	4	–	–	–	4
Powhatan	**483**	**78**	**979**	**187**	**1,727**
Pueblo	**59,533**	**3,527**	**9,943**	**1,082**	**74,085**
.Acoma	3,956	312	304	56	4,628
.Arizona Tewa	433	59	34	5	531
.Cochiti	889	70	80	10	1,049
.Hopi	11,111	1,918	1,794	452	15,275
.Isleta	3,652	150	578	41	4,421
.Jemez	2,583	105	153	15	2,856
.Keres	4	–	5	–	9
.Laguna	6,244	507	636	78	7,465
.Nambe	441	21	75	9	546
.Picuris	254	18	50	1	323
.Piro	179	17	36	4	236

.Pojoaque	211	4	25	3	243
.Pueblo	2,037	498	1,389	320	4,244
.San Felipe	2,606	69	78	3	2,756
.San Ildefonso	494	5	20	–	519
.San Juan Pueblo	1,274	54	121	13	1,462
.San Juan	226	41	50	7	324
.Sandia	389	32	60	7	488
.Santa Ana	589	15	42	1	647
.Santa Clara	1,104	40	123	6	1,273
.Santo Domingo	4,282	80	1,218	11	5,591
.Taos	2,014	140	383	44	2,581
.Tesuque	383	14	26	2	425
.Tewa	917	275	445	91	1,728
.Ysleta Del Sur Pueblo of Texas	1,840	66	451	25	2,382
.Zia	1,590	41	1,169	20	2,820
.Zuni	9,094	458	488	82	10,122
Puget Sound Salish	**11,034**	**226**	**3,212**	**159**	**14,631**
.Marietta Band of Nooksack	–	–	–	–	–
.Duwamish	166	4	159	7	336
.Kikiallus	4	–	5	–	9
.Lower Skagit	–	–	–	–	–
.Muckleshoot	1,327	18	134	6	1,485
.Nisqually	437	28	143	17	625
.Nooksack	710	23	303	10	1,046
.Port Madison	7	2	2	–	11
.Puget Sound Salish	1	–	2	–	3
.Puyallup	1,652	45	389	35	2,121
.Samish	242	8	242	7	499
.Sauk Suiattle	114	4	27	2	147
.Skokomish	706	19	120	9	854
.Skykomish	5	5	3	–	13
.Snohomish	484	30	420	24	958
.Snoqualmie	301	14	190	9	514
.Squaxin Island	594	10	137	5	746
.Steilacoom	119	2	116	–	237
.Stillaguamish	103	1	27	–	131
.Suquamish	608	13	154	7	782
.Swinomish	703	11	109	13	836
.Tulalip	2,252	32	334	14	2,632
.Upper Skagit	471	13	186	14	684
Quapaw	**1,151**	**249**	**619**	**164**	**2,183**
Quinault	**2,377**	**100**	**574**	**105**	**3,156**
Rappahannock Indian Tribe	**269**	**6**	**109**	**10**	**394**
Reno Sparks	**36**	**15**	**14**	**–**	**65**
Round Valley	**260**	**42**	**55**	**11**	**368**

	One tribe reported	Two or more tribes reported	One tribe reported	Two or more tribes reported	
	(1)	(2)	(3)	(4)	(5)
Sac and Fox	4,206	380	1,714	278	6,578
.Sac and Fox	2,313	273	993	160	3,739
.Sac and Fox Nation, Oklahoma	533	7	69	6	615
.Sac and Fox Nation of Missouri					
in Kansas and Nebraska	79	1	11	–	91
.Sac and Fox Tribe of the					
Mississippi in Iowa	1,281	99	641	112	2,133
Salinan	366	35	253	27	681
Salish	3,310	210	1,101	118	4,739
Salish and Kootenai	3,464	39	687	13	4,203
.Salish and Kootenai	3,464	38	687	11	4,200
.Pond d'Orielles Band of					
Salish and Kootenai	–	1	–	2	3
Schaghticoke	256	4	229	9	498
Seminole	12,431	2,982	9,505	2,513	27,431
.Big Cypress	–	–	–	–	–
.Brighton	–	–	–	–	–
.Florida Seminole	493	6	91	6	596
.Hollywood Seminole	–	1	–	1	2
.Oklahoma Seminole	374	4	47	1	426
.Seminole	11,556	2,981	9,358	2,502	26,397
.Dania Seminole	3	–	9	4	16
.Tampa Seminole	–	–	–	–	–
Serrano	263	89	65	12	429
.San Manual Band	58	8	14	–	80
.Serrano	199	93	51	12	355
Shasta	436	110	344	61	951
.Shasta	418	108	339	61	926
.Quartz Valley	18	2	5	–	25
Shawnee	5,773	495	4,301	432	11,001
.Absentee Shawnee Tribe of					
Indians of Oklahoma	1,701	20	264	2	1,987
.Eastern Shawnee	1,022	33	340	12	1,407
.Shawnee	2,987	441	3,664	416	7,508
.Piqua Sept of Ohio Shawnee	63	1	32	4	100
Shinnecock	1,239	87	1,299	133	2,758
Shoalwater Bay	129	1	30	3	163
Shoshone	7,739	714	3,039	534	12,026
.Duckwater	139	1	11	–	151
.Ely	100	1	33	1	135
.Goshute	222	47	41	5	315

.Shoshone	6,672	726	2,791	516	10,705
.Skull Valley Band of Goshute Indians	14	–	4	–	18
.Death Valley Timbi Sha Shoshone	201	17	76	2	296
.Northwestern Band of Shoshoni Nation of Utah (Washakie)	132	15	53	14	214
.Wind River (Eastern Shoshone)	110	1	14	–	125
.Yomba	102	–	14	1	117
TeMoak Tribes of Western Shoshone Indians of Nevada	949	14	219	7	1,189
.TeMoak Tribes of Western Shoshone Indians	926	9	204	2	1,141
.Battle Mountain	5	–	12	1	18
.Elko	15	4	2	4	25
.South Fork	–	–	–	–	–
.Wells Band	3	–	1	–	4
.Ruby Valley	–	1	–	–	1
.Odgers Ranch	–	–	–	–	–
Paiute Shoshone	3,112	57	349	21	3,539
.Duck Valley	120	15	11	1	147
.Fallon	532	3	36	1	572
.Fort McDermitt Paiute and Shoshone Tribes	306	7	12	1	326
.Shoshone Paiute	1,943	52	267	13	2,275
.Bishop	157	–	9	–	166
.Lone Pine	10	–	8	–	18
.Big Pine Band of Owens Valley Paiute Shoshone	33	2	6	5	46
Confederated Tribes of the Siletz Reservation	1,909	37	732	29	2,707
Sioux	108,272	4,794	35,179	5,115	153,360
.Blackfoot Sioux	412	26	914	67	1,419
.Brule Sioux	73	3	37	8	121
.Cheyenne River Sioux	9,064	45	845	10	9,964
.Crow Creek Sioux	2,550	21	235	9	2,815
.Dakota Sioux	1,739	237	674	146	2,796
.Flandreau Santee Sioux	336	28	54	6	424
.Fort Peck Sioux	2,233	13	136	3	2,385
.Lake Traverse Sioux	21	1	8	–	30
.Lower Brule Sioux	1,687	18	197	2	1,904
.Lower Sioux Indian Community of Minnesota Mdewakanton Sioux	418	3	66	2	489
.Mdewakanton Sioux	436	25	232	11	704

	One tribe reported	Two or more tribes reported	One tribe reported	Two or more tribes reported	
	(1)	**(2)**	**(3)**	**(4)**	**(5)**
.Miniconjou	35	2	16	1	54
.Oglala Sioux	22,157	582	3,259	252	26,250
.Pine Ridge Sioux	771	51	162	14	998
.Pipestone Sioux	1	1	–	–	2
.Prairie Island Sioux	219	6	25	1	251
.Shakopee Mdewakanton Sioux Community (Prior Lake)	95	9	37	–	141
.Rosebud Sioux	14,037	139	1,251	43	15,470
.Sans Arc Sioux	1	4	–	2	7
.Santee Sioux of Nebraska	1,987	130	698	54	2,869
.Sioux	21,886	3,883	19,378	4,275	49,422
.Sisseton Wahpeton	5,115	27	631	2	5,775
.Sisseton Sioux	672	10	145	9	836
.Spirit Lake Sioux (formerly Devils Lake Sioux)	2,430	23	142	–	2,595
.Standing Rock Sioux	8,714	76	680	11	9,481
.Teton Sioux	5,326	914	4,306	636	11,182
.Two Kettle Sioux	1	1	1	–	3
.Upper Sioux	84	3	16	–	103
.Wahpekute Sioux	–	–	–	–	–
.Wahpeton Sioux	64	5	37	–	106
.Wazhaza Sioux	–	1	1	–	2
.Yankton Sioux	4,941	44	760	19	5,764
.Yanktonai Sioux	2	–	3	1	6
Siuslaw	23	3	8	2	36
Spokane	2,198	26	418	11	2,653
Stockbridge Munsee Community of Mohican Indians of Wisconsin	2,012	124	1,267	174	3,577
Tohono O'Odham	17,466	714	1,748	159	20,087
.AkChin	492	4	13	3	512
.Gila Bend	26	1	4	–	31
.San Xavier	4	1	2	–	7
.Sells	5	10	2	–	17
.Tohono O'Odham	16,937	702	1,727	156	19,522
Tolowa	649	91	195	25	960
.Tolowa	503	83	165	23	774
.Big Lagoon Rancheria	4	–	1	–	5
.Elk Valley Rancheria	15	2	4	–	21
.Smith River Rancheria	127	6	25	2	160
Tonkawa	241	27	58	7	333

CherAe Indian Community of Trinidad Rancheria	6	2	9	–	17
Tygh	8	–	14	–	22
Umatilla	1,549	143	302	39	2,033
Umpqua	736	21	283	11	1,051
.Cow Creek Umpqua	516	13	155	7	691
.Umpqua	220	8	128	4	360
Ute	7,309	715	1,944	417	10,385
.Allen Canyon	–	–	–	–	–
.Uintah Ute	875	28	99	3	1,005
.Ute Mountain	1,478	12	64	–	1,554
.Ute	3,839	634	1,622	411	6,506
.Southern Ute	1,117	41	159	3	1,320
Wailaki	965	307	388	72	1,732
WallaWalla	143	46	83	14	286
Wampanoag	2,336	70	2,050	138	4,594
.Gay Head (Aquinnah) Wampanoag	328	1	78	1	408
.Mashpee Wampanoag	157	6	101	8	272
.Wampanoag	1,764	69	1,803	137	3,773
.Seaconeke Wampanoag	71	–	57	–	128
.Pocasset Wampanoag	13	–	7	–	20
Warm Springs	2,804	157	192	26	3,179
Wascopum	219	85	70	24	398
Washoe	1,186	423	310	55	1,974
.Alpine	11	1	33	1	46
.Carson Colony	3	1	16	–	20
.Dresslerville Colony	1	–	–	–	1
.Washoe	1,170	421	254	53	1,898
.Stewart Community	1	–	3	1	5
.Woodsfords Community	–	–	4	–	4
Wichita	1,395	120	371	50	1,936
.Wichita	1,386	119	354	45	1,904
.Keechi	6	1	5	1	13
.Waco	2	–	10	2	14
.Tawakonie	1	–	2	2	5
Wind River	12	–	–	1	13
Winnebago	7,409	322	1,814	155	9,700
.Ho Chunk Nation of Wisconsin	3,707	150	718	46	4,621
.Nebraska Winnebago	350	–	29	2	381
.Winnebago	3,284	308	1,040	162	4,794
Wintun	2,058	550	1,073	198	3,879
.Wintun	1,967	412	1,053	154	3,586
.Cachil Dehe Band of Wintun Indians of the Colusa Rancheria	11	1	8	–	20

	One tribe reported	Two or more tribes reported	One tribe reported	Two or more tribes reported	
	(1)	(2)	(3)	(4)	(5)
.Cortina Indian Rancheria of Wintun Indians	51	–	2	–	53
.Rumsey Indian Rancheria of Wintun Indians	28	139	10	44	221
Grindstone Indian Rancheria of Wintun Wailaki Indians	**13**	**3**	**3**	**–**	**19**
Wiyot	**444**	**60**	**149**	**21**	**674**
.Table Bluff	26	6	3	–	35
.Wiyot	402	52	145	20	619
.Blue Lake Rancheria	15	4	1	1	21
Yakama	**8,481**	**561**	**1,619**	**190**	**10,851**
Yakama Cowlitz	**5**	**–**	**2**	**–**	**7**
Yaqui	**15,224**	**1,245**	**5,184**	**759**	**22,412**
.Barrio Libre	–	–	2	–	2
.Pascua Yaqui	3,692	58	423	14	4,187
.Yaqui	11,500	1,252	4,752	759	18,263
Yavapai Apache	**879**	**27**	**170**	**–**	**1,076**
Yokuts	**2,924**	**536**	**904**	**132**	**4,496**
.Picayune Rancheria of Chukchansi Indians	853	250	356	60	1,519
.Tachi	381	108	72	9	570
.Tule River	719	19	118	7	863
.Yokuts	904	274	341	86	1,605
.Table Mountain Rancheria	9	1	2	–	12
Yuchi	**302**	**114**	**132**	**35**	**583**
.Yuchi	291	114	120	34	559
.Tia	7	–	7	–	14
.Wilono	–	–	1	–	1
.Anstohini/Unami	4	–	4	1	9
Yuman	**7,295**	**526**	**1,051**	**104**	**8,976**
.Cocopah Tribe of Arizona	679	16	103	10	808
.Havasupai	576	36	16	6	634
.Hualapai	1,419	84	124	15	1,642
.Maricopa	255	75	65	10	405
.Fort Mojave Indian Tribe of Arizona	1,437	216	215	38	1,906
.Quechan	2,080	87	420	25	2,612
.Yavapai Prescott Tribe of the Yavapai Reservation	818	74	105	6	1,003

Yurok	**4,098**	**382**	**1,170**	**159**	**5,809**
.Resighini Rancheria	14	–	2	–	16
.Yurok	4,084	382	1,168	159	5,793
American Indian,					
Tribe Not Specified/[3]	**103,174**	**89**	**80,163**	**85**	**183,511**
Alaskan Athabascan	**14,520**	**815**	**3,218**	**285**	**18,838**
.Ahtna	178	88	40	9	315
.Alaskan Athabascan	8,168	927	2,115	283	11,493
.Alatna Village	27	2	1	–	30
.Alexander	9	2	14	–	25
.Allakaket Village	159	5	1	–	165
.Alanvik	–	–	–	–	–
.Anvik Village	15	–	1	2	18
.Arctic Village	10	1	5	1	17
.Beaver Village	103	15	36	4	158
.Birch Creek Tribe	10	1	62	–	73
.Native Village of Cantwell	37	–	–	–	37
.Chalkyitsik Village	5	–	–	–	5
.Chickaloon Native Village	74	–	2	1	77
.Native Village of Chistochina	7	–	–	–	7
.Native Village of Chitina	41	13	26	3	83
.Circle Native Community	83	–	12	–	95
.Cook Inlet	116	54	36	17	223
.Copper River	4	1	2	–	7
.Village of Dot Lake	32	–	8	–	40
.Doyon	1,017	113	156	49	1,335
.Native Village of Eagle	54	57	26	12	149
.Eklutna Native Village	43	2	17	2	64
.Evansville Village (Bettles Field)	21	–	1	–	22
.Native Village of Fort Yukon	117	–	9	5	131
.Native Village of Gakona	8	–	5	–	13
.Galena Village (Louden Native Village)	97	2	6	1	106
.Organized Village of Grayling (Holikachuk)	54	10	7	8	79
.Gulkana Village	58	–	1	–	59
.Healy Lake Village	2	–	4	–	6
.Holy Cross Village	109	1	2	–	112
.Hughes Village	4	7	4	1	16
.Huslia Village	253	–	5	–	258
.Village of Iliamna	23	2	2	–	27
.Village of Kaltag	36	9	7	–	52
.Native Village of Kluti Kaah (Copper Center)	38	42	2	–	82

	One tribe reported	Two or more tribes reported	One tribe reported	Two or more tribes reported	
	(1)	(2)	(3)	(4)	(5)
.Knik Tribe	90	14	14	2	120
.Koyukuk Native Village	239	9	27	1	276
.Lake Minchumina	5	–	–	–	5
.Lime Village	1	–	–	–	1
.McGrath Native Village	57	–	13	–	70
.Manley Hot Springs Village	2	–	1	–	3
.Mentasta Traditional Council	9	1	2	2	14
.Native Village of Minto	232	4	5	1	242
.Nenana Native Association	75	6	9	–	90
.Nikolai Village	11	2	19	–	32
.Ninilchik Village Traditional Council	130	7	34	2	173
.Nondalton Village	203	1	2	–	206
.Northway Village	31	–	5	–	36
.Nulato Village	380	1	26	–	407
.Pedro Bay Village	32	–	22	–	54
.Rampart Village	34	–	2	–	36
.Native Village of Ruby	23	1	9	–	33
.Village of Salamatoff	39	–	9	–	48
.Seldovia Village Tribe	101	5	39	2	147
.Slana	–	–	5	–	5
.Shageluk Native Village	127	–	–	–	127
.Native Village of Stevens	15	1	3	–	19
.Village of Stony River	15	1	–	–	16
.Takotna Village	28	–	1	–	29
.Native Village of Tanacross	117	1	6	–	124
.Tanaina	32	34	27	13	106
.Native Village of Tanana	69	12	13	1	95
.Tanana Chiefs	46	6	13	–	65
.Native Village of Tazlina	32	1	1	–	34
.Telida Village	–	–	–	–	–
.Native Village of Tetlin	137	1	13	–	151
.Tok	3	–	3	2	8
.Native Village of Tyonek	73	7	17	1	98
.Village of Venetie	274	6	16	1	297
.Wiseman	–	–	–	–	–
.Kenaitze Indian Tribe	506	20	173	7	706
Tlingit Haida	**14,825**	**1,059**	**6,047**	**434**	**22,365**
.Angoon Community Association	85	7	1	–	93

.Central Council of the Tlingit and Haida Indian Tribes	65	5	10	–	80
.Chilkat Indian Village (Kluckwan)	142	–	4	–	146
.Chilkoot Indian Association (Haines)	19	–	7	1	27
.Craig Community Association	94	2	26	1	123
.Douglas Indian Association	4	1	9	–	14
.Haida	1,239	1,766	727	532	4,264
.Hoonah Indian Association	250	12	40	1	303
.Hydaburg Cooperative Association	171	–	11	–	182
.Organized Village of Kake	214	8	43	–	265
.Organized Village of Kasaan	8	2	6	–	16
.Ketchikan Indian Corporation	555	10	101	4	670
.Klawock Cooperative Association	205	3	23	–	231
.Pelican	1	2	6	–	9
.Petersburg Indian Association	1	1	–	–	2
.Organized Village of Saxman	284	1	17	1	303
.Sitka Tribe of Alaska	331	14	69	5	419
.Tenakee Springs	10	–	8	–	18
.Tlingit	9,413	2,494	4,450	837	17,194
.Wrangell Cooperative Association	1	–	1	–	2
.Yakutat Tlingit Tribe	89	1	10	2	102
.Juneau	5	12	3	3	23
Tsimshian	**2,177**	**388**	**663**	**132**	**3,360**
.Metlakatla Indian Community, Annette Island Reserve	706	252	85	16	1,059
.Tsimshian	1,284	561	568	138	2,551
Sealaska	**341**	**57**	**111**	**15**	**524**
.Sealaska	278	52	87	12	429
.Sealaska Corporation	63	5	24	3	95
Southeast Alaska	**26**	**6**	**66**	**–**	**98**
.Southeast Alaska	26	6	62	–	94
.Skagway Village	–	–	4	–	4
Eskimo Tribes	**5,658**	**1,686**	**2,112**	**364**	**9,820**
.American Eskimo	9	–	15	1	25
.Eskimo	5,649	1,686	2,097	363	9,795
Greenland Eskimo	**3**	**–**	**4**	**–**	**7**
Inuit	**534**	**68**	**359**	**54**	**1,015**
Inupiat Eskimo	**16,047**	**845**	**2,282**	**191**	**19,365**
.Native Village of Ambler	190	5	8	–	203
.Anaktuvuk	–	–	–	1	1
.Village of Anaktuvuk Pass	7	–	–	–	7
.Inupiat Community of the Arctic Slope	25	5	5	4	39

	One tribe reported	Two or more tribes reported	One tribe reported	Two or more tribes reported	
	(1)	(2)	(3)	(4)	(5)
.Arctic Slope Corporation	605	360	66	14	1,045
.Atqasuk Village (Atkasook)	2	4	1	–	7
.Native Village of Barrow					
Inupiat Traditional Government	171	38	19	2	230
.Bering Straits Inupiat	608	60	127	7	802
.Native Village of Brevig Mission	262	–	4	–	266
.Native Village of Buckland	352	9	3	–	364
.Chinik Eskimo Community					
(Golovin)	142	6	24	–	172
.Native Village of Council	108	5	4	–	117
.Native Village of Deering	17	1	3	1	22
.Native Village of Elim	303	3	7	–	313
.Native Village of Diomede					
(Inalik)	84	3	7	1	95
.Inupiaq	2,582	373	534	63	3,552
.Inupiat	2,405	656	657	64	3,782
.Kaktovik Village (Barter Island)	2	–	–	–	2
.Kawerak	11	7	1	–	19
.Native Village of Kiana	379	7	14	–	400
.Native Village of Kivalina	338	2	–	1	341
.Native Village of Kobuk	96	–	–	–	96
.Native Village of Kotzebue	364	47	34	5	450
.Native Village of Koyuk	250	–	3	–	253
.Kwiguk	247	–	2	–	249
.Mauneluk Inupiat	–	–	–	–	–
.Nana Inupiat	1,255	125	215	25	1,620
.Native Village of Noatak	407	7	9	–	423
.Nome Eskimo Community	659	24	210	8	901
.Noorvik Native Community	63	23	–	1	87
.Native Village of Nuiqsut					
(Nooiksut)	5	26	–	–	31
.Native Village of Point Hope	598	8	26	–	632
.Native Village of Point Lay	3	–	–	–	3
.Native Village of Selawik	239	4	12	1	256
.Native Village of Shaktoolik	182	2	5	1	190
.Native Village of Shishmaref	493	1	5	–	499
.Native Village of Shungnak	340	36	80	14	470
.Village of Solomon	22	–	15	–	37
.Native Village of Teller	178	1	3	–	182
.Native Village of Unalakleet	665	10	36	–	711

.Village of Wainwright	220	–	4	–	224
.Village of Wales	58	1	36	–	95
.Village of White Mountain	285	15	39	5	344
.White Mountain Inupiat	–	–	–	–	–
.Native Village of Mary's Igloo	49	2	–	–	51
.King Island Native Community	256	22	51	1	330
Siberian Eskimo	**1,381**	**9**	**37**	**3**	**1,430**
.Native Village of Gambell	633	1	3	–	637
.Native Village of Savoonga	618	2	2	–	622
.Siberian Yupik	130	6	32	3	171
Cupiks Eskimo	**49**	**8**	**9**	**2**	**68**
.Chevak Native Village	33	5	9	2	49
.Native Village of Mekoryuk	16	3	–	–	19
Yup'ik	**21,212**	**895**	**1,996**	**134**	**24,237**
.Akiachak Native Community	538	1	13	–	552
.Akiak Native Community	9	2	7	–	18
.Village of Alakanuk	674	4	18	–	696
.Native Village of Aleknagik	70	123	6	3	202
.Yupiit of Andreafski	83	2	–	–	85
.Village of Aniak	201	2	15	1	219
.Village of Atmautluak	70	37	–	–	107
.Orutsararmuit Native Village (Bethel)	287	15	39	–	341
.Village of Bill Moore's Slough	58	–	–	–	58
.Bristol Bay	557	26	81	5	669
.Calista	393	60	28	9	490
.Village of Chefornak	340	–	9	–	349
.Native Village of Hamilton	24	–	1	–	25
.Native Village of Chuathbaluk	128	–	9	1	138
.Village of Clark's Point	16	3	9	–	28
.Village of Crooked Creek	4	–	7	–	11
.Curyung Tribal Council (Native Village of Dillingham)	482	19	86	15	602
.Native Village of Eek	50	6	2	–	58
.Native Village of Ekuk	31	–	6	–	37
.Ekwok Village	23	1	4	–	28
.Emmonak Village	705	13	13	–	731
.Native Village of Goodnews Bay	206	–	5	–	211
.Native Village of Hooper Bay	897	3	20	–	920
.Iqurmuit Traditional Council	206	–	–	–	206
.Village of Kalskag	86	–	3	–	89
.Native Village of Kasigluk	537	–	3	–	540
.Native Village of Kipnuk	460	4	4	–	468
.New Koliganek Village Council	159	–	–	–	159
.Native Village of Kongiganak	130	–	6	–	136

	One tribe reported	Two or more tribes reported	One tribe reported	Two or more tribes reported	
	(1)	(2)	(3)	(4)	(5)
.Village of Kotlik	28	381	3	7	419
.Organized Village of Kwethluk	173	299	1	2	475
.Native Village of Kwigillingok	20	–	1	–	21
.Levelock Village	12	1	2	–	15
.Village of Lower Kalskag	6	–	–	–	6
.Manokotak Village	74	1	15	4	94
.Native Village of Marshal (Fortuna Lodge)	276	1	176	1	454
.Village of Ohogamiut	37	–	–	–	37
.Asa'carsarmiut Tribe	657	2	22	–	681
.Naknek Native Village	119	11	24	1	155
.Native Village of Napaimute	11	2	3	–	16
.Native Village of Napakiak	298	1	3	–	302
.Native Village of Napaskiak	373	4	2	–	379
.Newhalen Village	123	5	14	–	142
.New Stuyahok Village	20	6	7	–	33
.Newtok Village	307	–	7	–	314
.Native Village of Nightmute	142	8	11	–	161
.Native Village of Nunapitchuk	441	–	5	–	446
.Oscarville Traditional Village	53	–	–	–	53
.Pilot Station Traditional Village	20	3	–	–	23
.Native Village of Pitkas Point	80	–	2	–	82
.Platinum Traditional Village	36	–	3	–	39
.Portage Creek Village (Ohgsenakale)	19	–	6	–	25
.Native Village of Kwinhagak	53	1	8	2	64
.Village of Red Devil	2	–	–	–	2
.Native Village of Saint Michael	215	5	30	–	250
.Native Village of Scammon Bay	55	–	–	–	55
.Native Village of Sheldon's Point	6	–	–	–	6
.Village of Sleetmute	2	1	–	–	3
.Stebbins Community Association	503	1	6	2	512
.Traditional Village of Togiak	369	3	26	–	398
.Nunakauyarmiut Tribe (Toksook Bay)	25	–	3	–	28
.Tuluksak Native Community	5	–	1	–	6
.Native Village of Tuntutuliak	331	1	3	1	336
.Native Village of Tununak	288	–	3	–	291
.Twin Hills Village	4	2	–	1	7
.Yup'ik	5,896	838	832	83	7,649

.Yup'ik Eskimo	1,800	95	356	29	2,280
.Native Village of Georgetown	–	–	–	1	1
.Algaaciq Native Village (St. Mary's)	211	7	10	–	228
.Umkumiute Native Village	121	37	–	–	158
.Chuloonawick Native Village	7	–	–	–	7
Aleut	**6,606**	**737**	**2,888**	**317**	**10,548**
Alutiiq Aleut	**319**	**11**	**51**	**8**	**389**
.Alutiiq	182	8	26	5	221
.Village of Afognak	78	3	14	2	97
.Native Village of Tatitlek	28	2	8	1	39
.Ugashik Village	30	–	3	–	33
Bristol Bay Aleut	**610**	**5**	**69**	**–**	**684**
.Bristol Bay Aleut	44	–	12	–	56
.Native Village of Chignik	37	1	3	–	41
.Chignik Lake Village	31	–	2	–	33
.Egegik Village	85	–	23	–	108
.Igiugig Village	70	–	6	–	76
.Ivanoff Bay Village	29	–	–	–	29
.King Salmon	60	–	1	–	61
.Kokhanok Village	11	2	3	–	16
.Native Village of Perryville	100	–	–	–	100
.Native Village of Pilot Point	85	2	7	–	94
.Native Village of Port Heiden	58	–	12	–	70
Chugach Aleut	**340**	**18**	**55**	**14**	**427**
.Native Village of Chanega (Chenega)	74	1	17	3	95
.Chugach Aleut	43	5	15	2	65
.Chugach Corporation	92	7	22	7	128
.Native Village of Nanwalek (English Bay)	79	3	1	2	85
.Native Village of Port Graham	51	4	–	–	55
Eyak	**379**	**21**	**144**	**8**	**552**
Koniag Aleut	**1,457**	**42**	**282**	**19**	**1,800**
.Native Village of Akhiok	73	2	5	–	80
.Agdaagux Tribe of King Cove	50	–	12	–	62
.Native Village of Karluk	40	–	1	1	42
.Native Village of Kanatak	38	–	10	–	48
.Kodiak	134	29	34	13	210
.Koniag Aleut	493	21	154	5	673
.Native Village of Larsen Bay	65	6	4	–	75
.Village of Old Harbor	221	1	31	–	253
.Native Village of Ouzinkie	154	4	18	–	176
.Native Village of Port Lions	155	2	4	–	161
.Lesnoi Village (Woody Island)	22	1	9	–	32

	One tribe reported	Two or more tribes reported	One tribe reported	Two or more tribes reported	
	(1)	(2)	(3)	(4)	(5)
Sugpiaq	27	2	3	1	33
Suqpigaq	1	1	–	–	2
Unangan Aleut	2,187	25	347	10	2,569
.Native Village of Akutan	62	2	1	–	65
.Aleut Corporation	230	2	28	–	260
.Aleutian	269	16	232	8	525
.Aleutian Islander	8	1	6	–	15
.Native Village of Atka	69	2	5	1	77
.Native Village of Belkofski	21	–	–	–	21
.Native Village of Chignik Lagoon	73	–	4	–	77
.King Cove	294	–	3	–	297
.Native Village of False Pass	34	–	–	–	34
.Native Village of Nelson Lagoon	63	–	3	–	66
.Native Village of Nikolski	22	2	1	–	25
.Pauloff Harbor Village	–	–	–	–	–
.Qagan Tayagungin Tribe of Sand Point Village	274	–	21	–	295
.Qawalangin Tribe of Unalaska	147	3	24	–	174
.Saint George	13	–	3	–	16
.Saint Paul	428	2	3	1	434
.Sand Point	6	–	–	–	6
.South Naknek Village	128	–	2	–	130
.Unangan	7	–	2	–	9
.Unalaska	3	–	3	–	6
.Native Village of Unga	29	–	6	–	35
.Kaguyak Village	3	3	–	–	6
Alaska Native, Tribe Not Specified[2]	5,957	364	1,908	113	8,342
Alaska Indian, Tribe Not Specified[2]	203	8	145	5	361
American Indian or Alaska Native, Tribe Not Specified[3]	511,960	–	544,497	–	1,056,457
Tribal Response, Not Elsewhere Classified[4]	6,430	48	5,950	63	12,491

– Represents zero or rounds to 0.0.

Notes:

1. The number and percent for total American Indian and Alaska Native tribes tallied do not add to the total American Indian and Alaska Native population.

This is because respondents may have reported more than one tribe. This is a tally of the number of tribe(s) reported rather than the number of American Indian and Alaska Native respondents reporting a tribe.

2. Includes respondents who wrote in the generic term "American Indian" or "Alaska Native" or "Alaska Indian."

3. Includes respondents who checked the "American Indian or Alaska Native" response category on the census questionnaire and did not include a specific American Indian or Alaska Native tribe.

4. Includes respondents who wrote in a tribe not specified in the American and Alaska Native Tribal Detailed Classification List for Census 2000.

Respondents who identified themselves as American Indian or Alaska Native were asked to report their enrolled or principal tribe. Therefore, tribal data in this data product reflect the written tribal entries reported on the questionnaire. Some of the entries (for example, Iroquois, Sioux, Colorado River, and Flathead) represent nations or reservations. The information on tribe is based on self-identification and includes federally or state recognized tribes as well as bands and clans.

Total persons in column 1 include people who reported only one American Indian or Alaska Native tribe or who checked the American Indian or Alaska Native response category but did not write in a specified tribe. For example, a respondent who reported as Fort Sill Apache would be counted one time in the Fort Sill Apache data line, one time in the total Apache data line, one time in the total persons data line, and one time in the total tribes tallied data line.

Total persons in column 2 include people who reported two or more American Indian or Alaska Native tribes. For example, a respondent who reported as both Fort Sill and Mescalero Apache would be counted one time in the Fort Sill Apache data line, once in the Mescalero Apache data line, but once in the total Apache data line, one time in the total persons data line, and twice in the total tribes tallied data line.

Total persons in column 3 include people who reported one American Indian or Alaska Native tribe or who checked the American Indian or Alaska Native response category, but did not write in a specified tribe, and who reported at least one other race. These races include white, black or African American, Asian, Native Hawaiian and other Pacific Islander, and some other race. For example, a respondent who reported as both "white *and* American Indian and Alaska Native," and wrote in Fort Sill Apache, would be counted once each in the Fort Sill Apache data line, in the total Apache data line, in the total persons data line, and in the total tribes tallied data line.

Total persons in column 4 include people who reported two or more American Indian or Alaska Native tribes and at least one or more other races. For example, a respondent who reported as both Fort Sill Apache and Mescalero Apache and as "white *and* black or African American *and* American Indian or Alaska Native" would be counted in both the Fort Sill Apache and Mescalero Apache data lines once, counted in the total Apache data line once, counted in the total persons once, and counted twice in the total tribes tallied data line.

Total persons in column 5 include a tally of responses for people who reported one or more American Indian or Alaska Native tribe(s) and one or more races. For example, a respondent who reported as both Fort Sill Apache and Mescalero Apache and as "white *and* black or African American *and* American Indian or Alaska Native" would be counted in both the Fort Sill and Mescalero data lines once, counted in the total Apache data line once, counted in the total persons data line once, and counted twice in the total tribes tallied data line.

Source: U.S. Census Bureau, Census 2000, special tabulation.

Internet release date: September 2002.

Last revised date: June 30, 2004.

(For information on confidentiality protection, nonsampling error, and definitions, see www.census.gov/prod/cen2000/doc/sf1.pdf.)

AMERICAN INDIAN URBAN CENTERS

ALASKA

Tlingit and Haida Central Council
320 West Willoughby Ave.,
   Suite 300
Juneau, AK 99801
Phone: (907) 586-1432
Website: http://www.ccthita.org

ARIZONA

Affiliation of Arizona Indian
   Centers
609 North 2nd Ave., Suite 90
Phoenix, AZ 85003
Phone: (602) 266-6245
Fax: (602) 266-6316
Website: None

Inter Tribal Council of Arizona
2214 North Central Ave., #100
Phoenix, AZ 85004
Phone: (602) 258-4822
Fax: (602) 258-4825
Website: http://www.
   itcaonline.com

Ki'Ki' Housing Association
P.O. Box 776

Sells, AZ 85634
Phone: (520) 383-2202
Fax: (520) 383-2259
Website: None

Native American Connections, Inc.
650 North 2nd Ave.
Phoenix, AZ 85003
Phone: (602) 254-3247
Fax: (602) 256-7356
Website: http://www.
   nativeconnections.org

Native Americans for Community
   Action, Inc.
2717 North Steves Blvd., Suite 11
Flagstaff, AZ 86002
Phone: (928) 526-2968
Fax: (928) 526-0708
Website: http://www.nacainc.org

Phoenix Indian Center
2601 North 3rd St., Suite 211
Phoenix, AZ 85004
Phone: (602) 264-7086
Fax: (602) 274-7486
Website: http://www.
   phxindcenter.org

Tucson Indian Center
97 East Congress Ave., Suite 100
Tucson, AZ 85702

Phone: (520) 884-7131
Fax: (520) 884-0204
Website: None

ARKANSAS

American Indian Center of Arkansas
1100 North University, Suite 133
Little Rock, AR 72207
Phone: (501) 666-9032
Fax: (501) 666-5875
Website: None

CALIFORNIA

Friendship House Association of
    American Indians, Inc.
333 Valencia St., Suite 400
San Francisco, CA 94103-3547
Phone: (415) 865-0964
Fax: (415) 865-5428
Website: http://www.
    friendshiphousesf.org

Indian Housing Authority of
    Central California
4702 North Bendel
Fresno, CA 93722
Phone: (559) 271-9004
Fax: (559) 271-0125
Website: None

Native American Health Center
3124 East 14th St.
Oakland, CA 94601
Phone: (510) 261-0524
Fax: (510) 261-0646
Website: None

Southern California Indian Centers
    Commerce
6055 East Washington Blvd., #700
City of Commerce, CA 90040
Phone: (323) 728-8844
Fax: (323) 728-9834

Website: http://www.
    indiancenter.org

Southern California Indian Centers
    Los Angeles
3440 Wilshire Blvd., #904
Los Angeles, CA 90010
Phone: (213) 387-5772
Fax: (213) 387-9061
Website: http://www.
    indiancenter.org

Southern California Indian Centers
    Orange County Corporate Office
10175 Slater Ave., Suite 150
Fountain Valley, CA 92708
Phone: (714) 962-6673
Fax: (714) 962-6343
Website:
    http://www.indiancenter.org

Southern California Indian Centers
    Riverside
1151 Spruce St.
Riverside, CA 92507
Phone: (909) 955-8029
Fax: (909) 955-3131
Website: http://www.
    indiancenter.org

United Indian Nations, CDC
1320 Webster St.
Oakland, CA 94612
Phone: (510) 763-3410
Fax: (510) 763-3646
Website: None

COLORADO

Denver Indian Center
4407 Morrison Rd.
Denver, CO 80219
Phone: (303) 936-2688
Fax: (303) 936-2699
Website: http://www.
    denverindiancenter.org

Denver Indian Health and Family
Services
3749 South King St.
Denver, CO 80236
Phone: (303) 781-4050
Fax: (303) 781-4333
Website: http://www.dihfs.org

ILLINOIS

American Indian Center
1630 West Wilson Ave.
Chicago, IL 60640
Phone: (773) 275-5871
Fax: (773) 275-5874
Website: http://www.
aic-chicago.org

INDIANA

American Indian Center
406 North Broadway
Peru, IN 46970
Phone: (765) 473-3010
Fax: (765) 473-3018
Website: http://www.
americanindiancenter.org

American Indian Center of Indiana,
Inc.
1026 South Shelby St.
Indianapolis, IN 46203
Phone: (317) 536-0240
Fax: (317) 536-0248
Website: http://www.
americanindiancenter.org

KANSAS

Mid-American All Indian Center
650 North Seneca
Wichita, KS 67203
Phone: (316) 262-5221
Fax: (316) 262-4216
Website: http://www.
theindiancenter.com

Pelathe' Community Resource
Center
1423 Haskell Ave.
Lawrence, KS 66044
Phone: (785) 841-7202
Fax: (785) 841-7255
Website: http://www.pelathe.org

MASSACHUSETTS

North American Indian Center of
Boston
105 South Huntington Ave.
Jamaica Plain, MA 02130
Phone: (617) 232-0343
Fax: (617) 232-3863
Website: http://
bostonindiancenter.org

MARYLAND

American Indian Center, Inc.
113 South Broadway
Baltimore, MD 21231
Phone: (410) 675-3535
Fax: (410) 675-6909
Website: http://www.baic.org

MICHIGAN

American Indian Services, Inc.
1110 Southfield Rd.
Lincoln Park, MI 48146
Phone: (313) 388-4100
Fax: (313) 388-6566
Website: None

Inter-Tribal Council of Michigan, Inc.
2956 Ashmun St.
Sault Ste. Marie, MI 49783
Phone: (906) 632-6896 or
(800) 562-4957
Fax: (906) 621-1810 or
(906) 635-4212
Website: http://www.itcmi.org

North American Indian Association
of Detroit
22720 Plymouth Rd.
Redford, MI 48239
Phone: (313) 535-2966
Fax: (313) 535-8060
Website: http://www.naiadetroit.org

South Eastern Michigan Indians
26641 Lawrence St.
Centerline, MI 48015
Phone: (586) 756-1350
Fax: (586) 756-1352
Website: None

MINNESOTA

American Indian Family Center
579 Wells St.
St. Paul, MN 55101
Phone: (651) 793-3803
Fax: (651) 793-3809
Website: http://www.aifc.net

Minneapolis Native American
Center
1530 East Franklin
Minneapolis, MN 55404
Phone: (612) 879-1700
Fax: (612) 879-1795
Website: http://www.maicnet.org

Minnesota Indian Women's
Resource Center
2300 15th Ave. S
Minneapolis, MN 55404
Phone: (612) 728-2000
Fax: (612) 728-2039
Website: http://miwrc.org

St. Cloud Indian Center
St. Cloud University
720 4th Ave. S
St. Cloud, MN 56301-4498
Phone: (320) 308-5449
Fax: (320) 308-5451

Website: http://www.
stcloudstate.edu/aic

MISSOURI

Heart of America Indian Center
600 West 39th St.
Kansas City, MO 64111
Phone: (816) 421-7608
Fax: (816) 421-6493
Website: http://www.
haicindian.com

MONTANA

Missoula Indian Center
Building 33
Fort Missoula, MT 59804
Phone: (406) 829-9515
Fax: (406) 829-9519
Website: http://www.
missoulaindiancenter.org

Montana United Indian Association
P.O. Box 786
Helena, MT 59601
Phone: (406) 443-5350
Website: None

NEBRASKA

Indian Center, Inc.
1100 Military Rd.
Lincoln, NE 68508
Phone: (402) 438-5231
Fax: (402) 438-5236
Website: None

NEVADA

Inter-Tribal Council of Nevada
680 Greenbrae Dr., Suite 280
Sparks, Nevada 89431
Phone: (775) 355-0600
Fax: (775) 355-0648
Website: http://itcn.org

Las Vegas Indian Center
2300 West Bonanza Rd.
Las Vegas, NV 89106
Phone: (702) 647-5842
Fax: (702) 647-2647
Website: http://www.
    lasvegasindiancenter.org

NEW MEXICO

Albuquerque Indian Center
105 Texas SE
Albuquerque, NM 87108
Phone: (505) 268-4418
Fax: (505) 268-8955
Website: http://www.abqndn.org

Farmington Intertribal Indian
    Organization
100 West Elm
Farmington, NM 87499
Phone: (505) 327-6296
Website: None

First Nations Community Health
    Source
5608 Zuni Rd. SE
Albuquerque, NM 87108
Phone: (505) 262-2481
Fax: (505) 262-0781
Website: None

NEW YORK

American Indian Community
    House
708 Broadway, 8th Fl.
New York, NY 10003
Phone: (212) 598-0100
Fax: (212) 598-4909
Website: http://www.aich.org

NORTH CAROLINA

Cumberland County Association for
    Indian People
2173 Downing Rd.

Fayetteville, NC 28312
Phone: (919) 483-8442
Fax: (919) 483-8442
Website: None

OHIO

American Indian Education Center
1700 Denison Ave., Ste. 102
Cleveland, OH 44109
Phone: (216) 351-4488
Fax: (216) 351-6623
Website: http://www.aiecc.net

Native American Indian Center of
    Central Ohio
67 East Innis Ave.
Columbus, OH 43207-0705
Phone: (614) 443-6120
Fax: (614) 443-2651
Website: http://naicco.tripod.com

OKLAHOMA

Native American Coalition Head
    Start
1740 West 41st St.
Tulsa, OK 74107
Phone: (918) 446-7939
Website: None

PENNSYLVANIA

Council of the Three Rivers
    American Indian Center
120 Charles St.
Pittsburgh, PA 15238
Phone: (412) 782-4457
Fax: (412) 767-4808
Website: http://www.angelfire.
    com/pa/COTRAIC

United American Indians of
    Delaware Valley
225 Chestnut St.
Philadelphia, PA 19106
Phone: (215) 574-9020
Website: None

SOUTH DAKOTA

American Indian Relief Council
P.O. Box 6200
Rapid City, SD 57709
Phone: (800) 370-0872
Website: http://www.airc.org

American Indian Services
817 North Elmwood
Sioux Falls, SD 57104
Phone: (800) 658-4797
Website: http://www.
   aistribalarts.com

TENNESSEE

Chattanooga Inter-Tribal Center
P.O. Box 1063
Chattanooga, TN 37401
Phone: (423) 624-3380
Website: http://cita.chattanooga.org

Native American Indian Association
   of Tennessee
230 Spence La.
Nashville, TN 37210
Phone: (615) 232-9179
Website: http://www.naiatn.org

TEXAS

Urban Inter-Tribal Center
209 East Jefferson Blvd.
Dallas, TX 75203
Phone: (214) 941-1050
Fax: (214) 941-1668
Website: None

UTAH

Indian Walk-In Center
120 West 1300 S
Salt Lake City, UT 84115-5899
Phone: (801) 486-4877
Fax: (801) 486-9943
Website: http://www.auch.org/
   health_centers/iwic.html

WASHINGTON

American Indian Community
   Center
905 East Third
Spokane, WA 99202
Phone: (509) 535-0886
Website: None

Northwest Urban Indian
   Community
120 State Ave. NE, #1455
Olympia, WA 98501
Phone: (360) 561-2889
Website: http://nwurbanindians.
   home.comcast.net

Seattle Indian Center
611 12th St. S, #300
Seattle, WA 98144
Phone: (206) 329-8700
Website: None

Tahoma Indian Center
1323 Yakima Ave.
Tacoma, WA 98405
Phone: (253) 593-2707
Website: http://www.ccsww.org/
   familyservices/southwest/
   pierce/es.php

United Indians of All Tribes
   Foundation
Discovery Park
P.O. Box 99100
Seattle, WA 98199
Phone: (206) 285-4425
Fax: (206) 282-3640
Website: http://www.
   unitedindians.com

WISCONSIN

United Amerindian Center, Inc.
407 Dousman St.
Green Bay, WI 54303
Phone: (920) 436-6630
Fax: (920) 433-0121

Website: http://www.
    unitedamerindiancenter.
    onbroadway.org

References

U.S. Census Bureau. "Facts for Features: American Indian & Alaska Native Heritage Month." (October 2003). Retrieved September 9, 2004, from http://www.census.gov/PressRelease/www/releases/archives/facts_for_features/001492.html.

U.S. Census Bureau. "Disability Status: 2000 Census—2000 Brief." (July 2004). Retrieved September 9, 2004, from http://www.census.gov/hhes/www/disable/disabstat2k/table2.html.

Support for this practice guideline was provided by a cooperative agreement (#H235K000002) with the U.S. Department of Education's Rehabilitation Services Administration.

Please contact the American Indian Disability Technical Assistance Center if there are any additions or corrections to be made to the list:

AIDTAC
University of Montana Rural
    Institute
52 Corbin
Missoula, MT 59812-7056
Phone: 406-243-4856,
    or 866-424-3822
Fax: 406-243-2349
TT: 406-243-4200
Website: http://aidtac.
    ruralinstitute.umt.edu

American Indian Policy Center
1463 Hewitt Ave.

St. Paul, MN 55104
Phone: 651-644-1728
Website: www.
    aipc@cpinternet.com

AMERICAN INDIAN TRIBAL COLLEGES

Bay Mills Community College
12214 West Lakeshore Drive
Brimley, MI 49715

Blackfeet Community College
P.O. Box 819
Browning, MT 59417

Cankdeska Cikana Community
    College
P.O. Box 269
Fort Totten, ND 58335

College of Menominee Nation
P.O. Box 1179
Keshena, WI 54135

Crownpoint Institute of
Technology
P.O. Box 849
Crownpoint, NM 87313

Diné College
P.O. Box 126
Tsaile, AZ 86556

D-Q University
P.O. Box 409
Davis, CA 95617
Dull Knife Memorial College
P.O. Box 98
Lame Deer, MT 59043

Fond du Lac Tribal and Community
    College
2101 14th Street
Cloquet, MN 55720

Fort Belknap College
P.O. Box 159
Harlem, MT 59526

Fort Berthold Community College
P.O. Box 490
New Town, ND 58763

Fort Peck Community College
P.O. Box 398
Poplar, MT 59255

Haskell Indian Nations University
155 Indian Avenue
Lawrence, KS 66046-4800

Institute of American Indian Arts
83 Avan Nu Po Road
Santa Fe, NM 87505

Keweenaw Bay Ojibwa
Community College
107 Bear Town Road
Baraga, MI 49908

Lac Courte Oreilles Ojibwa
Community College
13466 West Trepania Road
Hayward, WI 54843

Leech Lake Tribal College
6530 U.S. Highway 2 NW
Cass Lake, MN 56633

Little Big Horn College
1 Forest Lane
Crow Agency, MT 59022

Little Priest Tribal College
P.O. Box 270
Winnebago, NE 68071

Nebraska Indian Community
College
P.O. Box 428
Macy, NE 68039

Northwest Indian College
2522 Kwina Road
Bellingham, WA 98226

Oglala Lakota College
P.O. Box 490
Kyle, SD 57752

Salish Kootenai College
P.O. Box 117
Pablo, MT 59855

Sinte Gleska University
P.O. Box 490
Rosebud, SD 57570

Si Tanka College/Huron University
P.O. Box 220
Eagle Butte, SD 57625

Sisseton Wahpeton Community
College
P.O. Box 689, Agency Village
Sisseton, SD 57262

Sitting Bull College
1341 92nd Street
Fort Yates, ND 58538

Southwestern Indian Polytechnic
Institute
9169 Coors NW
Albuquerque, NM 87184

Stone Child College
RR1, Box 1082
Box Elder, MT 59521

Turtle Mountain Community
College
P.O. Box 340
Belcourt, ND 58316

United Tribes Technical College
3315 University Drive
Bismarck, ND 58504

White Earth Tribal and Community
  College
210 Main Street South
P.O. Box 478
Mahnomen, MN 56557

American Indian

College Fund

National Headquarters
8333 Greenwood Boulevard
Denver, CO 80221
Phone: (303) 426-8900
Fax: (303) 426-1200
Website: info@collegefund.org
New York Office
21 West 68th Street
Suite 1F
New York, NY 10023

Phone: (212) 787-6312
Fax: 212-496-1050

AIHEC

121 Oronoco Street
Alexandria, VA 22314
Phone: (703) 838-0400
Fax: (703) 838-0388

White House Initiative on

Tribal Colleges and

Universities

330 C Street SW, Room 4050 MES
Washington, DC 20202
Phone: (202) 260-5714
Fax: (202) 260-5702

COMMON QUESTIONS IN REGARD TO NATIVE AMERICANS

Are Indians U.S. citizens?

Yes. Before 1924, when the U.S. Congress extended American citizenship to all Indians born in the territorial limits of the United States, citizenship had been conferred upon approximately two-thirds of the Indian population through treaty agreements, statutes, naturalization proceedings, and by "service in the Armed Forces with an honorable discharge" in World War I. Indians also are members of their respective tribes and thus have dual citizenship.

Can Indians vote?

Yes. Indians have the same right to vote as other U.S. citizens. In 1948, the Arizona Supreme Court declared unconstitutional the disenfranchising interpretation of the state constitution, and Indians were permitted to vote as in most other states. A 1953 Utah state law stated that persons living on Indian reservations were not residents of the state and could not vote, but that law was subsequently repealed. In 1954, Indians in Maine who were not then federally recognized were given the right to vote, and in 1962 New

Mexico extended the right to vote to Indians. Indians also vote in state and local elections and in their affiliated tribal elections. Each tribe, however, determines which of its members are eligible to vote in its elections. This qualification is not related to the individual Indian's right to vote in national, state, or local (non-Indian) elections.

Do Indians have the right to hold federal, state, and local government public offices?

Yes. Indians have the same rights as other citizens to hold public office. Indian men and women have held elective and appointive offices at all levels of government. Charles Curtis, a Kaw Indian from Kansas, served as vice president of the United States under President Herbert Hoover.

Indians have been elected to the U.S. Congress over a period of more than eighty years. Ben Reifel, a Sioux Indian from South Dakota, served five terms in the U.S. House of Representatives. Ben Nighthorse Campbell, a member of the Northern Cheyenne Tribe of Montana, was elected to the U.S. House of Representatives in 1986 from the Third District of Colorado and is currently serving in the U.S. Senate. He is the only American Indian currently serving in Congress.

Indians have also served in and now hold office in a number of state legislatures. Others currently hold or have held elected or appointed positions in state judiciary systems and in county and city governments, including local school boards. Larry Echo Hawk, an enrolled member of the Pawnee Tribe, served as attorney general of Idaho from 1992 to 1994.

Do Indians pay taxes?

Yes. They pay the same taxes as other citizens with the following exceptions: federal income taxes are not levied on income from trust lands held for them by the United States, state income taxes are not paid on income earned on an Indian reservation, state sales taxes are not paid by Indians on transactions made on an Indian reservation, and local property taxes are not paid on reservation or trust land.

Do laws that apply to non-Indians also apply to Indians?

Yes. As U.S. citizens, Indians are generally subject to federal, state, and local laws. On Indian reservations, however, only federal and tribal laws apply to members of the tribe unless Congress provides otherwise. In federal law, the Assimilative Crimes Act makes any violation of state criminal law a federal offense on reservations. Most tribes now maintain tribal court systems and facilities to detain tribal members convicted of certain offenses within the boundaries of the reservation.

How is Indian gaming regulated?

Indian land is not under state law unless a federal law places it under state law. The Supreme Court held that even if a tribe is under state law, the state gaming regulations do not apply on Indian trust land.

In 1988 Congress passed the Indian Gaming Regulatory Act, which allows traditional Indian gaming, as well as bingo, pull tabs, lotto, punch boards, tip jars, and certain card games, on tribal land. However, it requires a compact between the tribe and the state for other forms of gaming, such as cards or slot machines. Today there are about 145 tribal-state gaming compacts. Nearly 130 tribes in twenty-four states are involved in some kind of gaming.

The National Indian Gaming Commission was established by Congress to develop regulations for Indian gaming. For more information, contact the National Indian Gaming Commission, 9th Floor, 1441 L Street, NW, Washington, DC 20005, (202) 632-7003.

Does the U.S. Government still make treaties with Indians?

No. Congress ended treaty making with Indian tribes in 1871. Since then, relations with Indian groups are by congressional acts, executive orders, and executive agreements. Between 1778, when the first treaty was made with the Delawares, and 1871, when Congress ended the treaty-making period, the Senate ratified 370 Indian treaties. At least forty-five others were negotiated with tribes but were never ratified by the Senate.

The treaties that were made often contain obsolete commitments that have either been fulfilled or superseded by federal legislation. The provision of education, health, welfare, and other services by the government to tribes often has extended beyond treaty requirements. A number of large Indian groups have no treaties yet share in the many services for Indians provided by the federal government.

The specifics of particular treaties signed by government negotiators with Indians are contained in the second volume of the publication, *Indian Affairs, Laws and Treaties*, compiled, annotated, and edited by Charles Kappler. Published by the Government Printing Office in 1904, it is now out of print but can be found in most large law libraries. More recently the treaty volume has been published privately under the title *Indian Treaties, 1778–1883* (U.S. Government Printing Office).

Originals of all the treaties are maintained by the National Archives and Records Service of the General Services Administration. A duplicate of a treaty is available upon request for a fee. The agency will also answer questions about specific Indian treaties. Write to: Diplomatic Branch, National Archives and Records Services, Washington, DC 20408.

Are Indians entitled to a free college education?

No. An individual does not automatically receive funding because of Indian ancestry. The Indian higher education program provides financial aid to eligible students, based on demonstrated financial need, who have plans to attend an accredited institution of higher education. A student must obtain an application packet and other financial aid information from their tribe, home BIA agency, or Area Office of Indian Education Programs. The Higher Education Grant Program is available to an individual who is a member of a federally recognized Indian tribe.

Source: Bureau of Indian Affairs, Great Plains Regional Office, 115 4th Ave. SE, Aberdeen SD 57401. Phone: (605) 226-7343, Fax: (605) 226-7446.

American Indian History Timetable

American Indian history is much older than American history. The following brief list offers a few events of historical pride and grief that remain etched in the cultural memory of American Indians.

650   A democratic political structure existed among the Copa 'N Maya. Nine men known as *hol-pop* ("he at the head of the mat") were representatives who met with the kings to make decisions and deliberate about social problems.

1000   The Iroquois League, the oldest political alliance in North America, is founded at about this time.

1638   The first reservation is established in Connecticut; remaining members of the Quinnipiac Tribe are placed on this reservation.

1763   Presbyterians from Paxton, Pennsylvania, murder three men, two women, and a boy, members of the Conestoga Indians, who were living in peace with white settlers. The Paxton boys were never prosecuted for their actions

1775   American colonists declare war against England. The colonies' provisional government—the Continental Congress—establishes three Indian commissions (northern, middle, and southern). Each commission is charged with preserving amiable relations with indigenous tribes and keeping them out of the violence. But many Indians ally themselves with the British, and many join forces with the American colonists.

1777   The Articles of Confederation organize the new government of the United States. The articles assume authority over Indian affairs except when the "legislative right of any State within its own limits (is) infringed or violated."

1778   The United States signs its first Indian treaty with the Delaware Nation; in exchange for access to that nation's land by U.S. troops, the United States promises to defend and admit the Delaware Nation as a state.

1787   Northwest Ordinance declares that beyond the Alleghenies, Indian land will never be taken "without their consent."

1789   The U.S. Constitution is adopted. Article I, Section 8, grants Congress power to regulate commerce among foreign nations and Indian tribes.

Congress places Indian affairs under the War Department.

1802   Congress appropriates over $10,000 for the "civilization" of Indians.

1803   As part of the Louisiana Purchase, the United States acquires lands on which numerous Indian tribes reside.

1815   The United States begins the process of removing Indians to western lands.

1824   The Bureau of Indian Affairs is created within the War Department.

1827   John Ross is elected president of the Cherokee Nation; he is the first president since the adoption of the nation's new constitution that year in New Echota, Georgia.

1830   Indian Removal Act, successfully pushed through Congress by President Andrew Jackson, forces relocation of nearly 100,000 Indians from eastern homelands to areas west of the Mississippi River.

1831   The U.S. Supreme Court, in *Cherokee Nation v. Georgia*, holds that Indian tribes are domestic, dependent nations, not foreign nations.

1832   Supreme Court rules in *Worchester v. Georgia* that Indian tribal lands are sovereign "domestic dependent nations" with rights that states cannot infringe upon. Andrew Jackson is reported to have remarked, "John Marshall has made his decision, now let him enforce it."

1835   The Treaty of New Echota is signed. Cherokees agree to westward re-moval.

1838   The Trail of Tears begins. The Cherokee and several other tribes (Chickasaw, Choctaw, Creek, and Seminole) begin their forced jour-ney to the Indian Territory (Oklahoma). The term *Five Civilized Tribes* originated because these five tribes modeled their govern-ments after American and state institutions and had been assimi-lated into the white culture. Cherokee Indians and the other tribes are forced to travel almost thirteen hundred miles without sufficient food, water, and medicine; almost one-quarter of the Cherokees do not survive the journey. The Potawatomis in Indiana experience similar hardships on their Trail of Death.

1847   Pueblos in Taos, New Mexico, ally themselves with Latinos to over-throw the newly established U.S. rule.

1848   The Treaty of Guadalupe Hidalgo is signed, bringing the Mexican War to an end. As a result of the vast amount of land ceded to the United States, many new Indian tribes fall under U.S. jurisdiction.

1849   The Department of the Interior is created, and the Bureau of In-dian Affairs is shuffled from the War Department to the Interior Department.

1853   The Gadsen Purchase is completed. More tribes come under the ju-risdiction of the United States.

1854   Several southeastern U.S. tribes (Cherokee, Chickasaw, Choctaw, Muskogee, and Seminole) form an alliance to defend themselves from further forced removal to the West.

1861   The Civil War begins. Various Indian tribes fight on both sides. Stand Watie, a Cherokee, becomes the only Indian brigadier general in the Confederate army; he leads two Cherokee regiments in the Southwest.

1864   Approximately eight thousand Navajos are forcibly marched to Fort Sumner, New Mexico, on the Navajo Long Walk; after three years of harsh imprisonment, the survivors are released.

1865   Confederate General Robert E. Lee surrenders to Union General Ulysses S. Grant at Appomattox; at General Grant's side is Colonel Ely S. Parker, a full-blooded Seneca.

1867   The Indian Peace Commission finalizes treaty making between the United States and Indian tribes.

1868   Laramie Treaty with the Lakota restricts settlement in by non-Indians in nearly all of Nebraska, South Dakota, Montana, Wyoming, and North Dakota, reserving these lands for the Lakota.

1869   President Ulysses S. Grant appoints Brigadier General Ely S. Parker to head the Bureau of Indian Affairs; he is the first Indian to fill this position.

1871   Congress passes legislation that ends treaty making between the United States and Indian tribes.

1876   Custer is prosecuted by the Cheyenne and Sioux for trespassing on the sacred lands, Paha Sapa ("Black Hills") of the Lakota Nation, and a death sentence is carried out by the Lakota and their allies.

1879   Most tribes have been concentrated on reservations, and boarding schools are established to take Indian children away from parental influence and "civilize" them.

1884   In *Elk v. Wilkins*, the U.S. Supreme Court holds that the Fourteenth Amendment's guarantee of citizenship to all persons born in the United States does not apply to Indians, even those born within the geographical confines of the United States.

1887   Allotment (Dawes) Act calls for distributing tribal lands to individual Indians in hopes of making them into farmers who would assimilate into the general society. Tribal land base is reduced from 137 million to 52 million acres, as most is sold or given to non-Indian settlers.

1890   Last major confrontation of Indian wars takes place at Wounded Knee Creek on the Pine Ridge Reservation in South Dakota. Twenty-two soldiers receive Congressional Medals of Honor for the slaughter of two hundred men, women, and children who were turning over their weapons to the soldiers. Frank Baum, the author of the *Wizard of Oz* who was writing for a paper in Aberdeen, South Dakota at the time, wrote that "it was the duty of the United States government to exterminate all Indians since they refused to join the civilized world."

1898   Curtis Act strips tribes of most government powers.

1901   Congress passes the Citizenship Act of 1901, which formally grants U.S. citizenship to members of the Five Civilized Tribes.

1921 Snyder Act gave the BIA permanent statutory authority to expend funds for programs and delivery of services "for the benefit, care, and assistance of Indians throughout the United States."

1924 Congress passes Indian Citizenship Act—all Indians become U.S. citizens. Some reject U.S. citizenship and maintain tribal citizenship only. Others, generally half-breeds or less and assimilated (such as my grandmother), reject tribal citizenship and assume U.S. citizenship. Still others (such as my grandfather) maintain both tribal and U.S. citizenship. Some (such as my daughters) hold tribal, Canadian, and U.S. citizenship.

1934 Indian Reorganization Act (IRA) ends allotment, and tribes are urged to adopt democratic government with elections for tribal councils.

1939 Chief Henry Standing Bear and other Sioux leaders appeal to Korczak Ziolkowski, who worked on the presidential sculptures at Mount Rushmore in ex-Sioux territory, to create a similar monument to Chief Crazy Horse. Ziolkowski began work in 1947; in 1998 his son Casimir continued work on the monument.

1944 In Denver, Colorado, the National Congress of American Indians is founded.

1948 Through judicial means, Indians in Arizona and New Mexico win the right to vote in state elections.

1949 The Hoover Commission recommends "termination," which would mandate that Congress no longer recognize Indian sovereignty, thus eliminating all special rights and benefits.

1953 Congress passes House Resolution 108, better know as the Termination Act, which called for the termination of tribal governments and lands and moving Indians to cities—relocation. Terminated Indians were no longer classified as Indians. The Poncas, for example, were terminated in 1964 and reinstated in 1990.

1958 Secretary of the Interior Seaton begins to retract the termination policy.

1961 More than 210 tribes meet at the American Indian Chicago Conference, where the Declaration of Indian Purpose is drafted for presentation to the U.S. Congress.

1965 Termination is ended as the War on Poverty begins pouring money into reservations for new homes, schools, and other facilities. The Santee-Sioux on the east side of the Brazile Creek in Nebraska built over one hundred new homes, a new tribal office, a factory, and a school with these funds. The Poncas on the west side of the Brazile Creek sold their tribal buildings and remaining 360 acres of ground to a non-Indian farmer for $15,000.

1968   Congress passes the American Indian Civil Rights Act, giving individual Indians constitutional protection against their tribal governments. This protection is the same as the protection the U.S. Constitution provides against state and local governments.

The American Indian Movement (AIM), based on the model of the black civil rights protest groups, protests the U.S. government's treatment of Indian people.

1969   Indian activists occupy Alcatraz Island as federal surplus property that under U.S. law may be returned to Indian ownership.

1960s   From the late 1960s to early 1970s, tribes begin to create tribal colleges to ease the transition from reservation life to mainstream colleges and universities. Twenty-seven such colleges are created.

1971   The Alaskan Native Claims Settlement Act is passed; it eliminates 90 percent of Alaskan Natives' land claims in exchange for a guarantee of 44 million acres and almost $1 billion.

1972   In protest of a history of broken promises to Indian tribes, two hundred Indians participate in the Trail of Broken Treaties march, ultimately occupying the Washington, D.C., office of the Bureau of Indian Affairs.

1973   Indian activists seize the village of Wounded Knee, South Dakota, and hold federal marshals and the national guard at bay for seventy days. Two Indians are killed and one marshal is paralyzed.

1975   The Indian Self-Determination and Education Act is passed, giving Indian tribal governments more control over their tribal affairs and appropriating more money for education assistance.

Two FBI agents, Ronald A. Williams and Jack R. Coler, were killed along with Joseph Bedell Stuntz, originally Joseph George, a young AIM member, at the Jumping Bull encampment on the Pine Ridge Reservation in South Dakota. Leonard Peltier is still (as of 2005) held in federal prison for the murder of the two FBI agents, despite evidence that his trial was unconstitutional.

1979   Seminoles open first high-stakes "Indian" bingo hall in Florida. Within five years, one hundred Indian bingo halls open across the country with a gross annual revenue of $175 million.

The U.S. Supreme Court awards the Lakota Nation $122.5 million in compensation for the U.S. government's illegal appropriation of the Black Hills in South Dakota.

1980   The Penobscots and Passamaquoddies accept monetary compensation from the U.S. government for their lands (the Massachusetts colony—now the state of Maine), which the government took illegally in 1970.

P. L. 93–638, the Self Determination Act, permits tribes to contract for direct funding from the federal government and to take over programs previously or currently administered by the Bureau of Indian Affairs and the Indian Health Service.

1983   President Reagan calls for Indian "self-sufficiency" and pursuit of private enterprise as budget cuts eliminate federal jobs on the reservations.

1986   Interior Department study recommends enterprise zones for reservations and greater Indian access to federal procurements as methods of attracting manufacturing to reservations.

Congress amends the Indian Civil Rights Act and grants tribal courts the power to impose criminal penalties.

1988   The Alaskan Native Claims Settlement Act is amended, giving Indigenous Village Corporations the option to sell their stock after 1991.

Congress officially repeals the thirty-five-year-old termination policy.

Self-Governance Act allows tribal governments to contract directly with the federal government for authority and funding to develop and implement governance agreements with the federal government.

Indian Gaming Act establishes an Indian Gaming Commission to regulate Indian gambling on reservations. Most tribal leaders are against this legislation, but Congress sees it as a compromise with non-Indian opposition to Indian gambling, mainly by the governors (who until now have had no control over Indian gambling in their states) and the churches (who have seen their bingo revenues fall because of the higher payouts allowed in Indian bingo halls).

1990   In *Smith v. Oregon* the Supreme Court rules that states have the right to ban or restrict the use of peyote in Native American Church ceremonies, since those who use it can be prosecuted under the state's drug laws unless the state legislature has passed statutes allowing for the use of peyote. Indian leaders and religious rights supporters see this as a major blow to First Amendment rights.

On November 15, President George Bush signed the Northern Ponca Restoration Act. After having been terminated, the Northern Ponca Tribe of Nebraska is federally recognized once again. Only 2 of the 108 tribes that were terminated in the 1950s and 1960s have not been restored to federal recognition.

1991 Seven tribes complete three-year demonstration projects on tribal self-governance. Each feels that they have taken the first step toward regaining tribal sovereignty. Bureau of Indian Affairs control over Indian tribes is being relinquished for tribal self-rule. Twenty-three more tribes have signed self-governance agreements with the federal government. Some tribes fear that abolishment of the BIA will lead to a reduction in federal funding for the tribes. They feel that self-governance may turn out to be another policy of "termination" in which federal funds to tribes will be terminated.

1992 Representative Ben Nighthorse Campbell, a Cheyenne from Colorado, is elected to the U.S. Senate.

1993 Ada Deer is appointed assistant secretary for Indian affairs by President Bill Clinton. She is the first Indian woman to hold the position.

1994 Three hundred representatives from the 545 federally recognized Indian tribes meet with President Bill Clinton, the first time since 1822 that Indians have been invited to meet officially with a U.S. president to discuss issues of concern to Indian peoples.

Clinton signs a law that provides Indians with federal protection in the use of peyote in religious ceremonies.

1996 Laguna Pueblo faces a legal challenge regarding its long-standing tradition of allowing only men on the ballot for tribal office.

The University of Arizona creates the first Ph.D. program in American Indian studies.

November is declared National American Indian Heritage Month by President Clinton.

President Clinton signs Executive Order S13021 supporting tribal colleges.

1997 For the first time in history, American Indians are included in the presidential inaugural festivities as special and individual participants. American Indians are in the parade and have an American Indian ball.

Alaska Natives take a case to the Supreme Court regarding their right to tax others on their land (44 million acres in Alaska). The question posed: Does "Indian country" exist in Alaska as a result of the 1971 Alaskan Native Claims Settlement Act?

1998   Four thousand Alaska Natives march in Anchorage in protest of Alaska legislative and legal attacks on tribal governments and native hunting and fishing traditions.

In a unanimous decision, the Supreme Court rules that, in the absence of a reservation, the Venetie Tribe of Alaska does not have the right to tax others on land conveyed under the 1971 Alaskan Native Claims Settlement Act. In essence, the Court decreed that "Indian country" does not exist in Alaska.

Clinton issues Executive Order No. 13084, "Consultation and Coordination with Indian Tribal Government," in which he pledges that the federal government will establish and engage in meaningful consultation and collaboration with Indian tribal governments in matters that will significantly impact their communities.

Interior Secretary Bruce Babbitt investigated in Indian casino scandal under claims that he denied a gaming license to several Wisconsin tribes because of White House pressure to satisfy competing Minnesota tribes, who made large contributions to the Democratic National Committee.

The Makah Nation of Washington State renews the traditional practice of whaling for the first time in seventy years despite protests from many environmental and other groups.

1999   Federal judge holds Secretary of Interior Babbitt and Secretary of Justice Rubin in contempt for failure to provide documents related to the Indian trust funds class-action lawsuit.

Clinton visits the Pine Ridge Sioux Reservation in South Dakota on a swing through some of the most impoverished communities in America. He is the first sitting president since Calvin Coolidge in 1927 to make an official visit to an Indian reservation.

2000   Executive Order 13175 on Federal Consultation and Coordination with Indian Tribal Governments is signed by President Clinton.

2001   President George W. Bush honors Navajo Code Talkers for their service in World War II.

2002   Tribal Colleges and Universities, Executive Order 13270, George W. Bush's Executive Order, is designed to ensure that tribal colleges and universities receive support from the federal government to assist these schools in providing high-quality educational opportunities for their students.

National Congress of American Indians promotes the Native Vote 2004 Campaign, a nationwide nonpartisan effort to mobilize the American Indian and Alaska Native vote.

Opening of the National Museum of the American Indian draws thousands to Washington, D.C.

2005   U.N. Draft Declaration on the Rights of Indigenous Peoples is completed. The United States indicates that it will probably support an extension of the Working Group on the draft declaration to continue its work for an additional period of time.

American Indians view the twenty-first century with both hope and fear: hope in the growth of their tribal languages, traditions, and sovereignty, and fear that the traumatic governmental policies of the past will visit them once more.

Sources

Dewing, Rolland. 1985. *Wounded Knee: The Meaning and Significance of the Second Incident.* New York: Irvington.

Fash, William L., Jr., and Barbara W. Fash. 1990. "Scribes, Warriors and Kings: The Lives of the Copa'n Maya," *Archaeology,* May/June.

McClain, Paula, and Joseph Stewart, Jr. 1998. *Can We All Get Along? Racial and Ethnic Minorties in American Politics.* 2d ed. Boulder, Colo.: Westview, 197–200.

National Congress of American Indians Website. 2004.

Native American Rights Fund. 2005. Case Updates. November. Boulder, Colo.: NARF Website.

O'Brien, Sharon. 1989. *American Indian Tribal Governments.* Norman: University of Oklahoma Press.

Wilkins, David. 2002. *Nations within States: American Indian Politics and the American Political System.* Boulder, Colo.: Rowman and Littlefield.

Index

About the Author

Dr. Jerry Stubben is an Extension State Communities specialist and research scientist at Iowa State University. He grew up on the Ponca and Santee-Sioux reservations in Nebraska and has published in the areas of tribal government; tribally based substance abuse prevention and treatment programs; American Indian spirituality, culture, and history; and the wisdom of indigenous peoples. He is most proud to be a member of the Osni Ponca Heduska (Warrior) Society and the grandfather of thirteen living future tribal leaders.

I dedicate this book to my grandson, My Son Stabler, who I look forward to being reunited with in the Spirit World and who guides me in all I do while I remain in this world.

Ahgaha Ska